Leisure and Recreation Management

Other Titles From E & FN Spon

Amenity Landscape Management
A resources handbook
Edited by R. Cobham

Arts Administration
J. Pick

Countryside Management
P. Bromley

Drugs in Sport
Edited by D. R. Mottram

The Golf Course
Planning, design, construction and maintenance
F. W. Hawtree

Managing Sport and Leisure Facilities
A guide to competitive tendering
P. Sayers

Recreation and the Law
V. Collins

Sport and Recreation
An economic analysis
C. Gratton and P. Taylor

Sports Geography
J. Bale

Leisure and Recreation Management

THIRD EDITION

George Torkildsen

E & FN SPON
An Imprint of Chapman & Hall
London · Glasgow · Weinheim · New York · Tokyo · Melbourne · Madras

Published by E & FN Spon, an imprint of Chapman & Hall,
2-6 Boundary Row, London SE1 8HN, UK

Chapman & Hall, 2-6 Boundary Row, London SE1 8HN, UK

Blackie Academic & Professional, Wester Cleddens Road, Bishopbriggs, Glasgow G64 2NZ, UK

Chapman & Hall GmbH, Pappelallee 3, 69469 Weinheim, Germany

Chapman & Hall USA., One Penn Plaza, 41st Floor, New York, NY10119, USA

Chapman & Hall Japan, ITP-Japan, Kyowa Building, 3F, 2-2-1 Hirakawacho, Chiyoda-ku, Tokyo 102, Japan

Chapman & Hall Australia, Thomas Nelson Australia, 102 Dodds Street, South Melbourne, Victoria 3205, Australia

Chapman & Hall India, R. Seshadri, 32 Second Main Road, CIT East, Madras 600 035, India

First edition 1983
Second edition 1986
Reprinted 1990
Third edition 1992
Reprinted 1992, 1993 (twice), 1994, 1995, 1996

Typeset in 10/12pt Palatino by Graphicraft Typesetters Ltd, Hong Kong
Printed in Great Britain by St Edmundsbury Press, Bury St Edmunds, Suffolk

ISBN 0 419 16760 9

A Catalogue record for this book is available from the British Library

Library of Congress Cataloging-in-Publication Data available

This book is dedicated to
my friend and colleague
RON PICKERING OBE
who died 13 February 1991

Contents

Illustrations

Chapter 1
This drawing encapsulates the essence of the book. (*Courtesy of George Torkildsen.*)

Chapter 2
Mother and children. Leisure experiences can be fostered from childhood. (*Courtesy of Judy Cass.*)

Chapter 3
Little children playing. Play in the basis for leisure enjoyment. (*Courtesy of George Torkildsen.*)

Chapter 4
Open parkland scene. (*Courtesy of John McCann.*) Action shots taken for the Physical Education Association. (*Courtesy of Alan Edwards.*)

Chapter 5
A wheelchair tennis player. (*Courtesy of All-Sport Photographic Ltd.*)

Chapter 6
Cowes Week. A wide variety of factors influence participation – poverty or wealth are two of the greatest. (*Courtesy of All-Sport Photographic Ltd.*)

Chapter 7
Lazing in the summer – Morecambe Leisure Park. [*Courtesy of Faulkner-Brown (architects).*]

Chapter 8
The Dome at Doncaster Leisure Park. [*Courtesy of Faulkner-Brown (architects).*]

Chapter 9
Disney World. Theme parks are one of the major trends entering the UK and Europe. (*Courtesy of Ron Pickering.*)

Chapter 10
Indoor bowls at a local authority leisure centre in Northavon. (*Courtesy of Northavon District Council.*)

Chapter 11
Rotary International events. (*Courtesy of Rotary International.*)

Chapter 12
Snooker at Hanbury Manor Golf and Country Club. (*Courtesy of Hanbury Manor.*)

Chapter 13
Cartoon from an original idea by Ted Blake. (*Courtesy of George Torkildsen.*)

Chapter 14
Ponds Forge International Sports Centre. [*Courtesy of Faulkner-Brown (architect)*.]

Chapter 15
Ski jumper. Managers as well as top athletes need to be excellant performers. (*Courtesy of All-Sport Photographic Limited.*)

Chapter 16
Co-Op Store, Hardware Department. (*Courtesy of Beamish Museum.*)

Chapter 17
International volleyball. (*Courtesy of All-Sport Photographic Limited.*)

Chapter 18
Catering management and staff. (*Courtesy of Hanbury Manor.*)

Chapter 19
'Golf for Beginners' under instruction. Training is required at all levels of management. (*Courtesy of Ron Pickering.*)

Chapter 20
Forest bicycle ride on hire bikes. (*Courtesy of Ron Pickering.*) Mother and baby at pool. (*Courtesy of George Torkildsen.*) Aerobics and junior athletics. (*Courtesy of All-Sport Photographic Limited.*)

Preface and acknowledgements

This book is written for people who are interested in exploring the fascinating world of 'leisure' and 'recreation' and its management. They may be students, lecturers, or researchers, leisure executives, managers, recreation officers, supervisors or trainee managers. They may be organizers and administrators, policy-makers, planners, or leisure architects. They may be people on the 'fringes' of leisure, including community workers, teachers and many others.

My motivation in writing the first book ten years ago, carrying the same title, stemmed from a preoccupation and overwhelming interest in leisure and recreation and its management. That motivation remains and, indeed, is enhanced. Having been involved for over 30 years as teacher, coach, manager, director, lecturer and consultant and having been part of the movement towards the development of the community leisure centre and the emerging 'profession' of leisure management, I have felt destined to write about it.

I thank all who helped in any way in the writing and production of this new book, through their work, support, information, advice, patience or understanding. The book could not have been written without the accumulated knowledge and experience gained over many years from a wide range of sources and very many people.

In particular, I wish to record my grateful appreciation to my friend and colleague **Gwynne Griffiths** who made a substantial contribution to the writing and critical editing of many aspects in the book.

In addition, my young leisure researcher, Jacqueline Cutts, was of great assistance, together with my administrative 'team' of Jan Allen and Sue Tarling and Pat Kendall and Helen Torkildsen. Thanks, too, go to Professor Ray Maw and Jane Foulsham, my mentors at the Polytechnic of Central London during much of the 1980s.

To all and many more, thank you.

This book, as widespan as it is, does not cover the whole range of leisure and its management and, being broadly based, it does not cover every area in depth. My hope, however, is that all readers will find something in this publication which is informative, interesting, stimulating and of value to them. To those entering the field of leisure management, I wish all success in their chosen career, and trust that the book instils some knowledge, a philosophical direction and engenders much enthusiasm.

George Torkildsen

Chapter 1

Introduction, structure and significance of the book

1.1 INTRODUCTION

Leisure and Recreation Management, published in 1983, was the first book of its kind in the United Kingdom. The second edition, published in 1986, carried substantial changes to some chapters and there have since been minor changes in subsequent printings.

The first book has motivated others to write a number of textbooks but these invariably have been related to specific subject areas such as facility operation, forecasting, economics, marketing, arts, tourism and the countryside. None has embarked on a more comprehensive coverage in one volume of leisure philosophy, planning and management.

The expressed demand for a wider perspective and updating of the first book has motivated me to write a new book under the same title. This new book totally restructures the first. It draws upon the areas in the first book which are still relevant; new features are introduced and more prescriptive approaches, together with practical applications, are included.

1.2 WHY THE CHANGES?

Every day each product or service gets relatively better or worse. As Tom Peters, noted for his bestseller *Passion for Excellence*, says, 'quality improvement is a never-ending journey'.

The leisure about which I write is both individual and universal. Global conditions affect each country far more now than in the past; the world economic climate, for example, has an impact on each nation.

Europe is entering a period of turbulent change. In 1990 the geographic map has been redrawn, and the potential break-up of the Soviet Union republics, a united Germany, the Single European Market and also the prospect of a single currency and the Channel Tunnel all herald substantial change and opportunity. While changes are largely political and economic, the leisure industry will be part of the new Europe and new world. The entry of Disney into France, and the British government's encouragement in attracting a giant tourist international project to Britain, illustrate the perceived need to move fast from a cosy, insular home leisure industry into Europe and the wider field.

The world of leisure and recreation planning and management in the United Kingdom also has moved substantially since the first book was written and at a faster rate than anyone had forecast. This is as a result of economic and social changes, including government policy in relation to local authority expenditures; new technology; the growth in tourism; the growth of the service sector economy and the commercial leisure industry; and the growing expectations of people for healthier life styles, leisure fashion, facilities, services and choices.

To have *leisure*, to do the things we want to do, free from toil, responsibilities or weighty obligations, is a dream most people might have but few achieve. Yet leisure for the majority in Western civilization is a reality.

There is a fast-emerging profession called Leisure Management, an industry employing approx. 1.6 million people in the United Kingdom, in 1990, and developing rapidly. But as an industry, increasingly driven by market forces and people's disposable income, the very nature of leisure itself – what it is and what it does for people – is often lost, and more often, misunderstood.

1.3 CHANGES FROM THE OLD TO THE NEW

This book embodies both the old and new: it is new, in that it takes account of trends in leisure, recent government legislation, the increase in commercial leisure and changes in approach towards management, service and customer care. New chapters have been written covering the leisure 'product', planning, trends, performance appraisal and leisure and recreation management; included also are practical case studies and exercises of value to all students of leisure management.

But the baby has not been thrown out with the bathwater! The best of the old survives. Fundamental philosophies and principles upon which to plan and manage survive, but through further research they are deepened and strengthened. Now what leisure is and what it means to people has, at least for me (and I hope for readers), even more significance than it had just ten years ago.

A new theory is proposed towards the effective management of leisure services and facilities in the belief that good theory leads to good practice. Clearer insights into what we are supposed to be managing are put forward, so that planning for and management of leisure and recreation may be processed upon firmer foundations.

The several chapters on aspects of operational management have now been revised to encapsulate the greater awareness of 'quality' management and the need for efficiency in times of stricter accountability. However, while efficiency is very important and the pennies must be accounted for, my overwhelming preoccupation is with *effectiveness*. Do leisure planners and managers provide opportunities that make for personally worthwhile and satisfying experiences, for the good of individuals and the community? If not, then it is no use having super-efficient services that are ineffective and fail to meet the needs of people they are intended to serve. This viewpoint sets the book on its course and provides the logic behind its structure.

The book seeks to answer some simple questions on a complex phenomenon: what is leisure and recreation? How is it planned and provided for, managed and controlled? How can greater opportunities be provided through improved management? The book links leisure philosophy, planning, provision and management into a framework of leisure opportunity for people within a community. It is concerned with approaches towards better management and performance. It is not, however, a technical textbook dealing with buildings, facilities, design, maintenance, catering, accounting, nor with arts, sports, tourism, countryside recreation and social recreation, in and of themselves. These aspects are covered by other specific publications and by national agencies and institutions.

Instead, this book is concerned with the leisure 'software' – namely, the quality of the experience, the principles underlying provision and the 'people approach' to planning, managing, leading and programming. What does the experience of leisure and recreation do for people, and why provide opportunities and management for it to occur? It is to these questions that the book directs itself and provides practical suggestions as to how good planning and management can create better opportunities for leisure and recreation to occur for even more people, more often.

1.4 IS THERE A NEED TO MANAGE LEISURE AND RECREATION?

This book is concerned generally with the planning for and management of 'leisure' and 'recreation', and specifically with the effective management of leisure services and facilities. Why this concern?

The first thing that could be said about provision and management is that nature provides us, in the natural environment, with abundant resources for recreation, so much so that, one could argue, there is no need for expensive additional facilities, services, programmes and management. Nature has provided fields, woods, rivers, beaches and sunshine. We have the challenge of the mountains, winter snow, the seas and the sky. There is beauty to behold, solitude in the country and peace away from the crowds.

The second thing that could be said is that we, as individuals, or with families or among our friends, should be quite capable of providing for all our recreational needs and for our children, or those unable to care for themselves, without additional facilities, services, programmes and management. Nature has provided us with the means to survive, to seek and explore, to find, to grow and to multiply. Certainly, it has provided us not only with the desire to play and to find recreation, but also with the human capacity and resourcefulness so to do.

Yet the demand for man-made additional resources for leisure and recreation is greater now than it has ever been. Access to the countryside is increasingly limited; footpaths are being destroyed; and playing fields are sold for development. Opportunities are often needed for children just to learn how to play with other children. Indeed, the problem is so acute that it has required government, institutional and voluntary agencies to promote the concept of the 'child's right to play'. The International Year of the Child (1979) focused attention on the plight of children in slums, in traffic-congested areas, in high-rise blocks of flats and in bad homes and housing conditions.

The energies of young people, increasingly apparently channelled into acts of needless violence or vandalism, evidence unsatisfied needs. Could leisure opportunities provide for the adventurousness, the noise, the speed and independence of youth and assist in meeting some of those needs? One could ask whether opportunities are also needed for adults, for families, for the loner, the lonely, the old, the handicapped and the delinquent to *experience* the satisfactions that leisure holds. Will such experience enhance their quality of life?

The assumption is made in this book, at the outset, that the cornerstone of leisure and recreation and its planning and management must be concerned, first, foremost and always, with *people* – not just resources, buildings and facilities, but with the question of human rights, the dignity and the uniqueness of the individual. It is from this standpoint that planning and management are debated and this thread, however tenuous, links discussion on principles, planning and management.

1.5 PROVIDING FOR PEOPLE

Leisure and recreation are made possible by means of a range of services and facilities, both indoor and outdoor, in and around the home, in the urban environment, in rural areas and in the countryside. A range of services and programmes is provided by the public, institutional, voluntary and commercial sectors to meet the diverse needs and demands of individuals, families, groups, clubs and societies.

Many demands are met through resources and equipment in the home. Some demands are met, in part, through outdoor facilities such as gardens and open spaces, allotments, play areas and sports grounds. Other demands are met, in part, through a range of indoor facilities for entertainment, art, music, drama, literary activities, education, sport and physical recreation, hobbies and pastimes. This range of activity requires general and specialist facilities in the form of halls and meeting rooms, libraries, theatres, museums, sports and leisure centres, swimming pools, community centres, entertainment centres, pubs, clubs, cinemas, concert halls, craftrooms and workshops. Recreation in the countryside requires good road networks, maps and signposting, stopping-off points, scenic viewing points, picnic sites, car parking, camping and caravan sites, clean beaches and lakes, water recreation areas, walkways, footpaths, nature reserves and many others.

Demands are met, however, not just by providing facilities, but in attracting people to use and enjoy them, through services, management policy and management action. The range of facilities in urban areas and in the countryside is increasing, and becoming more sophisticated. With it come greater opportunities and greater problems – problems which leisure professionals must help solve through improved planning and management.

1.6 PURPOSE AND SIGNIFICANCE OF THIS BOOK

Leisure and recreation management, the kind which purports to meet the needs of people, must have concern with leisure philosophy, planning, provision and management. The purpose of this book is to explore these fields, to describe, to inform, to challenge and to provide linkages between these aspects, with a view to improving and enhancing leisure and recreation management.

New ground is broken in forging bridges between leisure philosophy, planning, provision and management. Three propositions are made and substantiated that:

1. providers should be concerned with the *quality* of experience for the individual and not just with the quantity of the facilities and the numbers attending;
2. leisure *opportunity* can lead to satisfying recreation experiences, which have positive effects on the quality of life of individual people; and
3. *management* exerts a powerful influence on both participation and non-participation.

Leisure planners, providers and managers are in key positions of creating resources and opportunities, which can help to enhance the quality of life for many people. However, little research has been undertaken relating to people's needs and leisure management and the implications upon the planning, development and operation of facilities. The complex network – linking people's needs, the provision of facilities to meet the needs and the management to render them effective – is an area yet to be adequately explored.

1.7 PLANNING AND STRUCTURE OF THIS BOOK

The structure of the book is illustrated in Fig. 1.1. Three focal points or axes, around which the structure hinges are: leisure and the needs of people, leisure planning and provision, and management.

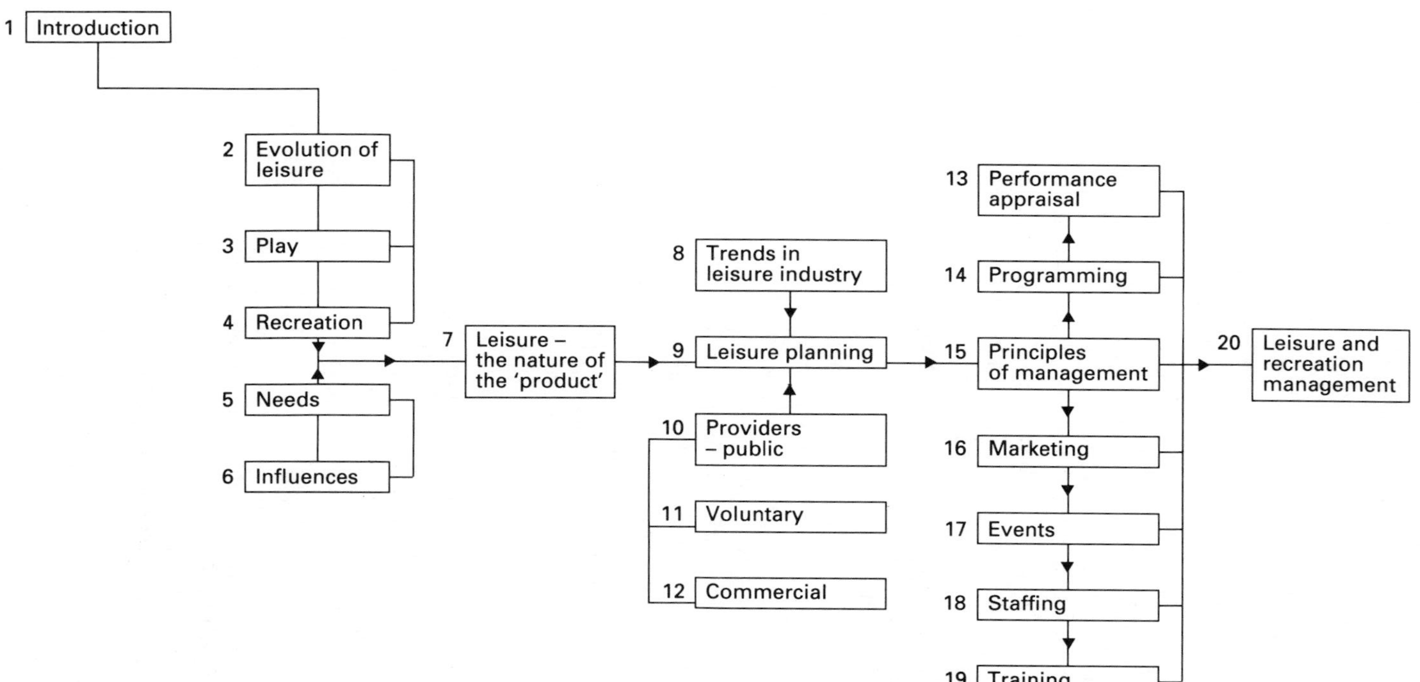

Fig. 1.1 The structure of the book.

1.7.1 Leisure and the needs of people

The first part of the book is written in five chapters and describes and explains three related recreation phenomena: *leisure, play* and *recreation*, and the needs of people and the factors which influence participation. The word 'leisure' is rarely used without invoking other words and concepts, the most frequent being 'sport', 'art', 'entertainment', 'recreation' and 'play'.

Furthermore, lack of attention has been accorded to relating the tangents of play, recreation and leisure into a cohesive and usable whole. The three concepts are used on the one hand to explain three distinct phenomena, yet on the other hand they are often used indiscriminately and frequently interchanged. As a consequence, clear understanding is limited and reliance is placed on generalized assumptions.

If leisure management is to blossom into a profession with a philosophy, an ethic and professional standing, it needs to establish itself as a discipline with a basic framework of terminology and understanding. At present, leisure theory, and consequently leisure planning, appear to be flowing in several diverse directions in search of such a cohesive perspective. If we can understand *what* it is and *why* people play, we shall then have a fundamental basis upon which planning should be based. If we know what motivates people to participate, then conflicts over priorities and facilities would be quickly resolved. On the other hand, if we have no basic insights into why people play and find recreation, then we cannot have any confidence either in the facilities we produce or the programmes we manage, for we will not know whether they are relevant or appropriate. Leisure, play and recreation are studied independently in Chapters 2–4 to show the similarities and differences between them.

Public community services are said to be based on the needs of people. Yet policy-makers, researchers, planners and managers have insufficient insights into people's needs. Clearly, the satisfying of people's needs through leisure opportunity is one of the principles behind providing services.

What are the factors which attract people to participate in recreation, and what factors militate against participation? Are management policy and operation significant influences on people, either to attract or inhibit participation? Chapter 5 describes some perspectives of people's needs and leisure. Chapter 6 considers some of the main factors which appear to influence and condition recreation activity choice.

In Chapter 7 an attempt is made to integrate the three concepts of leisure, play and recreation, taking into account the needs of people and influences upon them. An attempt is also made to explore whether there is an integrated base from which leisure planning and management should stem and the implications are examined as they relate to leisure opportunity and services, particularly in the public sector. The beginnings of a new theory are formulated, which encapsulates the inner core of play, recreation and leisure and becomes the basis for describing the leisure 'experience'.

1.7.2 Leisure planning and provision

The second part of the book is written in five chapters: planning for leisure, trends in leisure and the main providers of leisure and recreation resources, facilities and services, namely the public, voluntary and commercial sectors.

Chapter 8 is concerned with the *planning process*. The planner's dream is to provide the right facilities, in the best location, at the right time, for the people who need them and at an acceptable cost. Leisure planning must therefore include knowledge of leisure–recreation–play, knowledge of people's needs and input from professionals and the community. Should leisure managers be involved in the planning process? A greater human perspective, and a people-oriented approach, is proposed and debated.

The way in which people use their time for leisure has been changing significantly over past decades and some important departures have occurred since the first edition of this book appeared ten years ago. These trends in leisure are described in Chapter 9.

Chapters 10–12 answer the question: who are the providers of leisure and recreation services, resources and facilities? Those involved in recreation policy, research and management must know about the world in which they live – namely, the market place, the providers and their influence. These chapters deal with the public and voluntary and commercial providers respectively. Public recreation is enabled, controlled and guided, to some extent, through a whole range of national agencies and these are briefly described.

1.7.3 The management of leisure

The third focus of the book is the part which, traditionally, is accepted as 'management'. A person is appointed to a position of, say, manager of a leisure complex and is told to get on with the job and *manage*. Many believe that leisure and recreation management starts from there. This book takes a different view. It is suggested that far from starting with the facility, leisure management starts with the people it is intended to serve and their needs and an understanding of the 'product', the market place, the providers and the planning process.

Management, including marketing and programming, it is contended, is a continual beginning-to-end process. The techniques of service and facility management, however, are an important and essential part of the process.

The objectives of Chapter 13 are to describe the principles of management, to consider some general management factors which apply to all managers, such as decision-making and leadership, and to look at specific management tasks in the leisure setting. Two main principles appear to be predominant: the need for objectivity (planning, controlling and evaluating), and the need to be people orientated – to have the ability to motivate and handle properly staff and customers. The chapter concentrates on managers' need to understand the processes and the people with whom managers work.

Chapter 14 moves from general management to specific management and with programming of leisure services and facilities in particular. Managers should have sufficient knowledge to assist policy-makers in establishing guidelines for effective programming. In addition, managers must have sufficient knowledge of programming strategies, approaches and methods, in order to direct staff in achieving the aims and objectives of the organization.

Facility and service management, in which good programming is essential, need practical approaches and processes to achieve balances and targets. Chapter 15 is devoted to one specifically designed process, a performance appraisal based on Management by Objectives, encapsulating policies, aims, objectives, targets and performance measures.

Chapter 16 explores the possibilities for improved marketing of services and products, particularly in the public sector. In the commercial world, marketing leisure products has proved to be an effective means of making greater profits. For services in the public sector could it mean greater success in meeting organizational objectives? Or are there institutional and ethical problems in marketing in the public sector? Should public service marketing be processed in a different way?

The planning, promotion and management of events have become increasingly important skills for leisure managers. The presentation of events on television has created a far more discerning and sophisticated public, who now wish to see events at their local theatre, park or leisure centre promoted with greater flair and professionalism. Chapter 17 gives practical help in planning and presenting events.

Chapter 18 considers staffing. One of the key areas in the management of leisure and recreation services, departments and facilities is the performance of the staff. The way in which staff are organized is a crucial factor in the performance and level of success of management. The principles of management which concern staffing are described;

some of the problems of staffing within recreation services are highlighted, staffing structures are examined and legislation relating to staffing is described briefly.

Training for leisure management is receiving much attention from government, agencies and institutions. But is training appropriate to the needs of leisure and recreation organizations and personnel? Chapter 19 provides a broad overview of the training scene in the United Kingdom with some critical observations and challenging questions relating to leisure management as an emerging profession. The old ways of developing our managers were never very good. Are they worse now?

Finally, in Chapter 20, all the strands of the book – leisure philosophy, planning, provision and management – are drawn together into a new theory and framework for community leisure services and facility management which provides the linkages and bridges the gap between theory and practice, born out of the belief that there is nothing more practical than a good theory.

1.8 QUALITY MANAGEMENT FOR QUALITY LEISURE

The structure of the book therefore is based on a belief in the value of leisure and recreation to individuals and the community. It links philosophy, planning, provision and management; its emphasis is upon the integral role of the manager and management in the process from policy through to application.

A Leisure Manager is not someone who graduates from college with a certificate; there are no instant managers. Nor is he or she someone who, through years of experience, can operate an establishment efficiently, but has no knowledge about the effectiveness of the operation, what are the needs of the consumers and how opportunities can be provided to meet these needs. Rather, a Leisure Manager is a person, younger or older, who has evolved with a mix of education and training inside and outside the job situation, and some experience, to become a person with motivation, ability and sufficient understanding to create and manage opportunities for people to experience leisure through a choice of activities – at whatever level is satisfying for them. Hence the bland statement that 'any good manager can manage anything' is not unequivocally supported.

Many employers equate management with administration and thus appoint administrators. While the good manager should be able to administer, organize and learn, administration is only one of the many functions of management. The emerging profession of leisure management is accumulating many good administrators. This book is written in the hope that the emerging 'profession' will accumulate many good managers.

The first tenet of management is to know what it is you are managing. What business are you in? The following chapters seek answers to the question: what is leisure?

Chapter 2

Leisure – towards a philosophy and understanding of its evolution

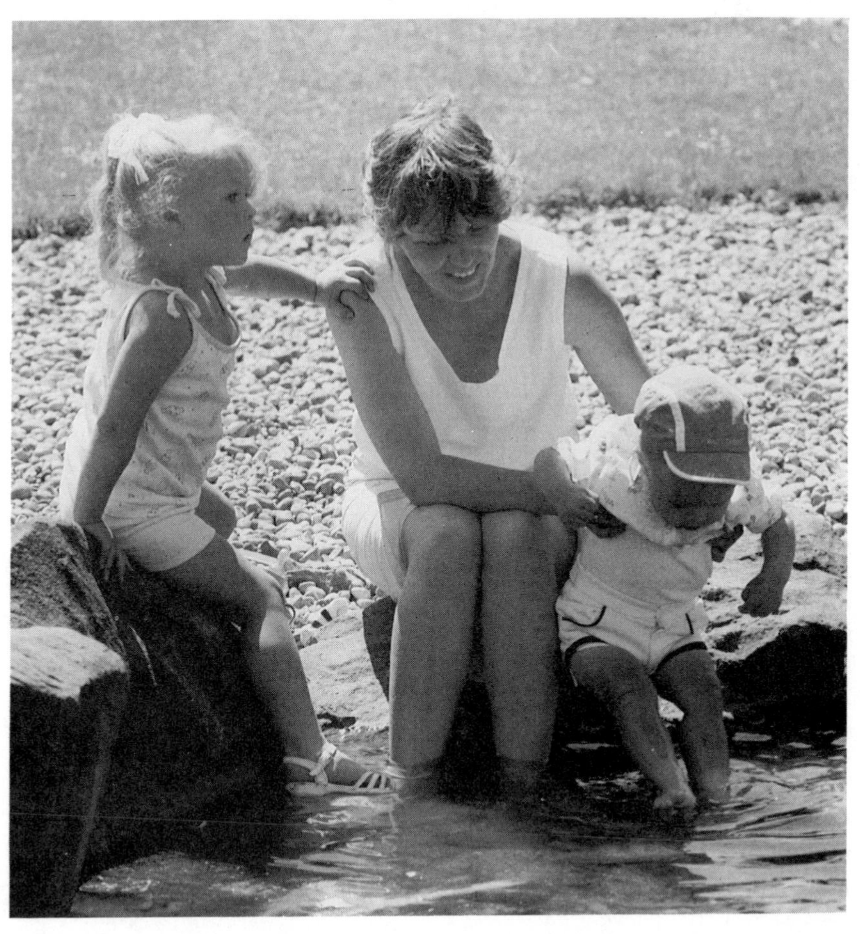

This chapter starts and ends with questions relating to a philosophy of life and leisure; and this first part of the book ends at Chapter 7 with the same question and some insights into it.

The chapter traces the evolution of leisure and its meaning and relevance today. *First*, leisure is seen in its historical perspective, from the Ancient Greek civilization to the Middle Ages to the Renaissance, the Reformation and Industrial Revolution and on to the 20th century. *Second*, a variety of descriptions and definitions are described. *Third*, the development of mass leisure and popular culture and the ensuing benefits and problems are considered. *Fourth*, leisure is viewed in the light of its relationship to the traditional concepts of work.

Having studied this chapter, the reader will know more about how it is that leisure has become significant in the lives of people; about its nature; and about its potential role in providing opportunities for personal well-being and self-fulfilment. The chapter illustrates how the freedom of leisure requires us to make good choices for ourselves and the community. It causes us to ask the question: how can leisure live up to its ideals and fulfil its potential to help people to become all they are capable of becoming? By keeping this theme as a recurring question throughout this book, readers will examine their own beliefs and discover ways to achieve leisure's potential.

2.1 A PHILOSOPHY OF LIFE AND LEISURE?

We may be unaware of it, but each one of us has a philosophy of life, no matter how vague and no matter how inarticulate we might be in defining it. It is our view of the world. What reality means for us is decided by our philosophy of life.

Now, to have 'leisure', to live the life we want to live, to do the things we want to do, freed from undue constraints, and to be all that we want to be, is a dream few achieve and some might not even want because with such freedom comes the responsibility to make 'good' choices. Yet, as we approach the year 2000, we have more knowledge, more resources and more opportunity than before, in which to have a fullness of living, undreamed of in time past. The question is: has leisure a central role in a way of life that harnesses opportunities for self-fulfilment, both at harmony with oneself and the world? Without an understanding of such leisure, albeit an ideal, the 'good life' for one and all, we cannot have sound principles on which to formulate policies for leisure planning, provision and management.

The philosophy – love of wisdom – of which I speak is nothing new. The Ancient Greek philosopher, Aristotle, described a philosophy, of which leisure was a cornerstone, as being about free and exalted souls. It is a far cry from trying to acquire happiness by buying more and language – 'pedagogy', 'gymnasium', 'stadium', 'decathlon', 'lyceum', 'academy', etc. As Goodale and Godbey [9] remind us, a symposium is a gathering of learned people to share ideas: 'to them it was a drinking party. The Greek *schole* became not only school but also *skole*, a drinking song. Ancient philosophers were full of life.' Alas, the leisure ideal died with the Ancient Greeks and little evidence of its resurrection is found until the birth of the university and the Renaissance.

2.2.2 The Romans

The empire of the ancient Romans established in 27 BC continued until AD 395, when it divided into Eastern and Western empires. The Roman culture spread across the known world. In ancient Rome military success and conquests led to affluence, a powerful nation and a move from agricultural democracy to urban populations with a class structure. Masses of the new urban population had considerable free time and as many as 200 holidays a year by the year AD 354. Leisure was important for the Romans, but its importance was different from that of the Greek leisure ethic. To the Romans leisure was important for fitness for work. Sports were practised for maintaining physical fitness and for war. Leisure was utilitarian rather than aesthetic. Baths, amphitheatres and arenas were constructed for the benefit of the mass of the population. In Rome itself there were over 800 public baths at little or no cost to the public.

Free time, however, became a problem. Emperors attempted to keep people content by providing free food and entertainment – 'bread and circuses'. Slaves not only toiled, but were also used for entertainment, which at first included music, drama and sports, but later included contests, simulated land and sea battles, chariot races and exhibitions of violence. Violent spectacles included animals and then humans; professional gladiators fought to the death. The Colosseum, built about AD 80, became the hub of life in Rome and large arenas, gymnasia, parks and baths were built in most large towns. The Circus Maximus could hold 385 000 spectators.

As Rome became more decadent it declined. Historians have suggested that the inability to cope with leisure was one cause for the fall of the empire [10]. Economically, and perhaps in other ways, the spectacles contributed to the financial ruin of the empire, as the aristocracy competed to outdo each other often to the point of bankruptcy.

Ancient Rome shows that mass leisure is no new phenomenon. It illustrates leisure in a social context of urbanization and the political use of leisure to quieten the masses. It also shows the massive investment in public recreation facilities and services and, above all, the growth of leisure *consumption* rather than participation.

Although, like the Greeks, the Romans built and planned for leisure, the stress was upon law and custom and consumption, a political instrument, as distinct from learning, discovering and enlightening. Later cultures used the example of Rome to show the consequences of uncontrolled misuse of leisure.

2.2.3 The Middle Ages

The fall of the Roman Empire and the spread of Christianity had profound and lasting effects on leisure and recreation. The Catholic Church taught that the purpose of life was to prepare for the next life. The early part of the Middle Ages from about 400 to 1000 is often called, aptly, the Dark Ages. For centuries it was for most people a time of relative drabness, and for many doom and gloom.

The first of the monasteries in the Western world was founded by St Augustine in North Africa. The monasteries represented an early sign of lives segmented into discrete parts. The Benedictines preached, 'Work do not despair'. Work became a virtue, as it is today, a far cry from Ancient Greek philosophy.

The monasteries expanded, preaching hard labour, good works and self-deprivation. As a reaction to the extremes and debased activities of the Romans, the church prohibited most kinds of leisure activity except those relating to worship and religious observance. Work was glorified; and idleness was evil. However, while music and morality plays flourished, social drinking, gambling and secular music were practised by the public often on 'holy'-day celebrations, and the aristocracy continued their leisure activities of hunting, falconry and holding tournaments. But life in the Dark Ages was harsh to the common man.

During the late Middle Ages up to approximately 1500 there were some relaxations from those strictures of the Dark Ages, but life for the masses remained much the same with religious festivals, cock fighting and other activities coming as breaks in the round of toil. However, throughout the Middle Ages leisure elitism, a modified Greek ideal for the landed gentry and political leaders, continued. Leisure activities included hunting, hawking, music and dance. Sports and jousting were a means of entertainment, but were primarily preparation for feuding noblemen and for war.

For the masses, leisure came through the church's 'holy'-days and from the trading markets – medieval leisure shopping! In the 13th and 14th centuries royal charters set up boundaries for the Great Fairs, attracting merchants from Europe and Asia. The Fairs attracted entertainers – singers, dancers, jugglers, magicians, fortune tellers, dancing bears and sports such as wrestling, archery, jousting, dog and cock fighting and gambling. Religious festivals and wakes, likewise, attracted entertainers and made for revelry. Gradually, the power of the church declined, but Europe was controlled by powerful monarchs.

2.2.4 Renaissance and Reformation

The two movements, one a cultural revolution and the other a work ethic and a moral way of life, developed in historical parallel. Over the centuries the power of the Catholic Church declined, permitting a reawakening in humanity and the arts. The 15th century marks the transition from the medieval world to modern Western civilization. This period of rebirth, developing in Italy and spreading across France and England is known as the Renaissance, the movement which helped to transform the medieval world and gave birth to modern times.

The spread of knowledge and liberalism – the liberal arts liberated from ignorance – broke through religious dogma. Liberal thought, however, opened up opportunity for both enlightment and extravagance and a breakdown in order and discipline. The Italian Renaissance collapsed through greed and excess. Upon its decline came other philosophies, including the philosophy of Niccolo Machiavelli – to gain power by whatever means, fair or foul.

It was not until the time of the Renaissance that leisure ideals became more generalized and more opportunities were available to the masses. The populace continued to enjoy both religious and secular festivals. The development of printing enabled literature to become available to a wider public since it had previously only been available to those who had studied in monasteries, universities and aristocratic homes. Music, drama and dance were professionally performed in theatres and education became more readily available. Later, educators such as Rousseau and Locke espoused the benefits of play in the education of children. During these times, the nobility became the patrons of the arts and the works of many of the great artists of that time hang in galleries all over the world today.

During the Renaissance, the Protestant Reformation took hold in many parts of Europe and later moved on to America. The liberalism brought about by the Renaissance had also encouraged a pleasure-seeking aristocracy, a public more prone to drinking, gambling and practising cruel sports and a worldly, often corrupt, church; these and other factors led to the Reformation. In the early 16th century, Martin Luther began a revolt against the established church in Germany, where marriages and divorces could be purchased and indulgences (monetary penance) could wipe clean the slate of sin, given sufficient payment!

Calvin and Knox began similar reformed churches. A time of austerity followed, with emphasis on religious matters and a diminishing of many leisure activities. In some communities, even children's play was discouraged as it was said to encourage 'idleness'.

A turning point in history came with Henry VIII's divorce from

Catherine of Aragon and marriage to Anne Boleyn. The Act of Appeals (1533) abolished the Pope's rights and the Act of Supremacy declared that the King of England was supreme head of the Church of England. The sale or destruction of all the religious houses and monasteries of the catholic church has had substantial implications on the tourism industry in Britain. By the turn of the century, England had rejected the authority of the papacy in Rome and the Anglican Church was established during the reign of Elizabeth I but, as now, rifts between warring religious factions continued. The Counter-Reformation of Ignatius Loyola, with the creation of the Jesuits, became a lasting legacy in Europe. The Tudor dynasty (1485–1603) ended with the death of Elizabeth I with England in turmoil. The Stuarts were one of England's least successful dynasties (though James I's reign brought some growth in political stability and a lessening of religious passions), Charles I was publicly beheaded and two decades of civil war and revolution changed again the course of history. To counteract the growing religious opposition to active leisure pursuits, James I of England issued the *Book of Sports* in 1618, making it legal for working people to play certain games outside church hours.

The Puritans, drawn from the poor and middle classes, were dissidents who sought to purify the church along the lines of Luther and Calvin and as a protest against the pleasures of the rich. They became entangled in the political struggle between Parliament and king, which was to lead to civil war, Cromwell's government and the Restoration, with the re-establishment of the monarchy under Charles II in 1660.

Early philosophy was based on subjective thought, ideas and religious precepts. The Renaissance had brought in its wake great discoveries in world exploration, science, medicine, astronomy, mathematics and philosophy. The greatest 'explosion' was in art and painting in northern Italy, with the works of Botticelli, Leonardo da Vinci, Michelangelo, Cellini, Carracci and hundreds of others.

As the movement spread across northern Europe, there came also philosophers Francis Bacon, Hobbes, John Locke and Spinoza, poets Spenser, Dryden and later Voltaire, the French dramatist and historian; and also there came great writers, Shakespeare and Molière, painters including Rembrandt and landscape architects like André le Notre with gardens designed for Louis XIV outside Paris at the Palace of Versailles, and later on Capability Brown.

René Descartes embodied the philosopher-scientist, as did da Vinci a century before. The world was becoming a smaller place with the adventures of explorers like the Spaniard Mendoza, the colonizer of South America; later Sir Francis Drake's voyage around the world; and the growth of world trade with trading companies such as the East India Company.

A non-stop scientific movement was being created. Not surprisingly, there was reaction to such rationality, for example, with the 'romantic movement' of Rousseau, the political philosopher and educator. His philosophy of the child of nature became one of the foundation stones of modern physical education. His ideas of a 'social contract' and political reform were significant in the lead up to the French Revolution against the monarchy and aristocracy, a revolution whose reverberations were to spread for over a century and beyond.

Despite being heavily suppressed by the Reformation, the cultural revolution of the Renaissance continued. In the 17th and 18th centuries parks and gardens were developed for the nobility who went hunting and fishing and enjoyed the beauty of the gardens. Commons and plazas were developed for the public. Holidays were declared by the kings and lords. The Tuileries and the Versailles gardens in Paris and the Tiergarten in Berlin, and Kensington Gardens in London, were gradually opened to the public.

Although the Renaissance brought about more freedom for leisure, the Reformation has been shown to have had an even greater effect on Western attitudes. The Reformation was a period which idealized work and distrusted the evils of leisure – a work ethic which has persisted throughout the 20th century. The Protestant ethic sought to condition leisure to behaviour fitting men and women for devotion and work. The humanism of the Renaissance sought the creativity and development of people through education and greater freedom in leisure. Regrettably, yet another revolution was to suppress still further the leisure development for the mass of the people.

2.2.5 Effect of the Industrial Revolution

The Industrial Revolution of the 18th and 19th centuries led to profound changes. Factories brought about the growth of cities. Populations were uprooted from the land, and from small towns and villages, to the cities. The consequent rise in urban population, overcrowding, poor housing, poverty, crime and the increase in working hours and child labour, all militated against leisure. British industrial history records examples of the hardship caused by the Industrial Revolution and the exploitation of the workers, poor wages and conditions of the miners, the cotton-mill workers and many others.

From the villages where people lived amid nature, where children could play in the fields and families could walk in the countryside people came to cramped conditions with little room to play and little time to enjoy leisure. Recreation areas were not planned. For children, often viewed as cheap labour, the consequences were devasting and many forms of play were condemned as evil.

From the mid-1800s to well into the 1900s a reform movement

sprang up. Reformers were deeply concerned about welfare, especially the welfare of children and they were deeply troubled by the conditions of an urban life bereft of opportunities for healthy exercise and play. The urban churches, in many cases, gradually began to recognize such problems and to come to terms with a new role in regard to recreation.

The reforms dealt more with the concept of recreation than leisure – 'wholesome' opportunities for activity after work which refreshed and renewed the worker for more work. The central element of the leisure philosophy of social reformers was that recreation served socially useful ends, a theme to continue throughout the 20th century. Even today, while there are undoubtedly generous motives based on human welfare, industrial and company recreation is still rationalized on the grounds of lower absenteeism, lower employee turnover, higher morale and higher productivity (Chapter 11).

It was in response to these appalling social conditions that the organized recreation movement began. At the turn of the century, an interest in leisure as it relates to industrial society was awakened. It was during this period also that several of the writings and theories of play and recreation began to emerge. The reformist movements were reactions to specific social situations. The Great Depression of the 1930s and world wars were to bring still further social emergencies.

Also re-emerging at this time was what Thorsten Veblen described as 'the leisure class'. Capitalism, urbanization and industrialization had brought about yet another division in society. In America, Veblen [11] began to identify weaknesses in the industrial system. He criticized the 'leisure class' and its 'conspicuous consumption'. With industrialism, the arbitrary division of labour and class continues to exist and to perpetuate itself. Status becomes symbolized by purchasing power and accumulation of wealth. To Veblen, writing at the turn of the century, leisure was perpetuated for the leisure classes.

It was out of times of hardship and social injustice that social pioneers influenced governments to act. In Britain public health and physical recreation, baths and parks and open spaces were gradually made available to the public. But leisure was never the right of the masses until it was won as a *separate* part of life from the excessively long working hours. The Saturday half-day was a significant turning point in Britain towards an acceptance of leisure for the mass of the people.

Gradually the working class began to demand leisure, not for any idealism or enlightenment, but for time off, because workers (and unions) were now selling their time. The demand for work and free time led to the organization of modern work and the world of public, voluntary and industrial recreation.

The 20th century has seen the growth of recreation, but more important, the need for play as a process of learning for the young and leisure for the sake of enjoyment rather than just for social welfare. Throughout the century there have been provided public parks, 'baths', pubs in their thousands, music halls in the first part of the century and after the First World War cinema and spectator sports and then the greatest hypnotic leisure attraction of them all – the television. Today technology has revolutionized leisure in its many forms. (Read Chapter 9 on the trends in the leisure industry.)

2.3 LEISURE: A VARIETY OF APPROACHES, DESCRIPTIONS AND DEFINITIONS

The English word 'leisure' appears to be derived from the Latin *licere*, 'to be permitted' or 'to be free'. Hence the French word *loisir*, meaning 'free time', and the English words 'licence' and 'liberty'. Thus the word 'leisure' is associated with a complexity of meanings in our language. Generally it is defined in terms of 'freedom from constraint', 'opportunity to choose', 'time left over after work' or as 'free time after obligatory social duties have been met'. However, according to the Parrys, leisure as a social phenomenon itself, 'involves social constraint and social obligation and can best be thought of as being embodied in a whole way of life. Such an idea immediately invokes the concept of culture' [12].

The concept of leisure permits widely varying responses. Leisure is commonly thought of as the opposite of work, but one man's work can be another man's leisure, and several activities combine both leisure and work characteristics. Freedom from obligation is often regarded as a key attraction of leisure, but many non-work activities – i.e. domestic, social, voluntary and community activities – involve considerable obligation. Some regard leisure as being an opportunity for relaxation and pleasure but often people spend their leisure time in dedicated service, study, personal development, hard training, discipline, stress and writing a book! The problems of definition and understanding are considerable.

Most theories have been developed in the 20th century. Many arose out of the troubles of the Industrial Revolution; hundreds of theories and descriptions of leisure have been written from then until now. From the mass of literature, five discernible, though overlapping, approaches are evident:

1. Leisure as time.
2. Leisure as activity.
3. Leisure as a state of being.

4. Leisure as an all-pervading, 'holistic' concept.
5. Leisure as a way of life.

2.3.1 Leisure as time

Within the broad framework of leisure defined as time there are many interpretations. Some make a very broad distinction, defining leisure as the time when someone is not working primarily for money [13]. With such a definition, however, we are left with a large proportion of people's time which is filled in a multitude of ways. Such a definition of leisure is far too broad to be of use and is only perceived in the context of doing 'work'.

The Dictionary of Sociology describes leisure as 'free time after the practical necessities of life have been attended to'. This gives 'surplus time' to do with as we please. Several other writers refer to leisure as free time or unoccupied time. The problem in viewing leisure as free time is that it is difficult to draw a line between necessities and spare time.

Parker [14] contrasts between 'residual' definitions and others. Residual time is the time left after taking out of total time everything that is not regarded as leisure. The Countryside Recreation Research Advisory Group defined leisure as 'the time available to the individual when the disciplines of work, sleep and other needs have been met'.

To Brightbill [15] and others, while leisure is concerned with time, it is only leisure if it falls into 'discretionary' time – i.e. time beyond existence and subsistence, 'the time to be used according to our own judgement or choice'. Hence three time-slots are identified: existence, subsistence and discretionary.

Yet the matter is complicated further: what is necessary for some will be discretionary for others and many necessary activities, for example, eating and sleeping may be chosen as discretionary activities. However, in general it appears that the word 'leisure' is correlated with positive or constructive behaviour. Free time appears to have some negatively charged characteristics. This aspect of leisure, as time, appears to establish leisure in a positive relationship to time. As Goodale and Godbey point out, in idealistic terms, 'we dis-locate leisure by consigning it to particular periods during days, weeks and years' [9].

2.3.2 Leisure as activity

A classical understanding of leisure is that it is made up of activities which enlighten and educate. Leisure therefore is made up of activities. Today we hear leisure described as a 'cluster of activities'.

Most industrialized popular culture is targeted for a middle-class, affluent urban audience, probably American, Japanese, British or French: 'As this material is beamed across the world, millions outside that target audience are exposed to it. To the extent they begin using it as a baseline against which to judge their own lives, one can predict an increase in feelings of dissatisfaction in such populations.'

The impact of television is illustrated dramatically in the showing of the 1990 Association Football World Cup, viewed across the world by an estimated audience of approaching 1 billion people, some of whom in poorer countries bought television sets for the first time. Lewis [46] sees a threefold outcome of popular Western culture beamed across the world: first, it will bring out feelings of personal inadequacy; second, a turning outward to forms of political unrest and dissensions; and third, developing countries will accept such popular culture as the goal towards which they should strive, at exactly the same point in history when the major economically developed countries are beginning to realize that the world does not have the energy, nor the resources, to support such life-styles of leisure.

Popular culture, however, has brought to the mass of people television, radio, popular music, fashion, sport and new life horizons. Mass leisure and popular culture are part and parcel of most civilizations today and must be fashioned to improve the quality of life for the great mass of people but, at the same time, must prevent the destruction of a nation's culture and heritage.

2.6 LEISURE: ITS RELATIONSHIP TO WORK

Other than the very essential, the ancient Athenians and Romans did not think much of work. Work was a curse: the Greek word for work, *ponos*, meant 'sorrow'. The philosophers agreed with the poets. The only solution, as most clearly expressed by Plato and Aristotle, was to have the vast majority, the slaves, provide the necessities and material goods for all, so that the minority – the citizens – could engage in leisure which produced the arts and sciences, politics, government and philosophy.

The relationship between the concepts of 'work' and 'leisure' has been well debated and documented, though there are no satisfactory universally accepted theses. We have noted that some societies, both ancient and modern, have made a clear distinction between work and leisure.

2.6.1 Work: a heritage of slavery, a tradition of paid employment

History has shown that the life of leisure could only be pursued by those who had sufficient free time and means to free themselves from the 'curse' of work. The blessing of leisure for some meant intensive work for many. The Greek aristocracy could not have pursued their leisure without widespread slavery; the English aristocracy could not have been the epitome of the cultured stock without suppression of the poor.

Bertrand Russell [51], in *In Praise of Idleness*, asserted that harm was caused by the belief that work was virtuous; the morality of work was the morality of slaves. Work was indeed slavery to the suppressed. The boys and girls who slaved in the coalmines and textile-mills in England just over a century ago had neither the time nor the energy to enjoy leisure.

The word 'work' covers a multitude of things. It is often used synonymously with words such as 'labour', 'occupation', 'employment', 'effort' and 'production'. Work may also be a time for personal development, creativity and other personal satisfactions. Marx's [52] ideal model of work was 'a process in which man and Nature participate, and in which man of his own accord starts, regulates, and controls the material recreations between himself and Nature'. However, modern work tends to contradict this ideal. Specialization, fragmentation, isolation, rigid time structuring, repetitiveness and depersonalization contribute to anonymity, a sense of helplessness and alienation for many workers.

To the public at large the question 'what is work?' is so obvious that definitions and understanding seem to be totally inappropriate. Work is paid employment. It is concerned with earning a wage, the money on which to live. In addition, work has been traditionally valued. It has been a means of self-identification. Traditionally too, work is what adults, particularly adult males, have to do. Leisure is something you don't have to do; traditionally again, it is conceived as freedom from commitment. Yet for those involved, many leisure activities require considerable commitment. It is clear to see that these two realms of 'work' and 'leisure' need to be considered not as dichotomized entities, but in far more fluid and complex dimensions.

2.6.2 The work–leisure dichotomy

People's lives are segmented in a whole variety of ways. One person, close to my heart, is a mother, grandmother, homemaker, part-time teacher, church steward, school governor, volunteer worker and recreational 'player' – all wrapped up in the same person. Work and play are becoming more and more alike; in some lives they are becoming, in a sense, fused. Focus here, however, is on only the segmentation of life into leisure and non-leisure.

In modern Western civilization different approaches to the work–leisure dichotomy are evident. As Parker [53] outlined:

'One (clearly declining) is that work is the serious business of life and leisure is subsidiary or even non-existent. The second is that leisure is the aim and purpose of life and work merely a means to that end. The third is a more integrated approach: work and leisure as reconcilable parts of a whole life, such as that of the craftsman or artist.'

'An important clue to the relative importance attached to work and leisure is the choice that people make between having more income or more leisure. In non-industrial societies people tend not to seek additional work after they have achieved a comfortable margin of income over what they consider to be necessary. But among the economically advanced nations more people prefer additional work (overtime or a second job) to more leisure'.

'Moonlighting' has become a familiar term. It was used in the British Parliament during the 1979 Budget debate which was denounced as a 'moonlighter's charter'. Although moonlighting does not appear to be a major problem to employers, it could grow to significant proportions. The move away from standard hours for some and flexi-hours for others, and the tendency to trade leisure for extra income, could become an issue in years to come.

From a sociological standpoint, Berger [54] identifies the primary differences between classical and Puritan attitudes. The Industrial Revolution produced an alteration in concepts of leisure and work which brought segmentation and separation. Leisure is no longer part of everyday life, but has become a relief from work, a reward and even rehabilitation. Berger asserts that there has been an alienation from work and loss of opportunities for personal achievement, identity and expression of prowess in work. The appeal to people by government and community to make wholesome use of leisure time, and to participate in community recreation programmes, he feels is ineffective because they fail to take credence of the social needs of leisure and the need to counteract work alienation. People will reject participation when it is beyond their means or when activities express values they do not recognize.

Some of the relevant factors in appreciating the juxtaposition of work to leisure in modern times are as follows:

1. Working hours determine how much time and money are available for leisure.
2. Work may determine the energies, enthusiasm and motivations left over for leisure.
3. Some work affords leisure opportunity during work hours or as part of work itself.
4. Some jobs are more akin to certain types of leisure occupation.

There are several arguments to suggest a fusion of work and leisure:

1. More people use free time for work purposes both for employment and for effort towards obligatory or non-obligatory actions.
2. Some work decisions are made with leisure in mind as one of the perks of the job.
3. Many leisure pursuits have become employment for some and extremely hard work for others.

Others, however, take the view that work and leisure are becoming more polarized. There is more free time available but not nearly as much as is popularly believed, perhaps no more than a few hours a week.

Two contrasting functions of leisure in relation to work have been put forward by Wilensky [55]: *spillover* and *compensatory*. People's work 'spills' over into leisure, or is a continuation of work, or there is a continuation of work experiences and attitudes. On a 'compensatory' level, leisure makes up for the dissatisfaction which is the outcome of work. Roberts [43] believes that leisure gives more meaning to a person's life than work but the job usually influences leisure behaviour more than vice versa. Bacon [56] found that there was little evidence to support the view that alienating work is associated with certain types of leisure behaviour. The things that people choose to do in their free time are unrelated to the nature of their employment.

In relation to work, Kelly [57] suggested three types of leisure activity: 'unconditional leisure' is independent of work and freely chosen; 'coordinated leisure' is similar to work such as undertaking a hobby; and 'complementary leisure' which is independent of work in form and content, but the need to take part is influenced by one's work such as being obliged to participate when it is expected of you.

Blauner [58] concludes that work remains the single most important activity for most people in terms of time and energy. Argyris [59] illustrates the difficulties of making leisure compensate for work: if people experience dependence, submission, frustration and conflict at work, and if they adapt to these conditions by psychological withdrawal, apathy and indifference, then these adaptive features will guide their leisure behaviour outside the workplace.

A case can be formulated to show work and leisure as opposites. However, this is a far from adequate formulation. Concepts such as *play, recreation* and *leisure* become relative terms. One man's play is another man's work: one man's leisure is another man's drudgery. In addition, the seriousness of work is seen in play and the play element in work.

2.6.3 Work, leisure and unemployment

Work has been traditionally valued. It has been a means of self-identification. A person's leisure appears to relate not only to indi-

Chapter 3

Play

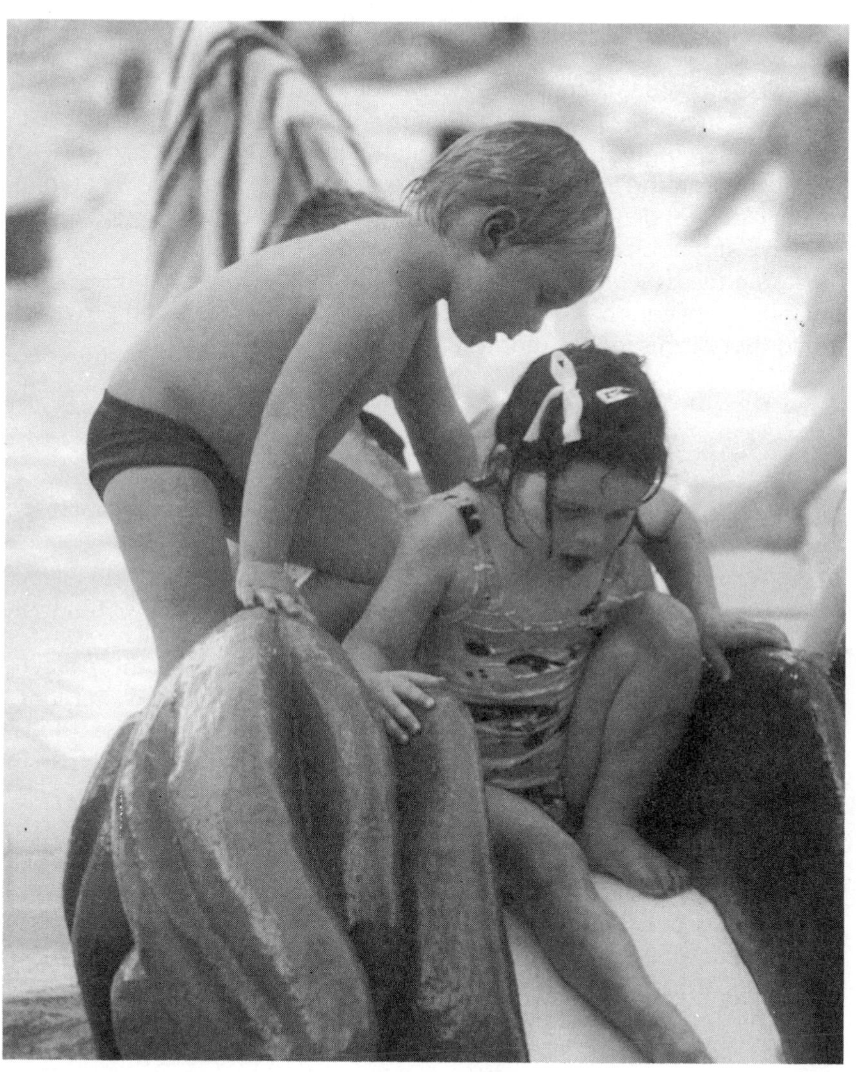

We have been concerned in Chapter 2 with the evolution of leisure and its role for the individual and the community. This chapter is concerned with the concept of *play*. It draws out the characteristics of play behaviour and attempts to understand what it is and why people play.

First, play is introduced to show that on the one hand it appears to be a simple phenomenon, yet on the other hand it is an extraordinarily complex one. *Second*, play is placed in historical perspective to show how it has been used and misused. *Third*, some of the theories of play – classical, more recent and modern – are described; and, *fourth*, play and playfulness are discussed in the light of their meanings and practical application.

Having studied this chapter, readers will be able to discern the special characteristics of play behaviour and its freedom of expression and its inner-consuming nature. Readers will be able to appreciate the role of play in the learning and socializing process of the young, and its potential in adult leisure, given the right climate in which to flourish. Readers will perceive similarities of play to leisure, yet there are cultural differences; those similarities and differences will be studied in Chapter 4. The practical implications of play theory on leisure planning and provision are further discussed in Chapters 7 and 8.

3.1 PLAY: A COMPLEX PHENOMENON

Our family dog, Sherriff, typical of so many animals, appears to be happiest (when not eating) at play – catching, fetching, teasing, playing games and having fun. The play of animals illustrates that play precedes culture and human civilization. Of all the animal kingdom, the latest of the species – human beings – play most of all.

Great discoveries have been made which help unravel the past. In tracing human development, anthropologists have found not only implements for work and survival, but also playthings – toys, dolls, hoops, rattles, marbles and dice. Long before the Hans Christian Andersen story of Pinnochio, our ancestors were inventive and creative toy makers. Playing musical instruments, dressing up in ornate costume, pageantry and dancing may have resulted from, initially, just playing, or having fun. In later times, scientific discoveries and inventions may well have been the outcome of playing with a hobby, with intense and absorbing enthusiasm.

So people play and appear to have done so from the dawn of man and woman. Why do they – is play the same phenomenon as recreation? Is it leisure? Why does one person choose one activity, and another something entirely different? To one, an activity may be play; to another, the same activity may well be drudgery. What determines the choice? Is it upbringing, ability, stature or status, education, employment, personality or the pressure of the social group or friends? Given the right ingredients, can choices be determined, predictions made and demands gauged? If so, major planning problems can be tackled realistically.

Play is a mystery and an enigma. It is understood yet misunderstood; known yet unknown; and tangible yet so internal to the individual that it is untouchable. Also it is utterly individual yet universal. The play of children is accepted, but the play of adults has perhaps a stereotyped image of muddy footballers on muddy pitches. However, play is not confined to the games of children, the sport of young men, the family outing or the Christmas party. Play can pervade all aspects of life; not just physical play, but also the play of the mind, the play of words and the play of communications with people. To Sebastian de Grazia [1]:

'The world is divided into two classes. Not three or five or twenty. Just two. One is the great majority. The other is the leisure kind, not those of wealth or position or birth, but those who love ideas and the imagination. Of the great mass of mankind there are few persons who are blessed and tormented with this love. They may work, steal, flirt, fight, like all the others, but everything they do, is touched with the play of thought'.

Play then can be evident in all walks of life, at home, at school, at work, in politics and unions, in religion, in business, in crime and vandalism, in international dealings and even in war. The film *Oh, What a Lovely War!* carried the caption 'the ever popular war game folks with songs, battles and a few jokes'. The problem with war is that for some it can be a game – it can be fun!

One of the distinguishing signs of the play world is its strict adherence to invented rules, which suspend the ordinary rules of real life. The attitudes encompassed in play rules carry over from the play world into the 'real' world. While boxers play to Queensberry Rules, soldiers play to the rules of the Geneva Convention and some criminals have a code of acceptable behaviour. Parliamentary and local government rules are cloaked in the playful seriousness of obligatory procedures, the 'Chair', the 'points of order' and the adherence to the 'laws of the game'. Sometimes, as with children's games, it would appear that the procedures are more important than the business itself. 'Fair play' is often play acceptable to the rules. In this context, it is curious to find how much more lenient society is towards the cheat than it is towards the spoilsport. As Huizinga [2] points out, the spoilsport shatters the play world and robs it of its illusion (*in lusio*, 'in play'); the game ends. (If I can't bat, I'll take my bat and go home.) The cheat, on the other hand, pretends to be playing the game and on the face of it acknowledges the magic circle, the rules; the game continues.

Suffice it to say, at this point, that play, normally reserved for the playground and playing field, is indelibly printed upon the lives of men and women, boys and girls. It spans the frivolous and the utterly serious, the shallow and the deeply emotional. Play is in the very nature of human beings. As life is a mystery, so is play. What explanation is there for the mystery?

3.2 PLAY IN HISTORICAL PERSPECTIVE

The roots of play philosophy and theory, like leisure, reach back to ancient times. In some respects, the classical era of Greece was also one of the most enlightened. Although child labour was common, children had an important place in classical society. Play was given a valuable position in the life of children, according both to Plato and Aristotle [3,4]. Play and leisure gave an opportunity to develop. The primary force was education (*paideia*), educating man in his true form, inculcating qualities of responsibility, of honour, loyalty, pride and of beauty. The philosophical writings which remain indicate the dedication to state and culture, the highest value being *productive citizenship*. It is not surprising therefore to note that play (*paideia*, i.e. the same word as education) was considered an aspect of enculturation and cultural reinforcement.

Play to the Greeks was associated with childhood. Yet the citizenship of adult life and the appreciation of aesthetics, music, art, athletics, drama and poetry might be seen as the products of play. Today we tend to look at the opportunities for play as incorporating free choice, freedom from compulsion, often spontaneity. But the Greek citizen was bound to social commitment. There was a belief in universal personality/character which was held to be true of all noble persons. Hence life's activities were structured to fulfil this ideal. Play, then, was a means of integrating children into Greek culture. The Ancient Greeks laid a foundation of thought regarding play that has endured to influence leisure and recreation today. The perfectability of human nature through play, its usefulness in mental, physical and social well-being and the necessity of social control were of great importance.

Later civilizations modified Greek attitudes towards play. The Roman culture exploited leisure and provoked a hedonistic philosophy, which abandoned the concepts of moderation and balance in play behaviour. The ensuing over-reaction to play left its mark on the cultures that followed.

The church took strict moral control over play expression. There emerged a suspicion of 'play' as a social threat. The Middle Ages marked a period of lack of any concept of childhood; children were viewed simply as small adults but with low status. Obedience to and passive acceptance of God's will characterized the ethos of these times; play, the active seeking of new experience, retained little place in the ideals of this world. The body was thought to detract from more spiritual activities, thus every effort was made to curb its impulses. The Reformation acted further to restrict play among those following its creeds. Work became all-important; consequently, play became separated from work behaviour, and was considered morally dangerous.

Important contributions in the 18th and 19th centuries to counteract the decline in play philosophy came from Rousseau, Froebel and Schiller. Rousseau in his revolutionary text *Emile* espoused the idea of the natural child – the child of nature; mankind should return to a state of nature marked by simplicity and freedom. Schiller [5] took a more aesthetic view of play, a new respect for play with a hint of Greek idealism: 'Man shall only play with Beauty, and he shall play only with Beauty ... Man plays only when he is in the full sense of the word a man, and he is only wholly Man when he is playing.'

Froebel [6] continues this philosophical direction. Play is the highest expression of human development in childhood.

'Play is the purest, most spiritual activity of man at this stage ... A child that plays thoroughly, with self-active determination, perseveringly until physical fatigue forbids, will surely be a thorough, determined man, capable of self-sacrifice for the promotion of the welfare of himself and others.'

Froebel emphasized a belief in self-esteem, self-determination and self-discipline. The Froebel Kindergarten was fashioned not only on age-related growth needs, but also on the need for opportunity for individual expression and spontaneity.

During the 19th century, the early education movement produced a new interest in play which culminated in a number of theoretical propositions attempting to explain and justify play. The ideas of Rousseau, and reformist and revolutionary ideas, forced society to accept two major changes: a distinction between the child and the adult, and the acceptance of play as an end in itself.

3.3 PLAY THEORIES

Play theories can be classified in a number of different ways. This section is divided broadly into three categories – classical, more recent and modern theories.

3.3.1 Classical theories

Many attempts have been made to explain the nature and function of play. The history of classical play theory has become relatively well known. Five of these theories are better known than the rest and survive in the literature today: the surplus energy, instinct, preparation for life, recapitulation and relaxation theories.

Schiller [5] saw play as non-survival – important, even aesthetic but essentially purposeless. Spencer [7] added two components: imitation, together with a physiological explanation. The *surplus energy theory*, sometimes referred to as the Schiller–Spencer theory, describes play as the expenditure of over-abundant energy which is unused in the normal processes of life sustenance.

The *instinct theory* suggests that play is caused by the inheritance of unlearned capacities to behave playfully. But this theory explains little, it ignores the fact that people learn new responses that we classify as play.

Groos [8] proposed that the play of children was practice for life. The *preparation theory*, based on Darwinian thinking, states that play is caused by the efforts of the player to prepare for later life.

Play is explained in the *recapitulation theory* as an outcome of biological inheritance. It is another Darwin-influenced theory. Children are a link in the evolutionary chain from animals to man, experiencing the history of the human race in play activities. Stanley-Hall [9] believed that play patterns were instinctive, generic expressions and re-enactments of early man's activities – i.e. a recapitulation of racial development seen in water play, digging in the sand, climbing trees and in tribal gangs.

Urban life puts people under extreme strain. The *relaxation theory* propounded by Patrick in *The Psychology of Relaxation* [10] proposed that playful activity was caused by the need to find compensating outlets to allow relaxation and recuperation from the tension and stress of work.

Most of the early theories were based on instinct as motivation of human play and these theories now only survive when they are incorporated in other theories of play behaviour. So today we find that play is considered to be much more complex than earlier theories suggested. All the older theories have some small merit, seeming to explain some aspects of behaviour, but they are over-optimistic in their simplicity. Each is relevant to different sets of problems. They take no account of individual differences. Ellis [11] suggests: 'Old soldiers never die' and they linger on in the literature as 'armchair theories'. They seem to explain, albeit curiously, some aspects of human behaviour, but they have logical shortcomings and are not substantiated by empirical findings.

3.3.2 More recent theories

In contrast to the classical theories, recent theories (after the turn of the 20th century) are concerned with attempting to explain the differences among the play of individuals. In his analysis of theories, Ellis [12] lists five major recent theories, namely generalization, compensation, catharsis, psychoanalytic development and learning. Other theories view play as an all-embracing phenomenon: as an end in itself, as the basis of civilization and culture, as the roots of social behaviour, as a reflection of society.

Two of the theories – *generalization* and *compensation* – rely on the belief that people's play choices are a result of the nature of their work. People who perform work tasks well, and are satisfied by them, will tend to behave similarly during their leisure time. The compensation theory suggests that adults select their leisure activities to compensate for the tendency of the work situation to deny satisfaction of their needs. These theories are over-simplistic, too general and take no account of pre-school play.

The *cathartic theories* of play stem from classical Greece where dramatic tragedies and some music were believed to purge the audience of their emotions. The belief was that giving vent to feelings and emotions releases them. Feshbach [13] questions the validity of the theory that the expression of aggression in a socially approved form will reduce the amount of socially disapproved aggressive behaviour. Aggression researchers are finding that frustration leads to heightened aggressive feelings, but that subsequent aggressive behaviour does not reduce aggression. Berkowitz and Green [14] indicate that 'aggression begets aggression'.

In the *psychoanalytic theories* of play concern for individual behaviour is clearly paramount. Interest stemmed from the observations of Freud [15], who observed that much play is motivated by pleasure. His ideas were later amended and formalized by Walder [16] to show that play has multiple functions and cannot be explained by a single function; that work was expanded still further by Erikson [17]. Hence the psychoanalytic theory goes beyond the pleasure principle to explain the play of children that is related to experiences that are not pleasant. There are encounters that they cannot control which are often unpleasant. To Freud, the opposite to play is not what is serious, but what is *real*.

Psychoanalytic theory suggests that children consciously add actual elements from their environment to their fantasies, mixing reality and unreality into their play. Adults are seen as more constrained by society, emphasizing their grasp of reality and hiding their tendency to deal with unreality in play. Thus adults are left with covert fantasies.

Walder [16] suggests that 'fantasy woven about a real object is however nothing other than play'.

The psychoanalytic methods of viewing the phenomenon of play led researchers like Melanie Klein to develop play therapy [18]. By playing out feelings, a child can bring them to the surface, get them out into the open, face them and learn to control or abandon them. When anxious, a child will prefer to play with items which are salient to the anxiety (e.g. hospitalized children prefer to play with toys relevant to the situation, namely doctors and nurses). However, the psychoanalytic theories are another set of partial theories, explaining some aspects of play behaviour.

Erikson [17] extended the ideas of infant development to stages of mastery and life development, taking into account effects of the environment. Play has a developmental progression in which a child adds new, more complex understandings about the world at each stage. He identified three stages: 'autocosmic' play concerns bodily play; the 'micro sphere' is playing with toys and objects; and the 'macro sphere' develops sharing. For the child, Erikson feels that play may be used to work through and master reality. The child finds identity through play. Infant play between mother and child is all-important; adult behaviour and attitude are also of great importance. He relates this interplay to ritualization; the ritual expression combines the elements of play and social tradition, providing individual identity in a structured and/or communal fashion.

The Swiss child psychologist, Jean Piaget [19], deals with play as an aspect of *intellectual development*. The structure of intelligence is a function of two co-existing processes which operate together to produce adaptation to the environment. These processes he called *assimilation* and *accommodation*.

Assimilation is a process whereby the child imposes on reality his or her own knowledge and interpretations and thus often alters reality to fit what is known from previous experience. In contrast is the process of accommodation, whereby the child alters existing cognitive structures to meet with the demands of reality. Hence the child modifies feelings and thoughts when confronted with an object which appears novel: what he/she thinks is known must be altered to match what is encountered in the environment.

According to Piaget the balance between assimilation and accommodation constitutes the basis of intelligence and all behaviour is the 'acting out' of this cognitive interplay. Play is characterized by the assimilation of elements in the real world without the balancing constraints of accepting the problems of accommodating them – i.e. the behaviour that occurs when assimilation predominates can be described as playful and when accommodation predominates behaviour is viewed as imitative. Hence play is manipulative. Children alter and restructure environment to match experience and existing knowledge: reality is altered; the child creates an imaginary play world.

Piaget believes that play eventually becomes a game played with rules and structure. Sutton-Smith [20] has raised many objections to this thesis. He believes that play remains important, does not become more realistic or rationalistic as intelligence develops, but remains symbolic, ritualistic and playful, even into adulthood. In essence, however, Piaget implies that play is the most effective aspect of early learning.

Thorndike, Hull, Skinner and others view play as learned behaviour, 'stimulus–response behaviour' [21]. A response has an increased probability of occurring if it is accompanied by a pleasant or reinforcing event. If play behaviour is learned behaviour, then the learning will occur as a result of a whole variety of 'reinforcers' and reinforcing systems, for example, parents, other children and other adults sharing the same cultural and environmental influences.

Empirical studies have been undertaken by Roberts and Sutton-Smith [22], an anthropologist and psychologist collaborating to study the role of games in various societies. They have shown that individuals in different cultures perceive games differently, depending on the values and attitudes prevalent, and that such games serve to relieve social conflict and consequently enhance socialization. They put forward a theory of conflict enculturation. Conflicts induced by social learning (e.g. obedience, achievement, responsibility training) lead to an involvement in 'expressive models', such as games, through which these conflicts are moderated, lessened and assuaged. A learning process occurs which has cultural value both to the players and to their societies. They tested the hypothesis by studying the difference in rearing patterns and games played by the children in three societies. Clear evidence was found for an association between the predominance of one type of game and a particular emphasis in the rearing patterns.

Jan Huizinga [23], a Dutch historian, in his masterly book *Homo ludens*, presents the cultural approach to play: 'Play is older than culture, for culture, however adequately defined always presupposes human society, and animals have not waited for man to teach them their playing.' Huizinga showed play to exist in every aspect of culture. He defines play as follows:

'Summing up the formal characteristics of play we might call it a free activity standing quite consciously outside "ordinary" life as being "not serious", but at the same time absorbing the player intensely and utterly. It is an activity connected with no material interest, and no profit can be gained by it. It proceeds within its own proper boundaries of time and space according to fixed rules and in an orderly manner. It promotes the formation of social groupings which tend to surround themselves with secrecy and to stress their difference from the common world by disguise or other means'.

To Huizinga, play is *self-justification*. It can be present in all aspects of life – i.e. in work, business, leisure, sport, art, literature, music, religion and even in war. He believed most former theories to be only partial theories, which justified play as a means to an end: play was seen to serve something which it is *not*, leaving the primary quality of play untouched. Moreover, civilization had compartmentalized play, had grown more serious, had put play into second place. For the full unfolding of civilization we cannot neglect the play element: 'genuine pure play is one of the main bases of civilization.' Observation of the play rules were nowhere more important than in relations between nations. Once the rules were broken, society would be in chaos.

Huizinga believed that to play we must play like a child. When, for example, the play spirit is lost from sport, sport becomes divorced from 'culture'. He gives no explanation as to why people play, but he does describe play vividly. One can deduce from his description a number of interrelated characteristics:

1. Play is a free, voluntary activity. There is more freedom in the play world than in the real world. We cannot play to order; if the player is forced to 'play', it changes its nature; it is no longer play.
2. Play is indulged in for its own sake. It is unproductive and non-utilitarian.
3. Play is not 'ordinary' or 'real'. The player steps outside real life into a temporary sphere. The player knows it is only pretending, yet it is often utterly serious.
4. Play has boundaries of space and time. It has its own course and meaning.
5. Play is creative. Once played, it endures a new-found creation: it is repeated, alternated, transmitted; it becomes tradition.
6. Play is orderly and creates order. Into an imperfect world and the confusion of life it brings a temporary, limited perfection.
7. Play is regulated. It has rules and conventions; they determine what 'holds' in the temporary world. The new legislation counts; deviation spoils the play.
8. Play is 'uncertain'. The end-result cannot be determined. When the result is a foregone conclusion, then the tension and excitement is lost.
9. Play is social. Play communities tend to become permanent social grouping even after the game is over (clubs, brotherhoods, gangs).

Groups are often esoteric or secret: 'It is for us, not for others.' Inside the magic circle there are the laws and customs which suspend the ordinary rules of life.

10. Play, then, is symbolic.

Huizinga's theory is a philosophical one. Play exists, it has always existed; it is its own justification. But self-justification is something that cannot be measured. It gives insights but not explanations.

The French sociologist, Roger Caillois [24], in *Man, Play and Games*, has presented a socio-culturally based theory of play building upon the theory of Huizinga. Caillois critically analysed the definition and redefined play as activity which is free, separate, uncertain, unproductive, governed by rules or make-believe.

Caillois developed a unique typology of the characteristic games of a society. Games are a culture clue, helping to reveal the character, pattern and values of a society. The basic themes of a culture should be deducible from the study of play and games no less than from the study of economic, political, religious or family institutions. He claimed that the destinies of cultures can be read in their choice of games: 'Tell me what you play and I will tell you who you are.'

The choice of games will reflect the society. Caillois identified four general classifications of games:

Agon (competition)	The desire to win by merit in regulated competition.
Alea (chance)	The submission of one's will to the luck of the draw.
Mimicry (simulation)	Assuming a strange personality.
Ilinx (vertigo)	The confusion that giddiness provokes.

Games in each of the four categories were put on to a continuum representing an evolution from childlike play (*paidia*) to adult play (*ludus*). The first encompasses the spontaneous, frivolous, exuberant play, the frolic and the romping. The second is more concerned with man the thinker; the pleasure is in resolving difficulties. It represents those elements in play whose cultural importance seems to be the most striking. Rules are inseparable from play, once play acquires an institutional existence.

According to Caillois, while the games reflect the functioning of a society, if corrupted, they indicate the weakness and potential dissolution of the culture. Although not completely explanatory, and often weak in accurate identifications of social expressions, Caillois's theory does illuminate another perspective for analysis of play.

3.3.3 Modern theories

There are few modern theories of play. Play is increasingly seen as a mixture of different elements. Two theories are considered: play as a stimulus-seeking behaviour, and play interpreted as playfulness.

(i) Play as stimulus-seeking behaviour

Michael Ellis's book *Why People Play* [11] is one of the most comprehensive and thorough studies of play in modern times. Ellis believes that there is no way of reaching any 'pure' definition and that the most satisfying explanation of play involves an integration of three theories: *play as arousal-seeking behaviour, play as learning* and *the developmentalist view of play*. There is considerable evidence to support the view that play enhances learning and development. The third aspect – the drive for optimal arousal – is advanced by Ellis.

Ellis shows that evidence is accumulating to explain some behaviour in terms of a drive to maintain optimal arousal. He defines play in this context as 'that behaviour that is motivated by the need to elevate the level of arousal towards the optimal'. Put another way, play is *stimulus-seeking activity* that can occur only when external consequences are eliminated: 'When primary drives are satisfied the animal continues to emit stimulus-seeking behaviour in response to the sensoristatic drive. The animal learns to maintain an optimal level of arousal.'

Researchers in arousal theory find that it is the stimuli that are complex, incongruous or novel that lead to arousal. In addition, the stimuli must have the ability to reduce uncertainty or carry information to the individual. Too much uncertainty and too much novelty will not be optimally arousing. Some intermediate level of information flow is optimally arousing. When situations are too complex, they have no arousal potential, and at the other end of the scale when the outcome is highly predictable, there is little uncertainty and the arousal potential diminishes. For example, the crossword in *The Times* will have no arousal potential for the easy-crossword dabbler; the gifted player will not be stimulated by the novice opponent.

The play 'spirit' for many adults is often the play of the mind. Reading a thriller, following the fortunes of a favourite team in the newspaper, reading up on the Stock Exchange, doing crosswords, playing *Trivial Pursuit*, problem-solving or just day-dreaming are all activities actively sought after by adults, in particular, who by virtue of their age have a richer store of experiences. However, stimulus-seeking behaviour means more than merely seeking exposure to any stimuli. The stimuli must have *arousal* potential. Knowledge seeking, for example, results in the reduction of conflicts, mismatches and uncertainties. Laughter, humour and smiling are created by situations such as novelty, surprise, incongruity, ambiguity, complexity – all of which possess arousal potential. Fun has arousal potential.

Play, then, to Ellis is stimulus-seeking behaviour, but not all such stimulus seeking is play. The behaviour that seems to be clearly *non-utilitarian* is play. This may appear to lead to an artificial divide between work and play but clearly such stimulus-seeking behaviour can be found in both work and play. The theory appears to handle the question of work and play equally well. Indeed, it questions the validity of separating work from play.

Thus Ellis provides an explanation for both special and individual motivation towards play, and also describes a researchable, physiological base for play. In terms of its value to people and society, play fosters individuality; it provides 'learnings' that reflect individual, unique requirements; and it prepares for the unknown. Play will not occur when the essential conditions necessary for play behaviour are absent. One of the most important aspects coming out of this work is the realization that people play when the control of the content of their behaviour is largely under their control. Players should therefore transcend the immediate constraints of the reality of the situation when playing.

(ii) Playfulness

The psychologist, J. Nina Lieberman [25], has studied a concept which she identified as *playfulness* and has observed and measured it in infants, adolescents, and adults. It is her thesis that playfulness is related to divergent thinking or creativity and that it has an important bearing on how we approach leisure. The three major components of playfulness are spontaneity, manifest joy and sense of humour.

Spontaneity shows itself in physical, social and learning dimensions and is a unitary trait in the young child. In the adolescent and adult, two separate clusters emerged in her studies which were labelled academic playfulness and social emotional playfulness respectively. The traits characterizing academic playfulness were alert, bright, enthusiastic, imaginative, inquiring and knowledgeable. The outstanding characteristics of social emotional playfulness were entertaining, extroverted, joking, light-hearted, witty, making fun of himself/herself. The latter was also given the overall label of 'bubbling effervescence'.

At the infant level Lieberman found that the more playful child was also the more creative boy or girl. This was expressed in fluency, flexibility, and originality of thinking. In terms of intelligence, we know that two-thirds of the population fall within the middle range of intelligence quotients; in the case of creativity, the evidence appears to suggest different degrees of endowment and in different areas, for example, in specific talents such as science, music, writing and painting. Playfulness can therefore be part of *any* individual's make-up. Moreover, because of its importance in a person's general approach to work and play, playfulness should, in Lieberman's submission, be encouraged and developed throughout the lifespan of people.

Assuming this to be the case, we have to ask ourselves how playfulness can be developed. To develop spontaneity, Lieberman believes that there needs to be emphasis on gathering and storing facts beginning as early as the pre-school level. Only if the child has a storehouse of knowledge is there a basis for parents and teachers to encourage playing with various permutations.

Manifest joy is the ability of showing pleasure, exuberance, friendliness and generally positive attitudes in everyday life. The joy that the adult shows at the child's growing competence will lead to the child's own sense of pleasure in his or her activities.

The ability of engaging in 'good-natured ribbing, gentle wit, creative punning, as well as poking fun at yourselves and others', Lieberman includes in the category *sense of humour*. To develop this, a climate needs to be created which encourages 'psychological distancing'. Evidence was found that the cognitively more mature children preferred less hurtful expressions of humour. Humour is dependent on mastery of the situation; mastery can then lead to fun in learning.

Following Lieberman's argument, as we continue to learn throughout our lifespan, we therefore need to practice the psychological distancing which allows us to take the task at hand seriously, but not ourselves; we need to free ourselves from being preoccupied with ourselves and with our own problems, in order to cope, to be resourceful and for leisure to function as one of the means towards what Maslow [26] terms 'self-actualization'. Maslow stressed the need for individuals to develop to their fullest degree of independence and creative potential.

The next logical step to ask is how playfulness can help in our approach to leisure. It seems self-evident that any individual whose approach to everyday living embraces spontaneity, manifest joy and sense of humour would be able to deal in a creative way with free time. It is apparent, though, that many individuals have these traits and are not aware of them, or do not realize the benefits of applying them to leisure. Other people will need actively to practice them in order to make them part of their everyday repertoire. To what extent we can discover ourselves, our skills and aptitudes and acquire the ability of stepping back and laughing at ourselves, is an area yet to be explored.

3.4 PLAY: SUMMARY

Play is important to the lives of people. It has personal meaning for each individual. Play behaviour appears to be possible in almost any life situation. It can be readily observed, particularly in children, but there is little agreement as to a definition or explanation of why people play.

There have been many theories of play. Classical theories may appear to have some 'common-sense' wisdom, but for the most part, they are archaic and not very helpful, with many logical shortcomings. Among the recent theories the learning, developmental and psychoanalytic theories show that play contributes to the development of intelligence and a healthy personality. Children gain pleasure, overcome unpleasant experiences and develop mastery of their physical and social environment.

Why play? There is no precise answer. Some claim that play is justification in and of itself without further rationalization, but animals play as well as humans and this seems to indicate that it performs some survival function. In addition, play does seem to be arousal-seeking behaviour, a seeking out of novelty, a preparation for the unknown and children, especially, learn and develop through play.

The descriptions and explanations of play have been in the past too simplistic and obtuse. They have been obscure because of our failure to recognize that play cannot be conceived as a simple concept. Play is a complex set of behaviours – 'a million permutations of human behaviour'. As play is utterly individual and play activity can be seen at any time and in all life situations, it follows therefore that almost any situation or activity can function for someone as a play activity if undertaken in the *spirit* of play.

There appear to be several accepted characteristics of play in the absence of an exact definition. Play is *activity* – mental, passive or active. Play is undertaken *freely* and usually spontaneously. It is fun, purposeless, self-initiated and often extremely serious. Play is indulged in for its own sake; it has intrinsic value; and there is innate satisfaction *in the doing*. This has implications on leisure policies. If, for example, one general principle encouraged play for sheer enjoyment or for the satisfaction in the doing, then no matter who wins, no one loses. When there is nothing to lose, we 'go for our shots' untroubled by the fear of losing.

The freedom to act and be ourselves is illustrated by Hoffer [27]:

'Men never philosophize or tinker more freely than when they know their speculations or tinkering leads to no weighty results. We are more ready to try the untried, when what we do is inconsequential. It is highly doubtful whether people are capable of genuine creative responses when necessity takes them by the throat'.

Necessity may not, then, be the mother of invention. Invention may be the result of the freedom afforded by leisure.

The study of play has taught us that the activity itself, rather than a useful outcome, is the motivating force. However, play does have important functions for learning, for social development and in co-operation in 'playing to the rules' as even the most simple of games teaches. Indeed, the play group, more than parents or teachers, appears to be the principal agent of learning to get on with each other. Play and games are vitally important in our culture.

Play transports the player, as it were, to a world outside his or her normal world. It can heighten arousal. It can be vivid, colourful, creative and innovative. Because the player shrugs off inhibitions and is lost in the play, it seems to be much harder for adults with social and personal inhibitions really to play. Playfulness is a very important part of 'healthy' and 'wholesome' living, and it has implications for leisure behaviour and opportunity. Those people whose living embraces spontaneity, manifest joy and a sense of humour are probably better able to deal with the freedom and choice that are present in leisure. Play most often refers to the activities of children or to the 'childlike' behaviour in grown-ups. In this chapter we have seen that all (young and old) can play, but as Millar suggests: 'Adults sometimes just play but children just play far more' [28].

REFERENCES AND NOTES

1. de Grazia, S. (1962), *Of Time, Work and Leisure*, Doubleday, New York, p. 359.
2. Huizinga, J. (1955), *Homo Ludens*, Beacon Press, Boston, Mass.
3. Aristotle (1926), *The Politics of Aristotle* (translated by Ernest Barker), Clarendon Press, Oxford.
4. Plato (1900), *The Republic of Plato* (translated by John Davis and David Vaughan), A. L. Burt, New York.
5. Schiller, F. (1965), *On The Aesthetic Education of Man*, Frederick Ungar, New York.
6. Harris, W. T. (1887), *The Education of Man* (ed., F. Froebel), D. Appleton, New York; see editor's preface.
7. See Lehman, H. S. and Witty, P. A. (1927), *The Psychology of Play*, A. S. Barnes, New York.
8. Groos, K. (1901), *The Play of Man*, Appleton, New York.
9. Stanley-Hall, G. (1920), *Youth*, Appleton-Century, New York.
10. Patrick, G. T. W. (1916), *The Psychology of Relaxation*, Houghton Mifflin, Boston, Mass.
11. Ellis, M. J. (1973), *Why People Play*, Prentice-Hall, Englewood Cliffs, N.J.
12. Ellis, M. J. (1973), uses the classification of 'classical' and 'recent' theories put forward by Gilmore, J. B. Play: a special behaviour, in Haber, R. N. (ed.) *Current Research in Motivation*, Holt, Rinehart and Winston, New York, 1966.
13. Feshbach, S. (1956), The catharsis hypothesis and some consequences of interaction with aggressive and neutral play, *Journal of Personality* **24**, 449–62.

14. Berkowitz, L. A. and Green, J. A. (1962), Simple view of aggression, *Journal of Abnormal and Social Psychology*, **64**, 293–301.
15. Freud, S. (1974), *The Complete Works of Sigmund Freud*, Hogarth Press, London.
16. Walder, R. (1933), The psychoanalytic theory of play. *Psychoanalytic Quarterly*, **2**, 208–24.
17. Erikson, E. G. (1950), *Childhood and Society*, Norton, New York.
18. Klein, M. (1955), The psychoanalytic play-technique, *American Journal of Orthopsychiatry*, **25**, 223–37.
19. Piaget, J. (1962), *Play, Dreams and Imitation in Childhood* (translated by G. Gattengno and F. M. Hodgson), Norton, New York.
20. Sutton-Smith, B. (1966), Piaget on play: a critique, *Psychological Review*. **73**, 104–10.
21. The authors' ideas are reviewed in Ellis, M. J. *Why People Play*, Englewood Cliffs, N.J., 1973.
22. Roberts, J. M. and Sutton-Smith, B. (1962), Child training and game involvement. *Ethnology*, **1**, 166–85.
23. Huizinga, J. (1955), *Homo Ludens*, Beacon Press, Boston, Mass.
24. Caillois, R. (1961), *Man, Play and Games*, Free Press of Glencoe, New York.
25. Lieberman, J. N. (1977), *Playfulness: Its Relationship to Imagination and Creativity*, Academic Press, New York.
26. Maslow, A. (1968), *Toward a Psychology of Being* (2nd edn), D. Van Nostrand, New York.
27. Hoffer, E. (1963), *The Ordeal of Change*, Harper and Row, New York.
28. Millar, S. (1968), *The Psychology of Play*, Penguin Books, Baltimore, Md.

Chapter 4

Recreation

The previous two chapters were concerned with the concepts of leisure and play. This chapter focuses upon *recreation.*

First, recreation is introduced to show that, like leisure and play, it is not a simple phenomenon and that confusion is evident in our definition and understanding of what it is. *Second,* the range of ideas and theories about recreation is reviewed very briefly. *Third,* a discussion and synthesis of ideas is attempted which differentiates between recreation experience, activity, process and structure. *Fourth,* a summary of findings and issues relevant to community recreation is presented.

Having studied this chapter, readers will be able to understand the conceptual and practical differences between recreation and play and leisure, and to appreciate their relevance in leisure planning and management. What will become clear to the reader is that recreation is perceived by most people as the organized leisure activities for personal and social benefits; yet for the professional manager recreation must be perceived also as having intrinsic value.

One of the key learning points is that programmes and activities should give potential participants a wide choice of opportunity to enable them to experience satisfactions and benefits which, in turn, help to meet individual needs. A further insight into what these needs are can be found in Chapter 5, dealing specifically with the needs of people.

4.1 RECREATION: AN OVERVIEW

The history of the organized recreation movement in the United Kingdom and in the United States is well documented, showing the early developments in the late 19th and early 20th centuries. There has been a close association with the recreation movement and the development of industrial society.

Many recreation theories view the concepts of play and recreation as one and the same thing. Others take the position that they are different entities. However, the view that recreation is *adult* activity and play is *children's* activity has been predominant.

The word 'recreation' stems from the Latin *recreatio,* 'restoration to health'. Hence traditionally the term has been thought of as a process that restores or recreates the individual. The historic approach in defining recreation has been to consider it as an activity that renews people for work, an approach to understanding recreation which has obvious limitations.

While some definitions refer to recreation as *restoration,* most focus on it as a form of *activity.* Others, while corroborating the activity approach, apply the condition to it of *social acceptance.* Most view the activity as unobligated. For example, the *Dictionary of Sociology* defines recreation as 'any activity pursued during leisure, either individual or collective, that is free and pleasureful, having its own immediate appeal, not impelled by a delayed reward beyond itself'. Hutchinson [1] supports the social acceptance theory; recreation is 'a worthwhile, socially acceptable leisure experience providing immediate, inherent satisfaction to the individual who voluntarily participates in activity'.

Some authors look to recreation as being morally 'sound' and 'mentally and physically upbuilding'. Romney [2] believes that recreation is not a matter of motions, but rather emotions: 'It is a personal response, a psychological reaction, an attitude, an approach, a way of life.'

Many recent definitions, however, do not regard recreation as being the opposite of working, nor as being morally sound or even as being activity at all; Avedon [3], and Gray and Greben [4], for example, look to recreation as providing personal well-being.

It is evident that there is considerable confusion both in a definition and an understanding of recreation. While it would be easy to say 'it is whatever you think it is', that is hardly a means of explanation. The confusion that does exist was portrayed dramatically in an editorial in *Parks and Recreation* [5], which listed approx. 200 words or phrases describing how recreation was perceived by different people!

4.2 RECREATION THEORIES

It is clear that recreation, like leisure and play, is also a far from simple concept to grasp and to understand. Indeed, hundreds of writers have attempted so to do and the literature is filled with a plethora of theories, a fact which cannot be escaped or ignored. There follows a brief summary of some of the definitions, which represent the range of ideas. More important, however, is the possibility that each description has some element of truth, which can aid our appreciation of what it is we are dealing with.

Hundreds of theories of recreation exist. They do not fall into any clear or logical categories. Most of them embrace a large number of interrelating elements, such as need-serving, satisfying, associated with activity, of value to society, and so on. Most theories, too, appear to overstress values, outcomes and 'wholesomeness'. The research is so confused and overlapping that an attempt is made below simply to highlight some of the main approaches to an understanding.

4.2.1 Recreation as needs-serving

Slavson [6] describes recreation as a 'need-serving experience'. Whatever the choice of recreation, each individual seeks to satisfy some inner need. Recreation is a response to pleasure cravings. But such a description concerns what recreation does, not what it is. Jacks [7] defines recreation as the 're-creation of something that gets damaged in human beings . . . the repair of human damage where it is repairable, and the prevention of it in the rising generation'. This also is an inadequate definition, in that it mixes biological need with social need.

Nash [8] also sees recreation as a means for satisfying the human need to express inner urges and drives. He evaluates activity in terms of the degree of creative social contribution. Recreation, therefore, serves both individual and society. Nash's romantic view of recreation is captured in his equating happiness within terms of recreation activity:

'The happy man paints a picture, sings a song, models in clay, dances to a call, studies the stars, seeks a rare stamp, builds a cabin, raises pigeons, digs in the desert, romps with his grandchild, reads the Koran, dreams of rushing rivers and snow-capped peaks . . . he has a hundred things yet to do when the last call comes'.

4.2.2 Recreation as leisure-time activity

By far the most widespread definitions and the ones most acceptable to providers of recreation services are that recreation is simply those activities in which people participate during their leisure. For example, the Neumeyers [9] define recreation as an activity, either individual or collective, pursued during one's leisure time.

The problem with this traditional view of recreation as activity is that it is heavily slanted in certain preconceived directions. Indeed, so much so, that to many people recreation is synonymous with *physical* recreation and sport. In addition, providers tend to provide for activities and feel they are providing for recreation, without knowing which activities are the most appropriate and whether they are meeting the needs of people. Moreover, there is no universally accepted definition of what constitutes people's leisure.

The Sports Council report, *Professional Training for Recreation Management*, describes recreation as 'the purposeful use of leisure time' [10]. Other official documents refer to it as 'the wholesome use of leisure time'. A Countryside Recreation Research Advisory Group report defined recreation as 'any pursuit engaged upon in leisure time, other than pursuits to which people are normally "highly committed"'.

4.2.3 Recreation as value to individual and society

Recreation has been dogged by having to live up to a standard of high moral and social value for the 'good' of the individual and society. The moral connotations are held strongly by many writers, such as Miller and Robinson [11], Meyer and Brightbill [12], Butler [13] and many others.

Miller and Robinson see recreation as the process of participation in leisure from a specific perspective of leisure values. Play is free, happy and expressive, behaviour that contributes to childhood development. Recreation does not necessarily contain play, but must always have a particular value framework related to appropriate and satisfying use of leisure.

Meyer and Brightbill propose that recreation contains the following characteristics and these contribute to fulfilling human needs – i.e. action, variety of form, motivation towards enjoyment, engagement during leisure, voluntary participation, universality, purposefulness, flexibility, creation of by-products. Recreation is also an attitude of mind regarding leisure behaviour and has a direct influence on those factors which create personality. It can produce feelings of well-being, satisfactions, pertaining to positive identity, growth, creativeness, balanced competition, character, mental capacity, dignity of the individual, physical conditioning, socialization and a coping attitude!

Not surprisingly, Meyer and Brightbill view recreation as a social force. But such value orientations placed on recreation are questionable. Such descriptions may well overstress presumed recreational benefits, and resulting services based on such presumptions might repel people rather than attract. However, there is no shortage of protagonists for such an orientation. Butler takes a similar view; he sees recreation as a force influencing people's lives, and as a system of services which provide 'wholesome' experience, to counteract disruptive social influences.

It is logical to perceive that from this value orientation 'wholesome' individual recreation will lead to recreation as an influence for social 'good'. From their viewpoint, community recreation is a means for improving and maintaining societal cohesion and the quality of life; its development is dependent on social participation. Hence community recreation is a system of services for wholesome, positively sanctioned activities.

4.2.4 Recreation as a re-creation

Most theorists have concentrated on the value of recreation, and the outcomes of recreation. They have not addressed themselves to the *recreation experience* itself. Shivers [14], in *Principles and Practices of Recreational Services*, focuses attention on 're-creation', although he treats play and recreation as virtually synonymous. Building on a theme of homeostasis (the process by which the body continues to produce the chemical balance necessary to maintain life, the process by which equilibrium is maintained), Shivers builds up to a definition of recreation based on the construct 'psychological homeostasis' – i.e. the satisfying of psychological needs, the process of mental balance.

He reasons that if homeostasis is the condition that motivates behaviour, it must also serve as the motivational stimulus for recreation. When there is imbalance, we move towards re-balance in which harmony and accord between self and the environment are found. Shivers claims that this balance may be restored through recreation. Recreation is 'any consummatory experience, non-debilitating in character' [15]. It produces unity and harmony within the individual. The unity of mind and body (psyche and soma) brought about at the time of 'consummation' is recreation. The distinguishing feature is its consuming and absorbing quality. It has the power to seize and hold one's attention to such an extent that the very meaning of subjective time and environment disappears from view. In this respect, it fulfils the need for psychological homeostasis. Hence the individual experiences a balance or temporary harmony at the point of complete fulfilment from which stems a feeling of *re-creation*, or re-birth. This realization of totality (i.e. complete integration by the individual within himself or herself) is the recreational focus.

The basic difference between recreational value and recreation itself is in time rather than degree. Recreational value will be noted after the consuming experience has occurred, whereas recreation itself occurs at the time of the experience. This unity of mind and body Shivers describes as the 'unity concept' of recreation.

This theory has value, in that it focuses our attention on what actually happens. However, there are a number of problems, for example, such complete absorption is rarely achieved and the theory begs the question whether every satisfying experience is recreation. However, if recreation is essentially an *experience*, it is central to the provision of recreation services. Yet very little is known about the 'experience', what it is and what it does for people. Furthermore, planners and providers have come far in the development of recreation facilities, programmes and services with so little understanding of the result that they are trying to produce!

There have been some investigations into people's perceptions of recreation and the experiences they encounter but the findings have no scientific validity and further studies are needed. One piece of research elicited from college students via self-reporting techniques the most significant and memorable recreation experiences they had ever had. The results were reported by Gray [16] (Table 4.1). Reactions to personal 'recreation experiences' indicate that recreation is a highly significant

Table 4.1 What is this thing called recreation?

- Heightened or reduced sensitivity to temperature, colour and smell
- Time distortion: 'Time stood still', 'An hour seemed like a minute'
- Anticipation and expectation
- Escape: 'Getting away from it all'
- Novelty; the sense of 'for the first time' brings freshness and uniqueness
- Relaxation, including release from social convention and personal demands
- Self-testing; challenge; and achievement, competence and self-worth
- Improved self-image: 'In the end we all experience only ourselves'
- Feeling a part of nature; beauty and awe Heightened appreciation and
- Heightened appreciation and unusual perception
- Culmination; a turning point; reward for extended preparation; a watershed life event
- Heightened insight; perspective clarity; illuminating experience; flashes of insight
- Order; regularity; clear and precise limits; rules
- Introspection; sorting out of life experience; release from sensory overload, contemplation; and communication with oneself
- Communion; love; friendship and identification with a group (perhaps the strongest single motivation for many recreation activities is the wish for social response)
- Personal development; learning; and extension of ability
- Refreshment; personal renewal; and recovery of powers
- Common experience; shared hardships; and teamwork
- Risk; apprehension; fear – being frightened is a part of the extraordinary experience
- Unity of mind and body; grace, coordination
- Feelings of excitement, freedom, control, power, creativity, inner peace, harmony, reward, competence; recreation experiences are a power stimulus to emotional response

Note: The table is an abridged selection and adaptation from *Parks and Recreation* [16].

component of total *life experience*. It also suggests that activities that do not generate some of these kinds of feeling may fail to produce a recreational result.

4.3 RECREATION: ANY KIND OF SATISFYING EXPERIENCE?

In broad terms, recreation can be considered as activity and/or experience. But is recreation *any* kind of satisfying experience? If so, recreation then becomes all of life's satisfying experiences. While philosophically this might be supported, in practical terms such a scope could make it far too wide and all-embracing to present and manage recreation. Taking Shivers's belief that recreation is any consuming non-harmful experience, it could be interpreted as everything and nothing as far as recreation management is concerned.

Gray and Pelegrino [17] have adopted a similar definition, which is psychological in nature; recreation is defined in terms of a person's experiences:

'Recreation is an emotional condition within an individual human being that flows from a feeling of well-being and satisfaction. It is characterized by feelings of mastery, achievement, exhilaration, acceptance, success, personal worth and pleasure. It reinforces a positive self-image. Recreation is a response to aesthetic experience, achievement of person's goals, or positive feedback from others. It is independent of activity, leisure or social acceptance.'

It is what happens *within* a person that determines whether or not recreation occurs. The unity within oneself, the mood and the situational elements themselves all go to make up the recreational experience. Hence participating in an activity does not in and of itself provide recreation. The psychological response of the individual is what determines what is recreation for him or her.

There is an apparent drawback to the school of thought that defines recreation as any experience at all: it loses any connection either to *leisure* or *activity*. Graham and Klar sum up the practical difficulties [18]:

'Should all positive feelings be categorized as recreation? Is the scientist's moment of discovery recreation? Or the student's feeling of satisfaction with a term paper well done? If we assume that recreation is independent of either leisure or activity, virtually all satisfying experiences become labelled recreation which seems too far reaching and presents barriers to communication since that is not the context in which most people view recreation.'

'Practically speaking, this definition will not be easily applied as it now stands since it incorporates so many types of experience. The psychological focus provided by Gray, however, is important and should be uppermost in the minds of leisure service practioners'.

In its interim report the Recreation Management Training Committee [19] stated as their reference point: 'We take recreation to mean any life-enhancing experience which is the outcome of freely chosen activity.' Here experience is allied to activity. Graham and Klar [20] take the matter closer to 'recreation' activity. It is imperative, they believe, to put the experience into a *recreation setting* to achieve understanding: recreation experience occurs as a direct result of involvement in a recreation activity. It is an emotional condition providing inner satisfactions and feelings of well-being. They define a recreation experience as:

'positive emotional response to participation in a recreation activity, defined as such by the individual or by a sponsoring agency or organisation. Responses associated with the recreation experience include feeling good about self and others, experiencing a sense of inner calm or personal satisfaction, or feeling an enriched sense of self-worth which results from motivators of either an intrinsic or extrinsic nature. There is a clear absence of stress and tension which produce anxiety; the joy of re-creative experience is achieved. The essence of the classical view of leisure is achieved'.

The principal difference between such a definition and that of Gray is that it is not independent of recreation activity. It is related both to leisure and activity. It therefore avoids the broadness of definition that views all positive experiences as recreation, which is extremely difficult to put into any operational context. Graham and Klar perceive recreation in narrower terms, but they retain the psychological component.

4.4 RECREATION: AN INSTITUTION AND A PROCESS?

Confusion exists in our understanding of how we can translate individual recreation into community-sanctioned activity. We have seen that recreation can be viewed as an activity and as an experience. Extrapolating the *recreation activity* focus, recreation is to do with promoting activities, providing facilities, programmes and opportunities. As such, recreation can be perceived as a *structure,* an institution. Following the *experience* focus, recreation is viewed as something which is personally motivated. In this sense, it can be perceived as a *process* of what happens to an individual. Thus on one hand recreation can be perceived as a directing social force, and on the other hand as an inner-directed experience.

4.4.1 Recreation as a social process

Recreation experience, according to Murphy [21], is a process whereby the human organism strives to reach optimal arousal levels, the primary ingredients of which are exploration, investigation, manipulation and learning behaviour. (Such a theory of recreation is akin to the play theory in chapter 3 put forward by Ellis.)

Murphy, like several writers before him, lists an impressive array of physical, psychological, social and educational values as the potential outcomes of recreation. He views recreation, for example, as a process towards self-realization, fostering interaction, novelty, challenge, diversity, adventure, identity and other qualities. It would appear that many of these needs are not being met through recreation programmes, and he believes that a shift of emphasis towards an enabler–community catalyst role, will come about as a reflection of changing social demands. He puts forward a humanistic perspective for recreation services and believes that basic needs can and should be satisfied through recreation participation. In these terms, recreation should be viewed from a process orientation, in order to see its role in the dynamics of change. Thus, to Murphy, recreation and leisure services are *processes*.

The process perspective includes aspects of psychological response rather similar to play – i.e. fulfilment, satisfaction in the doing. Recreation requires freedom and activity and seems to absorb the participant to the point of complete involvement. A related element appears to be creativity both in process and outcome and recreation may well culminate in *peak* experience.

4.4.2 Recreation as a social institution

Kraus [22] takes some important and differing views from many of the foregoing authors. Recreation is more than a conceptual framework, a kind of activity or a condition of existence. Instead it refers to all the *social institutions* which have been formed to meet the leisure needs of people. It includes activities and organizations which are sponsored by government at various levels, schools, churches, industries, voluntary agencies and the business world – all of which provide varied recreational opportunities [23].

Kraus challenges many of the theories put forward: voluntary participation is dependent on available choices; immediate gratification does not necessarily occur with many activities that take time to master before they become fully satisfying; and participating without extrinsic motivation is questioned – people engage in activities, often with goals in mind, and are motivated by external reasons. Community-based recreation is concerned with reinforcing the prevalent value system and must therefore provide a structured and manageable service which often precludes such aspects as voluntary, immediately satisfying and intrinsically based participation.

Avedon [24] supports the social institution argument. He points out that, as in the case of other social institutions, 'recreation has form, structure, traditions, patterns of operation and association, systems of communication, and a number of other fixed aspects'. Kraus [25], in the second edition of *Recreation and Leisure in Modern Society* concludes that recreation has emerged as a 'significant' social institution: 'Once chiefly the responsibility of the family, the church or other local social bodies, it has now become the responsibility of a number of major agencies in our modern industrial society.'

The *Dictionary of Social Sciences* defines an institution as 'an aspect of social life in which distinctive value-orientations and interests, centering upon large and important social concerns, generate or are accompanied by distinctive modes of interaction'. The term 'institution' is therefore different from the term 'association'. An *association* is essentially composed of people, while an *institution* is essentially composed of interactions and interrelationships. They are social patterns that have distinctive value orientations, they direct the behaviour of human beings and characteristically tend to be permanent and to resist change. They exist because they have been reasonably successful in meeting societal needs. Recreation in a collective social setting can thus be perceived as a social institution.

4.5 RECREATION: SUMMARY

'Recreation', like any other word, is an abstract symbol, having many meanings, depending on the context in which it is used. It has perhaps a ring of condescending moral, puritan authority: whether you like it or not, take it; it does you good. In this context, physical recreation, is close to the outmoded concept of 'muscular Christianity'. The word 'recreation' suggests leisure activities, recuperation, relaxation, pleasure, satisfaction – but these do not reveal its nature. It is traditionally seen as an action performed. Its outward manifestation indeed is that, but it contains a more inclusive meaning as well. Recreation for the individual can be a matter of emotions rather than motions.

Recreation as a concept of activity is understood. Recreation as an inner personal experience is yet to be understood, but it is from an *individual*, as well as collective orientation, that community recreation planning, programming and management should rebuild if people's needs are to be met.

The term 'recreation' can be used in a variety of ways. One may look at it within its traditional, institutional framework of activities, programmes, facilities and in the context of *Homo ludens*, 'man the player'. Recreation can also be considered as an activity performed, a set or cluster of activities or leisure-time expressions. It has also been defined as a social institution and as a professional service. This stance is understood and generally accepted by society. However, what the experience of recreation is, and what it does for people, is of the essence to purposeful planning and management of recreation.

From its re-creative centre, recreation can be seen as the 'new man feeling', the 'aah feeling', the job well done, success, the top of the mountain or 'Eureka!'. The experience is the moment itself; recreation value is post-experience: a game of squash (under this definition), where the player feels let down with a poor performance or poor attitude, would not be recreation. A mother who normally is reinvigorated after a weekly relaxing sauna but has had to cut short her visit because the children are to be home early from school may lose the completeness of the recreative experience.

Why recreation? There is no accepted scientific explanation. It is generally accepted that while we need to maintain a state of biological equilibrium, psychologically too we need to restore a mental balance. However, we also seek some degree of stress or activity that provides meaning to existence. Stress in effort helps to provide a form of biological and psychological 'tone', analogous to muscle tone. Effort, however, must be recognized by the individual as worthwhile, whether 'work' or 'leisure'.

In terms of recreation management, recreation is not only individual, but also collective and deeply entrenched in systems of public recreation, sport, art, physical education, planning and management. The complexity and the interrelationships make it almost impossible to construct a unified theory. One definition which meets many of the points put forward in this chapter relating to the multi-faceted phenomenon of recreation and which comes close to an all-round description is proposed by Kraus [25]:

'Recreation consists of activities or experiences carried on within leisure, usually chosen voluntarily by the participant – either because of satisfaction, pleasure or creative enrichment derived, or because he perceives certain personal or social values to be gained from them. It may also be perceived as the process of participation, or as the emotional state derived from involvement.'

'When carried on as part of organized community or voluntary agency programmes, recreation must be designed to meet constructive and socially acceptable goals of the individual participant, the group and society at large. Finally, recreation must be recognized as a social institution with its own values and traditions, structures and organizations, and professional groups and skilled practioners'.

Hence recreation can be viewed as *personal experience* (what it does to a person); as *activities* (the forms it takes); or as an *institution* (the structure in which it is made available to the community). Taken yet another way recreation can be viewed as a *process* (what happens to an individual), and as a *structure* (the framework in which recreation is practised). Its relationship to play and leisure is discussed in Chapter 7.

REFERENCES AND NOTES

1. Hutchinson, J. L. (1949), *Principles of Recreation*, A. S. Barnes, New York, p. 17.
2. Romney, G. O. (1945), *Off the Job Living*, A. S. Barnes, New York, p. 14.
3. Avedon, E. (1974), *Therapeutic Recreation Service*, Prentice-Hall, Englewood Cliffs, N.J.
4. Gray, D. E. and Greben, S. (1974), Future perspectives, *Parks and Recreation*, July, 27–33 and 47–56.
5. Gray, D. E. and Greben, S. (1979), Wanted: A new word for recreation *Parks and Recreation*, 9, No. 3, March, p. 23.
6. Slavson, S. R. (1948), *Recreation and Total Personality*, Association Press, New York.
7. Jacks, L. O. (1932), *Education through Recreation*, Harper and Row, New York.
8. Nash, J. B. (1953), *Philosophy of Recreation and Leisure*, C. V. Mosby, St Louis, Mis.
9. Neumeyer, M. and Neumeyer, E. (1958), *Leisure and Recreation*, Ronald Press, New York.
10. Sports Council (1969), *Professional Training for Recreation Management* (Chairman, D. D. Molyneux), Sports Council, London, p. 5.
11. Miller, N. P. and Robinson, D. M. (1963), *Leisure Age: Its Challenge to Recreation*, Wadsworth, Belmont, Calif.
12. Meyer, H. D. and Brightbill, C. K. (1964), *Community Recreation*, Prentice-Hall, Englewood Cliffs, NJ.
13. Butler, G. (1968), *Introduction to Community Recreation*, McGraw-Hill, New York.
14. Shivers, J. S. (1967), *Principles and Practices of Recreational Services*, Macmillan, New York.
15. *Ibid.*, p. 90.
16. Gray, D. (1980), *Parks and Recreation*, March 62–4, 94.
17. Gray, D. and Pelegrino, D. (1973), *Reflections on the Recreation and Park Movement*, William C. Brown, Dubuque, Iowa, p. 6.
18. Graham, P. J. and Klar, L. R., Jr (1979), *Planning and Delivering Leisure Services*, William C. Brown, Dubuque, Iowa, p. 7.
19. Department of the Environment (1978), *Recreation Management Training Committee: Interim Report*, Discussion Paper (Chairman, Anne Yates), HMSO, London, p. 5.
20. Graham, P. J. and Klar, L. R. Jr (1979), *Planning and Delivering Leisure Services*, William C. Brown, Dubuque, Iowa, p. 8.
21. Murphy, J. (1975), *Recreation and Leisure Service*, William C. Brown, Dubuque, Iowa.
22. Kraus, R. (1971), *Recreation and Leisure in Modern Society* (1st edn), Goodyear, Santa Monica, Calif.
23. *Ibid.*, p. 263.
24. Avedon, E. (1974), *Therapeutic Recreation Service*, Prentice-Hall, Englewood Cliffs, NJ. p. 47.
25. Kraus, R. (1978), *Recreation and Leisure in Modern Society* (2nd edn), Goodyear, Santa Monica, Calif.; 1st edn., 1971, p. 37.

Chapter 5

Leisure and the needs of people

In Chapters 1–4 we have dealt with three separate yet overlapping concepts: leisure, play and recreation. However, they are of limited value unless they help to meet some of the needs of individual people and thereby the good of the wider community.

Community leisure and recreation services are said to be based on the *needs of people*. Yet policy-makers, planners and managers have insufficient insights into people's needs. How can leisure, play and recreation meet their needs? In order to know this, we must know as much about the needs of people as we do about leisure. This chapter therefore attempts a brief overview of people's needs in relation to leisure.

First, some theories about human motivation are introduced, and the question is debated: do leisure needs exist? *Second*, an identification is made of many of the social needs: normative, felt, expressed, comparative, created, false and changing needs in leisure. *Third*, the difference between needs and demands is raised, together with their relevance to leisure services in the community.

The understanding of needs is fraught with difficulties, different interpretations and different psychological approaches. However, the satisfying of people's needs through leisure opportunity is one of the principles behind providing services.

Having read this chapter, readers will be able to distinguish needs from demands. They will be able to understand how leisure opportunity – sensitively managed – can help to meet some of the social and physical needs of people and the importance of offering different kinds of activity and experience to different people, at different stages in the life-cycle.

5.1 HUMAN MOTIVATION AND NEED

One simple view is that human need is something that is missing, *a deficit*. It has been defined as 'any lack or deficit within the individual either acquired or physiological' [1]. Needs here are distinguished from drives and are seen as preceding them; they are the cause of motivation, rather than the motivation itself. Others equate the need with the motivating force [2].

McDougal [3] attempted to explain behaviour by reducing it to a series of innate, but modifiable, *instincts*. Instinct theory has now been generally discarded, but McDougal's theory was in many ways a watershed in motivational theory. It led to the further efforts of behavioural scientists to discover why we behave as we do. It also led many psychologists to look for more widely extended, diffusive concepts which explain human motivation. One of the central ideas to be salvaged from McDougal's theory was that of the purposeful, *goal-directed* characteristic of the greater part of human behaviour.

Drive is goal-directed; it releases energy. It is generally considered to be the motivating factor within human personality. There appear to be different sorts of drive such as the drive for food, the drive for sex, the exploratory drive, and so on. Summarizing the concept, Young [4] says: 'Drive is a persisting motivation rather than brief stimulation. Drive is an activating energising process.'

Many psychologists who see the motivational aspect of human needs as drives do so in conjunction with the concept of *homeostasis*. People have a fundamental need to maintain a state of relative internal stability. Needs can therefore be perceived in terms of the elements that disturb homeostasis; drives are the forces which impel the individual to regain the equilibrium that has been lost.

Homeostasis is easiest to understand in terms of physiological needs, for example, the relief of cold or hunger. Needs which are social in nature, such as the needs for achievement, self-fulfilment and acceptance, are less easily accounted for in terms of homeostasis. However, as indicated in the discussion on recreation in Chapter 4, the principle of 'psychological homeostasis' was used by Shivers as *the* basis of 're-creation'.

All human behaviour is motivated, according to Freudian theory. Nothing happens by chance, not even behaviour which appears to be 'accidental'. Thus we often remark on the 'Freudian slip'; everyday errors, accidents and slips of the tongue, far from being just 'accidental', are *caused* by underlying and unconscious wishes or intentions [5].

In terms of motivation, Freud saw two fundamental driving forces in human beings: the *sexual* and the *aggressive*. The basic drives which motivate all behaviour operate unconsciously at a basic level of the psyche known as the *id*. They are not fixed patterns of behaviour, but function through 'external' demands and constraints – i.e. the 'realities' of the outside world. The two psychic structures which channel and modify the basic drives are the *ego* and *superego*. They direct the basic drives into socially acceptable channels.

Freud placed great emphasis on the developmental stages of early childhood, but little on the later life-cycle stages. Erikson [6], however, viewed development as a process which continues throughout the life-cycle. His theory of development demonstrates that needs themselves are developmental.

It appears to be a reasonable conclusion that need is concerned with motivation: 'In theories of motivation need is seen as a state or force within the individual. This can be either a deficit state leading to a search for satisfaction, or else a stage of psychological incompleteness leading to a movement towards completeness' [7]. In either case, need is a motivational concept referring to the processes – conscious or unconscious – involved in goal-orientated behaviour.

5.1.1 Do leisure needs exist?

In management and leisure discussion the most often cited theory pertaining to needs is that of Maslow [8,9]. He suggests that needs are hierarchically ordered. At the base of the hierarchy are the primary physiological needs of the human being (e.g. food, sleep, sex, shelter), and at the apex of the hierarchy are those needs which are related to the psychological factors of self-actualization such as creativity and sense of achievement. According to Maslow, the lower needs must be satisfied before any of the higher needs come into play .

There are a number of problems in the application of Maslow's hierarchy; for example, needs are not necessarily hierarchically ordered, nor divided into sectors, but are often overlapping and occur simultaneously. However, the theory emphasizes the *developmental* needs of the individual. Need is no longer seen by Maslow as the reduction of some state of tension or the return to homeostatic equilibrium. Instead people are seen as striving towards the fulfilment of more positive growth. Many others with a humanistic approach to psychology also emphasize the human need for self-actualization and growth [10]. Maslow's hierarchy is also a useful way of identifying and categorizing the different types of need that individuals have.

Tillman [11], building on this theme, examined needs and identified ten which he felt are important in determining the 'leisure needs' of people, namely:

1. New experiences like adventure.
2. Relaxation, escape and fantasy.
3. Recognition and identity.
4. Security – being free from thirst, hunger or pain.
5. Dominance – to direct others or control one's environment.
6. Response and social interaction, to relate and react to others.
7. Mental activity – to perceive and understand.
8. Creativity.
9. Service to others – the need to be needed.
10. Physical activity and fitness.

However, the concept of 'leisure needs' is misleading. People have needs, which can be satisfied in a variety of ways. One way of meeting some of them may be through leisure opportunity: *leisure needs as such may not exist.*

5.2 SOCIAL NEEDS

Bradshaw's conceptualization of needs is concerned with the problems that arise in identifying different types of *social* need [12]. He suggests that social needs be classified into four categories: normative; felt;

expressed; and comparative. He explores a system by which the overlapping considerations of the four approaches to 'need' can be utilized to form a model to assist in making objective assessments of 'real' need.

Mercer [13], and later McAvoy [14] and Godbey [15], have applied Bradshaw's concepts to recreation. Godbey and others have expanded the number of classifications in the social needs model by adding additional categories: created needs; changing needs; and false needs.

5.2.1 Normative needs and leisure

Normative needs represent value judgements that are made by professionals in the recreation and leisure field (such as criteria for open-space standards). These normative needs, stated as standards, are usually expressed in quantitative terms.

The use of normative needs as the major determinant of leisure provision can be challenged on a number of points. The development of standards is often based on small-group value orientations, often arbitrary and biased. They cannot be valid to the population as a whole. (A full discussion of the problems and benefits of standards is presented in Chapter 8.)

5.2.2 Felt needs and leisure

The problem in determining *felt needs* is that people find difficulty in articulating their needs, which are influenced by one's aspirations and cultural environment. Felt needs can be defined as the desires that an individual has but has not yet actively expressed; they are based on what a person *thinks* he or she wants to do.

According to Mercer [16], felt needs are largely learned patterns; we generally want what we have become used to having. In many cases, felt needs are limited by the individual's knowledge and perception of available recreation and leisure service opportunities. However, mass communication has expanded the individual's potential for knowledge and experiences ordinarily outside his or her realm of existence. Thus felt needs, on the one hand, are limited by an individual's perception of opportunities; but, on the other hand, they can be based on what a person imagines he or she would like to do.

The concept of felt needs can be of use to the recreation and leisure service for two reasons. First, it enables people to express desires of what they would like to do. Second, individuals are likely to be happier participating in what they perceive they want to do during their leisure than if leisure options are simply dictated to them.

5.2.3 Expressed needs and leisure

Those activities in which individuals actually participate are *expressed needs*. They provide the manager with knowledge about current leisure preferences, tastes and interests. Expressed needs are felt needs 'put into action'. However, if leisure resources, programmes and services are based solely on expressed needs (what people are doing), the practitioner may preclude the initiation of new services and programmes. In addition, participants' behaviour is limited by the specific programmes that are available. Expressed need itself does not give a total picture of involvement *potential*. Factors of cost, access, weather and fashion may induce number fluctuations. New and novel provision may create its own demand, where none existed previously. Yet programming based on expressed needs may tend to favour those who shout loudest!

5.2.4 Comparative needs and leisure

Often an individual or organization will compare itself with another individual or organization. This may be done purely out of interest, or it may serve to help to identify deficiencies. The *comparative needs* approach can be applied to services, facilities, resources and programmes. For example, there may be differences in the services provided for special groups (e.g. the disabled, the elderly, the mentally retarded and ethnic and racial minorities) and those provided for the rest of the population.

Care must be practised when utilizing the comparative needs method in needs assessment and programme planning. One cannot assume that what works well in one situation will automatically be effective in another.

5.2.5 Created needs and leisure

Godbey [17] has expanded on Bradshaw's taxonomy of social needs by adding a fifth, *created needs*. The concept implies that policy-makers and professionals can create leisure interests and values independent of what people do, or what they want to do. Created needs refer to those recreation activities which organizations have 'introduced to individuals and in which they will subsequently participate at the expense of some activity in which they previously participated'. In other words, created needs refers to those programmes, services and activities solely determined by the organization and accepted by the participant without question, desire or prior knowledge.

According to Edginton *et al.* [18], the created needs approach can be useful to the participant and to the organization as a method of defining needs:

'Many individuals are grateful to organizations for helping them identify an area of interest that previously they had not considered. In a sense, the approach is a form of leisure education that is an important component of the philosophy of recreation and leisure service organizations. The organization also benefits by serving as an agency that creates opportunities for stimulation and enrichment. As a result, individuals may look to the organization as a vehicle for providing innovative experiences'.

Implicit in the created needs approach is the notion that the professional's knowledge is sacrosanct, but this is a wrong assumption. The participant also has the ability to diagnose his or her felt, expressed and comparative needs. As with the other approaches, the created needs method should be used in conjunction with all the available tools for defining and interpreting needs.

5.2.6 False needs and leisure

Needs may be created which are inessential, which are in fact *false needs*. Young [19] points to the distinctions between what an individual is aware of needing and what others may think is needed. This raises the issue of the value which is placed on need by the individual and by outsiders. These values may differ.

Marcuse [20] developed the concept that society encourages the individual to develop certain sorts of 'need', which are not in any sense essential but which serve the interests of society as a whole. Thus people acquire the 'need' for cars, television or videos which it is in the general interest of society to promote. Such needs Marcuse calls false needs for the reason that they are not strictly essential. In fact they are hard to prove different from other sorts of need but, for Marcuse, they represent undesirable values.

5.2.7 Changing needs in leisure

Rhona and Robert Rapoport in *Leisure and the Family Life Cycle* [21] claim that although every person has needs, these needs *change* as one progresses from one phase of life to another. The key concepts which reflect the developmental nature of the changes in the life-cycle are *preoccupations* – 'mental absorptions', interests and activities.

Preoccupations arise at a deep level of motivation. Some preoccupations might be present throughout the life-cycle but tend to become particularly salient at a given phase. The preoccupations attributed to each stage in the life-cycle are worth considering since they are of fundamental importance if providers are to make the most appropriate provision for different segments of the population. The major stages reported in Kew and Rapoport [22] are outlined below:

(a) Stage one – youth (school years)

- Emergent personal identity.
- Tendency to fight against authority.
- Exploration – experimentation and sexual, physical, mental and emotional stimulation.

(b) Stage two – young adult (school-leaving to settling down)

- Development of a social identity.
- More intimate and committed relationships.
- Tendency to reintegrate with family previously rejected.

(c) Stage three – establishment (extended middle age)

- Commitments to life investments of work and family.
- Importance to productivity and performance.
- Later tendency to question ideals and commitments, perhaps leading to disillusionment and depression.

(d) Stage four – final phase (between end of work and of life)

- Emphasis on achieving social and personal integration.
- Attempts to achieve harmony with surroundings.
- Major reorganizations of attitudes and demands.
- Great variety of interests, dependent on very many factors.

The Rapoports believe that recreational activities arise out of *interests*, and interests arise out of preoccupations. There is no one-to-one relationship between preoccupations and interests, and particular interests can be satisfied through different activities. However, it appears that specific 'clusters' of interests are clearly related to each major life-cycle phase. The Rapoports' thesis is that all people have a quest for personal identity. At the root of their search, people have fundamental preoccupations. Specific preoccupations can be experienced through a variety of interests, and expressions of interest may be facilitated through specific activities.

Each person is seen as having a 'career' consisting of separate but interrelated strands. Three major strands relate to *family*, *work* and *leisure*. Each life strand therefore produces changes in preoccupations, interests and activities at life crises such as at marriage and at the birth of children.

5.3 NEEDS, DEMANDS AND LEISURE AND RECREATION SERVICES

Leisure policy-makers, researchers, planners and managers often equate 'needs' with *demands*. But there is a very real difference between the two. Lowry and Curtis [23] believe that a common error of regarding demand and need as synonymous should be avoided: they see 'need' as the more fundamental concept and 'demand' is perhaps generated by need.

5.3.1 Needs and leisure demands

Researchers have generally been concerned with establishing recreation demand, rather than understanding people's need. Large-scale surveys in Britain, for example, have identified certain demands but have not discovered what motivates people to recreation, why people participate and what are the most important influences on participation: 'Whereas a "need" appears to be conceptually "woolly" and operationally elusive, "demand" appears tangible, measurable, even predictable' [24].

In recent years, however, there has been a growing dissatisfaction with macro-social demand studies, and a feeling that if researchers are to provide information of real value to policy-makers and planners, they must look for approaches that are also of relevance to the people being researched. Knetsch [25] calls into question the concept of demand: 'The myth persists that somehow we are able to multiply population figures by recreation activity participation rates obtained from population surveys and call it demand.'

5.3.2 Needs and the effective service

Effectiveness and efficiency are not one and the same thing. An *effective* leisure service could be described as one that ensures that the right opportunities are provided, at the right time and in the right place, based on the needs of the people it is intended to serve. This is, of course, impossible to achieve in the sense that any collective service cannot be all things to every person. Yet the approach which encourages ways for people to attain self-fulfilment can be stressed. If not, providers may provide a service and ensure its smooth running but the service could be *ineffective*: 'Of the two, the provision of an effective service is the more important, as it is better to provide an effective service that meets needs, however inefficiently, than to provide a super efficient service that meets nobody's needs' [26].

Although little direct research has been undertaken on the 'social' need of the individual being a prime motivating factor, Crandall [28] has reviewed relevant existing research. He concludes that the success of many leisure and recreation services may depend more on their ability to bring together compatible people than on their programmes and facilities.

And although Maslow's hierarchy of needs has been criticized on the ground that the self-actualizing needs are largely culturally determined, it is generally accepted that people have a need for psychological growth and that a social need is a basic survival need. Maslow's basic survival needs, physiological, safety and social needs, correspond with the hygiene factors of Herzberg [29], who regards them as preventative, in that they do no more than prevent unhappiness, while the higher needs of Maslow may be equated to some extent with the motivator factors of Herzberg. Hence both Maslow and Herzberg see a person's ultimate need as being that of *self-actualization*, and Farina [30] sees this need as the 'goal of leisure'.

5.4 SUMMARY: LEISURE AND PEOPLE'S NEEDS

No single theory and no clear consensus exist relating to people's needs. In theories of motivation need is seen as a force within the individual to gain satisfactions and completeness. There appear to be many levels and types of need, including the important needs of self-actualization and psychological growth. 'Leisure needs' as such may not exist, rather there are human needs which can find satisfaction through leisure opportunity.

The concept of social need incorporating normative, felt, expressed and comparative needs has been enlarged to include created, false and changing needs. Needs appear to change in relation to one's life stage, and one's preoccupations, interests and activities at that stage. It has been hypothesized that needs can be created but, in so doing, can result in some 'false' needs being brought about, with both positive and negative results for the individual and society.

Leisure planning and management exist, in large measure, to provide opportunities for individual satisfaction and development. Everyone has a quest for personal identity. Can this personal need be met, in part, by effective leisure planning and management? What stands in its way? Chapter 6 identifies some of the many influences.

Needs assessment should allow for a broad base of public involvement. It is suggested that such an approach will:

1. Provide an increase in individual and community input and involvement in planning and decision-making.
2. Provide the planner with a better understanding of the community and individuals within it.
3. Provide information as to the activities in which people are involved, the activities in which they would like to be involved and how these can be planned and provided for within an overall leisure delivery system.
4. Provide supportive facts and ideas on which to base decisions in the planning process.

Two most important factors have emerged, which argue against the focus of current recreation planning policies on standards of provision. First, people have *diverse* needs. Second, these needs *change* or take on greater or lesser degrees of importance according to one's stage in the life cycle. The individual chooses on the basis of certain personal and social elements current in his or her life.

Needs assessment attempts understanding of individual and group behaviour as it relates to recreation and leisure. It accomplishes several things. Through such assessment, recreation planners and managers can become aware of people's underlying motivation, interests, opinions, habits, desires and knowledge regarding recreation and leisure. Practical ways of gathering such data include demographic characteristics, time use, leisure behaviour and opinions and attitudes. Hedges (27), for example, sought to develop a technique for more accurate charting of people's leisure patterns through their lives, namely their 'leisure histories'. It has become abundantly clear, however, that methods must include both quantitative and qualitative assessments.

In terms of need, people are three-dimensional. We are like *everybody* else, requiring the basic needs of security, belonging and shelter; we are like *some* other people sharing the same wants, the same groups and the same interests. We are like *no other person*, a unique individual – the only one. Leisure opportunity could enable us to become a three-phase person: to become all we think we are capable of becoming.

REFERENCES AND NOTES

1. Morgan, C. and King, R. (1966), *Introduction to Psychology*, McGraw-Hill, New York, p. 776.
2. Murray, H. (1938), referred to in Institute of Family and Environmental Research and Dartington Amenity Research Trust (IFER/DART) (1976), *Leisure Provision and Human Need: Stage 1 Report* (for DoE), IFER/DART, London, Item 2.8.
3. McDougal, W. discussed in Institute of Family and Environmental Research and Dartington Amenity Research Trust (IFER/DART) (1976), *Leisure Provision and Human Need: Stage 1 Report* (for DoE), IFER/DART, London, Items 2.10 and 2.11.
4. Young, P. T. (1961), *Motivation and Emotion*, Wiley, New York.
5. Freud, S. (1974), *The Complete Works of Sigmund Freud*, Hogarth Press, London.
6. Erikson, E. H. (1959), Identity and the life cycle. *Psychological Issues*, **1**, No. 1.
7. Institute of Family and Environmental Research and Dartington Amenity Research Trust (IFER/DART) (1976), *Leisure Provision and Human Need: Stage 1 Report* (for DoE), IFER/DART, London, Item 2.46.
8. Maslow, A. (1954), *Motivation and Personality*, Harper, New York.
9. Maslow, A. (1968), *Towards a Psychology of Being*, Van Nostrand, New York.
10. E.g. Carl Rogers (1961), referred to in Institute of Family and Environmen-

tal Research and Dartington Amenity Research Trust (IFER/DART) (1976), *Leisure Provision and Human Need: Stage 1 Report* (for DoE), IFER/DART, London, Item 2.22.

11. Tillman, A. (1974), *The Program Book for Recreation Professionals*, National Press Books, Palo Alto, Calif., pp. 57–8.
12. Bradshaw, J. (1972), The concept of social need. *New Society*, **30**, No. 3, 640–3.
13. Mercer, D. (1973), The concept of recreational need. *Journal of Leisure Research*, **5**, No. 1.
14. McAvoy, L. H. (1977), Needs and the elderly: an overview. *Parks and Recreation*, **12**, No. 3, 31–4, 35.
15. Godbey, G. (1976), *Recreation and Park Planning: The Exercise of Values*, University of Waterloo, Ontario, January, p. 2.
16. Mercer, D. (1973), The concept of recreational need. *Journal of Leisure Research*, 5, No. 1, 39.
17. Godbey, G. (1976), *Recreation and Park Planning: The Exercise of Values*, University of Waterloo, Ontario, January, p. 13.
18. Edginton, C. R., Crompton, D. M. and Hanson, C. J. (1980), *Recreation and Leisure Programming*, Saunders College, Philadelphia, Pa, p. 91.
19. Young, P. T. (1961), *Motivation and Emotion*, Wiley, New York.
20. Marcuse, H. (1964), *One Dimensional Man*, Sphere Books, London.
21. Rapoport, R. and Rapoport, R. N. (1975), *Leisure and the Family Life Cycle*, Routledge and Kegan Paul, London.
22. Kew, S. and Rapoport, R. (1975), Beyond palpable mass demand, leisure provision and human needs – the life cycle approach, paper presented to Planning and Transport Research and Computation (International) Company Ltd, Summer Annual Meeting.
23. Lowry, G. and Curtis, J. (1973), Satisfying leisure needs, in Lutzin, S. G. (ed.) *Managing Municipal Leisure Services* Institute of Training in Municipal Administration (ITMA), International City Management Association.
24. Institute of Family and Environmental Research and Dartington Amenity Research Trust (IFER/DART) (1976), *Leisure Provision and Human Need. Stage 1, Report* (for DoE), IFER/DART, London, Item 3.14.
25. Knetsch, J. L. (1969), Assessing the demand for outdoor recreation. *Journal of Leisure Research*, **1**, No. 2, 85.
26. College, S. (1977), Recreation Research in local authorities: a practitioner's view, in Veal, A. J. (ed.) *Recreation Research in Local Authorities*, CURS, University of Birmingham.
27. Hedges, B. (1986), *Personal Leisure Histories – Social and Community Planning Research*, Sports Council/ERSC, London.
28. Crandall, R. (1977), Social Interaction, Effect and Leisure, Institute of Behavioural Research, Texas Christian University, unpublished.
29. Herzberg, F. (1968), *Work and the Nature of Man*, Staples Press, London.
30. Farina, J. (1974), Toward a Philosophy of Leisure, In J. F. Murphy, *Concepts of Leisure Philosophical Implications*, Prentice-Hall, Englewood Cliffs, NJ.

RECOMMENDED ADDITIONAL READING

Stockdale, J. E. (1985), *What is Leisure? An Empirical Analysis of the Concept of Leisure and the Role of Leisure in People's Lives*, Sports Council/ESRC, London.

Chapter 6

Leisure: factors which influence participation

Leisure patterns are not fixed or predetermined for either individuals or groups, though, once established, they can become part of the rhythm of our way of living. Not only are there a multitude of factors which influence choice and participation, but also there is a complex relationship between them. In analysing people's needs in leisure, we have seen how misleading it can be to rely on only those factors which are easily quantifiable. There are both individual and social influences.

Because of the links and relationships between various influences, it is difficult to classify or group the factors with any accuracy. For the purpose of this chapter, three broad groupings are suggested: personal factors, social and circumstantial factors, and opportunity factors.

The first group of factors relate to the individual: his or her stage in life, needs, interests, attitudes, abilities, upbringing and personality. The second group relates to the circumstances and situations in which individuals find themselves, the social setting of which they are a part, the time at their disposal, their job and their income. The third group relates to the opportunities and support services available to the individual: resources, facilities, programmes, activities and their quality and attractiveness, and the management of them.

Having read this chapter, readers will be aware of the range of influences that are brought to bear on individual people in making choices of leisure activity. Leisure professionals will realize that they have no influence on some factors and little on others. However, they will be able to gauge what influences they have got in terms of planning, providing opportunities, creating the right environments and managing services and facilities.

6.1 RANGE OF PERSONAL, SOCIAL AND OPPORTUNITY FACTORS

Recreation policy and planning are by no means simple. There is a complex mixture and interaction when thinking about the factors which affect participation. In Table 6.1 some of the discernible factors are outlined which individually, jointly or collectively affect participation. This listing is not comprehensive, nor is it a classification but an illustration of the complexity and variety of influences which bear on an individual. In addition, even if people have identical circumstances and opportunities, still one person may choose one activity and another something entirely different. Nevertheless, by understanding some of the correlations between personal circumstances and participation, Leisure Managers can foresee some of the constraints and difficulties encountered by some people, and management attitudes can be modified accordingly.

Table 6.1 Influences on leisure participation

Personal	*Social and circumstantial*	*Opportunity factors*
Age	Occupation	Resources available
Stage in life-cycle	Income	Facilities – type and quality
Gender	Disposable income	Awareness
Marital status	Material wealth and goods	Perception of opportunities
Dependants and ages	Car ownership and mobility	Recreation services
Will and purpose in life	Time available	Distribution of facilities
Personal obligations	Duties and obligations	Access and location
Resourcefulness	Home and social environment	Choice of activities
Leisure perceptions	Friends and peer groups	Transport
Attitudes and motivation	Social roles and contacts	Costs: before, during after
Interests and preoccupations	Environment factors	Management: policy and support
Skill and ability – physical, social and intellectual	Mass leisure factors	Marketing
Personality and confidence	Education and attainment	Programming
Culture born into	Population factors	Organization and leadership
Upbringing and background	Cultural factors	Social accessibility
		Political policies

6.2 INDIVIDUAL, PERSONAL AND FAMILY INFLUENCES ON LEISURE PARTICIPATION

The personality of an individual, his or her needs, interests, physical and social ability, the culture into which one is born and a person's will and purpose in life, and a whole range of personal factors, could influence choice and participation. Three factors are further considered below: age and stage in family life-cycle, gender and education.

6.2.1 Age and stage in the family life-cycle

Age has an important influence on leisure participation but its effect will vary depending on the person and the type of activity. For children, there is a rapid change in the space of a few years from toddler to pre-school to junior to teenager – each calling for very different kinds of provision. Even for adults, there is a marked change with age, with participation in most active leisure pursuits declining sharply as people grow older.

The availability of time also has an influence on recreational participation and the greatest amount of free time appears to be concentrated at the ends of the age continuum with the adolescent and the retired having considerably more time at their disposal than the middle age group who live under a greater degree of time pressure. Further, with the increased purchasing power of teenagers and the popularity of commercial entertainment amongst this age group, there is a greater age segmentation in leisure choice. A sharp fall with age occurs, for example, in cinema-going, which is predominantly a young person's leisure pursuit.

The *General Household Surveys* [1] emphasize the general decline in active leisure participation with increasing age but also reveal that some home-based activities, such as gardening and do-it-yourself, are most popular with the middle-aged. Some activities are relatively 'inelastic' with the change of age. These are generally regarded as home-based activities, such as television watching and reading; other activities, such as membership of voluntary organizations, have a curvilinear trend, with a slight increase in participation rates in one's late pre-retirement and early post-retirement phase.

Age should not be considered in isolation, however. Age may be less restrictive than life-cycle changes, such as getting married and having children; for some, participation may increase with age as a result of the children leaving home or a person retiring from work. Although age may influence the level of fitness and energy, a reduction in family and work responsibilities may more than compensate for this. The type of leisure activity is also likely to be influenced by stage in the family life-cycle. For example, single people may be more likely to go to a dance or a club, while a family may be more likely to visit the seaside.

6.2.2 Gender and leisure participation

The leisure patterns of males and females show similarities and differences. However, two major obstacles have faced women: family commitments, particularly looking after children, prevent many women from participating outside the home, and for many older women, an upbringing that did not include pursuits like physical recreation within their compass.

In the study *Leisure in the North West* [2] it was found that gender makes little difference in participation rates for either full-day or half-day trips and excursions, but that there is a marked contrast to the impact of gender on sport and physical recreation. The ratio of men to women was 61:39, even though women outnumbered men by a ratio of 54:46 in the sample. This finding is consistent with both Sillitoe [3] and the *General Household Surveys*, which show that of all the sporting activities, only keep fit/yoga had a higher participation rate among females.

Max Hanna [4], found that while gender has been of fundamental importance in differentiating leisure activities, the two sexes appeared increasingly to share activities as more opportunities for women are opened up. Extending Hanna's thesis would suggest that many of the social filters, which can operate against female participation, will diminish and disappear. On the other hand, policies of provision appear in some cases to discriminate against women (e.g. male-dominated activity programmes). This being the case, it could lead to even greater dissatisfaction at the current patterns of supply and correspondingly high levels of demand. The problem is further compounded, in that many other life factors militate against leisure equality. For example, when a woman goes out to work, as well as maintaining a house and family, the extent of her leisure time is eroded since responsibilities for domestic work within the home are not normally abdicated.

Within the 'cultural' field of leisure women are the predominant users. Mann [5] found that for all theatre audiences in Leeds the highest proportion were women; at the ballet they comprised 73%; drama had a female audience of 69%; and opera 59%. This is supported by Davey [6], in Hornchurch, and by the Mass Observation Study in Birmingham [7].

Women are without a car more often than men, and in view of the dependence of sports and arts participants on the motor car, this is probably one of the factors that inhibits female participation. Green *et al.* [8], in a thoughtful and forceful study of women's leisure experiences in Sheffield, illustrate the damaging influences upon the leisure potential for women: 'the constraints and social controls on women's freedom to spend their leisure time as they may choose can be seen as a direct result of the operation of economic, political, and cultural forces, which exemplify the oppression of women under capitalism.'

Clearly, women have had, and continue to have, greater constraints placed upon them than men. However, one of the misleading factors in looking for similarities and differences stems from the fact that most surveys have studied traditional recreation activities – i.e. sport, day trips and theatre – and organized activities like classes, clubs, team games and committed activities. Once a wider view of leisure is taken, encompassing the whole range of activities in and around the home, holidays, socializing, entertainment, excursions or walks in the park, a totally different picture starts to emerge.

Looking at the broader spectrum, it would appear that overall participation rates do not differ substantially between men and women; women take a greater part in 'cultural' activities, men take part substantially more than women in active sport and sports spectatorship. When taking all leisure pursuits into account, then the *similarities* in leisure participation between the sexes are more striking than the differences [9].

6.2.3 Education and educational attainment and leisure

The *type* of education, the *length* of education and the educational *attainment* of people are closely related to upbringing, class, occupation, income and other factors. In terms of leisure participation, the better qualified tend to be male, young, in non-manual occupations and enjoying higher incomes: 'All these factors are reflected in higher participation rates for those with qualifications than for those without and, in general, the higher the qualification, the greater the degree of participation' [10].

Education influences to some extent, the *type* of leisure choice. Considerable evidence is available to support this view, from national surveys such as the *General Households Survey* and from specific research into leisure facilities such as libraries, theatres and recreation centres. For example, there is a sharp differential between members and non-members of the public library when related to educational institution and *level* of educational attainment.

Possibly, the biggest influence is within the arts. Mann [5], in Leeds, found that 57% of the whole drama audiences, 42% of opera audiences and 33% of ballet audiences were now at or had been at university or a college of education. At Birmingham, the Mass Observation Study found that the influence of education attainment was of greater significance than social class [7]. With the exception of the pantomime, all audiences had higher proportions of people who had completed their full-time education at 19 years of age and over. With sports and recreation centres, the bias is still significant although not to the same extent [11,12].

6.3 SOCIAL AND SITUATIONAL CIRCUMSTANCES AND LEISURE PARTICIPATION

The whole range of social and situational circumstances as they affect leisure participation include the home, school, work environment, income, mobility, time, social class, social roles and group belonging. This availability is, of course, a major determinant of leisure behaviour. Working women have the least unobligated time of all groups, mainly because of home obligations. Retired people and unemployed men have the most time for leisure, but much of it may remain simply as free time. In this brief section these aspects are further considered under three headings: income, social class and social climate.

6.3.1 Income and leisure participation

General Household Surveys have examined *household* income. They show that income levels are closely linked to participation rates, and for almost all the leisure activities they examined, the proportion participating rose with income.

In only three activities (bingo, needlework and going to clubs) did participation not increase with income. Even where little or no financial outlay is incurred, such as walking, participation rates were also higher. Middle-income groups, however, were more prominent in fishing, billiards, darts and bingo. With betting, bingo and doing the pools, participation rates fell among those with higher-than-average incomes.

Over an average working life, white-collar workers earn appreciably more than blue-collar workers and often attract hidden benefits (e.g. perks, pensions, less unemployment), all of which add to one's life style. It is perhaps not surprising that since income correlates with both education and social class, the higher-income group has the higher participation rates in many recreational activities. Even with facilities and activities provided by the local authority, such as for arts and sports, more people with higher incomes are attracted.

If lower-income groups are to be attracted in larger numbers to community recreation, then greater social service approaches would need to be applied, for example, through differential subsidies, cheaper admissions, positive discrimination towards those who are disadvantaged, outreach programmes, the loaning of equipment free of charge, taster courses at minimal costs, community programming application, community bus services to facilities, improved marketing such as 'passports for leisure', incentives and, above all, sensitive and appropriate management. Some 'passport' schemes involve the collection and completion of a detailed form, obtaining a photograph and processing these in person at the civic offices. The target market – those in greater need – has been hardly touched, in some areas, despite good overall numbers joining the schemes. The process of joining appears to have produced the opposite effect to that intended.

The choice of activities and the amount of money that people can spend on entrance fees, equipment, travel, and so on, is dependent on the extent of people's *disposable* income. Those on unemployment benefits or state pensions may have little or no disposable income. Families with highest incomes tend to spend a smaller proportion of their income on essentials such as food and clothing and a greater proportion on non-essentials such as recreation. Manual workers, when presented with a choice between more income and more leisure, generally choose the former; consequently, they have to undertake overtime which, in turn, diminishes the disposable time available for recreational participation.

Personal property has much to do with leisure. However, what were once luxuries and leisure items are now considered almost as necessities. 'Necessities' such as alcohol, tobacco and petrol and relatively insensitive to financial change; large, discrete items like holidays (and house improvements) are vulnerable. People who earn or have more money have greater personal property and the wherewithal to permit a wider choice of leisure pursuits. Owning a large house with a garden, and driving a second car may immediately open the door to leisure activities which will be denied those living in a high-rise flat, without personal transport and with a low income.

6.3.2 Social class and leisure participation

The nature and meaning of social class is generally regarded as being problematic. 'Social class' can be regarded as 'a grouping of people into categories on the basis of occupation' [13]. Because of the interrelationship between social class and income, education and mobility, it is generally considered that social class, as determined by *occupation*, is the most influential factor in determining recreational participation. Occupation is not therefore an independent characteristic, but is closely associated with other factors.

In the *General Household Survey* (*GHS*) [14] it was found that generally, 'it was professional workers who tended to have the highest participation rates in leisure activities and unskilled workers who had the lowest rates. Particularly striking are the differences in participation levels for outdoor sports (over half of professional workers, falling to under 20% for unskilled workers)'. Even playing and watching football were more popular among professional and skilled manual workers, and the pattern is not confined to sport and the arts. Outings, sightseeing, entertainment, gardening and do-it-yourself showed similar bias. Even knitting and needlework were more popular among female professional workers. According to the *GHS*, only two activities are more popular among manual workers: betting/doing the football pools and playing bingo.

A number of other studies have been undertaken that give pointers to the importance or otherwise of social class and participant leisure activities. Libraries, the theatre, arts, sport, countryside recreation, clubs and adult education have been covered. There is considerable evidence to show that in general such leisure pursuits are followed far more by non-manual workers but some argue that the biasing is not as great as many claim [15].

Studies of sport and recreation centres show similar participation patterns [11]. And at some centres follow-up studies some years later have shown that while the number of manual workers had increased, the *proportional* level of their use had declined [16].

As with other activities, participation in informal outdoor recreation activities is dependent on availability and location of facilities. Hence in high-density residential areas that are predominantly working class, such as the London Borough of Islington, which has the least amount of open space of any London borough, it is highly likely that its residents will use open spaces to a lesser degree than those residents in the outer London boroughs.

Sillitoe [3], in his national survey, found that 'there is a tendency, in all areas, for overall club membership rates, especially among women, to be higher in the non-manual occupational groups'. Boothby and Tungatt [17], investigating a range of different clubs in Cleveland, support the findings claiming that the socio-economic status of members was heavily biased towards non-manual workers, with the exception of football clubs; but even these show a considerable under-representation with the unskilled manual section.

Hutchinson [18] found that adult education students were more likely to be from the higher socio-economic groups, with the exception of those who attend the Workers' Educational Association, where they tend to have a greater percentage of manual workers among their registered students, though this was by no means representative of the population. Hutchinson claims that 'half the adult population is inhibited in involvement in adult education by attitudes that are probably deeply rooted in social circumstances and earlier education'.

6.3.3 Social 'climate' and leisure participation

The IFER/DART researchers [19] refer to the concept of 'social climate', a complex of factors in addition to those which relate to age, gender, income, occupation and education. The attitudes and values of people in their social setting are seen as enabling or inhibiting factors concerned with leisure choice. Isobel Emmet's study, in 1970 [20], is pertinent to an understanding of social climate. She argues, for example, that providers act both consciously and unconsciously as *social filters*, controlling who uses particular facilities and affecting the behaviour of those people. The social filters let through and channel different groups to different facilities. There appear to be both formal and informal social filters. The filters are influential in people's adopting of attitudes and behaviour appropriate to the situation. Behaviour patterns become habits. As Leigh [21] points out, 'The habits of leisure are habits of mind as well as habits of behaviour'.

Despite the cheapness of such activities as rambling, climbing, tennis and camping, these activities remain relatively 'middle-class' occupations. Free museums and subsidized theatre lack working-class patronage, as do evening institute classes. More manual workers may be playing golf but this is mainly on public golf courses, while some private clubs are becoming more expensive and more exclusive. Also the professional classes are finding an increasing number of esoteric and expensive ways of occupying their leisure time. Leisure between the classes differs not only in kind, but also in quantity. The recent *General Household Surveys* conclude that the middle classes are not only more active culturally, socially and intellectually, but they also play more sport and travel more widely.

6.4 OPPORTUNITY AND LEISURE PARTICIPATION

It is no good providing opportunity unless good advantage is taken of it. Opportunity – making it possible for a person to participate or be involved – can be, in many instances, even more important to community participation than personal, social and circumstantial influences, despite current studies which show the strongest correlation between participation factors, already discussed. Opportunity can come in a variety of forms: available resources and services, political policies, management styles and systems, community leadership and support, accessibility, and so on. It is most likely that opportunity will entail various interrelated components.

From his study in Greenwich, Gwynne Griffiths [22] arrives at the conclusion that the key factor that influences recreation participation is *accessibility* in its various forms. By accessibility, Griffiths does not refer simply to access and mobility, rather accessibility is defined as the 'ability to participate' where the constraints to participation have been eliminated. He divides accessibility into four main divisions: perceptual accessibility; physical accessibility; financial accessibility; and social accessibility.

6.4.1 Perception and leisure participation

Perception refers to the world as it is *experienced* – as it is seen, heard, felt, smelt and tasted. Consequently, the way an individual perceives the world will largely determine his or her behaviour. The way people perceive leisure provision (facilities, activities, etc.) may influence their participation, more than the actual form of provision. Leisure provision is concerned with providing satisfying 'experiences' for people; facilities, programmes and activities are means to achieving this. People who do not feel properly identified (or feel ill at ease) with the style of management and organization, or with others using the facilities, will be deterred; indeed, *preconceived* ideas about a leisure facility will influence a person's decision whether or not to make even an initial visit to see it, let alone use it!

Perception is increasingly being used in recreational planning, especially in the field of countryside recreation. Burton [23], in her studies relating to perceptual capacity, found that one's perception of crowding in the countryside was related to one's level of educational attainment. Individuals of high educational attainment were more sensitive to crowding and thought of it as unpleasant; others actually preferred high levels of use. Like the countryside, people have varied perceptions about the city: 'Some people see the city as a place for having fun, for going out on the town; others feel oppressed by the tightly packed nature of its dwellings, excited by the hustle and bustle of city life or overwhelmed by its pressures' [24].

Perceptual capacity as such appeared to have little effect on recreational participation within Griffiths's study [22], but the perception of one's *actual* neighbourhood appeared to have a significant effect on inhibiting recreational participation. The vast majority of those interviewed perceived their neighbourhood as being violent and the elderly were fearful of venturing out of the house at night. Even the close proximity of the police station to the library and the adult education institute had little influence on encouraging use of facilities at night.

Consequently, how the public perceive their neighbourhood and the facilities can either encourage or inhibit recreational participation. As with attitudes, where a negative aspect is perceived, its modification may be difficult to eradicate. *Positive* perception of recreation opportunity will enhance the desire and motivation to participate, will attract people and make them more aware of opportunities available.

6.4.2 Access and supply and leisure participation

Recreation participation undertaken outside the home involves some travel – i.e. walking, cycling, bus, taxi, car, train or plane. The method of travel can affect the level of satisfaction: one method will take more time; it can determine distance and destination; apart from walking, all other means of travel incur financial cost; the method of transportation will lesson or heighten the experience. For example, travelling to a recreation centre, during the rush hour, by public transport for a prepaid 5.30 p.m. court booking, could be harrowing.

The *Fair Play for All* study [25] appears to confirm this: 'though low mobility can act as a deterrent, higher mobility is not necessarily a pre-requisite of greater participation: rather it can reduce some of the inconvenience associated with travel.' Families with cars have reported greater participation over almost the whole spectrum of activities than families without cars. The mobility conferred by the ownership of a car has revolutionized people's use of leisure time. According to the *General Household Survey*, 60% of households in Britain had use of a car. For almost every activity, with the striking exception of bingo, the chances of participating in leisure activities was increased for car users by between 50% and 100%.

Accessibility to recreation provision is influenced, however, by other important factors apart from transportation. The actual *location* of a facility is of the utmost importance and will affect use; the rate of use of the facility falls progressively as one moves further away from the facility. Veal [26] found with regard to postwar swimming pool users that people living within 1 km of the swimming pool were four times more likely to use it than those who live between 1 km and 2 km away, and sixteen times more likely than those living between 3 km and 4 km away from the pool. *Distance decay*, whereby usage falls as the distance grows between the user's home and the facility, shows up in many examples – e.g. the use of national museums, urban parks and the use of water resources. Maw's study of swimming pools showed not merely the effect of distance, but also the significance of public transport as a means of access, particularly for the young. Those who lived near to the main bus or tube routes to Swiss Cottage, London, came to the baths there more frequently than those (within the same distance) who did not [27].

In terms of *travelling time*, the catchment area of even the largest recreational facility is comparatively small. Understandably, the catchment area of community centres and libraries, especially in the urban areas, is very local. Where local provision does not exist, facilities need to be located on bus routes, preferably at a nodal point of a bus network. Griffiths's study [22] illustrates the point:

'the location of the bus stop immediately outside the library is indeed an asset and the proximity of the zebra crossing also aids the accessibility especially for the children and the elderly, but unfortunately the bus services are not geared up for recreational use as their service deteriorates in the evenings and at weekends, when most people have their greater leisure time'.

Hence access and mobility are crucial elements relating to leisure opportunity. It is a sobering thought to consider that, according to *Fair Play for All*, three-quarters of non-car-owning households in the country are among the poorer 50% of households. In terms of facilities provided with public money, policies should exist which ensure the location of facilities on main transportation routes or within easy reach of the greatest number in the community [27]. Where there is easy physical access, and where local residents can walk to a facility, the recreationally disadvantaged (i.e. the elderly, car-less, lower-income groups, women with small children) could have far greater potential use. In a study undertaken in Belfast [28], it was found that by 1988 many parts of the city had higher levels of sports participation than had been recorded in any other part of the United Kingdom. The reason was clear: between 1977 and 1984, Belfast had become the best-provided city in terms of indoor sport facilities per head of city population. Local *opportunity* had led to greater participation across a broader section of the community. All these aspects are important in the context of planning for leisure, discussed in Chapter 8.

6.4.3 Awareness and leisure participation

One accessibility factor that is frequently ignored in considering the linkage of demand for and supply of leisure activities is awareness. If people do not know that something exists, then obviously they will not go to visit it, unless they stumble upon it. Because individual leisure facilities are not sought in the same way as a shopping centre or place of work, knowledge about them (particularly in urban areas) derives indirectly from seeing them, hearing about them or reading about them. It has been shown that people passing a leisure facility *en route* to work or the shops will be more likely to use that facility than a comparable one nearer home: they have become more aware of it. This factor has obvious implications with regard to the location of activities, as well as advertising and other marketing methods.

6.4.4 Management and leisure participation

People's use of leisure facilities is determined, as we have seen, by a number of discrete and interrelated factors. The management aspects of facility provision and leisure opportunity are no less important.

It has been abundantly clear that the presence or absence of facilities and opportunities, and their accessibility, quality, pricing structures and policies, could have substantial influences on leisure participation. For example, the pricing, administrative and booking structures at a leisure centre could consciously or unconsciously establish a type of social filter.

Planning and management policy determine, in the first place, what facilities are to be provided. The attitude of the providers is therefore of crucial importance. The *way* in which a facility is managed can also have a profound effect on the extent that it is used, and by whom it is used. Not only is management attitude and policy shown in the atmosphere created, the 'image' and pricing policy, but also in the skill of programming for the people the facility is intended to serve: programmes geared towards males are likely to result in male-dominated programmes.

This conclusion is reinforced by three studies. The IFER/DART [29] report on one survey on male and female levels of satisfaction with local sports facilities, suggested that there are significantly more 'very satisfied' men and 'very dissatisfied' women. At Harlow Sportcentre and the Abingdon Leisure Centre [16,30], where positive discrimination was made in favour of mothers with young children through 'ladies activities', crèche and social activities, the proportion of mothers with children attending the centre was far above the national 'average' reported by Sillitoe.

The need to socialize with others is a major motivating factor in influencing one's leisure choice. The activity itself may well be of quite secondary importance compared to getting out of the house, having the children looked after for an hour and meeting and talking with people in the coffee bar. Management needs to be aware of these motivating factors in deciding management policy, programming and in providing an atmosphere of social warmth and welcome.

6.5 SUMMARY: FACTORS WHICH INFLUENCE AND CONDITION PEOPLE'S PARTICIPATION IN LEISURE

Many discrete and complex, and often interrelated factors, condition people's choice and participation in leisure activities. Furthermore, there are the strongest links between leisure and other elements of life.

A person's age and stage in the family life-cycle, such as marriage, parenthood and retirement, affect opportunity and participation. Taking the widest view of leisure, the similarities in participation rates between men and women are more striking than the differences, though there are many specific differences in arts and sports, for example, and inequalities both within and between the sexes. The type and level of education people have undertaken has a profound effect on leisure participation. Education and recreation share in the same concern for the development of the 'whole' person – body, mind and spirit – through different approaches. The amount of income and property a person has influences leisure participation. Since income correlates with education and social class, higher-income groups have the higher participation rates in most active recreation activities.

Participation is closely and positively related to social status and the prestige of one's occupation. The 'middle classes' are not only more active culturally and intellectually, but also travel more and play more sport, compared with the 'working classes'. The way people perceive leisure provision influences participation. Preconceived ideas, too, can have important positive or negative effects.

Car ownership has revolutionized people's leisure opportunities. The accessibility of facilities and their location, and an awareness of opportunities, are important considerations. People's use of facilities and services is affected, to a considerable degree, by management policy and management activity. Facilities must be both accessible and acceptable. The attitudes of providers and managers, and the quality of management, will help more people to find satisfying experiences through leisure and recreation opportunity.

While there are many constraints to leisure choices (and, in practice, few people are free agents to choose whatever they will), leisure can offer significant opportunity for individual action and for personal decision, should opportunity permit and the individual wish to exercise such choice. As choice has to do with the individual, then two factors have to be stressed. First, there is a strong link between leisure and other elements of life; and second, because it 'matters' to the individual, the *quality* of the experience is of paramount importance.

In Chapter 2 it became clear that the freedom to choose was an essential feature of leisure. But choice, as we have seen, is conditioned by myriad factors, many of which are interrelated. However, the amount of choice has increased for most people. All leisure activities therefore must actively compete with other activities, and for a share of leisure time and disposable income. (These matters are taken up in Chapter 16 on marketing leisure.)

Finally, from observation and working experience of people's use of leisure, it is clear that a great many people overcome the limitations of a poor education, family obligations and personal handicaps, and even overcome the obstacles of low income, insufficient facilities and resources, to find themselves preoccupying satisfying interests, self-fulfilling experiences and 'mountains to climb'. Leisure and recreation management has much to offer in the way of enabling people to discover themselves, to reach beyond their immediate grasp.

REFERENCES AND NOTES

1. Office of Population Censuses and Surveys, Social Survey Division, *General Household Survey*, 1983, 1986, HMSO, London.
2. Patmore, J. A. and Rodgers, H. B. (eds) (1972), *Leisure in the North West*, North West Sports Council, Salford.
3. Sillitoe, K. K. (1969), *Planning for Leisure*, HMSO, London.
4. Hanna, M. (1975), *Leisure*, IPC Sociological Monograph No. 12; see Institute of Family and Environmental Research and Dartington Amenity Research Trust (IFER/DART) (1976), *Leisure Provision and Human Need: Stage 1 Report* (for DoE), IFER/DART, London, Item 628, for fuller evaluation.
5. Mann, P. H. (1969), *The Provincial Audience for Drama, Ballet and Opera* (survey in Leeds), University of Sheffield.

6. Davey, J. (1976), Promoting a Regional Theatre: Queens Theatre, Hornchurch, Polytechnic of North London, Diploma in Management Studies (R.), unpublished.
7. Mass Observation (UK) Ltd (1974), *The Potential for the Arts in Birmingham*, Peter Cox Associates, Leamington Spa.
8. Green, E., Hebron, S. and Woodward, D. (1987), *Leisure and Gender – a Study of Leisure Constraints and Opportunities for Women*, Sports Council/ESRC, London.
9. Zuzarek, J. (1977), Leisure trends and the economics of the arts, in Smith, M. A. (ed.) *Leisure and Urban Society*, LSA, London.
10. Office of Population Censuses and Surveys, Social Survey Division (1979), *General Households Survey 1977*, HMSO, London, p. 130.
11. Built Environment Research Group (BERG) (1978), *Sports Council Study 15. Sport for All in the Inner City, Sobell Sports Centre*, Sports Council, London.
12. Built Environment Research Group (BERG) (1978), *Sports Council Study 14. Sport in a Jointly Provided Centre, Medway Sports Centre, Reading*, Sports Council, London.
13. Reid, I. (1977), *Social Class Differences in Britain: A Source Book*, Open Books, London.
14. GHS (1983), in Central Statistical Office (1985), *Social Trends 1985*, HMSO, London.
15. Groombridge, B. (1964), *The Londoner and his Library*, Research Institute for Consumer Affairs, London.
16. Built Environment Research Group (BERG) (1977), *Sports Council Study 13. The Changing Indoor Sports Centre, Harlow, 1968, 1973*, Sports Council, London.
17. Boothby, J. and Tungatt, M. (1977), *North East Area Study Working Paper 46, Clubs for Sports and Arts: Results of a Survey of Facilities, Members and Activities in Cleveland County*, University of Durham.
18. Hutchinson, E. (1970), Adequacy of provision. *Adult Education*, March.
19. Institute of Family and Environmental Research/Dartington Amenity Research Trust (IFER/DART) (1976), *Leisure Provision and Human Need: Stage 1 Report* (for DoE), IFER/DART, London, Item 6.20.
20. Emmet, I. (1971), The social filter in the leisure field. *Recreation News Supplement*, No. 4, 7–8.
21. Leigh, J. (1971) *Young People and Leisure*, Routledge and Kegan Paul, London, p. 124.
22. Griffiths, G. T. (1981), Recreation Provision for Whom?, unpublished dissertation, Cranfield Institute of Technology.
23. Burton, R. C. J. (1973), A new approach to perceptual capacity: Cannock Chase research project. *Recreation News Supplement*, No. 10, December, 31–7,
24. Rapoport, R. (1977), Leisure and urban society in *Leisure and Urban Society* (ed. M. A. Smith), Leisure Studies Association, London.
25. Hillman, M. and Whalley, A. (1977), *Fair Play for All. A Study of Access to Sport and Informal Recreation, 43*, Broadsheet No. 571, Political and Economic Planning (PEP), London.
26. Veal, A. J. (1973), *Ashton-under-Lyne Swimming Pool Study: First Interim*

Report, Centre for Urban and Regional Studies, University of Birmingham; see also Veal, A. J. (1979), *Sports Council Study 18: New Swimming Pool for Old*, Sports Council, London.

27. E.g. Maw, R. and Cosgrove, D. (1972), *Assessment of Demand for Recreation – a Modelling Approach*, Working Paper 2.72, Polytechnic of Central London.
28. Roberts, K., Dench, S., Minten, J. and York, C. (1989), *Community Response to Sports Centre Provision in Belfast*, University of Liverpool.
29. See Institute of Family and Environmental Research/Dartington Amenity Research Trust (IFER/DART) (1976), *Leisure Provision and Human Need: Stage 1 Report* (for DoE), IFER/DART, London, Item 6.19.
30. Torkildsen, G. (for Harlow and District Sports Trust) (1984), Survey of Harlow Sportcentre, unpublished; and interview, *Leisure Management*, **5**, No. 4, 8–11, April 1985.

RECOMMENDED ADDITIONAL READING

Glyptis, S., McInnes, H. and Patmore, J. A. (1987), *Leisure and the Home – a study of Home-based Leisure, based on a study of 500 households*, Sports Council/ ESRC, London.

Stockdale, J. E. (1987), *Methodological Techniques in Leisure Research – a Review of Current Methodological Techniques*, Sports Council/ESRC, London.

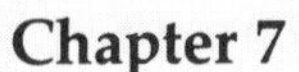
Chapter 7

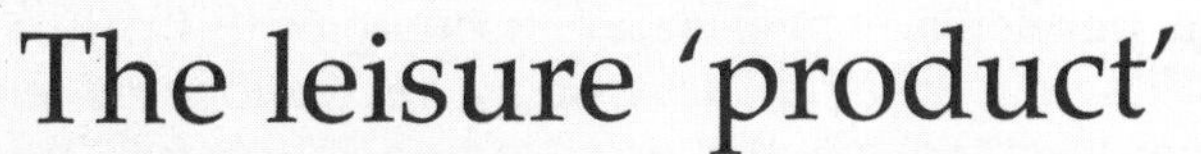
The leisure 'product'

Here the word 'product' has been put in inverted commas because leisure is not a product as such, but it can be a way of living, of experiencing satisfactions, developing interests and personal growth. It can be perceived as being at its core an amalgam of play, recreation and leisure. This chapter opens up an entirely new approach towards the effective management of leisure and recreation services and facilities available to the general public.

In Chapters 2–4 we have studied leisure, play and recreation as discrete entities; and in Chapters 5 and 6 attention has been focused upon the needs of people, how leisure opportunity might help in meeting some of the needs and what influences were brought to bear in achieving this.

This is a pivotal chapter in the book. It integrates play, recreation, leisure and the needs of people; anticipates the role of planning and management; and provides the bridge from theory to practice.

First, play, recreation and leisure are analysed summarily. *Second*, the elements common to all are identified. *Third*, the pieces are put together and the construct 'the pleisur principle' is created to describe what is at the heart of 'leisure'. *Fourth*, the problems and barriers to an integrated approach are highlighted and the assumptions on which to plan for leisure are listed. *Fifth*, the implications of such an approach are emphasized, which lead to worthwhile activities and the 'good life' of leisure. *Sixth*, the first phase of a new approach to a new theory is proposed as one of the foundation stones of effective community leisure management, giving emphasis to a more people-directed service.

Having read this chapter, readers will be able to appreciate the need for an integrated philosophical base as the platform for effective leisure management and its implications upon community leisure services. They will learn about the essential ingredient of leisure – the innate fulfilling experience. They will be able to discern for themselves what kind of opportunities, activities and approaches are more likely to meet the different needs of different people. Readers will also be made aware of the substantial barriers to providing leisure services to meet the needs of people. Readers will now be in a position to study more meaningfully the planning for and management of leisure, which occupy the remainder of this book in Chapters 8–20.

7.1 INTRODUCTION

Leisure as a way of life – living in relative freedom to choose what we do and enjoy an inner harmony with ourselves and the world around us – is an ideal which few may achieve. Many people, however, will experience leisure from time to time, and the achievement of self-actualization or self-fulfilment – the goal of leisure – will move individual people towards the leisure ideal. What is at the heart of this experience? Is the experience of play, recreation and leisure one and the same thing? In order to answer those questions, we need to examine the similarities and differences between play, recreation and leisure and to look for the common elements.

7.2 PLAY AND ITS IMPLICATIONS FOR LEISURE SERVICES

The uniqueness and worth of each individual is the cornerstone of our culture. Ellis [1] states: 'Ideologically a human is most human when at play, as defined by out culture.'

Play is activity, physical or mental, freely chosen and indulged in for its own sake. It has intrinsic value and personal meaning for each individual. Play is life vividly expressed. The motives and feelings of ordinary life are lived through quickly, in abstract, but without the everyday contingencies of anxiety and fear. The major outcome of play is a feeling of regeneration. One is revived. As Sutton-Smith puts it: '"vive" leads to revival. One judges he has had fun' [2].

The implications of play for leisure and recreation services could be profound, yet play does not appear to have a central place in the institution of leisure and recreation services other than children's play. However, if people's lives are enriched by play – physically, intellectually and spiritually – and if play raises the tone of life and brings colour into people's lives, then it is indispensable to the well-being of individual people, and also of society. Therefore leisure professionals need to create situations and promote those factors that give the opportunity for play to occur and limit those factors militating against it.

Can Leisure Managers 'organize' programmes to produce optimally arousing situations, offer opportunities for innovative experience where individuals control the content of their behaviour? Can we implant into recreation programmes the necessary ingredients such as exploration, investigation, manipulation, creativity and learning? For example, graded levels of instruction lead to complexity and creative problem-solving, clubs of like-minded people act upon each other to provide necessary complexity and well-presented events produce the drama for heightened arousal and awareness.

Society has need of many more innovative and vital people. Yet extending playfulness contributes to non-conformity, and some communities may well wish to limit it. The playfulness of young people – in growing up and mixing, in noisy rebelliousness and in their experimentation and testing the limits of the system – may be difficult at times for parents, schools and society in general to cope with. Leisure opportunities can give room to unfold to some of the necessary adventurous behaviour patterns, without the inhibiting, everyday constraints.

Play, in common usage, is clearly understood. Activities are seen as playful, non-productive, not instrumental in the process of survival – just play. In societies with a strong streak of puritanism, play, by virtue of its being unrelated to survival and production of profit, stands outside and inferior to the processes of work.

Play is often assumed to be free, the player not motivated by the end-product of the behaviour. By this argument, play cannot be controlled, planned, forced and still remain play. However, we can never be totally free, for we are always controlled to some extent by our environment. In addition, there are many examples of play being motivated by the end-product.

We refer to sport as being played by players. The study of play causes us to ask the question: how much do players in sport really play? The importance of the outcome, the external rewards (points, trophies, titles, press photographs and status) may make it all too externally serious to play, particularly when, for example, going through a losing streak in the competitive league. External pressures may then sap the *playfulness* of play. It is easy to overstate the case – the spirit of play still abounds at all levels. Nevertheless, it seems clear that the product orientation of winning, rather than process orientation of playing well, plus the imposition of structures not of one's own making, can change the nature of the play experience. For games to remain in the domain of play, players should become part of the process of setting up structures, rules and controls. Indeed, administrators and officials of sports and arts may also be players – playing as much as the participants themselves. In spectator sports play elements may well be seen as much on the terraces as on the court. Yet tribal loyalty and gang warfare at soccer matches illustrates the way in which the play spirit can be destroyed by taking the game out of the play world into the real world of 'dog eat dog'.

7.2.1 The child's right to play

This book contends that play should be part of our leisure throughout life. However, play for children is essential. Lloyd George attached the highest priority to play: the right to play is a child's first claim on the community; it is nature's training for life, 'No community can infringe that right without doing deep and enduring harm to the bodies and minds of its citizens'. In Britain The *Children Act 1989*, is to be implemented as a whole in October 1991; the Act will provide a more integrated approach to issues relating to children, in particular, the balance between family autonomy and the protection of children.

Children's play can help to determine the type of people they are and the type of adults they will become; therefore we need to provide a carefully considered and guided variety of (freely chosen) activities for their development. Appropriate public provision for play is of the utmost importance. What was appealing to children before, or even yesterday, may not be appropriate today. There is a genuine concern that play areas and equipment need a refreshing and innovative approach.

It is salutory to consider the statements of Lady Allen of Hurtwood in *Planning for Play* [4], and their validity today:

'The need for *places* where children can participate in natural play activities as individuals and in groups is a consideration which should be given a very high priority. There are so few places where children can be themselves. Most that is interesting and stimulating around where they live has disappeared under concrete or other cold and uninteresting material. Housing now is functional, practical and clinically designed. There are very few places, if any, where children can indulge in private fantasy and creative play which often is noisy and messy. In almost every country of the world children live through long, empty hours, and they are criticised when they fail to develop positive interests and activities that involve effort and skill. But what are they to do? In Britain, their age shuts them out from Youth Clubs; they have few places outside their homes where they can meet friends; their homes are often too tidy or too crowded for exciting work that may be messy; gardens are virtually non-existent. These children have no alternative but to use the street, with all its perils and frustrations. City children of school age who play in the streets often suffer from aimless boredom, or else they invent interesting and exciting activities which land them in the juvenile courts where much commendable initiative and enterprise has to be squashed. Valiant efforts are made by voluntary organisations to encourage young people to help themselves, but government and local authorities lend almost no support and waste their opportunities. A sense of responsibility cannot be inculcated in the young if the chances to practise it are eliminated, and it is up to the planners to provide these chances. Not all the so-called "youth problems" are the fault of the young'.

Today, in Britain, the situation is little changed in most areas. 'Latchkey' children are commonplace. Out of 7 million schoolchildren, there are only places for after-school care for about 8500 during term time [5]. There are not enough play schemes and most are underfunded, in unsuitable premises, with unqualified staff. As more women are attracted back to work, the situation can only get worse.

7.2.2 Adults need to play too

As adults, we also need to play. But rather than take the opportunities for play, we seem destined to search for ways to make all our time useful. The inability to find meaning in activities, in themselves, appears to drive many of us towards escape, to amusement and entertainment and some to drink!

'We are all of us compelled to read for profit, party for contacts, lunch for contracts, bowl for unity, drive for mileage, gamble for charity, go out for the evening for the greater glory for the municipality, and stay home for the weekend to rebuild the house, minutes, hours and days have been spared us. The prospect of filling them with the pleasures for which they were apared us has somehow come to seem meaningless, meaningless enough to drive some of us to drink and some of us to doctors and all of us to satisfaction of an insatiate industry' [6].

The study of play teaches managers that the important thing, whether it be with children or adults, is to invest considerable decision-making power in the hands of the participants. This is why some people like to belong to small autonomous groups, where they can feel creative and identified, where they can be masters of their own destiny, even for a short period of their routine lives. Recreation programmers would be foolhardy to omit autonomous groups, clubs and associations from their recreation programmes.

Another lesson from the study of play is to resist the temptation of controlling, administering and providing 'on a plate'. The process of controlling the content of our behaviour (i.e. ourselves) is important for the play element to flourish. More emphasis must be given to participation, rather than outcomes, and to a much broader range of activities that provides intrinsically rewarding play.

A child's world should be a world filled with wonder and excitement. Most adults appear to be separated or exiled from this childlike world. Yet we all need freedom and motivation to choose things of joy and wonder – to have one foot in the child's world. Despite their class culture, the Ancient Greeks' idea that life should be lived as play had merit; when they said 'Whom the gods love die young', perhaps they meant in Lord Stankey's words that those favoured by the gods stay young until they die.

7.3 RECREATION AND ITS IMPLICATIONS ON LEISURE SERVICES

Recreation can be described and defined in a number of ways. Two main ways of perceiving recreation are from an *activity* focus (the activities which we call recreation) and from an *experience* focus (the experience we enjoy from actively or passively taking part). From an activity base, recreation is seen to be an activity related to sports, games, art and other leisure-time pursuits. In this respect, recreation is *product-oriented* and concerned with facilities and programmes. The activity focus presents recreation as a structure, a framework and as a *social institution* in society.

The experience focus is *process-oriented* and the concern is on what an activity does for a person. Its concern is with self-fulfilment. A recreation experience can occur in varying degrees depending on the level of satisfaction experienced, much the same as other feelings, which may be of stronger or weaker intensity. This is consistent with the theory of self-actualization advanced by Abraham Maslow. Hence recreation can be regarded as a *means* to an end, or as an *end* in itself.

Looking at recreation experience, it follows that whatever activity or situation renews, revises, refreshes and re-creates for the individual, is a recreation for him or her at that time. This has far-reaching implications for recreation services. Any activity implies no right or wrong, no good or bad; no moral issues are at stake. But society will not allow just *any* activity. Even while many liberal views are held in Western society, individuals are still constrained, and inevitable so, in what is and what is not acceptable behaviour.

Throughout its history, recreation has kept its moral tag and this has been part of its *non-appeal* for many people. Modern society, with its wide interpretation of what is moral and what is socially acceptable, casts doubt as to the value of interpreting recreation with high ideals of morally sanctioned behaviour.

In recent times, greater attention has been given to the debate as to whether recreation is primarily determined by the nature of the activity, the attitude of the player towards the activity or the player's psychological state during the activity. Inherently there is a belief in the right of the individual to self-expression, the expanding of experiences and horizons, but within society's social ethic.

7.3.1 Recreation: practical considerations

The leisure professional has to live in a world of recreation traditions, systems, institutions and facilities, together with vociferous demands, employers, budgets and politicians. A Recreation Manager cannot therefore present a complex picture of what recreation is. The problem in viewing recreation solely as experience is that it is almost impossible to define operationally, and it is difficult to communicate with understanding. We therefore need to find tangible criteria on which to base planning, management and programmes. For the leisure professional to communicate with policy-makers and public alike, it may be appropriate and beneficial to talk in terms of recreation experience arising out of recreation or leisure activity.

Although recreation can occur at any time, and almost any situation can function for it to occur, it is during free time for leisure that re-creation is more likely to come about. Furthermore, recreation experience is more likely to be 'felt' if the following factors are incorporated into recreation programmes and activities:

1. Recreation is personal, therefore activities should be concerned with individual satisfactions.
2. Recreation is concerned with freedom, therefore programmes should offer a satisfactory choice.
3. Recreation is refreshing, therefore activities should have immediate value, be novel and stimulating.
4. Recreation can be found in any activity, physical, social, intellectual and spiritual, therefore programmes must be concerned with the whole person.
5. Recreation is creative, therefore programmes should have concern for the indirect benefits and creations which arise from the activities.
6. Recreation will often arise through play, therefore opportunities for participation in the spirit of play, with the players in control, need to be encouraged.
7. The fullest recreation experience is found in oneness and unity, therefore activities should be sought which give opportunity for 'peak' experiences.

Most people find no difficulty in identifying informal games of soccer, volleyball or netball as recreational, or in perceiving swimming, cycling, climbing and arts and crafts as recreation activities. These are the activities that have been offered by recreation administrators, clubs and organizations. Recreation has become institutionalized in so far as we have a common understanding of the services, activities and events offered as part of the recreation service.

7.4 LEISURE AND ITS IMPLICATIONS FOR LEISURE SERVICES

Leisure can be perceived in a variety of ways as time, as activities, as a state of being, as experience, as a way of life or as a framework of opportunity to participate.

In order to measure it more easily, leisure has been thought of by many leisure professionals, sociologists and planners, and by many individuals themselves, as a quantifiable period of time. However, even narrowing the concept down to a measure of time, there are still complex anomalies.

If leisure is a period of time, then any activity performed in that time can become a basis for an individual's leisure. This has far-reaching consequences for planners, policy-makers and managers. How do people use that time? Should Recreation Managers influence choices? Leisure time may not come up in appropriate blocks of time. Regardless of time availability, there is often lack of motivation, insufficient money, resources and facilities or poor mobility. Home-based leisure may be partly the result of insufficient time-blocks and the fact that home leisure is cheapest. For example, television viewing is cheap, convenient and satisfying. Leisure, in reality, comes about through a conglomeration of activities: television, hobbies, drink, sex, gambling, roaming, lazing, reading, do-it-yourself, gardening, families, holidays, social visiting, church-going, service-giving, social contacts, physical recreation, arts and crafts and music-making.

But as we have seen, leisure is not just time or activities; it is also concerned with the experience during the time and during the activities. Lately, theorists are thinking not so much in terms of activities in given times, but linking recreation and leisure into satisfying or life-enhancing experiences. How do people perceive leisure and what does it mean to them? If leisure is to fulfil its potential to meet the needs of people, then we must know as much about people and about the nature of leisure, as we do about the activities we so often refer to as 'leisure'. If leisure is a human phenomenon – more than time, activity or experience – it has to perform a function for people. It has to provide opportunity. Managers must help to provide and enable people to take advantage of that opportunity.

7.4.1 Leisure opportunities

Opportunities afforded through leisure have awakened for many a spirit of self-development, adventure and creativity. Economists and sociologists may tell us that we have not reached the 'age of leisure', but it is clear to see that many people are in search of new leisure identities. The tenth London Marathon attracted 60 000 applications and 35 000 of them were accepted to run. Between them they raised millions of pounds for charity. Race organizer, Christopher Brasher, commented: 'Make no mistake, it is hard, desperately hard, to run 26 miles 385 yards and the only reward for the masses is that every single one of them is a winner.'

The increasing army of joggers, orienteers, climbers, hang-gliders, cavers, skin-divers, parachute jumpers, surfers, sailors, dancers, amateur historians and archaeologists, painters, writers, actors, fitness fanatics, tri-athletes and meditators shows that people are looking for new and innovative activities and experiences. But what are all these people searching for, while sometimes risking their lives, money and loved ones? Maslow described it as a *peak experience*, brought about by 'affirmation of our identity and confirmation of our existence'.

Peak moments are some of those high moments in life when one is totally immersed in an activity, at one with the world and with oneself. Top-class skiers say they have the sensation of blending into the mountain; runners, having gone through the pain barrier, have described a feeling of 'floating'; and top gymnasts have achieved a moment of sheer 'perfection'.

Although such experiences cannot be *made* to happen, some conditions can create an enabling environment. Most people (drug free!) reporting 'highs' in, say, sport or music have achieved some mastery, a high level of skill.

Well-conditioned athletes (e.g. keep-fit exponents or dancers) can achieve a great feeling of joy in movement (and so can we all, at times). Often outdoor activities, battling with the elements, or being surrounded by natural beauty, may cause us to reach beyond our ordinary urban existence. Many peak experiences (e.g. mountaineering, parachute jumping, white-water canoeing) involve risk. It is clear that recreation and leisure activities have much to offer in helping people reach beyond themselves. Spectators and supporters can share in moments of achievement but it is the *doers* – those participants motivated by intrinsic rewards – who will gain greatest satisfaction and who are the ones more likely to achieve peak experiences or feelings of re-creation or oneness.

More than peak experiences, however, many people are looking for self-fulfilment, maybe to be or to become 'somebody' – all they are capable of becoming. The spirit is caught in the poem by Robert Browning: 'Ah, but a man's reach should exceed his grasp. Or what's a heaven for?' Is this not akin to the leisure ideal of the Ancient Greeks, but more so because it widens the scope of their narrow choice?

The search for identity is important in understanding leisure behaviour. It is a search for the *whole* person, not a split person. This idea is exemplified in the growth of spiritual and meditative movements. Some Eastern disciplines and philosophies, for example, emphasize a unification of the body, mind and spirit, through movement, meditation and deep relaxation. These Eastern cults, which promise a unity with oneself and with the universe, have captured the imagination of the Western world, perhaps because of the vacuum created by our artificial splitting of the body from the mind and spirit.

It is clear, then, that leisure offers opportunities for enrichment. But the time for leisure potential can also bring problems because freedom not only allows us, but also forces us, to make choices.

7.4.2 Leisure problems

While time for leisure can be used to enrich the lives of many people, for others it may be a curse upon them. For example, it is a time to be lonely for many. For some it is an opportunity for vandalism, warring factions and gangs looking for excitement and trouble. The extraordinary lengths taken by governments and the football fraternity to head off trouble erupting at the World Cup in Italy, in 1990, are an indictment against the way in which we have failed to meet the needs of some young people and failed to inculcate the ability to choose and to act wisely.

In some cases, leisure has taken on the mantle of business and work. The inability to relax, even for a moment, is a common complaint and evidence of neurotic disturbance; even leisure time is taken at a work-rate pace. Some find it hard to take holidays, suffer from after-work irritability and the 'Sunday neurosis'. Most suicides occur during weekends, holidays and vacations. The attraction of 'moonlighting' – the second job – is not *just* for money. It indicates the relative importance given to work compared with leisure. Apparently up to 8 million Americans need psychiatric assistance every year, 125 000 are treated in hospital for depression and 50 000 commit suicide.

While leisure opportunity contains a time element, leisure behaviour must not be time conscious, if people are to play and find satisfying preoccupations, interests and leisure in their lives.

7.5 SIMILARITIES BETWEEN PLAY, RECREATION AND LEISURE

The conceptual and institutional differences between the three phenomena have been highlighted in preceding chapters and summarized in this chapter. However, in many instances they overlap to different degrees, like an eclipse.

Several words, ideas or themes are used frequently in describing each concept, including the following:

1. *Freedom* The free expression of play; the free choice of recreation; the freedom of choice in leisure.
2. *Self-expression* Each emphasizes individual self-expression.
3. *Satisfaction* Play is characterized by satisfaction in the doing, manifest joy; recreation and leisure are both satisfying to various degrees.
4. *Quality* The quality of experiencing is important to all.
5. *Self-initiated* Play is usually self-initiated, and leisure and recreation also appear to be so in large measure; recreation, however, can also be other-directed.

6. *Absence of necessity* Play avoids external pressure, it cannot be forced and remain play; leisure has the same connotations; in recreation too there is an absence of necessity, but a level of obligation may be attached to it in its institutional setting.
7. *Playfulness* Play, though often serious and intense, is abundant in playfulness, in fun; recreation is often playful but many elements are so product orientated and competitive that they appear to be more akin to work; leisure is freer and 'looser' and therefore exhibits more playfulness.
8. *Any activity* In its purest terms almost any activity can function as a play, recreation or leisure activity for someone; this is most evident in play activity; the same can be said of recreation and leisure from an 'experience' focus; recreation, however, is more socially constrained in its institutional setting.
9. *Experiencing* Again, in its purest terms, each has an inner dimension; play is totally absorbing in the doing ('lost in play'); re-creation can be an inner-consuming experience of oneness; leisure can be the perception of freedom for the sake of doing or experiencing.

These similarities emphasize that play, recreation and leisure are integrated and they appear, collectively, to have an inner core.

7.6 DIFFERENCES OF PERCEPTION AND EMPHASIS

Play, recreation and leisure are both different from and similar to each other; they have their own idiosyncrasies, but there are also more subtle differences of emphasis.

Play gives a strong emphasis to the qualities of being childlike, spontaneous, purposeless, unreal ('only play'). It has justification in and of itself. It is a single, all-embracing concept. Children at play do not compartmentalize themselves into physical, mental and spiritual beings. They play in a 'whole-person' way. This holds true for some adults too. One only has to observe a senior citizen's talent contest to see the similarities. In adult life, play may provide the best opportunity for people to regain the unity of body, mind and spirit.

Play, then, can be described as activity, freely chosen and indulged in for its own sake for the satisfaction it brings in the doing; it exhibits childlike characteristics of spontaneity, self-expression and a creation of its own special meaning in a play world.

Recreation, unlike play, appears to need to be justified, 'keeps youth off the streets', 'produces good citizens'. It carries greater social responsibilities than 'leisure'. It has concern for community well-being, which is epitomized in 'therapeutic recreation', 'industrial recreation',

'recreation counselling'. Recreation, is thus a social institution, a structure for recreation organisations, services and activities.

Re-creation is the second meaning, and it is about experiencing. In its purest sense, it is characterized by an inner-consuming experience of oneness that leads to revival. It is re-creative. Like all feelings, it can have different strengths. At its highest, it can be a 'peak' experience. Recreation experience therefore renews, restores and recharges the batteries – in our waking moments. Like sleep, it is a process of re-creating!

Leisure is perceived in different ways – time, activity, experience, state of being, a way of life, and so on. It is in a way multidimensional. It can encompass play and recreation activity. It can also function as the psychological perception of freedom to choose and to do and to experience. It also has the capacity to be perceived as a way of living – a 'leisure ideal', in the Ancient Greek sense of the term. Leisure, then, can be perceived as experiencing activities, chosen in relative freedom, that are personally satisfying and innately worthwhile and that can lead an individual towards self-actualization and, ultimately, a self-fulfilling life.

Hence play, recreation and leisure exhibit a *sameness* at their core. And at the core they can be interlocked into one meaning, which is greater than the sum of the three individual parts. Take this everyday situation by way of illustration: a friend attends an aerobics session for a variety of reasons, which she may not be able to explain. Do we describe this as the period of time, the activity, her attitude towards the activity, the spirit in which it is undertaken, the psychological state during the activity, the physical effort expended, the aches and pains, the experience of 'feeling great', the fun, the social experience, the sheer freedom of getting away from home obligations or simply the joy of movement? What the total experience (the total 'package') does for her, and what she feels about it, are of the essence. The satisfying experience will want to be bought again. The interest can take hold and can change a life-style. Hence leisure can begin to become a way of living; it can also provide a new identity.

Some people – young people in particular – are now freer to try to discover themselves. Who am I? What am I here for? They are looking for ultimate experiences, often with dangerous consequences. Where does leisure and its management come into the search for identity? What is the Leisure Manager's role in this 'revolution of rising expectations'?

Leisure professionals need to have concern therefore with the qualities of the activities and their meanings for people and in the *use* of time – not just with the activities, *per se*, or the time itself.

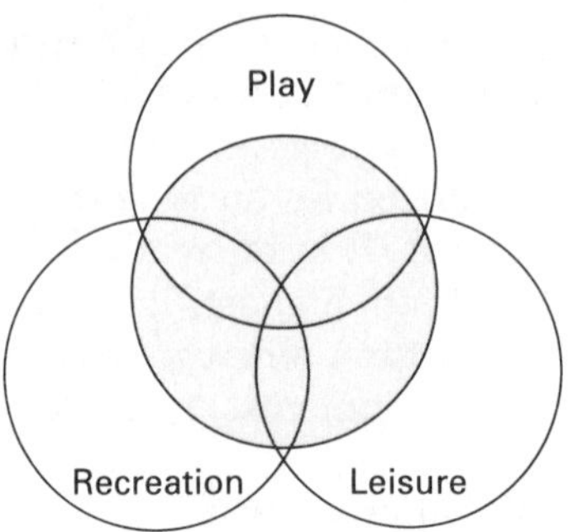

Fig. 7.1 'Pleisur' at the heart of play, recreation and leisure experience.

7.7 THE INNER CORE – THE LEISURE EXPERIENCE

An inner – consuming experience may occur in the process of play, recreation or leisure. This experience I shall now call 'pleisur' (a derivation and an acronym for the words 'play', 'leisure' and 'recreation') as these is no word in the English language to describe it. Indeed, the experience goes beyond the description afforded by words – it is experience, wordless.

What implication does this 'discovery' have for the management of leisure? Put simply, the 'pleisur principle' implies that, in meeting the needs of people, the quality of the experience is more important than the activities themselves, the numbers attending or the income generated. Furthermore, managers must take into account that different people have different needs, which change according to their circumstances and stage in life. The quality of the experience is of greatest importance for 'pleisur' to occur. The activity itself may be secondary to what it does for a person, or what it means to him or her.

If, as leisure professionals, we want to provide a choice of activities and opportunity for people to experience and develop leisure potential, then 'pleisur' is more likely to occur for individual people if the setting and circumstances are favourable. For 'pleisur' to be experienced there need to be:

1. the right conditions;
2. satisfaction in the doing or experiencing; and
3. positive outcomes.

The right conditions There need to be sufficient levels of some of the following ingredients:

- freedom
- choice

- absence of necessity
- self-initiating
- spontaneity

Satisfaction To be satisfying, there need to be levels of some of the following experiences:

- self-expression
- challenge
- novelty
- stimulation
- playfulness
- quality experiences (ideally, peak experiences)
- re-creative moments

Positive outcomes To be effective, there should be some positive outcomes, for example:

- physical
- emotional
- social
- psychological wellbeing
- level of achievement
- heightening of self-esteem

'Pleisur' experiences give satisfactions. Satisfactions lead to consuming interests. Individuals become more of what they are capable of becoming. This can lead to life-enhancing experiences, a goal of leisure.

7.8 BARRIERS TO PUBLIC SERVICES DESIGNED TO MEET NEEDS

Were it all as simple as that! Regrettably, there are a number of individual and institutional barriers to providing integrated services based on the needs of people. The reasons are complex.

Individual people are not free agents and are limited in their response to leisure services and programmes; some of the factors responsible for this situation are:

1. People have physical, mental and social limitations.
2. Their environments limit choice (e.g. family, peer group, culture, resources).
3. Leisure for some is being eroded through many obligations or through insufficient blocks of time or through enforced free time, without the means or motivation to use it.
4. The choice of activities is limited to those that are socially desirable.
5. The play spirit is eroding as play activities become work-like and highly structured.

6. Opportunity for peak experiences, excitement and adventure are limited for most.
7. A culture of 'win at all costs' militates against playing for its own sake.

Playing, experiencing satisfactions and achieving have much to do with the processes of learning, knowing ourselves, being motivated, reaching beyond our grasp and becoming balanced individuals. However, activities such as sport can be practised in such extremes that they can work not for the good, but for the bad, and where the spirit of goodwill and fair play are submerged and dominated by over-zealous competition and cheating – winning at all costs.

Do leisure professionals adequately consider people's needs in formulating programmes? Are people given sufficient opportunity to seek personal fulfilment in their leisure? Does a rationale exist to justify public and private expenditure to support an institution for leisure services? Traditionally, public authorities have not been orientated towards a 'holistic', people-directed approach; they have directed their efforts towards the provision of facilities, activities and programmes without involving people in the plans. A more *qualitative* approach – what it does for the whole person – will reorientate professional values. This will, in turn, affect the principles and aims of leisure services and programmes. Again, this will affect objectives, programmes and activities. There is some evidence of this multi-faceted approach, particularly in areas of social disadvantage. Senior citizens' programmes can include not only recreational activities, but also health, nutrition, medical care and voluntary employment, making use of skills and talents. This multi-service approach also has benefits in assisting young people, who may be out of a job and who feel they have lost their identity and their usefulness.

It is apparent that there are not only personal and social barriers to integrated services, there also exist strong organizational and institutional barriers. Commercial organizations are concerned with financial profits; monetary results therefore are the ultimate goal. Many voluntary organizations and institutions are concerned with their own organizations, their own autonomy and their own programmes, in isolation to the needs of the larger community. Public authorities provide fragmented services between authorities, between tiers in the same authority and sometimes within the same department. Fragmentation of services can lead to lack of continuity and duplication. It is not uncommon to find people going from one local authority department to the next, to find a satisfactory solution to a problem. Organizations, professions, voluntary bodies and public departments all have a tendency to isolate themselves and operate independently. They may not collaborate for fear of not receiving proper credit. Most organizations are prestige-oriented. Even public departments compete among themselves for kudos. The lack of cohesion and customer care may deprive the individuals whose needs may go unheeded. In public services there is often lack of accountability, through lack of evaluation. Services flow on and departments remain very busy, but do they accomplish what they are supposed to do? Participant needs may go unmet, even though the intent is to fulfil them.

Hence, while an integrated approach to leisure service is desirable, there are personal limitations and traditional, organizational and institutional barriers in the way of such an approach. To provide appropriate services, principles must be founded on the best theoretical framework, the obstacles and limitations should be recognized and assumptions made on which services and programmes can be developed.

7.9 LEARNING TO CHOOSE

Leisure implies freedom. Freedom implies choice. Choice enables people to be involved in activities which are either personally worthwhile and which lead to good citizenship or which are of doubtful value.

In the United Kingdom, in the 1990s, some new leisure provision increasingly panders to the apparent need for entertainment and diversion? 'Provide slides and rides; people will pay for the pleasure.' In balance, this is fine. We need amusement and fun. Yet consider, does the individual who flits from experience to experience, like an impulse buyer in a supermarket, have the opportunity to gain an appreciation of the activity which will make it, in Godbey's words, 'intuitively worthwhile'? For most people, enjoyment and satisfaction in an activity increase as knowledge and skill increase. Whether gardening, playing the violin, cooking, playing tennis or collecting antiques, all are enriched by an increase in knowledge and skill:

'Leisure involves sacrificing that which is potentially good for that which is potentially better. The lack of willingness to sacrifice one desirable activity in order to undertake another, however, suggests an inability to obtain leisure [7].'

As Jacob Bronowski [8] pointed out, appreciation is essentially an act of re-creation; a deep sense of appreciation envelops us and lifts us to a higher plane where we discover that there is peace, beauty and joy in this world. And that may carry over into increased appreciation of life itself. That is leisure's promise.

It seems hard for us to appreciate and accept the gift of leisure. Ideally, leisure can be a way of living the 'good life' for individuals and communities. But as Goodale and Godbey point out, only we can determine for ourselves what that will be. However, education and knowledge will help to give the opportunity and ability to make good choices. Education can help make us free, and freedom forces us to make choices because the world of opportunities opens up before us. But education should not be limited to finding jobs. Schools and colleges are not employment agencies. The more we learn about ourselves, how to choose to find fulfilment, the better society we create.

7.10 ASSUMPTIONS ON WHICH TO BUILD SERVICES AND PROGRAMMES

People have diverse needs, and different people have different needs, which change according to their circumstances and stage in life. Old people have different needs from the young; disadvantaged people have different levels of need compared to those highly advantaged. People have a whole range of needs, some of which are basic to survival, some are essential to cope with living in an uncertain social world and some are at the apex of a complex human network bringing balance, harmony and self-worth to individual people. It is particularly in this latter category where leisure opportunity can help people to meet some of their needs. Leisure therefore is linked, inextricably, to other elements of life. For example, leisure for the vast majority of disadvantaged groups is likely to remain low, while major life constraints persist such as lack of income, poor housing and the unrelieved pressures of parenting.

In order to provide public-integrated leisure services based on the needs of people, authorities must make a number of assumptions on which to base principles, aims and objectives; for example:

1. That the services are intended to meet individual needs, so that a person can choose activities, in relative freedom, and fulfil needs in the way he or she chooses.
2. That programmes have concern with the whole person.
3. That services help to redress the balance of lost time, lost opportunity, lack of awareness and lack of ability and of know-how.
4. That services are open to all citizens.
5. That priorities should be balanced to serve the greatest number and those in greatest need, recognizing that those in greatest need may well be in the minority.
6. That services should be comprehensive and not separate pockets of competing interests.

Superimposed on these factors is the overriding assumption that leisure needs management and, furthermore, that it can be managed. The question is: can leisure, with emphasis on freedom, be organized, planned and managed? The activity can be. The experience cannot. However, opportunities can be enabling:

1. Leisure Managers can market, involve people and then create an environment where personally worthwhile choices can be made and satisfying experiences are more likely to occur.
2. Leisure Managers can extend the range of activities to offer a wide and varied choice.
3. Groups can be enabled to participate through supportive services.
4. Other groups can be encouraged to fashion their own destiny.
5. Work conditions can be improved to give people a greater chance of self-expression, recreation activity and recuperation. Leisure Managers can advise employers.
6. Education can be extended to inculcate leisure skills (physical, social, cultural and intellectual) which can help people to realize their potential. Leisure managers can work in consulation and co-operation.

In these and other ways, management can help to extend opportunities. The assumptions provide principles on which to force a reorientation towards a *people approach* to leisure services. The reorientation stems from the belief that each individual has worth and has a need to express himself or herself, and that society will benefit from citizens who have the ability, adaptability and resourcefulness to cope, create and find fulfilment.

Leisure time without the opportunity, the means and the ability to cope can be a two-edged sword. Along with a marked increase in leisure participation, there has been a marked increase in antisocial behaviour, particularly in those areas where leisure opportunity is low. Free time has not solved the social problems of loneliness, poverty or job satisfaction. Indeed, *leisure time* may have exacerbated those problems. Can *leisure opportunity* help to solve some of them? Opportunity for leisure has no value to people, of course, unless advantage is taken of it. This is where the leisure professional has a special role to play, that of enabling people to take up the opportunities by effective and sensitive marketing.

The job of the manager is to help people to take advantage of that leisure opportunity. That opportunity can be seen as a favourable or advantageous combination of circumstances; it can be a suitable activity, occasion or time, an opening, a chance, a break. It allows the time and access to do and to behave in ways that we want to, and which we find satisfying – i.e. to play, to rest, to enjoy, to contemplate, to work, to serve and to be ourselves.

The study of leisure shows how important it is to deal with men and women as complete, whole persons. In addition, it is important to look at leisure and work not as two discrete, mutually exclusive components of life. The interrelationships and the overlapping between the two are evident: 'Man was not born to work. Rather man was born with an innate capacity for effort, which can be dissipated in any activity be it sailing, cooking, sex, chess, Frisbee or art' [9].

The leisure we are talking about in this chapter can be for some a way of living, and for most a major sphere of life that brings innate satisfaction. It is not just a series of activities, not just uncommitted time; nor is it just experiencing satisfactions. Rather it is a personal opportunity to experience, behave and act in ways which are internally satisfying. To be able to grasp leisure opportunity, people must develop preoccupations and interests which can be expressed through leisure activities. These activities need resources, organization, planning and management.

7.11 TOWARDS A NEW THEORY AND NEW PRACTICE

Hence, to provide for, plan and manage leisure, we must start from a philosophy for living the 'good' life, the satisfying life. But why start from theory? Surely our experience and practical knowledge are sufficient on which to plan? I believe that while technical know-how is important, as a basis for effective management, it is wholly inadequate. If, however, we have an acceptable theory, if we know what motivates people and what demotivates, then we are better able to plan and manage effectively. If we have no basic insights and explanations into why people play and find recreation, we cannot be confident that the resources and programmes we provide are either relevant or appropriate.

The value of a theory is the degree to which it explains and predicts. Alas, no theory or explanation has been put forward which explains leisure satisfactorily. This, however, makes it possible for 'philosophers' to consider new approaches. The latest thinking, combining the old with the new, can be drawn together in a new theoretical framework. The output from the theorist should then be the input for the practitioner – the practising manager. Leisure professionals can help bridge the gap by becoming theory–practice orientated – i.e. putting into practice good theory.

Here, we are at a pivotal stage in this book – and from which a new approach to leisure planning and management can be forged. We have considered leisure and its inner core 'pleisur' and suggested that some of the needs of people might be met by providing opportunity to choose activities which are personally fulfilling and worthwhile, and for leisure and 'pleisur' to occur.

I put forward three propositions which are fundamental to a people-centred approach to leisure management:

First, providers of resources should be concerned with the quality of the experience for the individual, not just with the quantity of facilities and the numbers attending.

Second, leisure opportunity can lead to satisfying experiences which, in turn, have positive effects on the quality of life of individual people.

Third, management policy and performance can be a powerful influence on people's participation and non-participation in recreation.

Any new leisure theory therefore should have concern with linking together leisure, people's needs and management and that, in meeting the needs of people, the quality of the experience and the satisfaction in the doing, and the positive personal outcomes, should be perceived as being more important than the activities themselves, the numbers attending or the income generated.

There is nothing more practical than a good theory! Or as Ted Blake says, 'To say it's OK in theory but no good in practice is a contradiction. If it won't work in practice, it can't be good theory.' The rest of this book illustrates how the theory can work in practice.

REFERENCES AND NOTES

1. Ellis, M. J. (1973), *Why People Play*, Prentice-Hall, Englewood Cliffs, NJ, p. 1.
2. Sutton-Smith, B. (1974), in the Education and Leisure Conference, Liverpool University; and also in *An Ideology for Play*, paper, Columbia University, New York.
3. E.g. Department of Health (1989), *An Introduction to the Children Act 1989*, HMSO, London.
4. Lady Allen of Hurtwood (1968), *Planning for Play*, Thames and Hudson, London.
5. Phillips, A. (1990), When play becomes a prison. *Observer* 15 April.
6. Kerr, W. (1962), *The Decline of Pleasure*, quoted in Goodale T. and Godbey, G. *The Evolution of Leisure*, Venture Publishing, State College, Pa, 1988, p. 178; distributed outside North America by E. & F. N. Spon, London.
7. Goodale, T. and Godbey, G. (1988), *The Evolution of Leisure*, Venture Publishing, State College, Pa, p. 218–19.
8. Bronowski, J. (1965), *The Science and Human Values* (rev. edn), Harper Torchbooks, New York.
9. Levy, J. (1977), A recreation renaissance. *Parks and Recreation*, December, p. 18.

RECOMMENDED ADDITIONAL READING

Making Sense of the Children Act, 1989, guide for the Social and Welfare Services by Nick Allen, Longman, Harlow.

Working with the Children Act, 1989, National Children's Bureau, 8 Wakeley Street, London.

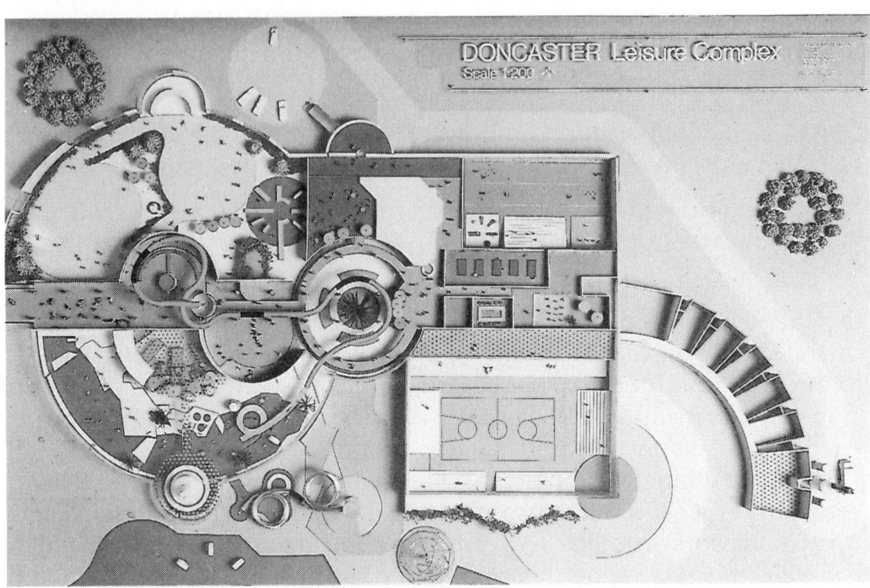
DONCASTER Leisure Complex
Scale 1:200

Chapter 8

Planning for leisure

The first part of the book, in Chapters 2–7, has been concerned with leisure and the needs of people. The second part deals with the planning process, with emphasis on the role of the public sector.

This chapter is written in the following sequence. *First*, planning for leisure is seen in historical perspective. *Second*, a seven-stage leisure planning process is proposed and described. *Third*, the philosophical approaches adopted by local authorities, from which policies for leisure planning flow, are debated; they include equitable distribution, expressed demand and social control. *Fourth*, the complexity of assessing potential demand is illustrated by a critique of a wide range of approaches. These include standards of provision, spatial analysis, hierarchy of facilities, national participation rates and expressed demand; and also relatively less used, yet more sensitive methods, Grid and Need Index approaches and a wide variety of public consultation exercises.

Having read this chapter, readers will understand more about the complex nature of leisure planning, seen from the viewpoint of leisure professionals. They will appreciate that leisure planning differs from 'general' or conventional planning. They will understand why it is of fundamental importance to work from a sound philosophical base, together with an orientation towards a people-involved process. Readers will learn about the various methods which can be used in assessing needs and demands and that no one method or one system will be sufficient on which to plan.

Planning for leisure will be seen as best involving a number of professional disciplines, including leisure. The Leisure Manager will be able to perceive the role that he or she can play in the process of assisting planners and policy-makers with planning for leisure to meet the needs of people.

8.1 HISTORICAL PERSPECTIVE

Planning has always been concerned albeit often peripherally with the provision of facilities for recreation. The evolution of the planning movement was closely associated with the 19th-century fight for the retention of open spaces and commons which were threatened by unplanned urban development. The movement has evolved from a concern for public health, education and moral standards to problems of inner cities and countryside recreation and conservation. Since the *Public Health Act 1848*, which authorized local authorities to provide public walks and pleasure grounds, successive Acts of Parliament such as the *Physical Training and Recreation Act 1937*, the *National Parks and Access to the Countryside Act 1949* and the *Countryside Act 1968* were formulated to meet changing demands. In this evolution, the planner's role has been strengthened by the profession's wide powers over the control of land use.

The various Acts of Parliament concerning leisure and recreation in England and Wales have placed statutory responsibility upon local authorities only to provide allotments, libraries, youth facilities and Adult Education facilities. However, no recommendations have been made with regard to the scale of provision required to fulfill this statutory obligation. This, coupled with the 'permissive powers' that relate to other forms of leisure provision, has resulted in considerable variation in the range and scale of provision made by different local authorities. The political philosophies of the respective councils has further exacerbated the situation, with Labour councils generally perceiving leisure and recreation provision to have a greater social service orientation compared to Conservative councils.

8.2 GENERAL PLANNING AND LEISURE PLANNING

The planner's objective is to provide the right facilities, in the best location and at the right time, for the people who need them and at acceptable cost. Dreams, however, seldom become reality. Planning is not a static process, but a dynamic and changing one. Planners should work with all the disciplines involved in creating amenities and opportunities for people in neighbourhoods, villages, towns, cities and in the countryside. Planners themselves are only part of the planning process. They do not directly acquire and manage land and amenities. They identify locations for facilities according to acceptable planning principles. They seek to minimize conflicts of interest, traffic, noise, pollution and congestion. Planners help to make towns functional, attractive and healthy places; they also have to safeguard public interest and help to conserve (and foster good use of) the countryside.

Gold [1] defines recreation planning as

'a process that relates people's leisure time to space. It is both art and science, using the methods of many disciplines . . . into developing alternatives for using leisure time, space, energy and money to accommodate human needs. The process results in plans, studies and information that condition the public policy . . . to provide leisure opportunity'.

These leisure opportunities are provided within the constraints imposed by central government (e.g. financial) and in accordance with local government policies at local level, for the common good of the community. Unfortunately, in practice, community needs are frequently overruled by central government. There are adequate examples of playing fields, designated in Local Plans, being permitted, upon appeal, to be used for housing and commercial development. The action of the Department of Environment in such circumstances has led to a belief that 'there is always a presumption in favour of allowing applications for development' [23]. A recent publication by the Sports Council, the National Playing Fields Association and the Central Council of Physical Recreation [23] strongly recommends that there should be a reversal of emphasis and a different starting point with the presumption being against the loss of playing fields for building development.

The social dimension of leisure planning emphasizes the difference between it and general planning. Leisure facilities, outside the home, in comparison to housing, retail outlets, roads, and so on, are non-essential facilities and have only a minority appeal to the community as a whole. Hence assessing the demand for a particular leisure facility is a complex and difficult process, particularly since there is a range of competing attractions for a person's leisure time.

Leisure planning as a discipline in its own right is not a new phenomenon. Indeed, leisure planning was to the forefront in the planning of the Garden Cities by Ebenezer Howard at the turn of the century and also he recognized the economic and social benefits associated with the dual use of school facilities. The first of many recreational standards of provision was established by the National Playing Fields Association (NPFA) in 1925. Leisure planning, however, is often a neglected area, despite the considerable advances made in recent years. Veal [2] states the problem:

'The problem with planning for leisure is that, generally speaking, the planning profession knows very little about leisure while the leisure professions know very little about planning. With some honourable exceptions, planners have tended to ignore leisure because they have had more pressing issues such as transport, housing or shopping to deal with. The leisure professions have ignored planning because they have been primarily concerned with management – the day to day operation of facilities and services. And yet the need for firmly based planning in the area of leisure is as great if not greater than in some other areas of public society. Leisure plans not only have to present politicians with proposals concerning the desirable quantity, types and distribution of facilities and services, they also very often have to present the case for any provision at all.'

The word 'management' is used, in this quotation, only in an operational context. This book takes the position that top-level management should be concerned not just with policy, planning and operational management, but also with inputs into policy and planning. Bereft of an input into policy, planning, outcomes and evaluation of services, the manager is rendered at best an efficient administrator, organizer and controller of users and personnel. The Leisure Manager should be involved in planning because an involvement at the earliest stage can ensure inclusion of the appropriate ingredients for leisure and elimination of factors not compatible with good management process and practice. An essential part of the planning process is to identify the needs of people and to provide products and services in response to those needs, so that individual self-fulfilment can be achieved.

Unfortunately, however, there are far too many examples of poor planning. The most common failure is that leisure facilities are often placed in the most inappropriate locations. All too often they are located on land which is owned by the local authority but not necessarily in an appropriate location. This, in many cases, is false economy because facilities suffer from poor accessibility. In such circumstances, they are unlikely to achieve optimum levels of usage and hence require increased levels of subsidy. Facilities located on the periphery of centres of population or away from main transportation routes or alongside physical barriers, such as rivers, inaccessible motorways or difficult road systems, suffer from poor access and inevitably result in a restricted catchment area.

A frequent fault in the early 1970s was that many leisure complexes were built that were too large for the community they were intended to serve. This inevitably resulted in high operational costs and, at times of economic constraint, many of these centres appear to have had an insecure future. Additionally, the accessibility of a large centre compares unfavourably with a distribution of strategically located smaller centres.

In the past decade, however, considerable strides have been made in the approaches to leisure planning. The present financial constraints imposed by central government upon local authorities and the effect of Compulsory Competitive Tendering (CCT) legislation are forcing local authorities to place greater importance upon leisure planning in an attempt to provide appropriate facilities that incur the minimum level of operating subsidy.

8.3 THE LEISURE PLANNING PROCESS

The leisure planning process, in conceptual terms, is a very simple model based on a four-stage cycle approach (Fig. 8.1), whereby the leisure needs and demands of a community are identified. From the resources available, facilities and/or services are selected to meet this requirement; these are subsequently implemented and the outcome is monitored. In reality, however, the process is far more complex and a fairly common approach is illustrated in Fig. 8.2. This involves seven

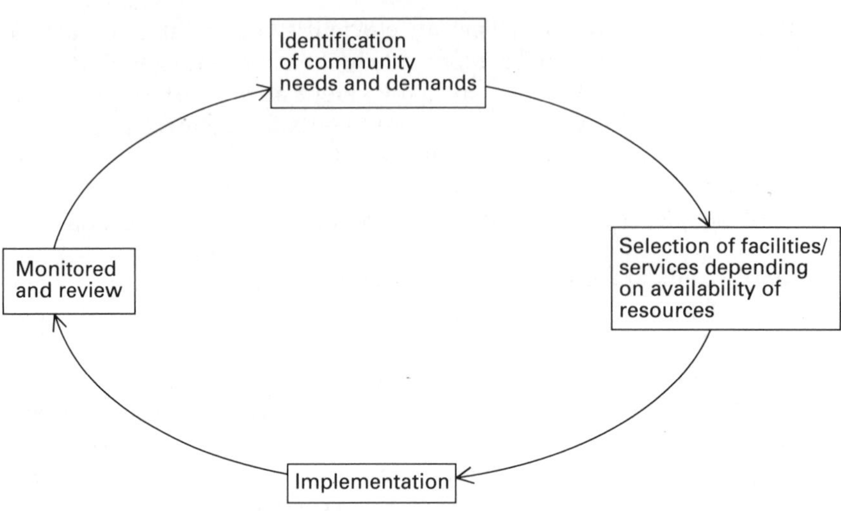

Fig. 8.1 Leisure planning process – simple model.

distinct stages that are undertaken in a systematic way. The seven stages are as follows.

Stage 1: determine council policies

The council's policy towards the allocation of leisure resources (i.e. the reasons behind its investment in leisure provision) is important as it can influence the type and range of facilities provided (i.e. their location and the way they are managed). Additionally, it is necessary to determine what the council's policy is in respect of partnership developments with other local authorities (e.g. local education authority) or with the voluntary and/or commercial sectors. Further, how the council perceives its role in the provision of leisure opportunities can also affect the type of facility provided, and by whom.

Stage 2: evaluate current leisure provision and services

A population survey will identify population concentrations and specific sections of the community that require special consideration, while a transportation analysis will highlight the accessibility of existing and potential leisure sites.

At times of economic constraint, it is important that existing facilities are used to the optimum level and wasteful duplication of facilities avoided. Hence it is necessary to evaluate the current service and, where possible, determine areas of spare capacity and where demand exceeds the available supply. This evaluation should also involve mak-

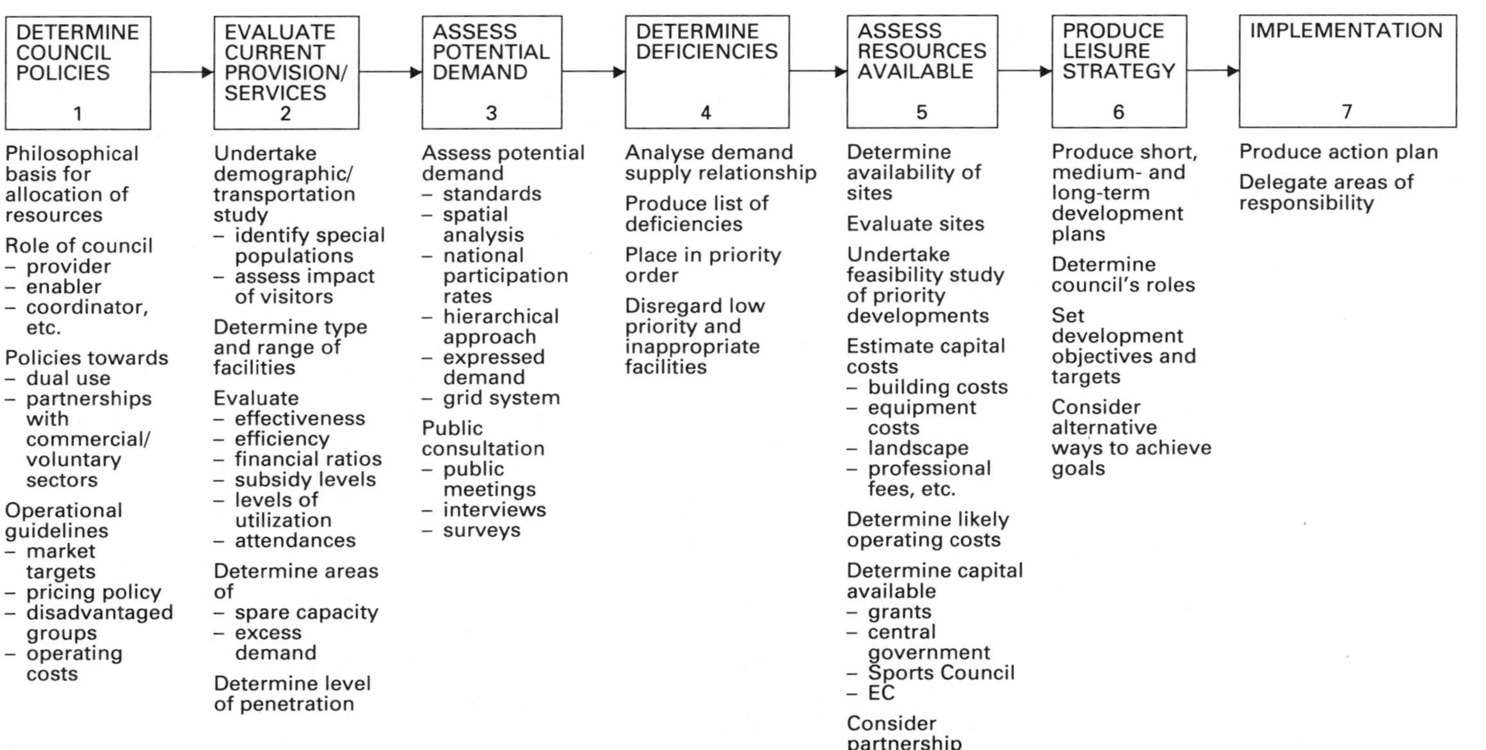
DETERMINE COUNCIL POLICIES 1
EVALUATE CURRENT PROVISION/ SERVICES 2
ASSESS POTENTIAL DEMAND 3
DETERMINE DEFICIENCIES 4
ASSESS RESOURCES AVAILABLE 5
PRODUCE LEISURE STRATEGY 6
IMPLEMENTATION 7
Philosophical basis for allocation of resources
Role of council – provider – enabler – coordinator, etc.
Policies towards – dual use – partnerships with commercial/ voluntary sectors
Operational guidelines – market targets – pricing policy – disadvantaged groups – operating costs
Undertake demographic/ transportation study – identify special populations – assess impact of visitors
Determine type and range of facilities
Evaluate – effectiveness – efficiency – financial ratios – subsidy levels – levels of utilization – attendances
Determine areas of – spare capacity – excess demand
Determine level of penetration
Assess potential demand – standards – spatial analysis – national participation rates – hierarchical approach – expressed demand – grid system
Public consultation – public meetings – interviews – surveys
Analyse demand supply relationship
Produce list of deficiencies
Place in priority order
Disregard low priority and inappropriate facilities
Determine availability of sites
Evaluate sites
Undertake feasibility study of priority developments
Estimate capital costs – building costs – equipment costs – landscape – professional fees, etc.
Determine likely operating costs
Determine capital available – grants – central government – Sports Council – EC
Consider partnership schemes
Change priority order if necessary
Produce short, medium- and long-term development plans
Determine council's roles
Set development objectives and targets
Consider alternative ways to achieve goals
Produce action plan
Delegate areas of responsibility

Fig. 8.2 Leisure planning process – a practical approach.

ing a performance appraisal of each element within the service and, in particular, examine its efficiency and effectiveness. Although a comparison of a specific facility with national norms is fraught with difficulty, because no two facilities are identical (they differ in design, philosophy of use, quality of management and staff and the environment in which the facility is located),valuable indications of the performance level can be obtained. Performance indicators can include various financial ratios (e.g. Income: Operating costs; Income: Staff costs, etc.), subsidy levels, levels of utilization of individual facilities and the penetration level within the local community. (Chapter 15 further describes operating ratios.)

Stage 3: assess potential demand

Although there is no single leisure planning technique that can accurately indicate what the potential demand may be for a particular activity or facility, a good indication can be obtained by using an array of leisure planning techniques. These include:

1. standards of provision;
2. spatial analysis;
3. national participation rates;
4. hierarchical approach;
5. grid system;
6. need index approach;
7. expressed demand incorporating public consultation.

(These methods are described in some detail later in this chapter.)

Stage 4: determine deficiencies

Comparing the level of potential demand with the actual provision should theoretically produce a list of deficiencies. Inevitably this list would be extensive and it would, moreover, be unrealistic for any authority to contemplate redressing the perceived inadequacies across the whole leisure spectrum. It will therefore be necessary to place the deficiencies in rank order of importance, determined by establishing a criteria based on council policies and the needs of the community. Facilities that are regarded as inappropriate for a specific area would be omitted from the list, together with those having a low level of priority.

Stage 5: assess resources available

It will be necessary to examine all potential sites for leisure development and these should be assessed in terms of their suitability (e.g. size, terrain, accessibility, environmental considerations) and a full feasibility study undertaken in order to be able to estimate the capital cost involved for each facility and its likely outcome in terms of attendance and net operating cost. Sources of capital funding will need to be investigated including possible grants from central government (or government agencies such as the Sports Council or the Countryside Commission) and the European Community, planning gain or partial funding arising from a partnership development. Upon completion of this exercise, it may be necessary to review the priority order.

Stage 6: produce leisure strategy

Arising out of the decisions made in the previous stage it should be possible to produce a leisure strategy incorporating short-, medium- and long-term development plans for the area with the council's role in these developments being clearly defined.

Stage 7: implementation

To implement the leisure strategy, it will be necessary to produce an action plan and delegate areas of responsibility to key staff. In order to ensure that the tasks are completed on time, it is advisable that a detailed *Critical Path Analysis Network* be drawn up. Naturally, the progress made will need to be monitored, together with the effect of the provision upon the community, and the leisure strategy periodically reviewed in the light of economic, social and environmental changes.

Many of the major elements in the planning process are further discussed in this chapter, including planning philosophies and policies and assessment of demand before giving specific guidelines on the implementation of a leisure strategy.

8.4 LOCAL GOVERNMENT – PHILOSOPHICAL BASIS FOR LEISURE PROVISION

It is perhaps surprising that many local authorities who spend many millions of pounds each year on the operation and maintenance of their leisure services do so with no stated philosophy for the allocation of such resources. In such circumstances, one is tempted to ask: 'why incur this expenditure?' 'Who are the beneficiaries?' 'What are the perceived benefits?', etc. It is acknowledged that much of the leisure provision is an historical inheritance, but this does not justify the continued expenditure without an explanation of its purpose.

Historically, a paternalistic concern for the health and welfare of the community was the major influence on recreation planning. The standard response was the provision of facilities such as parks, playing fields and swimming pools, and these remain today as primary areas for local authority provision and finance. Stated planning policies currently appear to be based on three philosophies or a combination of two or more: equitable distribution, expressed demand and social control.

8.4.1 Equitable distribution

In this context, leisure participation is seen as being of intrinsic value to the participant, with the community also benefiting from the resulting spin-off. However, equity is by no means synonymous with equality – equal distribution of facilities does not necessarily provide either equal opportunity or equal participation.

As we have seen in Chapter 6, the social inequality that exists in our society manifests itself with the more affluent sections predominantly represented as users of public sector facilities. This situation has been brought about largely by a degree of inaccessibility associated with many municipally managed leisure facilities, particularly to the less affluent residents within the community.

Accessibility, in this context, covers its widest application – geographical, financial, social and psychological accessibility. While good management with enlightened policies (e.g. large discounts offered to disadvantaged groups) can do much to improve the financial and social accessibility, planners should also consider the leisure needs of the less affluent and less able members of society in providing appropriate facilities at locations that the non-mobile can reach with the minimum of effort. The public transport system is geared to the requirements of the commuter and not to the needs of the leisure participant. Indeed, when people are most free the public transport system is at its worst, and when the level of inconvenience exceeds the perceived enjoyment that a person will obtain from leisure participation, then he or she will discontinue. Therefore, to provide an equitable distribution, there must be a policy of positive discrimination in favour of the disadvantaged in order to ensure equality of opportunity.

8.4.2 Expressed leisure demand

Planning policies based on the expressed demand of its residents are attractive to local government decision-makers. If there is a demand for a particular type of facility and it is used to the optimum, then councils are more likely to say: 'we have provided what was demanded – we have therefore met community wishes.'

The use of petitions, staging public meetings or having perhaps a media-inspired campaign can certainly influence planning decisions, particularly when a council election is imminent. Pressure groups, however, tend to be represented by the better educated, more articulate and the more affluent, and their influence is far greater than the proportion of the electorate they represent.

In contrast, those with the greatest leisure needs are unlikely to be heard, and without the advocacy of the professional leisure leaders, such expression of demand can be misleading. Likewise an assessment of demand based on the membership of a club as an index of growth in demand of a particular activity can also be misleading, as it does not necessarily reflect the level of active participation.

The use of surveys does not necessarily reflect what a community 'demands'. If the size of the sample is small, minority activities may be over-emphasized or be omitted altogether. Additionally, the responses to questions on 'demand' tend to be subjective in nature, as the respondent is required to make projections about his or her future levels of leisure time and disposable income. Further, where the respondent has no experience of a particular activity, there is no way of knowing whether the person concerned will find the activity satisfying. Hence the provision of leisure facilities based on the expressed demand of its residents needs careful consideration; and other forms of demand assessment need to be undertaken to confirm or refute these claims.

8.4.3 Social control

There is a strong and instinctive belief that the provision of sports and leisure opportunities will alleviate anti-social behaviour and many ills of the world. This belief is well established in the minds of local authority members and at central government level. The government White Paper, Sport and Recreation, claimed that such provision was a means of 'reducing boredom and urban frustration' and stressed its contribution 'to the reduction of hooliganism and delinquency among young people'. This belief was also stressed in more recent reports and White Papers, such as *Policy for the Inner Cities* [4] and the Report of the Scarman Inquiry [5].

Although claims are made [6,7] to support this belief, it is suggested that these are simply correlations and not proof. A more important issue, however, is what kind of facilities and services are likely to attract those persons who are, or are likely to become, delinquents: is the present type of public sector provision perceived by this market target as attractive; and what are the facilities being used by the potential delinquents? Until answers to these questions are forthcoming, such a philosophy for the allocation of leisure resources appears to be a hit or miss affair and as such can be inappropriate and expensive.

8.5 ASSESSMENT OF LEISURE DEMAND

As we have previously stated, there is no single correct method of assessing the level of potential leisure demand for a given community, but a good indication of the probable demand for a particular activity can be obtained by using a range of different planning techniques. Leisure behaviour is by no means predictable; it is rather a matter of

Table 8.1 Standards of provision

Category/facility	*Standard*	*Recommended by:*
Outdoor recreational 'playing' space	6 acres (2.42 ha) per 1000 population	NPFA
Outdoor equipped playgrounds	0.5–0.75 acres (0.2–0.3 ha) per 1000 population	NPFA
Casual or informal play space within housing areas	1.0–1.25 acres (0.4–0.5 ha) per 1000 population	NPFA
Athletics and miscellaneous	0.5 acres (0.2 ha) per 1000 population	NPFA
Allotments	0.5 acres (0.2 ha) per 1000 population	Thorpe Committee
Golf courses	1 9-hole course per 18 000 population	Sports Council
Metropolitan parks	150 acres (61 ha minimum) within 2 miles (3.2 km) of population	Greater London Development Plan (GLDP)
District parks	50 acres (20 ha) within 0.75 mile (1200 m) of population	GLDP
Local parks	5 acres (2 ha) within 0.25-mile walking distance (400 m)	GLDP
Small local parks	Under 5 acres (2 ha)	GLDP
District indoor sports centres	1 per 40 000–90 000 population, plus 1 for each additional 50 000 population (17 m^2 per 1000 population)	Sports Council
Indoor swimming pools	1 25 m pool and 1 learner pool per 40 000–45 000 population (5 m^2 per 1000 population)	Sports Council
Squash courts	1 court per 6000 population	Squash Rackets Association
Indoor bowling rinks	4, 6 and 8 rink centres to serve populations of up to 30 000, 44 000 and 59 000 respectively	Sports Council
Ice skating rinks	1 in conurbation of 250 000 within a 5-mile radius	National Skating Association of Great Britain
Community centres	1 per 10 000 population	National Federation of Community Centres
Libraries	1 per 15 000 within 1-mile walking distance of all	Bourdillion Report

Table 8.1 (Cont.)

Category/facility	*Standard*	*Recommended by:*
District libraries	1 per 12 000 population, 60 h opening per week	Library Advisory Council
Branch libraries	1 per 4000 population, 30 h opening per week	Library Advisory Council

Note: This table outlines some of the 'standards' frequently used by local authorities c 1990 even though some of the authorities now no longer quote standards.

personal choice and the situation is further exacerbated if one's preferred choice is not available and one has to seek a substitute activity. Provision should not therefore be based upon a simple set of measurements, criteria or rules.

8.5.1 Standards of provision

Surprisingly, one of the most developed and widely accepted approaches to the 'equitable' distribution of recreational services is the use of scales of provision, standards and norms (Table 8.1). Many standards are not based on empirical research, but on long-accepted assumptions of what is 'needed'.

For some unexplained reason, standards have a fascination for planners and politicians. They have the almost hypnotic effect of drawing attention to themselves as a magnet. Veal [2] captures this paradox of leisure standards:

'Leisure planners love standards. This is one of the great paradoxes of our time. When government Ministers try to tell local authorities how to organize their affairs they rise up as one and complain of threats to local democracy. And yet in the area of leisure provision, the one area where local authorities are virtually completely free from government interference, they frequently look nervously over their shoulders to ensure that they are sanctioning their activities'.

Standards, however, are necessary, important and useful when they have been based on sound methodology and are used with flexibility, local knowledge and wisdom. Tempered with wise judgment they have considerable advantages. They give yardsticks against which to measure existing provision, they are easy to understand and communicate and they cover many of the facilities provided by local authorities. Veal lists the advantages of standards: simplicity, efficiency and equity, in that they can lead to the same level of provision from area to area; authority, in that they act as an external authoritative source; and measurability, where progress can be monitored and assessed.

Gold and Mercer [8,9] criticize standards for not being supported by empirical research; beliefs or myths have become accepted and with time have become institutionalized. They believe that the people who develop the standards differ in their social background from the majority of the population and, by implication, impose their own standards upon the population. They also argue that standards across the board do not take into account areas of deprivation, factors of accessibility, socio-economic or demographic differences. Hence, while standards have some advantages they have many disadvantages, including the six discussed briefly below:

1. institutionalized;
2. variable;
3. lack validity;
4. misinterpreted;
5. quantitative;
6. inappropriate.

First, they become institutionalized as if written on tablets of stone. Once entrenched, they become authoritative, unmovable and are given far greater strength and importance than they merit.

The best known and most frequently applied recreation standards in Britain are those of the National Playing Fields Association (NPFA). Founded in 1925, the NPFA first established its 6 acres of outdoor recreational playing space per 1000 population in 1937. Reviews were undertaken in 1946, 1955, 1971 and 1986 to account for changing conditions. This target, however, has remained intact, and the 6 acres are representative of:

1. *Youth and adult use*
   1.6–1.8 ha (4.0–4.5 acre) per 1000 population.
2. *Children's play area*
   0.6–0.8 ha (1.5–2.0 acre) per 1000 population.

Unfortunately, this standard has been the subject of some criticism [11], and the 1986 review was not based upon any empirical research, but on a consensus of opinion of the planning authorities surveyed; this is hardly surprising since this standard has become institutionalized after being in existence for over 50 years.

However, it is not just the long-established standards that become authoritative. The Sports Council in 1972 (the year in which it obtained its Royal Charter) published *Provision for Sport* [12], which estimated the shortfall in England and Wales for indoor swimming pools, indoor sports centres and golf courses. The method of assessment (which in the case of the indoor sports centres was based upon research undertaken at only five centres) became a standard that is still used by many local authorities, although the Sports Council have tended to move away from standards in recent years. Today, however, these standards have little relevance, with swimming participation having increased twofold in the past decade while the current demand for golf is apparently insatiable.

Second, standards vary. Different authorities have different standards for the same leisure facility. Most major pursuits requiring public recreation facilities have standards – pitches, pools, indoor sports centres, libraries, and so on. Yet all have a variety of standards. For example, there are four standards for allotments. One 'official' standard is given in Table 8.1 as 0.5 acres per 1000 population. However, the National Allotments and Gardens Society has a standard of 2.0 acres per 1000 – i.e. four times as great as the 'official' standard. This promotes the question: whose standards? Who should make the standards? Should it be central government, local government, national agencies, governing bodies or the local community? At present, in many areas of leisure provision nobody has a mandate to dictate what the standards should be.

Third, as Veal [2] rightly points out, it is the problem of validity that is the greatest difficulty with standards. The way they are derived is open to question and none more so than many of the major physical recreation standards of playing fields, swimming pools and indoor sports centres. Playing space standards, for example, are based on participation rates, but participation is largely dependent on the level of supply. The number of swimmers will depend on the number of pools, their location and accessibility, whether they are all open to the general public, the strength of swimming in the area, the type of pool, the marketing and quality of provision, whether instruction is good and cheap and whether the water is warm!

To make assumptions that only so many people will play sports and so many people will swim is not only misleading, it perpetuates the traditional system of planning based on artificial standards. The jogging movement and the 'fun runs', and the growth of indoor bowls and squash, all show how misleading fixed standards can be. Hence some standards of just a decade ago are no longer valid or appropriate. Alas, even those minimum standards have still in most cases to be met.

Other standards such as those appertaining to public open space cannot be achieved in many of our inner cities. In London the initial standard of 7 acres of public open space per 1000 population has been substantially reduced to meet the specific circumstances of different boroughs and neighbourhoods.

Fourth, while standards are usually fairly easy to understand, they can be misinterpreted and used as a justification for taking no further action. Some authorities have been known to interpret standards to suit their own purposes, not those of the community; they do not wish to be seen as failing to provide. For example, some authorities may show that they have more than adequate indoor playing space but analysis might reveal that most of the total space is made up of small units quite unsuitable for activities in demand, or that access by the general public is restricted.

Fifth, standards are inanimate, inhuman. They assume a 'need' for a facility rather than a need which might be fulfilled in a variety of ways. They are concerned with quantitative and not qualitative aspects of provision. They take no account of the leisure potential of the specific areas – i.e. local needs, local priorities, local differences and local environments and conditions.

Sixth, while many leisure pursuits are amenable to standards of provision, many are not. Water recreation, tourism, heritage, entertainment and arts have no comprehensive basis for evaluation.

In summary, it is clear that standards of provision, whether local, regional or national, can be a very crude assessment of demand. As they are based on national information, they often bear little relationship to local circumstances; they deal in quantities, thereby ignoring the quality of provision, aspects of distribution, use and management. The ready acceptance of artificial standards prevents planners from considering the unique qualities and possibilities of each situation. Ready acceptance may preclude more dynamic, flexible and responsive approaches to planning.

Standards of provision can be used as a starting point by providing a useful benchmark for measuring the adequacy of facilities in an area and for identifying sub-areas that may be under- or overprovided, while recognizing that most standards indicate minimum levels of provision. From this initial assessment, the need for further provision can be identified and more detailed standards of locally formulated criteria can then be used to test the feasibility of particular schemes.

8.5.2 Spatial analysis

In recent years, extensive user surveys have been taken of many leisure facilities, and from these an indication of the size of a leisure facility's catchment area can be made. By using this approach, the geographical area covered by the facility's perceived catchment area can be identified, with areas beyond that, theoretically, not being served. The limitations associated with this approach are considerable and include:

1. No consideration is taken of the quality of the existing facility or whether it currently has considerable spare capacity, or if the demand for its use exceeds the supply available.
2. It assumes that the density of population is evenly distributed, while in reality (particularly in the inner city areas) there are pockets of heavily populated areas and other areas, incorporating parks, where fewer people reside.
3. The catchment areas of leisure facilities are not necessarily circular in nature and are distorted due to many factors. Physical barriers which have to be crossed such as rivers, railway lines and busy motorways can restrict a catchment area, while access to a facility along a major road can extend the catchment area along its route [13].
4. The assumption that similar-sized facilities will have identical catchment areas is fraught with problems as the respective populations may differ in size, affluence (and hence mobility) and social composition. These factors will undoubtedly influence the perceived attraction of the facility to its potential users.

Much of the above criticism can be overcome if a user survey is conducted of the existing facilities and action taken dependent on its findings. Additionally, if the level of penetration and frequency of visit is determined in relation to distances travelled by the users to the facility concerned (by using enumeration districts or grid squares), this (with some modification to account for the increased attraction factor) can be used to project the likely attendance should a new facility be developed.

An example of how this can be applied is shown in Fig. 8.3, where in an imaginary situation a local authority is contemplating developing a further swimming pool in the southern part of the district. The user surveys conducted at the existing pools over a given week are revealed in Table 8.2, with Pools A and B being the existing pools.

From the analysis of the survey results the percentage of users from the different catchment areas can be determined, together with the penetration/weekly visits expressed in percentage terms, and the expected weekly visits can be calculated, given the population within the perceived catchments of the proposed pool. This can be calculated, based on the average performance of the existing facilities. It should be stressed, however, that this assumes that the population profile and accessibility is constant and no consideration has been given to the increased attraction effect of the new pool.

This *spatial analysis approach* model has been further refined by the Scottish Sports Council in conjunction with Planning Data Management Services, Edinburgh University. The model consists of three principal components: demand, supply and catchment areas. The model

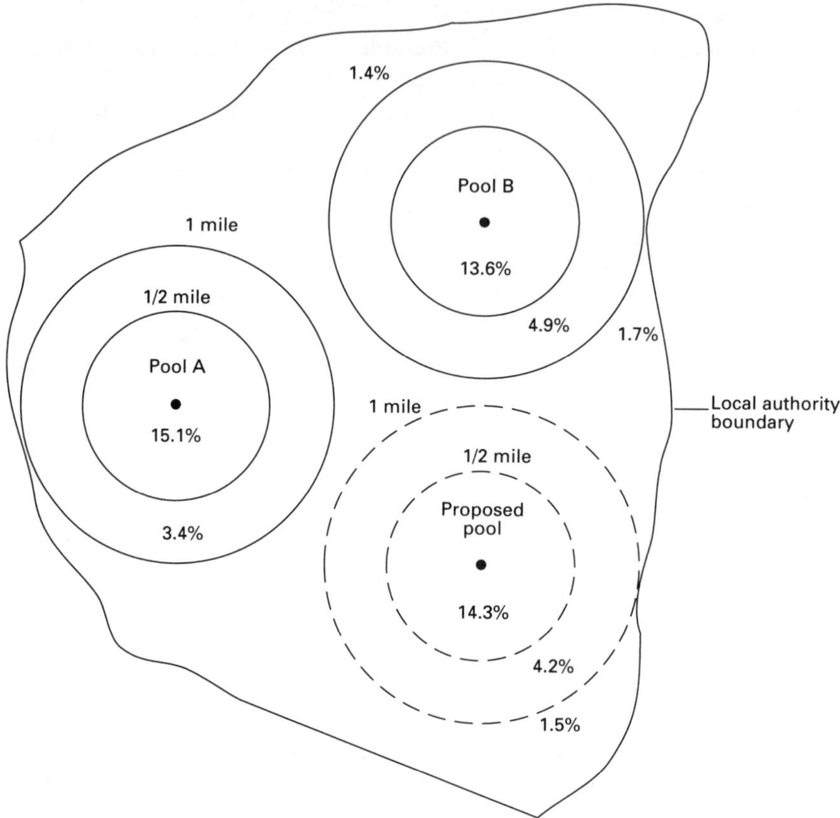

Fig. 8.3 Penetration/visits per week (%) from perceived catchment of existing pools and proposed pool.

Table 8.2 Survey results – two imaginary swimming pools

	% users from catchment			*% penetration*		*Visits within catchment*	*Total weekly visits*
Facility	½ m	½ m–1 m	1 m+	½ m	½ m–1 m	1 m+	
Pool A	71	20	9	15.1	3.4	1.4	3900
Pool B	67	23	10	13.6	4.9	1.7	3500
Proposed Pool	69	21	9.5	14.3	4.2	1.5	?

has basic assumptions which reduce its effectiveness in reality: all participants within a catchment have equal accessibility, all facilities exert similar attractions and the current pricing policies remain unchanged. Yet it remains a valuable aid to planners in establishing priorities and identifying areas of deficiency. The model has been used by the Grampian Regional Council to determine the requirements of the Aberdeen Area [14] and by the Sports Council for Wales in its national strategy for the ten years 1986–96 [15]. A variation of the model is currently being contemplated by the Sports Council for use in England.

8.5.3 Hierarchy of facilities

A modified version of the standards approach is the *hierarchy of facilities approach*, normally applied to a range of facilities for a given population size. Its application has been greatly used in the development of new towns where the planning of leisure facilities is a prerequisite of the population getting to the towns. Probably of greater value is its use for small communities, where the range of facilities perceived to be required by a smaller population is likely to be less controversial. An example of a hierarchy of facilities is given in Table 8.3, which was developed specifically for use in the small communities along the Lambourn Valley in Berkshire [16].

Such an approach used for small-scale community facilities has more validity than most other approaches. However, if it is used for large-scale projects, then the limitations associated with the use of standards (e.g. validity, inflexibility, inapplicability, lack of concern for accessibility, quality of provision, quality of experience, etc.) equally applies to this planning approach.

An example of the hierarchy approach that has some merit is the Hierarchy of Parks developed by the Greater London Council [17]. This was established as a result of extensive user surveys of London parks that identified the catchment area of different-sized parks and led to the development of a strategy for parks by the GLC and most of the London boroughs.

8.5.4 National participative rates

Large-scale national or regional participative surveys can be used to determine what the potential demand may be for a given community based on the findings of the survey. It should, however, be stated that the level of participation is largely dependent upon the level of provision and does not take into consideration potential or deferred demand. Additionally, such surveys do not normally indicate the participation rates within different types of neighbourhood.

Table 8.3 Suggested hierarchy of leisure provision for rural communities

Community size	*Recommended facilities*	*Examples of activities that could be offered*	*Additional comments relating to location*
1 Hamlet/small village, 100–500 population	1 Village hall – suitable for social functions. Kitchen, snooker table depending on demand and local tradition	1 Meetings, dances/disco, concerts, table tennis, youth club, voluntary organizations, e.g. scouts, adult education classes	1 Centrally located – preferably linked to community open space
	2 Community open space, 2–3 acres, with children's play area with equipment	2 Children's play, football and cricket, informal recreation, village festivals, carnival, etc.	2 Location – centrally avoiding the necessity for children to cross main roads. Possibly linked to primary school
	3 Mobile library service – van	3 Books, records, tapes, etc.	3 Preferably linked to form focal point of village
2 Medium-sized village, 500–1500 population	1 Community hall (15–20 m × 10 m × 6.7 m), with kitchen, toilets, temporary stage, changing facilities, storage areas. Bar facilities depending on demand, car parking	1 Recreation, badminton, keep-fit, yoga, aerobics, meetings, drama concerts, dances/discos, youth clubs	

2 Community open space, 3–7 acres, including football pitch with pavilion, (or linked to community hall), children's play area with equipment, seats, floral beds. Space for tennis and/or bowls, depending on local demand	2 Children's play, football club level, informal cricket, informal recreation, village festivals, carnival, pony club	
3 Mobile library service – trailer library	3 Books, records, tapes, etc.	
4 Community mini-bus – availability for hire – provision dependent on public transport service and facilities available within village	4 Organized visits in connection with sporting, art, entertainment and social events	4 Hire costs and maintenance schedules important
5 Mobile recreation service	5 Offering sports and arts activities, particularly for the very young, females, etc. unemployed and the elderly	5 Depending on the range of opportunities available and the degree of initiative and leadership within the village. One half-day visit per week

Table 8.3 (Cont.)

Community size	*Recommended facilities*	*Examples of activities that could be offered*	*Additional comments relating to location*
3 Large village, 1500–2500 population	1 Community hall (20 m × 10 m × 6.7 m), marginally larger than that required for a medium-sized community, plus bar facilities	1 A range of sports (including gymnastics, martial arts, badminton, possibly 4-a-side soccer, etc.), arts and social recreation	1 Location – centrally, focal point of public transport
	2 Community open space, 9–14 acres, 2 or more football pitches, 1 cricket square, bowling green, 2 hard/tarmacadam surfaced tennis courts/netball courts. Pavilions for changing, plus bar refreshments facilities. Children's play area – with kick about and equipment	2 Activities to include club football/rugby, cricket, bowls, tennis, netball	2 Depending on the availability of open space. It might be necessary to have the facilities at more than one location. Each site should have pavilion with changing facilities
	3 Library – fixed accommodation	3 Books, records, tapes, etc.	3 Opening times staggered throughout week to meet different people's needs
	4 Mobile recreation service – depending on the facilities within the village and whether they are professionally managed	4 Sport and recreation activities	4 Visit restricted to half-day a week

4 Small country town, 2500–6000 population	1 Sports Hall (26 m × 16.5 m × 7.6 m), depending on the size of community, consideration to be given to ancillary facilities such as weight training area, 2 squash courts	1 Increased range of sporting activities including 5-a-side football, cricket, indoor bowls, basketball, volleyball, weight training, squash, archery, tennis	1 For economic reasons dual use with a secondary school or a large sports club/voluntary organization should be explored
	2 Swimming pool (25 m)	2 Swimming, life saving	2 As above; provision only if dual-use arrangement can be achieved
	3 Community hall/arts centre – to include stage and projection facilities, plus meeting rooms, kitchens, bar, toilets, craft workshop	3 Meetings, drama, concerts, cinema, whist drives, bingo, table tennis, adult education classes, displays	3 Linked to other community provision – improve spin-off and awareness
	4 Community open space (15–40 acres), including park area, children's play areas with equipment, 4 football/rugby, hockey pitches, 2–4 tennis courts, bowling green and pavilions with refreshments, 1 cricket square, multi-purpose floodlit hard all-weather area	4 Children's play, town show, carnival, soccer, rugby, cricket, bowls, tennis, netball, 5-a-side soccer, training purposes	4 Children's play areas, easy access to housing estates. Playing pitches best located near sports hall – economics of scale and spin-off
	5 Library facilities – branch library	5 Books, cassettes, records, video, pictures	5 Permanent accommodation – spread opening hours
	6 Mobile recreation service	6 Sports/recreation activities	6 Programmed to meet specific market segments, e.g. unemployed – off peak times/one day per week

Table 8.4 General household survey 1986, results extracts

Active sports, games and physical activities	*(a) % of adults participating in the 4 weeks before interview*	*(b) Average number of occasions of participation per participant in 4 weeks*	*(c) Average number of occasions of participation per adult per year*
Outdoor			
Walking 2 miles or more (incl. rambling/hiking)	19.1	8	20.0
Football	2.7	5	1.9
Golf	2.7	5	1.6
Athletics – track and field (incl. jogging)	2.6	9	3.0
Swimming (incl. public pools)	2.4	7	2.2
Tennis	1.4	5	0.8
Bowls	0.9	6	0.8
Camping/caravanning	0.8	6	0.6
Cricket	0.8	4	0.4
Horse riding	0.7	7	0.6
Snow sports	0.5	4	0.2
Sailing (excl. windsurfing)	0.5	3	0.2
Rugby	0.4	5	0.3
Climbing/potholing	0.3	3	0.1
Rowing/canoeing/punting	0.3	4	0.1
Hockey	0.2	[4]	0.1

The most appropriate source of information in this respect is the *General Household Survey* (*GHS*), which is undertaken by the government's Office of Population Censuses and Surveys. Every three years, the survey has questions relating to leisure activities which cover active participation in sports, games and physical activities, watching spectator sports and participation in other leisure activities, including entertainment and day visits. The survey also determines the frequency of participation. The sample size is in the region of 25 000 and is confined to those aged 16 years and over. The main results of the 1986 survey are given in Table 8.4.

An illustration of how the *GHS* results can be used is given in the following example:

For a community of 50 000 adults (aged 16 and over) how many squash courts should be provided to meet the leisure demands of its residents?

Table 8.4 (Cont.)

Active sports, games and physical activities	*(a) % of adults participating in the 4 weeks before interview*	*(b) Average number of occasions of participation per participant in 4 weeks*	*(c) Average number of occasions of participation per adult per year*
Indoor			
Swimming	9.5	3	4.1
Snooker/billiards/pool	9.3	7	7.9
Keep fit/yoga	3.3	6	2.7
Squash	2.4	4	1.3
Badminton	2.1	3	0.9
Gymnastics/athletics	1.9	9	2.1
Bowls/tenpin	1.5	4	0.7
Table tennis	1.1	5	0.7
Self-defence (excl. boxing, fencing)	0.4	6	0.3
Ice skating	0.3	2	0.1
Boxing/wrestling	0.0	[12]	0.1
Fencing	0.0	[2]	0.0
Other indoor sports/games	1.4	4	0.7
At least one activity	28	–	–
Total (all activities)	–	–	26

Notes:
Sports, games and physical activities:
(a) Participation rates in the 4 weeks before interview.
(b) Average frequency of participation per participant in the 4 weeks before interview.
(c) Average frequency of participation per adult per year.
Persons aged 16 and over.
[ ] = figure based on fewer then 50 participants.

Using the *GHS* data, this would suggest that the requirements are for 6 courts.

Number of games per week =

$$\frac{2.4\% \text{ participation rate} \times 50\,000 \text{ population} \times 1 \text{ (frequency of participation)}}{2 \text{ players/game}}$$

= 600 games/week

Assume capacity of squash court to be

$$= 14 \text{ h/day} \times 7 \text{ days/week} \times 1.5 \text{ games/h} \times 65\% \text{ level of utilization}$$
$$= 95 \text{ games/week}$$

$$\text{Therefore, number of courts required} = \frac{600}{95} = 6 \text{ courts.}$$

It is possible to refine this approach further by making minor adjustments to take into consideration the sex, age and socio-economic background of the residents. Additionally, should the regional variations in participation rates be available, this would make the projections more accurate. And in addition to the limitations associated with this approach, as stated earlier, it tends to be unreliable with regard to minority activities, due to the size of the sample.

There is also a further application that combines this approach with the spatial analysis. An example is where a local authority wants to provide, say, squash courts or sports halls on the sites of its many existing swimming pools. From the perceived catchment area, the population can be determined and the required number of squash courts and/or sports halls calculated.

Another national survey that can be used in this approach is the *Target Group Index* (*TGI*), which is a national consumption survey funded by the British Market Research Bureau. It is an annual survey with a 24 000 adult sample taken in 200 parliamentary constituencies. The advantage of using the *TGI* is that it is linked with *ACORN* (which is the acronym for *A Classification of Residential Neighbourhoods*), and is available from CACI, a company authorized to use the census data. By using the activity index for each ACORN type of household, the potential demand for a particular activity can be determined.

Unfortunately, this approach has many disadvantages. In addition to those associated with the *GHS*, the main disadvantages relate to the actual wording of the self-completing questionnaires and the lack of precision in the data collected. While the *GHS* determines what activities the respondents participate in, in the four weeks prior to being interviewed, the *TGI* is more open ended such as: 'Do you ever . . .' [18]. The consequences in the different approaches to the surveys are reflected in the results, with the participation rates in the *TGI* sample being around 200% to 300% higher than those found by the *GHS*. Also the reliability of some of the data is in question as the results relating to some of the minority activities are not consistent.

8.5.5 Grid approach

The *grid approach* is more of a management technique than a planning approach, but it has an important function in specific situations. A suitation where it is frequently used is where planning criteria have been established for a range of possible developments on a particular site. A further application is where the facilities within a park or geographical zone have to meet the demands of all sections of the community. By dividing the community into different categories, deficiencies can be determined. An example is the division of the community into age or life-cycle groups such as those included in the grid approach example in Table 8.5.

Table 8.5 Example of grid approach

	Community Sections							
Facilities/areas	A	B	C	D	E	F	G,	etc.
1	/	–	/	/	–	/	–	
2	/	/	–	/	/	–	–	
3	–	–	–	/	/	–	–	
4	–	–	–	/	–	/	/	
etc.								

A Pre-school children (under 5)
B Young children (5–12 years)
C Early teenagers (13–16 years)
D Late teenagers (17–19 years)
E Young adults (20–25 years)
F Single adults (19 years plus)
G Young childless married couples
H Young married couples with children
I Family couples with older children
J Post family or mature couples
K Elderly couples or adults.

A further planning application of this technique within the overall planning approach is that it can be used to place a list of facility/service deficiencies into a priority ranking list or to select the most appropriate site from a range of possibilities (Fig. 8.4). An example of a priority-criterion ranking system is given in Table 8.6.

This system eliminates most bias and can incorporate within it the importance that the council places on a specific element by giving it an additional weighting.

		Proposed facility						
		Sports Centre	*Community Arts Centre*	*Artificial pitch*	*Swimming pool*	*Riding Centre*	*BMX track*	*Entertainment Hall improvements*
1	Unmet Needs	X	X	X	X	X	X	X
2	High Demands	X	X	X	X	X	X	•
3	Replace	X	•	•	•	X	•	•
4	Benefit Deprived Area	X	X	X	X	•	X	•
5	Benefit Target Groups	X	X	X	X	X	X	X
6	District Service	X	X	X	•	X	X	X
7	Different Age Groups	X	X	X	X	X	•	X
8	High Level Usage	X	X	X	X	X	•	X
9	Nil/Little Capital	•	•	•	•	•	X	•
10	Low Revenue Expend.	•	•	•	•	X	X	X
11	Grant Aid/ Sponsor	•	X	•	X	•	•	•
12	Reduce Vandalism	X	•	•	X	•	X	•
13	Weighting Factor	3	3	2.5	2	2	2	2.5

Fig. 8.4 Example of how to implement grid systems in determining priorities for additional facilities.

Table 8.6 Priority-criterion ranking system for new public sector developments based on a policy of community recreation effectiveness

---

1 Does the proposed facility meet a previously unfulfilled leisure need within the locality?
2 Has there been a high level of expressed demand for the facility?
3 Does the facility replace and/or renew an existing facility with a high value to the community?
4 Does the facility specifically benefit persons from a leisure deprived area?
5 Does the facility substantially benefit specific target groups such as children, the elderly, disabled?
6 Will the proposed facility be regarded as a district facility – i.e. to meet the needs of the whole district?
7 Does the facility meet the needs of different age groups?
8 Is the facility likely to attract a high level of usage?
9 Will the facility involve the council in nil or minimal capital investment?
10 Will the facility involve the council in nil or minimal revenue expenditure?
11 Will the facility attract substantial (i.e. 50%+) grant aid and/or sponsorship?
12 Is the facility likely to make a contribution to reduce the level of vandalism and delinquency within the district?

8.5.6 Need index approach

The *need index approach* not only determines whether a deficiency exists, but simultaneously places the different deficiency areas into a priority ranking. The basic concept behind this approach is simple and can be illustrated as follows:

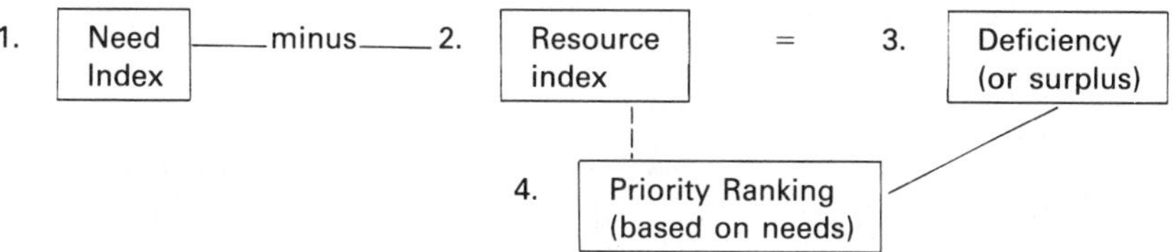

At present, most of the methods of assessing demand concentrate upon the relationship between resources available and potential users and little emphasis is attached to the concept of need. It is logical to assume that the different factors prevailing in different areas imply that those areas with a low resource level, as well as a high level of need, should have a higher priority than areas with a high level of resources and a low level of need. This can be achieved by using this approach.

The use of this approach is best illustrated when applied to children's playgrounds, particularly to small study areas. In an urban environment, a cluster of census enumeration districts can be used as units of small study areas. Within these designated areas, it is necessary to develop a resource index and a need index.

To develop the need index, it is necessary to identify factors that affect children's opportunity to play, together with indicators of social deprivation:

1. Number of children.
2. Incidence of high-rise flats.
3. Lack of gardens attached to dwellings/flats.
4. Dwellings lacking basic amenities.
5. Incidence of council dwellings.
6. Number of unemployed.
7. Socio-economic groupings.
8. Ethnic population.
9. Economically active females.

Information relating to the above elements can be obtained from the census data or the council's land use register, or with the aid of data provided by agencies approved by government, such as CACI.

In developing the resource index, it should be stated that there are four factors that are of significance in developing such an index. These are:

1. the location of the playground;
2. the size of the playground;
3. the range and nature of the facilities within the playground;
4. whether the playground is supervised

and to each of these individual elements points are allocated, based upon a weighting system.

However, before worthwhile comparisons can be made, the totals for the respective indexes have to be converted to a comparable form. This can be achieved by using a statistical tool known as the 'C-scale', which converts the data range for each index into a scale on a 0–100 continuum. By subtracting the index need from the resources need for each study area, a surplus or deficiency point can be determined and then the study area can be placed into deficiency priority ranking.

Although this method has its limitations, largely based around the subjective nature of determining the resource play index points, it is a method that does concern itself with the concept of need and has the potential for refinement and improvement.

8.5.7 Expressed demand

The level of demand for existing facilities can provide a useful guide as to whether additional facilities are required in an area. The analysis of a sports centre's booking sheets can reveal the amount of spare capacity available, or whether the demand for specific facilities exceeds the supply available.

The recently published *The Playing Pitch Strategy* [23] recommends a model approach for assessing the demand for playing pitches based on the expressed demand as indicated by the number of teams requiring pitches within the study area. Whilst this approach is superior to the use of standards, inadequate guidance is provided on how to determine the level of latent demand and how to project future changes in demand.

The projection of future demand based on the trend extrapolation of previous performances is occasionally used, although in most cases it is used in a negative way – e.g. projecting when an old facility may not have an adequate demand to justify its continued operation.

An equally neglected technique is that of observation, although it is far from being an accurate method of demand assessment. The counting of users of busy facilities, such as playgrounds, parks and beaches, is difficult because the participants are not static and are not in uniform groups. The tendency for the researcher, where large numbers are involved, is to count in multiples of ten or more, hence the findings tend to be only a crude indication of the actual attendances. Additionally, the actual counting itself is rarely free from the bias of the researcher.

8.5.8 Public consultation

Not only is it politically desirable to consult the people the provision of leisure facilities is intended to serve, but more important, the planning process itself is incomplete unless people are consulted about their leisure needs and demands, their perception of existing facilities and services and their expectations of future provision. Without such consultation, the planning process is one of providing *for the people*, as opposed to planning *with the people*. Planning for the people presupposes that those concerned with leisure planning know more about the requirements of people than the people themselves.

As with other methods, public consultations are not without their shortcomings. These are normally associated with the expressions of demand not being representative of the community, as a whole, and with the subjective nature of many of the responses made. The major methods of consulting with the public are described briefly below and include:

1. Community demand survey.
2. User survey.
3. Organization survey.
4. Public meetings.
5. Working parties.
6. Interviews.

(i) Community demand survey

All too often, local authorities demand very large surveys to be undertaken, while from a statistical point of view, comparatively small surveys can provide the necessary information at a high level of confidence. For example, Table 8.7 shows that for a town with a population of 100 000 residents, a survey with a sample of 1067 respondents will give a tolerated error of 3% at a 95% level of confidence [20].

Table 8.7 Statistical significance of sample sizes for a population of 100 000

Tolerated error (%)	*Confidence limits* 95 Samples in 100	99 Samples in 100
1	9604	16 587
2	2401	4 147
3	1067	1 843
4	600	1 037
5	384	663
6	267	461
7	196	339

The manner in which the survey is conducted can be problematical as the *face-to-face interview* approach can be both time-consuming and expensive to administer. The face-to-face interview approach is normally the best if the interviewers are adequately trained, although the place of contact is also important so as to keep levels of refusal to a minimum. In order to avoid unnecessarily alarming residents, particularly the elderly, household interviews are best undertaken following an introduction from a friend or an associate. This, of course, requires even more time.

The *postal survey* is much easier and cheaper to administer, although it too is not without its limitations. The response rate can be in the region of only 10%–30% (or even less), unless some interest has been created in the local media or an incentive is associated with a return of the questionnaire; even so, response rates are low. Using a random selection of residents from the Electoral Register does not in itself guarantee good and unbiased response – up to 10% of the electorate may no longer be residents.

A *telephone survey* is comparatively easy to undertake, provided the questionnaire is short and simple. The problems associated with this method of research are those of contacting the selected people and getting accepted. Many sales personnel use the telephone in an attempt to sell products such as double glazing and kitchen refurbishments, hence there may be some resentment by residents to this form of consultation. Telephone surveys require skilful and sensitive telephone research staff. Five other survey methods are briefly described below.

(ii) User surveys

User surveys conducted in a face-to-face approach can be most informative, providing information on the user profile, the facility's catchment area (and also the areas not being served), participation data (e.g. activities, frequency), perceptions of the facility and how it is managed and expectations for the future. Hence such surveys can be useful in improving the efficiency and effectiveness of the existing service, as well as obtaining the opinions and attitudes of users and residents regarding future provision.

The limitation with such research is that children tend to be under-represented among the respondents and the stated occupation of many of the respondents tend to be elevated. User surveys, where the questionnaires are self-administered, tend to be less representative and the response rate is greatly reduced.

(iii) Survey of clubs, societies and organizations

The voluntary organizations for the sports and arts are the backbone of leisure provision in the United Kingdom. Hence, in any leisure planning process knowledge of their collective contribution to providing recreational opportunity is required, so that the full spectrum of the leisure provision in a particular area can be determined. A survey of local clubs and societies can provide valuable information regarding the leisure opportunities programmed for their members, their membership levels, their resources and their current and future requirements. Additionally, the larger clubs provide an insight into the attitudes and opinions of a section of the community.

The drawbacks with undertaking this form of research are that the local council's data base of clubs and societies is generally inadequate and often changes in club officials go unrecorded. Additionally, there is normally a delay in the responses because of the seasonal nature of the clubs and, in some cases, the need to discuss the questionnaire at a committee meeting. Further, too many clubs are inward looking and are not prepared to look at aspects beyond those that directly affect their members.

(iv) Public meetings

Although opinions given at public meetings are not necessarily those representing all the community, they do give an indication of the strength of the support or opposition to a particular proposal. Good promotion is necessary to ensure that adequate attendances are achieved at the meetings and that those who 'shout loudest' or have vested interests do not hold sway.

(v) Working party approach

A much under-used approach is that of a working party approach whereby members of local clubs, residents associations, etc., together with officers and members from the local council are officially formed into a working party that has executive powers to make decisions and use the budget provided. Examples of where such an approach has been activated include the designing of a new park and the conversion of an old school into a community centre. It is important, however, that such working parties have authority to make decisions, or they simply become talking shops!

The advantages associated with this approach are considerable. It is democracy at work and, hopefully, the realistic expectations of the local community can be fulfilled. Unfortunately, in such a situation, decision-making can be slow and the commitment of its members will be on the wane if progress is not seen to be made. But the greatest problem may be associated with many members making unrealistic demands that require excessive amounts of space and finance to fulfil.

(vi) Interviews

Interviews with community leaders (political, ethnic and religious and business), including teachers, youth leaders, social workers, police and the business community can be an invaluable source of information.

Likewise, informal interviews with shopkeepers, publicans, post workers – all those who come into contact with a wide range of residents – and ordinary residents, helps to build a picture of how different people perceive the current provision and how it is managed and what deficiencies they think exist. A 'living-in' approach for some of the research time will assist in identifying issues and deficiencies from a resident's viewpoint.

8.5.9 Assessment of demand: summary

It is clear that, at present, there is no one way of determining the level of potential leisure demand for a particular activity. All the approaches described in this section have different degrees of limitations, and in order to be able to make a fairly accurate projection of the likely demand for a specific activity, it is necessary at present to use a range of different leisure planning techniques. All too frequently, the public are omitted from the planning process, with the planners stating what people should have, as opposed to determining what the people would like, and examining whether this is valid and possible. *Planning for people means putting people into the planning process*. To make future leisure provision more appropriate and meaningful, a greater understanding is required of people's needs and demands, what leisure means to people and the role it plays in their lives.

In *Leisure and the Family Life Cycle* [21], the Rapoports and Strelitz look beneath the surface of leisure planning and reveal underlying predispositions towards leisure: planning for people's leisure should not be undertaken simply by 'feasible' extensions of what already exists and is known to be workable and on hunches about what people's needs are; social research must look beyond mass demand and begin from the 'people's side of the equation'. They suggest that by building up knowledge and information about people in leisure, by learning about their motivations, preoccupations, interests and activities and injecting their knowledge into the planning process of large-scale fact finding, small-scale local findings and community projects, decision-makers will have a broader platform on which to plan policies.

More recently, Brandenburg *et al.* [22] have developed this model further in the understanding of why a person adopts a particular activity (Fig. 8.5):

'The process commences with preoccupations and interests. Four conditions, opportunity, knowledge, favourable social milieu and receptiveness, are deemed necessary and sufficient to enable an interest to be expressed through adoption of a specific activity. These conditions are focused upon a specific activity by one or more key event(s), which may at the same time modify the conditions themselves. The decision to actually adopt that activity finally rests on the extent to which the individual anticipates satisfaction through participation. Participation, in its turn, may lead to clarification, development or change of preoccupations and interests.'

While various research projects have revealed much about the conditions (opportunity, knowledge, favourable social milieu and receptiveness) that influence actual participation, further research is required for a greater understanding of the impact of the 'key events'.

8.6 SUMMARY: PLANNING FOR LEISURE

Leisure planning has been, until recently, a much neglected discipline and there are numerous examples of poor leisure planning in the

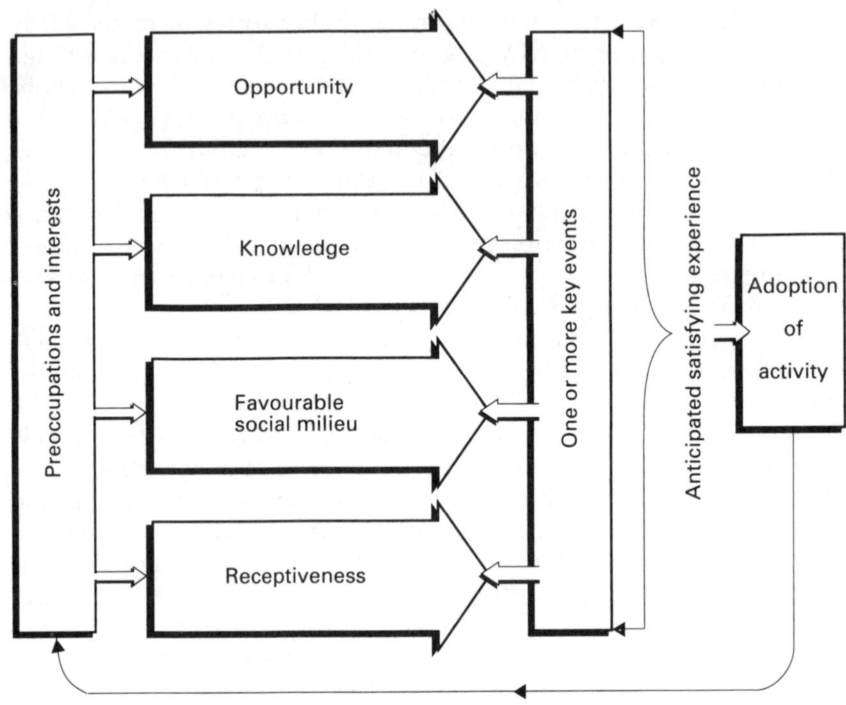

Fig. 8.5 A conceptual model of the recreational activity adoption process developed by Brandenburg *et al.* [22].

United Kingdom and elsewhere. Leisure planning differs fundamentally from general planning as leisure, outside the home, is a minority activity and the potential participant has to choose between a range of opportunities.

The suggested *leisure planning process* that can be implemented in a local authority setting is illustrated in Fig. 8.2 and involves seven distinct stages. An integral, but often ignored, stage is the evaluation of current provision and services which can identify areas of spare capacity and where the demand exceeds the supply available.

The nature and scale of leisure provision by many local authorities is the result of inheritance and possibly this may be the reason why many councils have no philosophy for the allocation of leisure resources (i.e. no stated purpose for the expenditure on leisure services), which in most large councils represents many millions of pounds each year. Where such philosophies exist, these fall into policies based on equitable distribution and/or expressed leisure demand and/or social control. Although the basis of these philosophies are sound, they appear to have been forgotten or neglected in their practical implementation.

With the assessment of demand, there is no one method of accurately determining the potential demand for a particular activity or facility. In this chapter we have examined eight different methods of assessing demand: standards of provisions; spatial demand; hierarchy of facilities; national participative rates; the grid approach; the need index approach; expressed demand; and public consultation. Although these approaches have their limitations, used collectively, they can provide a good indication of the level of deficiency. To develop a more accurate method of assessment, greater research is needed into why people choose a particular activity.

Planning the facilities themselves, in urban and rural settings and designing them to meet the physical, social and environmental needs of a catchment area, are important areas not covered in this book. In this chapter the planning process and methods have been debated. The following chapters deal with leisure provision and management.

8.7 ASSIGNMENTS

The following assignments are meant to test the reader's planning knowledge and the answers are provided at the back of the book.

8.7.1 Assignments

(i) Blackroad Sports Centre – additional squash courts
The manager of the Blackroad Sports Centre has, along with the other managers, been pressurized to reduce the centre's net expenditure by either increasing the centre's level of income or by reducing the centre's level of expenditure. His/her response to this has largely been restricted to the suggestion that the Council should build a further two squash courts at the centre which, he/she claims, would provide a significant increase in income even after payment of loan charges. He/she further claims that there are no squash courts within 3 miles of the centre and that the current demand at peak times frequently exceeds the supply available.

The Director of Leisure Services is not convinced by the claims made by the manager and from an analysis of a random selection of booking sheets, found that 60% of the utilization fell at what was regarded as peak times, namely:

Weekdays – 5–11 pm
Weekends – 9 am–5 pm
(the centre is open from 9 am to 11 pm daily).

The Director also contacted a leading squash court builder and was informed that the cost of building the courts only (i.e. excluding changing accommodation, viewing gallery, etc.) was approximately £40 000 per court.

Task: You are requested to undertake a feasibility study for a further two squash courts at the Blackroad Sports Centre to determine whether such a provision would generate a significant surplus after the payment of loan charges and all costs have been apportioned. You should attempt to determine the likely demand in the area; an estimation of the additional income to be generated and the additional costs involved.

Additional information

1. *Squash – hire charges* – £2.80 per court (40 min). No discounts given.
2. *Population* – the population within a 3 mile catchment area is 16 400.
3. *Financial performance of centre – last year's actuals*

Income	£
Wet facilities	
Education	7 514
Spectators	17 475
Child swim	32 778
Adult swim	15 471
Lessons	1 605
Miscellaneous	1 720
Dry facilities	
Sports Hall (4 badminton courts)	27 360
Squash (2 courts)	14 600
Weights	1 927
Bar/Cafeteria	9 426
Bowls Hall (4 Rinks)	28 342
Gross income	158 218
Expenditure	
Employees	214 563
Premises	236 009
Supplies and services	32 149
Transport	100
Establishment expenses	19 671
Gross Expenditure	502 492
Net Expenditure	344 274

(ii) Soccer pitch provision

In a Borough with an adult resident population of 200 000, determine what the theoretical demand is for soccer pitches based on the *General Household Survey* results.

REFERENCES AND NOTES

1. Gold, S. M. (1981), Meeting the new recreation planning approach. *Parks and Recreation*, May 53–6, 74–80.
2. Veal, A. J. (1981), *Planning for Leisure: Alternative Approaches*, Papers in Leisure Studies No. 5, Polytechnic of North London.
3. *Sport and Recreation*, Command 6200, HMSO, London, 1975.
4. *Policy for the Inner Cities*, Command 6845, HMSO, London, 1977.
5. Lord Scarman (1981), *The Brixton Disorders, 10–12th April 1981*, Report of the Right Honourable Lord Scarman, HMSO, London.
6. Griffiths, G. T. (1981), Recreation Provision for Whom? unpublished dissertation, Institution of Technology, Cranfield.
7. Munn, J. M. (1976), *Neighbourhood Opportunity. An Equation with Vandalism, Delinquency and the Quality of Life*, Torfaen District Council.
8. Gold, S. M. (1973), *Urban Recreation Planning*, Lea and Febiger, Philadelphia, Pa.
9. Mercer, D. (1973), The concept of recreational need. *Journal of Leisure Research*, **5**, Winter, 37–50.
10. NPFA (1989), *The NPFA Six Acre Standard*, National Playing Fields Association minimum standards for outdoor recreational playing space, NPFA, London.
11. Patmore, J. A. (1972), *Land and Leisure*, Penguin, Harmondsworth.
12. The Sports Council (1972), *Provision for Sport – Indoor Swimming Pools, Indoor Sports Centres, Golf Courses*, HMSO, London.
13. Maw, R. and Cosgrove, D. (1972), *Working Paper 2/72; Assessment of Demand for Recreation – a Modelling Approach*, Polytechnic of Central London.
14. Grampian Regional Council (1988), *Aberdeen Area Urban Sports Study, Report of the Working Party*, Grampian Regional Council, Aberdeen.
15. The Sports Council for Wales (1985), *National Strategy 1986/1996*, Consultative Document, Sports Council for Wales, Cardiff.
16. Torkildsen, G. (1987), *Lambourn Valley Recreation Study* (commissioned by Newbury District Council), LMGT, Harlow.
17. Greater London Council Planning Department (1968), *Surveys of the Use of Open Space*, GLC, London, Vol. 1.
18. Shaw, M. (1984), *Sport and Leisure Participation and Life Styles in Different Residential Neighbourhoods, an Exploration of the ACORN Classification*, Sports Council/SSRC, London.
19. Pickering Torkildsen Partnership (1986), *Study of Leisure and Tourism in the City and District of St Albans* (commissioned by the City and District of St Albans), PTP, Harlow.
20. Kelsey, C. and Gray, H. (1985), *Master Plan Process for Parks and Recreation*,

American Alliance for Health, Physical Education, Recreation and Dance, Reston Va.

21. Rapoport, R. and Rapoport, R. N. (1975), *Leisure and the Family Life Cycle*, Routledge and Kegan Paul, London.
22. Brandenburg, J. *et al.* (1982), A conceptual model of how people adopt recreation activities. *Leisure Studies*, **1**. No. 3, September.
23. Sports Council, National Playing Fields Association and Central Council of Physical Recreation (1991), *The Playing Pitch Strategy*, Sports Council, London.

Chapter 9

Trends in the leisure industry

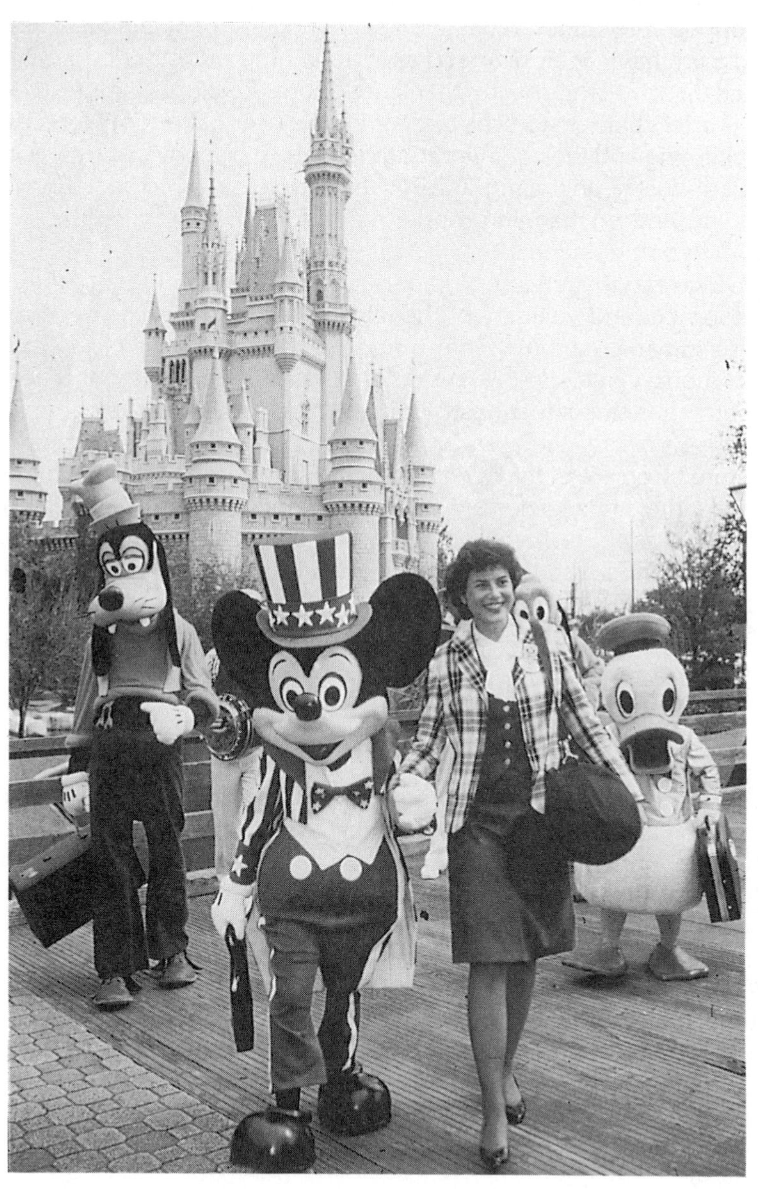

Up to this point, this book has been concerned with leisure, people's needs and the planning process to meet needs and demands. The emphasis has been on what should be and what could be, given the right circumstances. We now move to what actually exists and is happening and turn towards the leisure industry and the providers of services and facilities.

In recent years, in the United Kingdom, the pace of change not only in leisure, but in our quality of life generally, has been rapid. We are now enjoying higher standards of living filled with goods, services, activities and opportunities that in past years seemed unimaginable. Underlying this growth have been several major, and numerous other minor, trends related directly or indirectly to leisure and recreation.

This brief chapter starts by explaining the uses of trends in forecasting and planning and then highlights some of the more obvious trends in the leisure industry, including its growth; people's new expectations, the changing and unchanging markets and facilities and also the overall growth in participation.

Having read this chapter, readers will be in no doubt as to the rapid development and volatility of the leisure industry, and the need to use forecasting and marketing information to plan appropriately for today's and tomorrow's leisure. Leisure Managers will appreciate the need to adapt to changing situations. What seems clear is that the commercial sector is currently the area for leisure facility growth. Managers must therefore be aware of the need to provide services, particularly for those caught in the gap between affluence and disadvantage. They will also be made aware of the demand for more individual and social leisure pursuits. Planners and providers of services and facilities, described in the chapters which follow, need to be able to use the knowledge of trends in the leisure industry to help to read the signs for future growth in the industry.

9.1 MAKING USE OF INFORMATION ON TRENDS

Exploring the past and predicting the future in terms of leisure provision and participation is itself a major growth area. 'Trends' ('to have a tendency or general direction'), as we have come to know them, have arrived as essential planning and management tools. Leisure commentators, forecasters, social scientists and researchers provide information on trends in areas such as leisure time, leisure participation, consumers' expenditure on leisure, leisure travel, government, commercial and voluntary sector involvement in leisure and the international aspects of leisure. Other commentators provide detailed economic, social and demographic trends which all impinge on leisure provision.

Trends are used in numerous ways, including:

1. To predict the future behaviour of customers.
2. To provide a guide to policy formulation and, in some ways, reduce the element of risk in decision-making.
3. To draw attention to specific problems or likely growth areas.
4. To monitor the reaction of customers to a service, facility or activity over several years.
5. To provide information for use in marketing of future facilities or programmes.

Trends are important indications of future needs and demands. However, they are normally indications of national movements. It is important for leisure planners and managers to remember that what is happening nationally may not be occurring locally. National trends need to be supplemented by local traits, and local needs and demands, to ensure a substantial degree of success in interpretation. Moreover, many of the 'trends', so called, are short-lived, emphasizing the volatility of the leisure industry.

The following sections outline the major general trends affecting leisure provision today and in the immediate future in the United Kingdom; they include:

1. Leisure as a growth industry.
2. Rising expectations.
3. Changing markets.
4. Growing awareness.
5. More facilities.
6. New technologies.
7. Blend of traditions and new fashions.
8. Growth in participation.

9.2 LEISURE – A GROWTH INDUSTRY

We have now reached a stage where almost a third of the year, and a similar proportion of consumer spending, is devoted to leisure. There is a continual move towards a shorter working week and to more holidays each year. It is said we are moving to the 'three 35s' – i.e. 35 years of working life, 35 working weeks per year and a 35-hour working week.

Between 1971 and 1989 household disposable income in the United Kingdom grew by £301.4 billion [1]. Spending on leisure topped £75.7 billion in 1989, approx. 16% of household expenditure. As disposable income continues to rise, the proportion attributed to leisure spending takes some 18% of each new pound, regardless of income levels.

During 1990, the rapid growth in leisure spending slowed down as outside variables such as the Community Charge ('poll tax') and high interest rates and mortgage rates came into force. However, over the past decade the volume of spending on leisure goods has grown at a faster rate than spending on non-leisure goods and will continue to do so, but only if the levels of service, facilities and customer care continue to increase at the same pace as they have over the past several years.

The combination of greater time and money on the part of the majority has elevated the importance of leisure for most people. In the UK, the 1980s was the decade of market forces, and the 'me first' culture, with the emergence of the 'yuppie' whose status depended on the amount of work, stress and money he or she could sustain. However, in the 1990s, when 'time starvation' – insufficient time to do all the things we want to do – will become a trade mark for a proportion of employers and full-time employees, recognition of status, in addition to professional roles, will come through leisure time 'occupations'.

Leisure itself could become either the social equalizer or a social divider (see Chapters 2 and 6 which indicate the influences, both for equality and exclusivity). For those who support campaigns such as 'Sport for All', leisure opportunities must provide for the greater good of the greater number. In a market-orientated culture, this becomes more difficult and the 'new' leisure can divide society still further. During the 1980s, in some respects, this did happen. Although an over-simplification, leisure may become dominated by two groups, those with the money but not the time and those with the time but not the money!

9.3 EXPECTATIONS ARE RISING

People's expectations of leisure are rising rapidly – what it is and what it means to them are now more important than ever before. Attitudes and perceptions of leisure and its relationship to work are shifting; customers are becoming more discerning and knowledgeable and therefore demand value for money. In terms of community leisure, residents thus expect to be provided with good facilities and a quality service. Further, value for money will become even more prominent as the rapid growth slows down as high interest rates and the community charge (or its successor) come into play.

Leisure provision and choice of activity are increasingly affected by outside variables. For example, they are increasingly influenced by the culture of *environmentalism*. Concern about the environment, and the way in which products and activities affect personal health, will rate high among consumer priorities through the 1990s. Those leisure activities that result in harming the environment, for example, motor sports, may suffer falls in participation unless active measures are seen to be taken to alleviate the problem of pollution. Developers applying for planning permission, particularly in the Green Belt, will face strong objections from local pressure groups and a less favourable attitude from local authorities. Leisure operators will have to consider how their provision of facilities and services fit in with prevailing attitudes.

9.4 THE MARKET IS CHANGING

The age profile of the United Kingdom is changing, with a dramatic fall in the 15–24 age group. Some sectors of the leisure market have been dominated by the preferences of teenagers; this section of the leisure industry, over the next decade, will be competing for an increasingly smaller share of the population. With the youth market no longer culturally and commercially predominant, adjustments of leisure provision, away from the youth to the older markets, will need to be made. For example, provision with a quieter, more sociable atmosphere, enabling people to carry out activities at their own pace, may be needed. Leisure providers will see themselves moving away from the standardized mass market provision towards more flexible provision for more segmented markets.

The leisure industry will increasingly have to cater also to the 25–34 age group (family formers) and beyond, particularly the over 60s. The leisure market in the United Kingdom is ageing; the affluent 'empty nesters' or 'woopies' (well-off-older-persons) are an increasingly important market in both numerical and economic terms. It is estimated that by 2001, there will be 4 million more people over 65 [2], indicating the 'greying' of our society. These people with small or repaid mortgages may even be gaining income at present as a result of high interest rates. Many older people are therefore becoming more affluent at a time in life when they have the freedom and time to enjoy leisure activities.

Running parallel with these changes, the population of children, under the age of 15, will dramatically increase; by 2001 there will be 1.2 million more [2]. The presence of children in the family can be an important influence on both the extent and type of activity – swimming, for example, is particularly orientated towards young children accompanied by a parent.

The family unit, however, is becoming more fragmented. Each member has a diverse range of opportunities and obligations, which means leisure time is often spent apart. There is also a growth of one-person households. Today, one in four people live alone and this is projected to continue.

Life-styles have changed and are changing further. There are changes in household structures away from the traditional family markets. There is a greater need to consider couples as a prime market and the needs of single-parent families, a growing disadvantaged market sector. Employment patterns have changed, from predominantly men in full-time employment to large numbers of women in part-time employment.

Under the Office of Population Censuses and Surveys' *Classification of Occupations* categories, society is becoming more 'middle class' with a projected growth in the number of people in the A, B and C1 socio-economic groups, to over 40% in the mid-1990s, from about 33% in the early 1970s. More people are employed in white-collar jobs. This changes attitudes to 'outside work' activities. 'Middle-class' life-styles lead to middle-class concerns in health and leisure.

Customers are becoming increasingly knowledgeable. The media and foreign travel constantly expose the market to the latest developments and opportunities in the leisure field. In the United Kingdom, there is an increasing, insistent demand for the provision of leisure facilities. Low levels of provision and poor-quality facilities will no longer be acceptable. Customers now expect more. However, in a market economy customers will also have to pay more.

9.5 MORE FACILITIES, NEW TECHNOLOGY AND INNOVATION

Over 1000 new local authority indoor sport and recreation facilities, and many diverse commercial attractions from snooker halls and health clubs to theme parks, have been built in the United Kingdom over the past two decades. Providers and managers are now far more aware of the life-cycle costs. Cheap buildings often need costly repairs in a matter of a few years. However, with the high cost of borrowing money, cheap buildings can serve a useful purpose and provide a return on investment. New types of facilities are being built, either to meet these growing expectations or to set new trends – e.g. 'leisure' pools, synthetic surfaces, fitness gymnasiums, 'leisure' ice rinks and indoor arenas.

The general public is becoming used to watching excellent events, primarily on television. The event business is now very big business, and new facilities are being provided to increase demand. The National Exhibition Centre, in Birmingham, has grown as an event centre, but the Wembley Stadium and Arena has dominated the scene for over 50 years.

The opening in 1989 of the London Arena with a seating capacity close to 13 000 has marked the start of a phase in the building of indoor arenas across the country, but also seems to illustrate the potential financial problems relating to the funding of such arenas. The Birmingham National Indoor Arena and Sheffield Arena were both opened in 1991. In addition, planned arenas include the London Dome, and many others in each major conurbation. A good number, however, will fail to surface as a result of planning permission being withheld and/or lack of adequate finance. The question must also be asked as to whether the British sporting and entertainments calendar could sustain so many indoor arenas. The impact that such provision will have upon the leisure needs of local communities is, at present, largely unknown.

In the United Kingdom, to date, Doncaster Leisure Park represents, perhaps, the most ambitious public sector driven leisure complex to be built. Its first phase, the Dome, offers as its core 'leisure ice', 'leisure waters' indoor and out, a 2000-seater sport and entertainments venue, extensive health and fitness facilities and a large central forum. In its wake is a host of large commercial leisure developments, primarily 'leisure waters' based. This may be an indication as to what is to be provided in future years but such facilities are only likely to be built as commercial or partnership enterprises.

9.6 THE TRADITIONAL AND THE FASHIONABLE

The market for sports and recreation has broadened significantly over the past ten years. Most of the traditional sports and recreation activities survive and prosper and there has been considerable growth in indoor recreation and outdoor 'risk' activities. Adventurous and individual activities, such as rock-climbing, canoeing, mountain biking and the tri-athlon, are becoming more popular.

Other activities have become fashionable as a result of the influence of television. In 1969 soccer ranked first as the sport most enjoyed on TV, while in 1989 it ranked fourth. In 1969 snooker ranked twentieth, while in 1989 it had moved into first position [2].

One interesting aspect of these activity trends is their essentially individual nature. The Mintel *Sports Equipment Report 1989/90* [4] highlights the move away from participation in competitive and team sports towards individual fitness activities such as swimming, keep-fit and tennis. For those who regularly take part in sport, swimming remains the most popular activity.

9.7 LEISURE PARTICIPATION IN THE UNITED KINGDOM

The Sports Council claims that 21.5 million adults and 7 million children participate in sport or exercise at least once a month. Future trends favour the success and growth of the sports sector. As work diminishes, in terms of hours spent per week, outside special interests become an important source of personal pride and status.

The *General Household Survey* undertaken in 1986 in Britain, which surveyed the leisure participation of the population aged 16 and over, showed adults participating in sport during the most popular quarter as:

Walking (2+ miles)	23%
Swimming	18%
Snooker and billiards	11%
Darts	7%
Golf	4%
Keep-fit/yoga	4%
Angling	3%
Football	3%
Squash	3%
Cycling	3%
Tennis	3%

Swimming is the most popular sport in Britain, after walking; factors attributed to this include the very strong attraction of water, its mass participation appeal, and individual or family orientation; and that it is inexpensive, requires no equipment and is easily available to the majority of the population. The traditional swimming market has, however, been segmented into those that wish to swim, dive or splash and have fun or improve health and fitness. The design of a proportion of swimming pools has therefore changed considerably in recent years from the standard rectangular shape to the modern free form, with the addition of flumes, slides, tropical islands and spas.

Center Parcs in Nottingham's Sherwood Forest and Elveden Forest, in Suffolk, are an example of a commercial holiday and short-break village which has at its hub a very large domed leisure water facility that appeals to a wide age range. This type of facility is becoming extremely popular, particularly with family groups. The Centre Parc concept, founded in Holland, arguably has been the most significant leisure development in recent times. It is a development that gives participants the opportunity to experience not only tropical water facilities, but also the opportunity to participate in a number of sporting and non-sporting pursuits in a clean, friendly and informal atmosphere.

During the 1980s total spending on cultural goods and services (i.e. admissions to live arts events and cinema, video cassette hire, pre-recorded video cassette purchases, CDs, vinyl records, pre-recorded cassettes, books) rose from £1 214 million to £3 350 million. Home-based culture accounted for almost three-quarters of total spent during 1988, and since 1980 live arts have experienced a 159% increase in box office takings. First indications are that more money is being spent on cultural pursuits. However, research by the Policy Studies Institute has shown that higher takings are the result of higher ticket prices, not wider participation. In short, the arts still remain an activity that is available to a minority. Those that are able and prepared to pay (i.e. those on higher weekly incomes and in higher socio-economic groups) will attend arts events much more than others.

In addition, government support for the arts rose during the 1980s from £110 million to £361 million. The direct benefits of this increased subsidy to the arts is therefore being felt by those who already participate and who are already financially sound.

9.8 INTEGRATED CITY DEVELOPMENTS AND MULTI-LEISURE COMPLEXES

A significant development in the United Kingdom during the 1990s that will influence leisure habits is a move away from the stand-alone facilities of the past to the integrated centre offering a range of leisure and non-leisure activities. This trend is exemplified by the shopping development at the Metro Centre, Gateshead, and the Meadowhall development, Sheffield, Tower Park, in Poole, Dorset, and the Rank Centre, Stoke-on-Trent, represent a yet newer concept which is primarily leisure based, as distinct from shopping based.

This movement towards multi-centre sites is seen as part of the reason behind the growth in out-of-home activities and the popularity of facilities such as ten-pin bowling and multiplex cinemas. Developers and operators are beginning to realize the economies of scale, in the form of central services and car parking, associated with putting a number of leisure attractions together.

The renaissance of ten-pin bowling is another leisure pursuit that has been transformed over the past few years, largely as a result of computer technology with visual scoring displays, and through a change of image from the structured, dull facilities dominated by league and club events to an activity that presents itself as a family-based pursuit in facilities that are bright and relaxing, with associated services such as restaurants and cafeterias. There were by 1990 approx. 100 new centres with a further 200–250 planned. Popular centres were attracting over 1000 people per day with an admission charge of around £3.50. It is predicted that this activity will continue to grow in popularity as its development becomes more and more 'bankable' with facility planners and financiers.

Multiplex cinemas are seen as another growth area. The first British multiplex opened in 1985, at The Point, Milton Keynes. By 1990 there were 30 trading with a further 25 planned. As cinema attendance figures continue to grow steadily, from an all-time low in 1983/84 of *c*.60m., to 88 million in 1989, faith in the industry is returning.

The growth in the popularity of activities such as ten-pin bowling and multiplex cinemas is seen as part of the movement towards multi-centre sites. Many new retail and leisure developments will emerge in the future as their viability is realized. Despite the rise of leisure activities orientated in or around the home (e.g. television, do-it-yourself and gardening) and the growing acquisition of leisure equipment (e.g. videos, music centres), activities outside the home are expanding.

9.9 HEALTH AND FITNESS AND NEW LIFE STYLES

The positive awareness towards health and fitness has seen a boom in the weights and aerobic exercise and dance-related activities, and in jogging, skiing and health and fitness generally. In a recent survey in the United Kingdom some 90% of a sample of 1000 senior executives were found to be overweight or physically unfit. There is an enormous market for health and fitness facilities and associated concerns. The market is buoyant and has spawned its own fashion-wear industry. There has been a rapid increase in private sector investment in this area, in the development of private clubs, and also in office and residential developments; and in sales of home, health and fitness equipment.

9.10 SUMMARY: TRENDS IN THE UNITED KINGDOM LEISURE INDUSTRY

Trends of the past decade have been just as significant as the decades before. In 1960 the community sports centre at Harlow set the trend in the United Kingdom for 'dry' sports. In the early 1970s the free-shape pool and sophisticated ambience of the Bletchley Centre set the style for leisure centres to come. In recent years, the creation of large indoor water parks, leisure ice rinks and fitness centres such as those found at the Barbican, London and Living Well in Milton Keynes have fueled the fitness boom. Leisure and retail complexes have burgeoned, with the Gateshead Metro as an outstanding example. The concept of Center Parcs has been revolutionary, and the most significant project in recent years. The fortunes of the ailing cinema and ten-pin bowling industries have been revived. Theme parks have been developed, with Alton Towers as the biggest draw, but many other potential projects have been still-born. New activities like indoor cricket will continue to be tested, but traditional sports like badminton and leisure activities like bingo will continue to be long-lived.

The prospect of a single currency and the Channel tunnel herald change and opportunity. While changes are largely political and economic, the leisure industry will be part of the new Europe and new world. The entry of 'Disney' into France is significant.

Though not covered in this brief section, the wider British tourism industry (Chapter 12), supporting 1.5 million jobs in 1990, has had a profound effect on leisure provision and management in holiday villages, hotels, theme parks and all the associated catering and ancillary facilities that go with these costly attractions. New commercial activities will continue, encouraged by the need to provide for leisure demands and the need for growth and jobs in the service industries.

The benefit of providing leisure opportunities, particularly those that meet the current demands for regular participation and growth, is that they will help to produce a healthier and more balanced community, with individuals obtaining more effective use of leisure time and greater personal fulfilment. However, simply providing entertaining and fun experiences, without personal growth potential, could militate against this.

New trends in the leisure industry are more likely to be dominated by the commercial sector in the 1990s. It is to be hoped that the public and voluntary sectors will continue to provide substantially not only to meet the needs of many millions of people, but to enable individuals and groups to find worthwhile and long-lasting interests and preoccupations.

Chapters 10–12 deal with the public, voluntary and commercial providers.

REFERENCES AND NOTES

1. Central Statistical Office (1991), *Social Trends*, **21**, HMSO, London.
2. English Tourist Board and Jones Lang Wootton (1989), *Retail, Leisure and Tourism*, London, ETB.
3. 'A last look at the old order of the TV world', *Guardian*, 6 June 1990.
4. Mintel (1990), *Sports Equipment Report 1989/90*.

RECOMMENDED ADDITIONAL READING

Cultural Trends in the Eighties, 1991, Policy Studies Institute, London.

Arenas – A planning, design and management guide, 1989, Sports Council, London.

Leisure in Britain by C. Gratton and P. Taylor, 1987, Leisure Publications Ltd, Letchworth.

Sightseeing in the UK, 1990, BTA/ETB Research Services, London.

Chapter 10

Leisure provision in the public sector

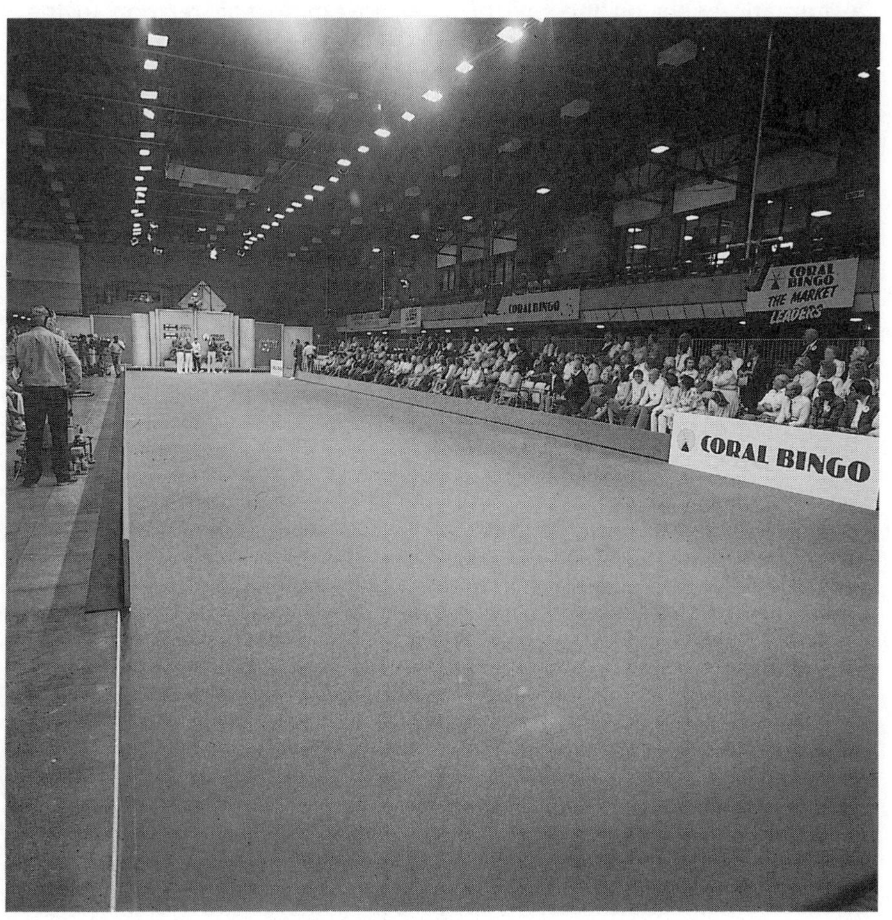

The previous chapters considered the complexities of the planning process and the growth in the leisure industry, and the chapters which follow will deal with management. Leisure has to be planned and managed. However, many of the resources and opportunities for leisure have to be provided for in the form of services and facilities. This chapter is concerned with public sector provision, while Chapters 11 and 12 deal with the voluntary and commercial sectors respectively.

The public sector is currently facing up to a period of substantial change. Successive legislation in the 1980s has had the effect of tightening councils' budgets and diminishing management control. *Compulsory competitive tendering* (CCT), in particular, is likely to have a dramatic effect on the role of local government in relation to the provision of facilities, services and opportunities for leisure and recreation.

This chapter is written in the following way: *first*, the local government role and range of services is put in the perspective of overall leisure provision. *Second*, the development of services and the enabling Acts of Parliament are described. *Third*, the influence and control of central government is explored. *Fourth*, aspects such as the reorganization of local government, joint provision and corporate management are shown to have substantial effects. *Fifth*, the complexities and problems within public sector leisure provision are highlighted.

This chapter will assist readers' understanding of the essential characteristics of the public sector, the range of provision and its development from early 19th century legislation, successive enabling Acts of Parliament and the reorganization of local government through to the current issues such as CCT.

Students will be made aware of the opportunities and traditional constraints on leisure through mandatory and permissive powers – the few 'must dos' and the many 'may dos'. The role of local authorities in leisure is essential, but it is changing with enabling and coordinating functions taking on greater importance in the 1990s.

10.1 PROVIDERS OF LEISURE SERVICES AND FACILITIES

People's leisure and recreation is made possible, in part, through a wide range of resources, services, facilities and management. A range of facilities is needed both indoor and outdoor, in and around the home, in the urban environment, in rural areas, in the countryside and on dry land and on water. A range of services and programmes is needed to meet the diverse needs and demands of individuals, families, groups, clubs and societies.

The providers of services and facilities for leisure and recreation come mainly from within the public, voluntary and commercial sectors. The pressure on land, and on financial capital, in the United Kingdom has encouraged some providers to combine efforts and pool resources. However, with some notable exceptions, habits die hard and changes come about very slowly. Even within the public sector, cooperative ventures between county councils and district councils have progressed little since the relative euphoria of the early joint provision leisure centres in the 1970s.

It is recognized from the outset that there is overlap between the public, voluntary and commercial sectors and that, in many cases, the three will be involved in the same kinds of provision and services. They are also increasingly dependent on one another. However, there appear to be fundamental and distinct differences in philosophy, objectivity and approach, which need to be understood in order to provide appropriate recreation services.

10.2 PUBLIC SECTOR SERVICES AND FACILITIES

In the United Kingdom, public services and facilities for leisure can be provided by a public authority or by legislation for the general use of the public. Some facilities are provided by public funds for a restricted use such as educational establishments, facilities for Her Majesty's Services and restricted forestry areas. Commercial operators have veered naturally towards those facilities and activities that give a good return on their investment. The increasing costs of land and construction have left the local authorities the task of providing more of the land-extensive facilities such as water recreation and parks, and more of the expensive buildings such as swimming pools, theatres, sports centres and concert halls.

Local authorities provide a wide range of facilities and services for leisure. They also provide – often indirectly – through financial and other support, through planning decisions and generally by acting as an 'enabling authority'. Local authorities thus play a major role in the provision of facilities and opportunities for public recreation.

Government agencies, like new town corporations, regional water authorities and national park boards, also have major roles in recreation provision. All these bodies have powers or duties to assist in or to initiate provision.

10.2.1 The range of direct provision by local authorities

The scope of recreation and leisure services within local authorities is very wide. However, there are a number of identifiable elements and spheres of influence; different authorities will have some or all of these elements depending on the location and the size of the authority, its policies and its responsibilities. These spheres and elements are shown

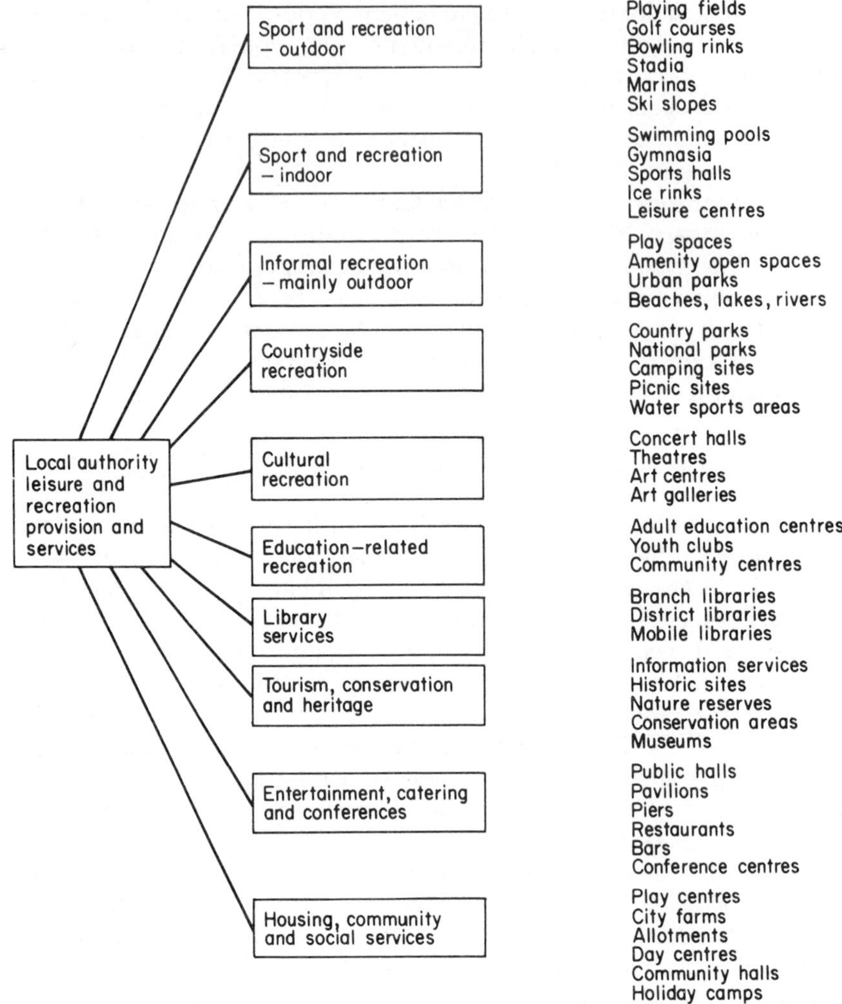

Fig. 10.1 Ten local authority leisure and recreation elements and spheres of influence.

in Figure 10.1. Many of the elements are combined or overlap; no two authorities are exactly alike either in provision or management. There are general similarities but specific differences.

Local authorities provide their range of facilities in a variety of ways. The public has free access to a large number of facilities, for which no direct payment is made, such as urban parks, playgrounds, libraries, picnic areas, nature trails, beaches and country parks. While the public does not pay directly for these amenities, it does so indirectly through taxes and the Community Charge, or 'poll tax', now subject to change. Local authorities also provide facilities such as swimming pools, playing fields, golf courses, marinas, arts centres, theatres and sports centres, where there is a direct payment by the user, albeit often at highly subsidized charge.

Local authorities are important providers of leisure, education, arts and cultural activities, through schools and colleges, art galleries, museums, concert halls and libraries. They have statutory duties to provide public libraries, though there are widely varying standards of provision. Youth and community services are provided usually through education, but the totality of services is a mixture of local authority provision and services provided by voluntary bodies.

While local authorities often look to commercial and voluntary sectors to provide for social activity and entertainment, they nevertheless do provide for entertainment, both directly and indirectly. Directly they provide, for example, through village and community halls; community centres are particularly widespread in new town developments. They also directly provide through the provision of civic halls which are used for entertainment, and urban parks with their bandstands and entertainment facilities. Many new leisure centres are also prime venues for public entertainment.

The vast majority of services, manpower and finance is used for the traditional, existing facilities. Despite the emergence of new facilities, such as indoor recreation centres and country parks, it is clear that it is the staffing and management of existing provision which predominate local authority recreation services. When education-related services and libraries are included in the comprehensive recreation coverage, then the picture becomes even more evident, with all the new areas of leisure expenditure taking up less than 10% of the total. In terms of expenditure on recreation, local authorities are dominated by two services: those relating to the libraries and urban parks.

10.2.2 Support and indirect provision

Local authorities are not simply providers of facilities. They have a support service to perform. They support organizations of all kinds – private institutions, voluntary organizations and even commercial bodies, when it is shown that greater service will be given to the public by so doing. The support given is basically of two kinds. The first is to make 'its own' facilities and equipment available for use, with or without charge. The second is to make financial grants.

The local education authorities are usually involved in support to youth and community services and organizations, for example, by making schools available for youth and adult classes, and by making capital and annual grants to community associations and other social groups. They may pay the salaries of wardens, leaders, teachers and managers of purpose-built community centres.

Local authorities have discretionary powers to assist in all manner of ways. They can assist trust bodies to provide theatres and sports centres, sports clubs to provide bowling greens and tennis courts and community groups to provide facilities for children's play, community arts or facilities which help the aged. The authorities also provide considerable support, indirectly, by sponsoring arts, sports and entertainment festivals and major events, by meeting deficits or by funding community events and activities.

Often, small services or small grants given to organizations to help to provide for themselves can benefit the community enormously. The redistribution of local authority funds for recreation based on individual, group and social need could enhance particularly recreation opportunity for the disadvantaged in the community.

The local authority planning function is crucial to recreation. As planning authorities, they can assist with the availability of land and resources. As housing authorities, they can assist with leisure in and around the home, in gardens and walkways, in play areas associated with high-rise dwellings and in access to community provision.

Local authorities give planning consent. They make decisions on development proposals and give consent for recreational facilities provided by other agencies. Planning authorities have to consider proposals in the context of broad overall and long-term policy. To consider leisure and recreation planning only in local terms would not take account of increased mobility, greater affluence and the movement across local authority boundaries. Countryside and regional facilities are particular areas of vulnerability for poor planning. Urban fringe leisure and recreation is gaining greater importance not only because of higher expectations, but also because of the cost of travel.

Another aspect of movement into recreational areas is holidaymaking, tourism and sightseeing. Since local government reorganization, many local authorities have taken up their greater powers relating to the enhancement of tourism.

This brief résumé is sufficient to show that local authorities are major providers of leisure and recreation opportunities through planning, facilities, services, budgets and support. They have a duty to provide recreation opportunities through education and libraries. They have very wide discretionary powers in England and Wales (unlike those in Scotland and Northern Ireland that have a duty to provide) to assist the arts, sports, informal recreation, countryside recreation, entertainment, conservation, tourism and youth and community services. In addition to these direct services, local authorities can assist leisure and recreation through many indirect ways, such as planning and housing and through social services that help the disadvantaged, who may need recreation services more than most, but who may make the least demand.

10.3 GOVERNMENT AND RECREATION: THE DEVELOPMENT OF LOCAL AUTHORITY SERVICES

Leisure and recreation services and facilities are subject, like all other services, to the laws of the land; while there is no comprehensive leisure or recreation Act, recreation is made possible and is guided and constrained by a whole variety of Acts, laws, statutes, government circulars and reports and regulations, both national and local.

Acts of Parliament impose duties or confer authority or powers to provide for recreation. Acts cover such diverse areas as allotments, swimming pools, parks, catering, clubs and associations, betting and gaming, public entertainment, libraries, licensing, preservation, waterways, employment, local authorities, institutions, charities and companies.

What is immediately evident in studying the public provision for recreation is that it is historical, traditional, institutional and facility orientated. Progress must be made within and through the system; changes will come about slowly. Despite the surge of new facilities in the 1960s and 1970s, the bulk of local government expenditure on recreation is still reserved for parks, pitches and pools, which is clearly a result of what exists, what is tradition, what local government is geared up to handle and what is known and understood.

10.3.1 The origins of recreation services

The origins of local authority recreation services as we know them today go back to the 19th century. To understand the rationale behind early legislation, it is necessary to comprehend the poverty and unhealthy and debilitating social conditions that prevailed at the time of the Industrial Revolution and the era of the puritanical work-ethic (Chapter 2). In such an era, there was a need for a fit, healthy nation.

The *Baths and Wash-Houses Act 1846*, from which many of our present-day recreation departments originated, was concerned primarily with personal cleansing and hygiene. However, swimming pools were built alongside these mainly for instructional purposes, but also for recreation. Today the recreation role is paramount and the 'baths' service in many cities embraces other indoor provision in the form of sports halls, squash courts and entertainment facilities.

Many parks departments also originated in the second half of the

19th century. Again, the movement was partly philanthropic and partly by the local authorities. Many bequests of land were received and acquisitions made. Parks departments, like the baths departments, expanded their sphere of authority and took over areas for organized outdoor sports and facilities for tennis, athletics, golf, boating, bowls and the range of outdoor entertainments and festivals.

The *Public Health Act 1875* was the first major statutory provision enabling urban authorities to purchase, lease, lay out, plant, improve and maintain land for use as public walks or pleasure grounds. Later statutes had to be passed to empower local authorities to set aside parts of such lands for the playing of games. In the *Public Health Act 1936* authority was given to provide public baths and wash-houses, swimming baths and bathing places, open or covered, and the right to close them to the public for use by school or club and to charge admission.

The *Physical Training and Recreation Act 1937* was introduced as a result of unrest in Europe. There was a need for a strong, fit nation. The Act was thus very much a movement towards national fitness, away from the Victorian idea of 'public walks and pleasure grounds'.

Local authorities could acquire land for facilities and clubs, with or without charge for their use. The 1937 Act was the first major Act to use the word 'recreation', but support from government had come not because recreation was fun and enjoyable, but on the grounds of social and physical health and welfare, character training and improvement.

10.3.2 Postwar improvements to recreation services

The recreation lobby continued promoting its arguments during and after the Second World War. Organizations such as the Central Council of Physical Recreation and the National Playing Fields Association played an effective, persuasive role.

The *Town and Country Planning Act 1947* made it possible for the development plans of local planning authorities to define the sites of proposed public buildings, parks, pleasure grounds, nature reserves and other open spaces or to allocate areas of land for such use. Powers were extended in the *Town and Country Planning Acts* of 1971 and 1974. The *National Parks and Access to the Countryside Act 1949* gave local planning authorities, whose areas include a national park, opportunity to provide accommodation and camping sites and to provide for recreation. The scope of countryside recreation was greatly enhanced with the passing of the *Countryside Act 1968*. The Act permits local authorities to provide recreation facilities; the 1949 Act placed a duty to manage national parks, along with other permissive powers. Importance has been given to the debate relating to use and abuse of the countryside, the preservation of heritage and the needs of conservation.

Local authorities have considerable powers to provide for recreation through education facilities, personnel and services. The successive major *Education Acts* of 1918 and 1944, coming after two world wars, gave education authorities permissive powers (in 1918) to create facilities for social and physical training and then in 1944 made it mandatory on all education authorities to provide adequate facilities for 'recreation and social and physical training' for primary, secondary and further education. This resulted not only in the growth of the Youth Service, adult education and physical education (and hence sport), but also in the growth of facilities such as sports grounds, swimming pools, larger gymnasia and some sports halls. However, it was not until many years later that additional finance through other local authority sources made it possible to increase greatly the standards of provision. Only by joint planning and provision between different tiers of authorities or between different departments were the larger community-based facilities made possible. Despite the progress throughout the 20th century up to this point, and despite the statutory and enabling Acts of Parliament, governments consistently viewed recreation as a beneficial means towards some other ends. The report of the Wolfenden Committee [1], published in 1960, led to the eventual recognition by Parliament of recreation in its own right.

10.3.3 The transition: an awakening to recreation

An acceptance of the benefits of recreation in its own right did not come until the 1960s. But the initiative did not come from the government. The Wolfenden Committee was appointed in October 1957 by the Central Council of Physical Recreation (CCPR) and produced its report, *Sport and the Community*, in 1960 [1], to examine the factors affecting the development of games, sports and outdoor activities in the United Kingdom and to make recommendations to the CCPR as to any practical measures which should be taken by statutory or voluntary bodies in order that these activities may play their full part in promoting the general welfare of the community.

The committee recommended the establishment of a Sports Development Council. Although the Sports Council was to be formed many years later, the recommendations were never implemented. The report, however, was a watershed in the eventual acceptance of recreation by Parliament.

The Wolfenden Report, and the Albermarle Report on the Youth and Community Service [2], stressed the need for more and better facilities for indoor sport and recreation. Even before the Wolfenden Report was published, the first community sports centre had been planned, had opened its first facilities and appointed its first manager. The centre was developed by a charitable trust, the Harlow and District Sports

Trust. The Crystal Palace National Sports Centre was also under construction and was eventually opened in 1964. Again, the spearhead was a voluntary organization, the CCPR, in collaboration with statutory authorities and government.

During the 1960s, in addition to new proposals for sport and recreation and for youth and community services, the expansion of education services, library services and the arts was also proposed. The Plowden Report, *Children and their Primary Schools* (1967) [3], advocated the development of community schools to encourage interaction between home and school and proposed that a policy of 'positive discrimination' should favour schools in neighbourhoods of social and home disadvantage.

The *Public Libraries and Museums Act 1964* repealed all other legislation, some going back to before the turn of the century. It placed a duty on every library authority to provide a comprehensive and efficient library service, to promote and improve the service. From April 1974 non-metropolitan counties, metropolitan districts and the London boroughs became library authorities. The Department of Education and Science's Circular 5/73, *Local Government Reorganisation and the Public Library Service* [4], stressed greater links between the major services for education, health and social services in encouraging activities for the whole community.

The arts have been the subject of numerous reports since the mid-1960s, for example, the 1965 White Paper, *Support for the Arts: The First Steps* [5]. The 1976 Maud Report [6], sponsored by the Calouste Gulbenkian Foundation, has been greatly influential. Redcliffe-Maud recommended that counties and districts should have a duty to ensure a 'reasonable range' of opportunity for arts enjoyment and that there should be a development plan for the arts with linkages to the education, libraries, museums and sport and recreation services.

Despite the acceptance of recreation and the enabling Acts of Parliament, many of the major proposals for sport, the arts, and the youth and community service were never introduced. In addition, in practical terms, local authorities and other providers had still to operate through a maze of Acts or sections of old statutes. They also had to operate through a proliferation of departments and, as Molyneux pointed out [7], the system allows and almost encourages separate policies, separate budgets and different attitudes and changing policies towards recreationists, particularly the clubs.

In 1968, with the establishment of a new county borough merging five former authorities, Tees-side County Borough established a major committee and matching department for the arts and recreation. The new department, headed by a chief officer, spanned former services covering the arts, libraries, museums and art galleries, entertainments, sport and physical recreation, baths, parks and catering. Similar restructuring followed in a number of other authorities and in London boroughs.

One of the major influences which led to these developments was the inquiry headed by the then John Redcliffe-Maud into the machinery of local government administration and this was reported in 1967 [8]; it recommended the streamlining of committees and departments. Recreation services were ready to begin to rationalize the total sphere of leisure and recreation.

10.3.4 Dual use and joint provision

The 1960s and 1970s witnessed not only the advent of new purpose-built facilities for recreation and the restructuring of local government administration, but also the recognition that thousands of schools and education facilities throughout the country were in essence embryo community leisure and recreation centres.

A department of Education and Science and the Ministry of Housing Local Government Joint Circular 11/64:49/64, *Provision of Facilities for Sport* [9], advanced a new policy guideline:

'In assessing local needs and the resources to match them, it is appropriate to consider how far facilities for sport and physical education already provided or in the course of provision at schools and other educational establishments can be shared with other users or can be economically expanded to meet those needs. Consultation with other authorities will be necessary, not only because facilities in one area may serve neighbouring areas; but also there will normally be more than one authority with powers to provide them.'

The Ministry of Housing and Local Government Circular 31/66, *Public Expenditure: Miscellaneous Schemes* [10], drew attention again to the savings which could be achieved by joint provision and the need for consultation with the new regional sports councils on new projects. The Department of Education and Science's Circular 2/70, *The Chance to Share* [11], gave more control to local authorities over their own local expenditure, free of government control, for locally determined schemes including almost all sport and recreation schemes. Local authorities could now go ahead in providing facilities, provided they stayed within their overall block allocation of capital investment.

10.3.5 Local government reorganization and its effect on recreation

A Royal Commission under Lord Redcliffe-Maud was established in 1966 to consider the structure of local government in England, outside

Greater London [12]. The commission proposed that the greater part of England should be divided into 58 unitary authorities. Public reaction to the unitary concept was, in general, unfavourable and three of the four local authority associations preferred a two-tier system. A government White Paper in 1970 [13] proposed a new structure based on 51 unitary areas and five metropolitan areas. In 1971 the new Conservative government's alternative proposals emerged in two White Papers – one for England and the other for Scotland – and a consultative document for Wales [14]. A compromise solution of a two-tier structure and a radical reorganization of boroughs and urban and rural districts was proposed.

The *Local Government Act 1972* gave effect to the proposals contained in the 1971 White Paper. The Act conferred no new powers, but transferred the previous powers to the new local authorities. The *Local Government (Miscellaneous Provisions) Act* 1976 brought together the various powers relating to the provision of leisure and recreation facilities. The Act consolidated most of the powers for leisure services other than those relating to 'cultural' and 'educational' services. The Act permits local authorities to provide such recreational facilities as it thinks fit, unlike the *Libraries Act 1964* which placed a duty on library authorities to provide services.

In 1974 six new metropolitan county councils were established and the 1400 existing district councils were reduced to 333. As far as recreation services were concerned, the greatest impact was felt in the 296 non-metropolitan district councils. These councils were now larger and more powerful and had, in many cases, inherited a range of facilities. Reorganization also encouraged the creation of new facilities, particularly indoor leisure centres before reorgnization actually took place.

Prior to local government reorganization in 1974, most local authorities were structured on the basis of a number of departments operating under the control of committees. The committees competed for their share of the available financial resources. The Bains Report [15] placed emphasis on the corporate approach to management. It was felt that, in this way, an authority could formulate more realistically its long-term objectives covering all services, and make forward planning projections. With increased facilities, increased awareness towards community recreation and the emergency of new larger departments, jobs were created for managers within recreation services and rapid promotions and movements of staff were prevalent throughout the United Kingdom.

The *Local Government Act 1972* and the *Local Government (Miscellaneous Provisions) Act 1976* provided the framework for local authorities with respect to the provision and administration of facilities for sport and recreation with the emergence of leisure services in their own right.

Local authorities are the largest providers of leisure facilities for sport and outdoor physical recreation and have traditionally been so. Central government has placed an obligation on local authorities, in England and Wales only, to provide leisure services in three specific areas: library services, the youth and adult education facilities and allotments, but no indications of the scale of provision are given. In Scotland and Northern Ireland local authorities also have a duty to make provisions in other areas of sport and recreation. Local authorities are therefore allowed to interpret the needs and demands of the community in different ways and, consequently, the level of provision varies considerably from one local authority to the next.

10.3.6 Housing and finance and the Education Reform Acts

The past thirty years, from the early 1960s onwards have seen a major expansion in the provision of recreation facilities and activities. However, successive legislation over the last years of the 1980s has had the effect of tightening councils' budgets and diminishing management control. The *Local Government Housing and Finance Act 1988* (containing provisions for the Uniform Business Rate and Compulsory Competitive Tendering, CCT) and the *Education Reform Act 1988* collectively are likely to have dramatic effects on the role of local government and recreation provision.

The *Local Government Act 1988* (Competition in Sport and Leisure Facilities Order 1989) imposed upon local authorities the necessity to offer the management of their sports and leisure facilities to competitive tendering; there are certain exceptions, such as dual use centres, which combine education and public provision. This is compulsory but not out-and-out privatization; local authorities will still have control over aspects such as pricing, programming and opening hours. Undoubtedly, this will result in some economic savings with many of the facilities being operated by commercial leisure companies or local authority Direct Service Organizations, who will have to improve their performance to provide more efficient services tailored to local needs. This will probably encourage an increased growth in commercial provision of the more profitable sports, while leaving the non-profitable sports to be provided more and more by the voluntary sector supported, hopefully, by local authorities.

The Community Charge, albeit subject to change, will also have effects on council spending. Non-statutory provision, such as leisure and recreation facilities, may suffer from cuts in expenditure.

The introduction of the *Education Reform Act 1988*, whereby each school (with its board of governors) has to be responsible for its own budget, may reduce the range of sporting experiences offered to schoolchildren and probably will prevent some local sports clubs from using school premises. The governing bodies of schools may be more cost-conscious and will also be much more aware of the costs involved in hiring other facilities for pupils. However, certain facilities, previously not available for community use, may become available, thus adding to the stock of local sports provision.

As a result of the constraining legislation imposed upon local government capital and revenue expenditure, as well as the effects of CCT, the expansion of sports provision within the public sector is likely to decrease unless partnership schemes with the commercial and voluntary sectors can be arranged or the public sector becomes more effective and efficient without forfeiting its social conscience.

10.4 THE FRAMEWORK UNDER CENTRAL CONTROL

Local government is required by law to conduct its business under the constraints and guidelines provided by Parliament. It must be, and must be seen to be, accountable to the public. The overall management hinges around three main structures: the committee structure, the officer structure and the departmental structure.

Local authorities have to provide certain services and therefore need certain departments. They have a duty to appoint certain officers and they have permissive powers to appoint others. Hence the structures in local government are made up with a mixture of 'have tos' and 'may dos'. This renders all local authorities similar; it also renders all local authorities dissimilar.

The work of a local authority cannot be undertaken without money and it is the financial considerations which loom largest at the end of the day. The local authority budget is the single most important function, the mainspring of its activities.

The local authority is a business organization. Finance is needed for recreation services and can be classified under two main headings: capital finance and revenue finance. Capital funding is accessible to local government from several sources, though capital expenditure is principally financed through borrowing sanctioned by central government.

As from April 1990, the capital control system has altered. Local authority capital receipts will be taken into account when the borrowing limit is fixed. Therefore, a percentage of such receipts will be earmarked to pay outstanding debts. Where sports facilities are provided by private developers in return for land, the notional value of the land will be taken into account and treated as a capital receipt.

Capital projects may be of local, regional or national importance. Depending on the amount of capital a local authority can borrow, certain projects may be controlled by the central government departments concerned, others may fall within the jurisdiction of the local authority. For these projects, each authority or group of authorities is given a block allocation for each year. This allocation has fallen sharply since the mid-1970s and recreation services have had to compete against many other even more pressing services. However, there are sources other than borrowing from which to finance capital expenditure. Some of the ways are outlined below, along with the main sources of capital funding:

1. Direct grant from central government.
2. Loans from central government.
3. Rate support grant.
4. Revenue contributions.
5. Capital receipts through the sale of land and other assets (greatly reduced under the new capital spending regulations).
6. Capital internal funds (e.g. Community Amenity Funds).
7. Loans from commercial concerns and a variety of joint arrangements with development companies and funding institutions.
8. User finances (e.g. lotteries).
9. Rates.

Finance from these sources is used to develop and construct amenities for use by members of the public, whether through clubs and organizations or by direct local government management.

Revenue finance is needed to support the ongoing running costs of the service and facilities. The finance is generated from:

1. *Users* – income from fees and charges and trading such as by admission fees, library fines, hire of facilities and catering.
2. *Grant aid* from central government – Urban Aid.
3. *Rates.*

Like capital expenditure, revenue expenditure has also been strictly limited in recent years.

Restrictions in powers of borrowing and spending, the decrease in financial allocations from central government and in the rate support grants limit severely the expansion of local authority leisure and recreation services. As we have seen, local authority capital expenditure on recreation facilities normally falls within the locally determined schemes sector for borrowing purposes. In times of economic restraint, it is this sector in which the most severe cuts are made. Other services receive greater priority. This state of affairs has prompted some local authorities to explore a variety of ways of funding new capital projects including:

1. Capital sales.
2. Formation of charitable trusts.

3. Joint schemes with commercial enterprise.
4. Lease and lease-back schemes.
5. Deferred purchase methods.
6. Partnership projects.
7. Commercial development where a developer purchases, develops and manages leisure projects and the council benefits from 'planning gain'.

10.5 MANAGEMENT IN LOCAL GOVERNMENT: THE POLICY – MAKERS

Management of local authority services is a highly complicated process. It revolves around the local authority structural framework and involves a large number of people: elected members, voluntary committee members, departmental staff, facility managers and staff, and all the organizations and programmes through which recreation is made available to the public. Elected members, however, are of utmost importance to the management of leisure and recreation services: they decide policy; they decide what is to be built and made available; and they budget and they control.

Councillors are citizens who devote part of their time to the service of local authorities. They are not salaried, but can be paid allowances. The business of local authorities takes time – is often arduous and complex. A councillor is a representative of his or her area. He or she is essentially a man or woman of the people, and should represent the community and involve the community. A councillor should be seen as making decisions not just *for* the community, but *with* the community.

Councils often provide facilities as an answer to presumed recreation need. But community support, community service and leisure opportunity may be the greater need for many people. A councillor's job involves using the local authority framework, departments and staff to determine needs and demands, establish policies, priorities and objectives, make decisions, implement measures to achieve them, monitor progress and make evaluations. In providing for recreation demand and need, councillors must be working with and through officers, with recreation-involved people in the community and with the public – the users of the services being provided.

In order to undertake those responsibilities, councillors need the ability, the professional guidance and the motivation to achieve results. Their decisions are based on intuition, 'feel', experience and gut-reaction. Their decisions are based, too, on some knowledge and information acquired from their officers but rarely, if ever, from training. Councillors have the authority and the power. They are 'trained' on operational experience. Leisure professionals must therefore inform, educate and influence councillors in the execution of their important task in the field of leisure and recreation.

10.6 CORPORATE MANAGEMENT AND COMPREHENSIVE DEPARTMENTS

Corporate management aims to provide a framework for local government business, whereby the needs of a community are viewed comprehensively; the activities of the local authority are planned and directed in a unified manner to satisfy those needs to the fullest extent possible within available resources. Corporate management requires a masterplan combining policy-making, corporate planning and collective management.

According to Seeley [16], 'corporate management constitutes a total system of management embracing planning the activities, undertaking and controlling them, and monitoring and modifying them in the light of experience, all within a concerted or corporate framework'.

The committee structure envisaged in the Bains Report has been used as a guideline by many authorities, but by no means all. Community recreation services can be greatly enhanced where corporate management includes a chief leisure officer within the management team.

The following arguments can be put forward for composite departments:

1. Better use can be made of existing resources.
2. By bringing together separate, disparate departments – parks, baths, museums and entertainment – there can be more effective development, siting and administration of new facilities.
3. Stronger linkage can be forged between 'district' plans and 'education' plans for better dual use and joint provision of facilities.
4. More effective liaison is afforded with planning, education and social services committees and their departments.
5. The aims and objectives can be thought out anew, particularly as leisure services under older systems had been established on other objectives.
6. A more effective link can be made between users of facilities, voluntary bodies and others.
7. More effective liaison can be forged with regional agencies like the regional sports and arts councils.
8. Better ways can be found to utilize commercial capital and expertise in the wider range of community recreation.
9. Comprehensive departments can look more effectively at total community plans and networks.

In some authorities, leisure services is a major directorate with principal officers, planners, researchers and managers. In other authorities, it still remains a fragmented service and is often splintered into several departmental responsibilities. In yet other authorities, recreation is seen as a unit, but is swallowed up within a general service department such as technical services or housing. In the larger authorities and the metropolitan districts, in particular, large departments exist, but there is often a traditional split between 'sports' and 'arts' departments. Hence recreation and leisure services are by no means standardized. Different areas have different needs and what is appropriate for one area may be inappropriate for another. The introduction of CCT a rationalization of services could improve recreation management efficiency. However, there is still a degree of uncertainty as to the outcome of CCT, and the effects that it will have on the management of leisure and recreation services.

10.7 THE COMPLEXITIES OF LEISURE MANAGEMENT IN LOCAL GOVERNMENT

Local authorities have an extremely important role to play in the provision and management of leisure and recreation. However, they are considerably constrained in what they can do and the way in which they can go about it. The problems are often complex and revolve around a number of separate and interrelated issues. Some of the problems are outlined below, and taken cumulatively, they show how difficult it is for authorities to provide what is needed, particularly in a society with growing expectations and widening freedom. The problem areas include:

1. Heritage of a traditional institution.
2. Fragmentation and lack of 'fit' between central and local government.
3. Concurrent powers within tiers of local government.
4. Permissive powers.
5. Departmental structuring difficulties.
6. Lack of rationale and objectivity.
7. Inarticulation between local government and the people.
8. Implementation of CCT legislation.

First, administration at all governmental levels is complex, often confusing and peculiar to the British government, tradition and way of life. Some of the strengths and many of the weaknesses stem from the way in which the pattern of active recreation pursuits developed. Organized recreation, for example, was originally a matter for private and voluntary effort. By the time 'statutory' provision began to supplement this, numerous agencies were already established and working in the field. They were uncoordinated and autonomous. When we look at facilities alone, even within the same authority, it appears that we have somehow managed to keep the left hand in ignorance of what the right hand is doing. Today it is now clear that for generations we have wasted many of our resources and facilities by keeping strict divisions between school, youth, community, young and old. Often the problem has been not a shortage of facilities, but rather administrative weakness and an inability to coordinate functions of separate departments within different tiers of local government.

The lesson for Leisure Managers is that authorities must make the fullest use of existing resources. It would also appear that local authorities have in the past concentrated too much on facilities and not enough on services and opportunities. If local authorities are to serve all sections of the community, including those who are disadvantaged, then supplying facilities alone is not enough. Community developments, partnerships, 'outreach' programmes, neighbourhood schemes, community leaders and 'animateurs' must be encouraged. Groups of many kinds can benefit not just from cash sums, but also from support in a variety of guises – e.g. staff, leadership, offices, administration, free publicity and 'moral' support.

The advantages of a fully integrated approach can be beneficial to neighbourhood and communities. Residents of deprived urban neighbourhoods are almost entirely dependent on public leisure facilities, whereas residents of more affluent neighbourhoods will have a wider range of leisure alternatives. Future facilities must be planned more effectively. This entails public participation, the involvement of leisure professionals throughout the planning stages, designing, siting and managing facilities effectively and developing community recreation programmes with which the community can identify.

Second, recreation administration is fragmented. Different Acts of Parliament and regulations govern separate services such as social, health, community, education, tourism, the countryside, sport and outdoor recreation and the arts. Tourism is a function of the Department of Employment; sport, physical education and the arts come within the remit of the Department of Education and Science; local government and the various roles that it plays with regard to leisure and recreation provision fall under the Department of the Environment. Other departments too, such as the Home Office, the Department of Health and Social Security, the Ministry of Agriculture, Fisheries and Food and the Department of Transport, are also involved in leisure provision; many of the functions, however, are devolved upon agencies such as the Tourist Boards, the Arts Council, Sports Council and Countryside Commission.

The multi-sector and multi-department approach of central government and the resulting complexity and overlap, constitute inherent problems between the 'fit' between central government and local government. Furthermore, most local authority functions, for example, libraries and adult education, have central government controls, guidance and sources for grant aid. However, this is not universally applied, for example, children's play, entertainment, catering and urban parks fall into several sectors and no one department takes overall responsibility.

Third, not only is there a lack of fit between central government and local government, there is lack of fit between levels of government within local authorities. The *Local Government Act 1972* invests in all the county councils and district councils equal powers to provide recreation and leisure facilities for the community. Thus county councils and district councils have concurrent powers which lead to overlapping and duplication. The exceptions to this general provision are education, libraries and national parks.

Fourth, in Scotland and Northern Ireland a duty has been laid on local authorities to provide recreation facilities, but in England and Wales local authorities are under no obligation to provide for recreation other than through education, libraries, allotments and some national parks. The 'duty to provide' was specifically rejected by the government in its 1975 White Paper, *Sport and Recreation*. Local authorities thus have permissive powers.

Fifth, at local level, leisure services can be combined through corporate management and comprehensive departments, or partially combined or remain separated into autonomous departments. Even where comprehensive recreation departments exist, they are known and have titles which vary from one authority to the next.

Sixth, it is not surprising that, given obligatory and permissive powers, we find problems over policy and priorities and a patchwork development of services. Local government departments have often been unclear about their rationale, aims and objectives. Aims are often all-embracing – 'to serve the whole community' – and can mean all things to all people. They are difficult to translate into operational objectives. Fundamentally the status of leisure is still problematic and planning for leisure is not a main priority for local government and features only peripherally in many structure plans.

Another fundamental problem is the inevitable bureaucracy which comes through public accountability, public service, institutionalized systems and approaches, which render the whole machinery a slow-moving animal, one which cannot readily respond to the needs of a fast-moving, changeable and flexible society.

Seventh, several management problems exist at an officer-manager level, and these have an effect on the face-to-face work with the community, as follows.

1. Officer and staff behaviour is often controlled and guided by formal, organization structures. This system of 'working to rules' can in-

culcate formal attitudes and responses to informal and flexible situations.

2. The formal approaches tend to make it difficult for local government to attract or to articulate with the socially disadvantaged, who find little identification with the services. The Department of the Environment (DoE) Report *Recreation and Deprivation in Inner Urban Areas* [17] describes the problems which arise when simple approaches to providing recreation facilities 'for the whole community', without considering the special needs of particular groups, are adopted. A similar lesson is drawn from the report *Fair Play for All* by Hillman and Whalley [18].
3. The 'apparent' constraints of public accountability, allied to local government 'standards' tend to make local authorities wary and uneasy concerning commercial investment. However, greater cooperation is now becoming essential in times of local government spending constraints.
4. Following local government reorganization, the speed with which new recreation departments came into existence meant that they were being founded on little that had been tried and tested. In addition, many new recreation personnel were recruited, often without relevant experience and with little qualification in the field. Senior posts were being created and promotions made with rapid movement of personnel following. The situation has stabilized considerably but there is yet insufficient exchange of management information or management education and training for those actually in the field. Complicating the whole scene in local government is the confusing array of 'professional' bodies involved in the field of leisure and recreation.

Eighth, meeting the competitive tendering requirements needs much effort and the time available is not great. The experience of the relatively few authorities which have voluntarily put the management of sports facilities out to contract has shown that there are pitfalls to be avoided. Many local authority officers are entering a new field and the degree of uncertainty that exists as to the outcome of CCT is still substantial.

10.8 SUMMARY: THE PUBLIC SECTOR AND LEISURE

Successive legislation over the past few years has (and will continue to have) a dramatic effect on local authority leisure and recreation provision. The new capital control systems which will constrain local government capital and revenue expenditure, along with compulsory competitive tendering, local management of schools and the Community Charge (now subject to change), will undoubtedly affect the expansion of leisure provision within the public sector. The result may well be a changing role for the local authority from that of provider (although in order to sustain its social conscience, this will remain) to that of enabler and, more important, coordinator. Partnerships will encourage the growth in commercial leisure provision, particularly in that of the more profitable activities, while equal support for the voluntary sector will enable the non-profitable activities to thrive.

The management of leisure and recreation at all levels of government is complicated by inherent and institutional constraints. In overall planning terms, recreation is not regarded as a main priority; until it is, a comprehensive policy is unlikely to emerge. In addition to the major constraining limitations on both borrowing and spending, key problem areas exist.

Local government, by the nature of its public accountability and bureaucratic systems, has been slow to adapt to changing demands. The systems are inflexible, compared with other systems of management. The CCT legislation is forcing local authorities to look afresh at their services and management.

Despite CCT legislation, however, recreation and leisure services are an area under less constraints from government. Flexible approaches are possible, and the public is able to take a greater share in the provision of resources to meet community demands and needs.

Local authorities have considerable permissive powers. They can act independently or in partnership; they can enable, support and encourage self-help and initiative. They equally have the power to help those who are unable to help themselves and to provide various opportunities which would be denied the community without local authority assistance.

One role which local authorities can take upon themselves is that of coordination. In all districts there are a whole range of providers, with a wide range of services and facilities. There is a need for coordination, support and enabling functions to be performed to make the best possible use of the immense voluntary, commercial, institutional and governmental services.

REFERENCES AND NOTES

1. Report of the Wolfenden Committee on Sport (1960), *Sport and the Community*, Central Council of Physical Recreation, London.
2. Ministry of Education (1960), *The Youth Service in England and Wales: Report of the Committee November 1958* (Albermarle Report), Cmnd 929, HMSO, London; Department of Education and Science (1969), *Youth and Community Work in the 70s*, HMSO, London.
3. Central Advisory Council for Education (England) (1967), *Children and their*

Primary Schools. Volume 2, Research and Surveys, for Department of Education and Science, HMSO, London.

4. Department of Education and Science (1973), *Circular 5/73: Local Government Reorganization and the Public Library Service*, HMSO, London.
5. Department of Education and Science (1965), *Support for the Arts: The First Steps*, Cmnd 2601, HMSO, London.
6. Lord Redcliffe-Maud (1977), *Local Authority Support for the Arts*, Gulbenkian Foundation, London.
7. Molyneux, D. D. (1968), Working for recreation. *Journal of Town Planning Institute*, **54**, No. 4, April, 149–56.
8. Ministry of Housing and Local Government (1967), *Management of Local Government. Volume I, Report of the Committee*, and *Volume V, Local Government Administration in England and in Wales*, HMSO, London.
9. Department of Education and Science and Ministry of Housing and Local Government (1964), *Joint Circular 11/64 and 49/64: Provision of Facilities for Sport*, DES, London.
10. Ministry of Housing and Local Government (1966), *Circular 31/66: Public Expenditure: Miscellaneous Schemes*, MHLG, London.
11. Department of Education and Science (1970), *Circular 2/70: The Chance to Share*, DES, London.
12. *Report of the Royal Commission on Local Government in England 1966–1969: The Redcliffe-Maud Report* (1969), HMSO, London.
13. *Report of Local Government in England*, Cmnd 4276, HMSO, London.
14. *Local Government in England: Government Proposals for Reorganisation*, Cmnd 4584, HMSO, London; *Report of Local Government in Scotland*, Cmnd 4583, HMSO, London.
    Welsh Office (1971), *The Reform of Local Government in Wales*, HMSO, London.
15. Study Group on Local Authority Management Structures (1972), *The New Local Authorities: Management and Structure* (Bains Report), HMSO, London.
16. Seeley, I. H. (1978), *London Government Explained*, Macmillan, London, p. 67.
17. Department of the Environment (1977), *Recreation and Deprivation in Inner Urban Areas*, HMSO, London.
18. Hillman, M. and Whalley, A. (1977), *Fair Play for All. A Study of Access to Sport and Informal Recreation*, Broadsheet No. 571, Political and Economic Planning, London.

RECOMMENDED ADDITIONAL READING

The Education Reform Act, 1988, and its Effects on the Leisure Industry, 1990, ILAM, Reading.

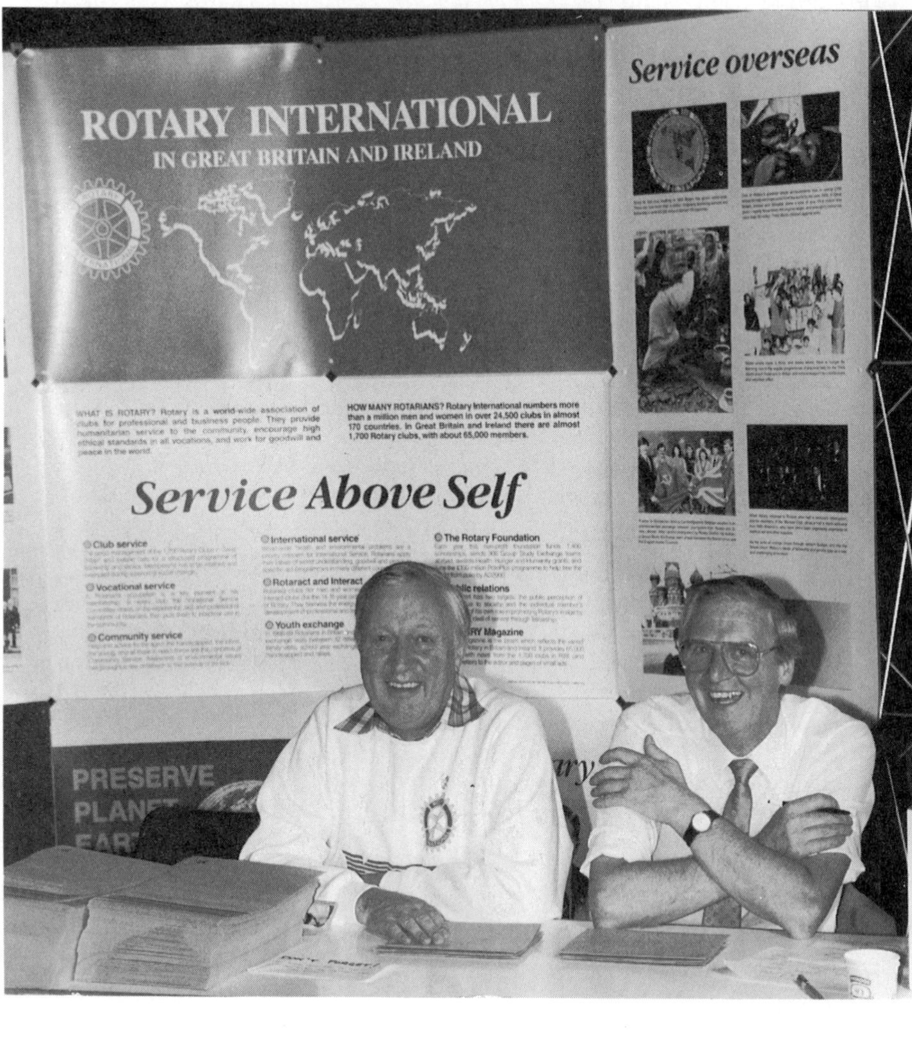
ROTARY INTERNATIONAL
IN GREAT BRITAIN AND IRELAND
WHAT IS ROTARY? Rotary is a world-wide association of clubs for professional and business people. They provide humanitarian service to the community, encourage high ethical standards in all vocations, and work for goodwill and peace in the world.
HOW MANY ROTARIANS? Rotary International numbers more than a million men and women in over 24,500 clubs in almost 170 countries. In Great Britain and Ireland there are almost 1,700 Rotary clubs, with about 65,000 members.
Service Above Self
Club service
Vocational service
Community service
International service
Rotaract and Interact
Youth exchange
The Rotary Foundation
Service overseas
PRESERVE

Chapter 11

Leisure provision in the voluntary sector

In Chapter 10 we have been concerned with the public sector. We now turn to aspects within the non-public sector, which is large, complex and diversified. It exists in collaboration with the public sector and is often interlocked with it.

This chapter deals with the voluntary sector. This chapter covers the following areas: *first*, a brief outline of the range of recreation provision in the voluntary sector is given. *Second*, voluntary organizations are seen in the context of their historical background. *Third*, the role of voluntary groups in society is examined.

In addition, two types of provider – charitable trusts, and industrial and company recreation clubs – are studied to understand their function and relevance to the community, but more important, to understand their approach to leisure and recreation management. Company clubs are invariably managed as non-profit-making organizations, hence in terms of management they can be equated with the voluntary sector rather than the commercial sector. Finally, a brief look is taken at some of the major national agencies that have an influence on leisure and its management.

Readers will learn that the voluntary sector has a substantial role to play in enabling like-minded people to fashion their own 'destiny', to choose to behave in ways which are worthwhile and satisfying to them; that is one of the hallmarks of leisure. Leisure Managers will appreciate the value in supporting and enabling voluntary groups to prosper and to relinquish the notion that the job of providers is to provide leisure 'on a plate'. For public sector Leisure Managers, the enabling and coordinating roles and links with the national and local agencies become important functions.

11.1 LEISURE AND RECREATION IN THE VOLUNTARY SECTOR

The resources, facilities and opportunities offered to people through the vast range of many thousands of voluntary bodies in the United Kingdom represent collectively a significant contribution to the field of recreation and leisure. Voluntary bodies vary greatly, from neighbourhood groups to national organizations. The voluntary sector is dominated by a vast array of leisure and recreation clubs and associations.

Sport is managed, in large measure, by local voluntary sporting clubs and associations, which are the backbone of sport in the United Kingdom. Governing bodies of sport are linked nationally by organizations such as the Central Council of Physical Recreation. The role of the Sports Council is to support sport and physical recreation groups at all levels, the vast majority being voluntary amateur groups.

Arts, community arts and cultural activities in their variety are largely catered for through local voluntary societies, associations and groups of many kinds. The regional arts boards themselves, while dependent on grant sources, are nevertheless voluntary bodies, supported by the Arts Council.

Informal outdoor recreation is encouraged through organizations such as the National Trust, Ramblers' Association, local walking and cycling and other clubs. Tourism is encouraged through voluntary organizations like the Youth Hostels Association.

Social recreation and leisure are catered for by a large number of social, entertainment or multi-activity organizations. Consumer organizations protect interests, particularly with leisure products. Women's Institutes, community associations, religious organizations, youth organizations and hundreds of others all go to make up the array of resources and opportunities for recreation and leisure participation. In nearly all cases, other than the conservation of buildings and lands, all these voluntary organizations are concerned with the interests of their members and users. They help to provide and manage leisure opportunity.

Private and institutional bodies, such as landowners, employers, universities, schools, colleges and institutes, make an important contribution to provision and services for recreation. Many firms provide social and sporting facilities. University extramural departments provide adult education classes. Many universities and colleges provide holiday residential courses, partly as a means of keeping residential accommodation and services open throughout the long vacations. The growth of the 'activity holiday' has been rapid in recent years. Private schools, like Millfield, have become famous for their 'schools of sport'. Private landowners also play a significant part in the provision for informal recreation. They own much of the rural land in the United Kingdom which is the setting for outdoor informal leisure and recreation. They also own and manage facilities for public leisure through historic houses, country parks and many of the great tourist attractions.

In many cases, voluntary bodies are inextricably linked to public providers and public money. Charitable trusts are often partly sponsored by local authorities and, in some cases, wholly subsidized. Advisory and counselling services such as the Citizen's Advice Bureaux, while volunteer based, are funded almost entirely by local authorities. Local councils support and initiate many thousands of voluntary groups and projects and, in many cases, fund and staff them. The interdependence between many voluntary bodies and public authorities is part and parcel of the wide framework of public community services, including leisure and recreation.

Some voluntary organizations are also dependent upon commercial bodies. Many 'art' and sporting institutions might perish without the financial backing and marketing skills of major commercial companies. At local level, many clubs rely on the brewer's contribution or the room at the back of the pub.

Further complicating the issue is the problem of demarcation between what is commercial and what is voluntary. Some private institutions and voluntary organizations adopt a style of management which, in certain elements, is wholly commercial. With some private landowners the earning of income is a major objective and therefore in terms of management they can be considered similarly to commercial bodies.

11.2 VOLUNTARY CLUBS AND ORGANIZATIONS IN HISTORICAL CONTEXT IN THE UNITED KINGDOM

Voluntary recreation and leisure groups have existed for centuries – but not in the number and variety of recent times. In the 18th century the coffee-house was for the 'gentlemen of leisure', a social group – a club in embryo. They were in theory open to all, but often developed into clubs for specified groups, with restricted membership. Today in the United Kingdom we still find that many private and institutional bodies confine the use of their facilities to certain groups of people.

Most national governing bodies for sport were also formed from the creation of interest groups of like-minded people such as the MCC (Marylebone Cricket Club), the founders of the game of cricket as it is played today. Leisure interest groups like the Royal Horticultural Society date back to 1804 and animal societies, such as the Royal Society for the Protection of Animals, to 1824. The Cyclists' Touring Club was formed in 1878. Indeed 50% of the national voluntary leisure groups identified by the English Tourist Board have been in existence for over fifty years [1].

In early-industrial Britain recreations were often communal affairs based on seasons, festivals and commemorative events. The sports, dances, processions and ceremonies were within the context of the whole community, as they are in underdeveloped, simple societies today. It was the rationalization of work that led to a separate and identifiable sphere of social life [2]. Simultaneously, the first half of the 19th century saw the disappearance of 'old playgrounds' which were not replaced by anything new until the growth of clubs and provision for recreation by voluntary bodies later in the century. Unions, factories and schools established their own football clubs; YMCAs and the Sunday School movement created clubs for recreation.

Clubs featured in the 18th and 19th centuries as important organizations in the recreative and social life of the community. The great expansion of clubs took place in the last quarter of the 19th century but this was not a long-term trend. Working men's clubs developed through several stages from the last quarter of the 19th century. The most significant development was the move towards professionally based entertainment. The switch produced a change in the membership participation from producer to consumer patterns. Despite these changes, activities such as snooker and darts have continued and with television exposure have increased.

Many voluntary movements and associations arose out of the Great Depression as responses to social injustice. For example, the National Association of Women's Clubs arose in that way. Many were post Second World War outlets for wives of the unemployed, and for unemployed women themselves.

Today the voluntary sector national organization groups and clubs are as strong as ever. In 1988 there were 560 000 Scouts and 682 000 Guides, 335 000 members of the National Federation of Women's Institutes, 540 000 members of the Royal Society for the Protection of Birds and a huge rise to 1 634 000 in membership of the National Trust. Membership of most environmental organizations has dramatically increased in recent years. For example Friends of the Earth's membership grew 65-fold from 1971 to 1988 [3].

Suffice to say, that the voluntary groups have a substantial part in providing opportunities for people's leisure, whether as participants, supporters or service-givers. The broad range of voluntary groupings is set out in Table 11.1.

11.3 LEISURE PARTICIPATION IN VOLUNTARY GROUPS

People go to extraordinary lengths and exhibit wide variations of behaviour in expressing their individual and collective needs in their leisure. People express themselves in all manner of participation groups, for example, there are religious, community and welfare groups, men's, women's, old people's and young people's groups, advisory and counselling groups or para-medical and military groups. Some people join clubs and associations that are culturally uplifting or educational. Some join acting, ballroom, jazz, dancing, keep-fit, slimming, singing, operatic or pop groups; others play sport in groups, sail the seas with yachting clubs and climb with mountaineering groups. Many groups identify themselves by wearing badges or special clothing; others have a uniform to create a new identity – a leisure identity, or even a way of living identity.

The range of groups is wide and diversified and no adequate classification has yet been made to cover all groups that exist. Several different types of grouping can, however, be identified; some of these are listed in Table 11.1 but the overlaps are many. For example, many uniform groups are youth groups, many women's groups are welfare

Table 11.1 Range of voluntary organizations

Community organizations	Community associations, community councils
Community actions groups	National Council for Voluntary Organizations, Inner City Unit, Inter-Action Trust Limited, Gingerbread
Children's groups	Fair Play for All, Pre-School Playgroups Association, Toy Library Association
Youth organizations	Scout Association, Girl Guides' Association, National Council for YMCAs, National Association of Youth Clubs
Women's organizations	National Federation of Women's Institutes, National Union of Townswomen's Guilds, Mothers' Union, Women's Voluntary Service (WVS)
Men's groups	Working men's clubs, servicemen's clubs
Old people's groups	Darby and Joan Clubs, Senior Citizens
Disabled groups	Gardens for the Disabled, Disabled Drivers' Motor Club
Adventure organizations	Outward Bound Trust, Duke of Edinburgh's Award, National Caving Association
Outdoor activity organizations and touring groups	Camping Club of Great Britain and Ireland, Youth Hostels Association, Central Council of British Naturism, Ramblers' Association, British Caravanners' Club
Sport and physical recreation organizations	Keep Fit Association, British Octopush Association, National Skating Association of Great Britain, Cycle Speedway Council, GB Wheelchair Basketball League
'Cultural' and entertainment organizations	British Theatre Association, Museums Association, English Folk Dance and Song Society, British Federation of Music Festivals
Educational organizations	National Institute of Adult Education, Workers Educational Association, National Listening Library
Hobbies and interest groups	National Association of Flower Arranging Societies, Citizens Band Association, Antique Collectors Club, Handicrafts Advisory Association for the Disabled, British Beer Mat Collectors' Society
Animals and pet groups	Pony Club, Cats Protection League
Environmental, conservation and heritage groups	National Trust, Friends of the Earth, Royal Society for the Protection of Birds, Keep Britain Tidy Group, Save the Village Pond Campaign, Rare Breed Society
Consumer groups	Consumers' Association, Campaign for Real Ale (CAMRA)

Table 11.1 (Cont.)

Counselling organizations	British Association for Counselling, Citizens Advice Bureau, Alcoholics Anonymous, Marriage Guidance Councils, Samaritans Incorporated
Philanthropic groups	Rotary International in Great Britain and Ireland, Inner Wheel, Variety Club of Great Britain, Golddiggers
Paramedical organizations	British Red Cross Society, St John Ambulance Brigade
Uniform groups	Voluntary Reserves, Territorial Army, Sea and Army Cadets, Air Training Corps
Religious groups	Methodist Church Division of Social Responsibility, Church Army, Church of England Children's Society
Political groups	Political parties, trade unions

groups, and so on. The list is by no means an attempt at classification or taxonomy; it is simply a means of showing the range and diversity of voluntary leisure groupings.

The English Tourist Board [4] identified the membership of 211 national voluntary leisure groups with over 8 million members collectively, of which 29% belong to youth groups, 27% to sports groups, 13% to conservation and heritage groups, 8% to touring groups, 7% to women's groups and 7% to animal or wildlife conservation groups. The National Trust is by far the largest national organization, with a membership rise of over 700% in 20 years. Well over 40% of the groups identified have memberships of over 5000. Over the long term (with exceptions such as some church, cycling, para-medical and women's groups), very few national groups have had a fall in membership.

The Leisure Manager has an important role in helping groups of people to negotiate with public bodies, planners, architects and other organizations. Supporting groups, by helping them to run their own projects, may be more important than providing projects 'on a plate'.

11.4 THE ROLE OF VOLUNTARY GROUPS IN SOCIETY

It is clear from the range and growing variety of leisure groups that such participative behaviour is important to people. What is the role of the voluntary group?

Modern life in Western civilization is more complex than life in underdeveloped societies. Voluntary groups have therefore to play a far greater role in modern society [5]. In simple societies there can be no real voluntary association or club-life, whereas in advanced society there exist numerous small-scale associations catering for varying numbers of individuals. In modern society people can behave both as individuals and collectively within groups. Leisure has importance, in that it has potential for both individual and group expression. Individuals can choose their group identity.

One of the motivations for corporate action in the recreation and leisure field is often that individuals and groups of people find themselves isolated and cut off from opportunity and support. Voluntary groupings are initiated at a grass-roots level. They usually start with people's felt needs, demands, wishes or inclinations. They are voluntary. They might become involuntary, according to Tomlinson [5], in either of two ways: by becoming commercialized and turning into entrepreneurial bodies, or by turning inwards and becoming secret societies.

In terms of the management of community recreation, the primary interest groups should feature strongly in any comprehensive community programme. People want to retain their individuality, yet many people too want to belong to groups. The Leisure Manager has the dilemma in planning and programming as to the extent to which provision should be made for group interests. Understanding group belonging and group behaviour will assist the manager in coming to terms with the problem.

At first glance, each club appears to be decidedly different from, another. A ladies' darts club meeting in the local pub, for example, might appear very dissimilar to the ladies' choral society meeting in the church hall. Hutson [6] has shown, however, that there are many basic similarities between all forms of clubs and voluntary associations: there are similarities in patterns of activity and the ways in which clubs develop and decline. She has shown how organizers tend to form a distinct, closely connected, elite within a town or region. Social class, life-cycle, physical mobility, kinship and sex roles affect both patterns of attendance and leadership. Voluntary associations tend to reflect 'the economic and social milieu' and tend to be dominated by a group of people of similar type. This leads to a proliferation of many small groups.

Like-minded people tend to gather together and form associations. Recruitment is normally along lines of friendship or kinship. Most clubs are social clubs, whether the primary activity is social or not. People who are felt 'not to belong' to the predominant group are often kept out through formal procedures. In the areas in Swansea studied by Hutson, there were often internal political pressures and several examples of cliques leaving a club as another clique took over.

These may be some of the reasons why newcomers, if they are in any numbers, tend to set up their own associations rather than join existing groups. While youth clubs were more socially mixed, and some associations claimed to draw members from all social categories, most clubs did not.

Study of the differences and similarities of clubs and associations reveals four important factors for the Leisure Manager to consider:

1. All the clubs tend to be, at least partially, exclusive. Many clubs, theoretically open to all in principle, have been able to 'guarantee' their exclusiveness with high enrolment fees, membership systems, etc.
2. Clubs are not static, but changing, organizations. The Wolfenden Committee Report (1978) on voluntary associations [7] found that, 'New organisations are formed to meet newly discerned needs, others die. Yet others change their emphasis or venture into fresh fields . . . There is nothing static about the scene.' The Leisure Manager should bear in mind therefore that new clubs, in particular, are likely to change in membership and will have different leadership patterns within the first few years. Shorter-term initial bookings of facilities and flexible and supporting management roles may need to be given.
3. Clubs display similarities in behaviour: they are social groupings. Sports clubs can be seen, in some sense, as less exclusive than some other clubs, but just like other leisure groupings, sport generates separate groups and activities for different social categories. The Queen's Lawn Tennis Club will attract a very different clientele compared to the club affiliated to the local community sports centre or park. Managers must not therefore neglect the important social aspects of group leisure participation.
4. Clubs are dependent on support services such as premises. Local authorities, commercial bodies and all the institutions who have premises and administrations can be important enablers in providing support services and premises. The local authority's coordinating role plays an important part in this respect.

One of the characteristics of leisure-time participation is that a considerable proportion of people take on new roles i.e. new leisure roles; indeed, they are no longer factory workers, bank clerks or housewives. They become instead leader, coach, club chairperson, golfer, sailor, official, youth worker, lay preacher or sergeant-major. In some cases, the adoption of new identities is intensified by the wearing of a uniform: the uniform is the symbol of the organization; it gives identity, and 'image' – it stands for something, a faith, a belief in what we are doing.

The taking on of new roles in leisure time is an interesting phenomenon and may be significant. There is commitment, purposefulness and responsibility. Are these meaningful roles absent from other aspects of everyday life? What does it tell us about having clearly defined group norms and cultures?

In summary, the voluntary sector is and remains the backbone of leisure and recreation organization and participation. The sector is vast, diversified and linked with both the public and commercial sectors. Voluntary organizations give people both the chance to participate and the opportunity to become involved in all levels of organization and management. They also give the opportunity to serve. In terms of community recreation, in its widest sense, managers must be aware that the voluntary sector, more than other sectors, holds many of the keys to individual self-fulfilment, one of the main goals of effective leisure and recreation management.

11.5 RECREATION CHARITABLE TRUSTS

The recreation trust system of management is a hybrid. It is normally conceived as private, independent initiative, but it normally needs financial assistance from statutory sources in the form of grants and loans, in order for it to survive and prosper, particularly in regard to community recreation. The trust is an administrative system for co-ordinating and managing facilities as a charity. Its formation involves legal formalities, bearing in mind that such a trust system carries organizational and financial benefits and must therefore be for the benefit of the public at large.

The establishment of a trust has the advantage that the projects initiated by it become eligible for grant aid for capital expenditure from sources not normally open to a local authority. This not only lessens the burden on the rates or community charge, but also as a voluntary organization with charitable status, a trust is entitled to 80% mandatory relief from rates and also to any discretionary relief which the rating authority might decide to allow (under sections 43 and 45 of the *Local Government Finance Act 1988*). Trusts can also be linked to supporters' clubs, lotteries, fund raising and other schemes. It would, however, be a mistake to think that the link with the local authority will always be wholly advantageous. At times of financial stringency, there could be withdrawal of financial support; and as elected representatives change over the years, there is a risk that support may be reduced or even withdrawn altogether. Undue levels of interference could apply in return, as it were, for financial assistance.

Apart from the financial benefits, trusts have social benefits. There is the advantage that the local community will help to share the responsibility for the provision and management of its facilities, instead of having them provided and managed solely by a local authority and financed entirely from rates. Many local authorities welcome joint committees, even when they (the local authorities) have provided much of the finance.

It is not inferred that one method of management is better than another or that there is a best solution; each method may be the right management in the particular circumstances. However, the trust system works successfully in many areas of social welfare and community recreation. For example, the start of the community recreation centre movement in the United Kingdom began at Harlow, in 1960, by means of a sports trust; it must, of course, be seen against a background of a rapidly developing town with resources of potential leadership from industry, education, local government and the professions.

11.5.1 Trust system advantages and disadvantages

The trust system has both advantages and disadvantages. In summary, some of these are:

(i) Advantages

- Direct access by senior management to executive control, cutting down levels of bureaucracy and streamlining decision-making.
- The trust system is flexible. The governing body can be built up on a widely representative basis to include all appropriate authorities, industry, commerce and local community.
- It represents partnership between statutory and voluntary organizations.
- It is eligible for grant aid and savings on the rates.
- As a voluntary enterprise, it can encourage a strong spirit of community endeavour. As such it may have to raise substantial local funds for capital and maintenance. Members of some trusts feel, in some way, that it is their own, and they have partly to pay for it and look after it. Many paid staff too can feel a greater sense of personal commitment.
- This spirit of voluntary enterprise can produce economies in operation.
- Its great strength could be in its contribution to the future. Being flexible and free from too many ties with authorities, the system lends itself to experimentation, new ideas and pioneer projects.
- As a voluntary self-governing project, it encourages leaders in commerce, industry, the professions and the community to want to be associated with it.
- Being a non-political body, the trust can establish a system of key

member stability and can build upon the experience gained over years of development. Local authority projects may well suffer from changes of either personnel or party political representatives more often than is good for the project.

(ii) Disadvantages

- There are usually insufficient capital resources. Often many savings have to be made, particularly in ancillary accommodation, which some local authorities may not be able to make.
- There are insufficient operational resources. If a comprehensive programme is to be given, the need may exist for guaranteed local authority financial assistance. A voluntary body, although it may be giving a much needed community service, can often be at the mercy of local and county councils, needing to approach them 'cap in hand' for assistance.
- Trusts constantly need to raise large sums of money from their resources and supporters.
- Often there are too few staff, many giving service beyond the 'call of duty'. Without the backing of a large authority, the workload is heavy on such staff.
- Members of the public in many urban areas have become used to the idea of having good recreation facilities. Many may not care or even know that a theater or sports centre is being run by a trust. To the public it is a public facility.
- Trust executives of a small governing body carry a heavy burden of responsibility.

The ideal trust should prove a flexible administrative instrument and one which might well command more support and interest from a local community than if it were purely a local authority responsibility. On the other hand, the project should in the long run benefit from the stability, continuity and financial resources of the local authority.

11.6 INDUSTRIAL AND COMPANY RECREATION PROVISION

Industrial and company recreation, by and large, is the provision of private facilities, ostensibly not provided for commercial gain, but for the workforce as private individuals. It is conceded at the outset that a happy workforce may achieve greater efficiency and output and thereby greater profits, but in terms of management, industrial provision is more akin to the private members' club than to the commercial enterprise.

The development of the industrial sports and social club in the latter part of the 19th century has often been attributed to the philanthropic motives of benevolent and paternalistic employers, influenced by religious and humanitarian ideals. However, underlying this, more practically orientated motives may have been at work, and certainly the development of industrial recreation into the 20th century is unlikely to be attributable solely to the altruistic behaviour of the employer.

A number of factors have been put forward as being influential in or motivating the decision by an employer to contribute large capital and recurrent expenditure towards the provision, maintenance and management of facilities for the recreational benefit of the employees. Six influencing factors can be identified:

1. Philanthropy.
2. Fitness for work.
3. Reduction in staff turnover.
4. Company image.
5. Company prestige.
6. Employee pressure.

The provision of company services and facilities is likely to have been influenced by a combination of these and other specific factors, not all of which will have been relevant at any one time.

11.6.1 Historical perspective

Whatever the motivation, the beginnings of industrial recreation provision in the United Kingdom started in the 19th century, probably with the founding of Pilkington's Recreation Club in 1847. The growth of company clubs in the latter part of the 19th and the early part of the 20th centuries was evident with the early days being dominated by such pioneers as Pilkington, Cadbury and Rowntree. The government-initiated Clarendon Report, going back to 1864, extolled the virtues of sport participation as a means of developing comradeship, team spirit and loyalty to an organization.

Following the First World War, many industrial clubs sprang up, often associated with religious and welfare organizations. However, the Great Depression caused a decline in the number of clubs owing to the closure of companies and impetus was only once again regained after the Second World War.

In general terms, there was a boom in industrial recreation provision in the 1950s, when profits were high and a spirit of altruism led to a spate of companies 'investing' in sports and social clubs. In the 1960s responsibility for the organization and management of many of these clubs changed from employer to employee, under the guidance of a sports and social secretary and/or committee structures. Finance remained a joint effort with the employers often providing for capital expenditure and/or an annual block grant. The employees contributed by membership subscriptions, lotteries, bar and vending profits.

Cullen [8], and Parker [9], reported a decline in the movement in the 1960s with some of the smaller companies being unable to sustain an acceptable level of interest among their employees, and consequently selling or using the facility's land for building development, and this is still partly the case. But the picture is a far from clear one. Cullen's 1979–80 industrial recreation survey [10] revealed that twice as many clubs were formed in the 1970s as disbanded, and these new clubs were 'by no means' connected solely with large companies (more than 1000 employees); few companies had disposed of recreation sites, and relatively few clubs reported a decrease in interest. In Cullen's survey practically all respondents either wholly or partly agreed with the statement: 'Almost irrespective of the level of employee interest in company sports and social clubs, these clubs and their facilities are now looked upon by company employees as a normal "fringe/welfare benefit" – a sort of background benefit which is always available to the employee, whether or not he or she actively uses the club and its facilities.'

None the less, changes in the British economy, allied to changes in employee recreation and where they reside in relation to the sports grounds, has led to the closure of some sports and social clubs. For example, with the advent of Saturday closure of the banks and the escalating house prices in the suburbs and in the areas where many of the sports clubs are located, the demand by employees, to use the sports facilities provided by the banks, has declined. This has been due largely to the increased travelling inconvenience and the cost involved. The declining number of participating members has coincided with the increasing cost of maintaining the grounds and the indoor facilities.

It is impossible to make an accurate estimate of the number of industrial sports and social clubs in the United Kingdom, let alone guess the numbers in Europe and elsewhere. In addition, the types of clubs vary enormously from industrial 'giants' to small local manufacturers; the programmes vary from a few activity sections to as many as 30 activity sections in a club and there are considerable differences in funding. The type and size of the company appear to have a bearing on provision; for example, with its greater financial and physical resources a firm with 2000–3000 or more employees can offer a wider range of activities and opportunities. The largest in the United Kingdom, the Shell Lensbury Club, is such an example.

11.6.2 Industrial clubs and community recreation

The goals of industrial clubs may vary, but in general clubs appear to aim at providing recreation opportunities for their company workforce.

It is strange therefore, bearing in mind the preponderance of working-class employees in manufacturing industries, that some of the finest facilities and programmes are clearly directed towards middle-class tastes, and that while more working-class people join company clubs than other clubs, nevertheless, professional and semi-professional employees predominate [11]. It would also appear that, in general, the majority of industrial workers do not participate in company-organized sport or recreation and often less than 10% of employees use company facilities [12]. This raises the contentious issue of under-use of industrial recreation facilities, and the possibility of shared use with the community in order to maximize facility potential.

A Regional Sports Council Survey [13] identified a willingness among the majority of industrial firms to make their sports facilities available to outsiders, but because the majority of sports facilities are maintained with the help of weekly contributions from employees, they were jealously guarded by the company club members themselves. Many club members are reluctant to share.

The practical problems of preservation of standards, employee safeguards, cost of additional use, bar and excise licences, security, staffing costs and legal and insurance problems are also put forward as reasons against involvement with the community, as is the problem of community clashing with company use, particularly in those industries where shiftwork is prevalent.

Another, perhaps major, but underestimated reason for 'keeping themselves to themselves', may be that the industrial sector provision offers recreational experiences which are different in kind from those offered in the public sector: – 'identification', 'small units', 'belonging', 'minority groups' (e.g. 'aero modelling catered for') and 'getting together with work colleagues' [10].

Most companies with their own leisure facilities provide access of some kind to individuals and groups other than their own employees, but this is usually carefully limited. Families, retired employees, members' guests and associate members are the main beneficiaries and large companies make available high-standard facilities for county matches, national sports coaching, sports festivals, and the like. Shared use, however, is the exception rather than the rule.

Managers or sports and social secretaries of the larger clubs have wider responsibilities than counterparts of the earlier years. As well as a knowledge of management techniques, licensing laws and financial control, the industrial Leisure Manager should also be providing a programme relevant to the needs of the company's workforce. The extent to which the manager simply performs a caretaker role, letting out the facilities to worker-organized clubs, or the extent to which he or she performs the role of enabler, actively promoting and encouraging participation through coaching schemes, special events and leagues, and for the unattached as well as the club user, is not clear and, again, is likely to differ from organization to organization. With exceptions, however, most programmes revolve around the traditional games and social activities.

11.6.3 Employee health and fitness

In recent years, the concept of 'corporate fitness' has slowly been gaining momentum in the United Kingdom as statistics become more widely publicized regarding the poor health of British workers and executives. For example, the World Health Organization shows British workers at the top of the table when it comes to heart disease and lung cancer. British industry loses over 27 million days per annum due to heart-related problems and a further 13 million days per annum are lost due to back-related problems. The DHSS's statistics show that in a company with 1000 employees, an average £2 000 000 per annum is lost as a result of circulatory disease.

A significant number of large corporations in the United Kingdom, including BP, Shell, Marks and Spencer, British Airways, British Telecom, STC and the Bank of England, and most of the major banks, offer employees extensive and often luxurious sports and social facilities in recognition of the considerable mutual benefits of corporate fitness to the employer and the employee. The Burton Group has established its own 'staff only' fitness club; and 'Busybodies' – and many other city firms in London and elsewhere – include corporate health club memberships within their remuneration packages. Exclusive London sports clubs, such as Cannons, Lambs and Cottons, have a very high proportion of corporate memberships.

11.6.4 Joint provision involving industry

Industry is involved in sport and recreation in a number of ways other than making provision solely for its own workforce. Essentially this involvement can be split up into two areas: promotion and sponsorship, and joint provision.

Joint provision of recreation facilities by industry and local authorities for use by both employees and the community was advocated by B. Seebohm Rowntree, in 1921, when in *The Human Factor in Business* he wrote:

'That adequate opportunity for wholesome recreation is desirable for all workers, especially in view of the shortening of the working week will not be disputed. The question is whether an employer has any responsibility in connection with the matter. I think the right answer is that if many of his workers live near the factory he should satisfy himself that adequate recreational facilities exist for them. He may do this in two ways: either he may provide adequate recreational facilities for his own employees only, or, by his influence and possibly also his financial help, he may assist communal effort to provide such facilities for the community as a whole. Strong arguments can be brought forward in favour of either course. In the case of a town where voluntary committees or local councils are seeking to provide playing fields, clubs and similar amenities for the general public, it is certainly a disadvantage if large employers refuse to co-operate in the public effort because they are concerned merely with their own employees'.

This view was endorsed in *The Pilkington Report* [14].

'the Study Group was firmly of the opinion that, in the logical development of sociological planning following all the improvements in the overall standard of living, it is no longer the function of private or public industry to provide recreational facilities for the exclusive use of their own work people but that they might well combine their resources with those of the local authorities in order to provide facilities which could be used and enjoyed by all'.

There have been a few successful collaborative projects – but too few to mention! One is left to ponder whether companies could apply the same drive and imagination in discharging responsibilities to employees and the community, as they do in meeting responsibilities to shareholders! If so, there could be a brighter future.

11.6.5 Industrial sports and social club of the 1990s

Philanthropy, a major early influence on the development of individual sports and social clubs, is no longer a common motive for provision of employee facilities. Fitness for work is increasingly perceived as the major justification. Economic realism has become the hallmark of the 1980s and 1990s. Corporate fitness concepts are slowly infiltrating into the boardrooms of the larger British companies from the United States and Japan. The arguments for corporate fitness are strong; the economic benefits can be substantial and company image and prestige can be enhanced at no real cost.

Large companies with or without established 'traditional' sports and social clubs, which tend to be centred on extensive bars and playing pitches, are increasingly looking to the health and fitness type of facilities. Some are providing their own facilities. Still more are arranging for corporate memberships of commercial clubs. Yet the corporate fitness market remains small relative to American and Japanese experiences.

The traditional sports and social clubs are, in many cases, going through a transitional stage. The days of liberal financial support from their sponsoring companies are over for many and clubs are increasingly being required to adopt more commercial approaches to management. Common trends include greater use of volunteer staff, higher subscription and activity participation charges, more and better-quality catering, more hires to outside organizations and a broadening of associate membership qualifications, section membership rules and guest allowances to increase revenue and reduce costs. A few have opened their entire facilities to their local communities, while large numbers have begun to permit a proportion of community memberships within certain activity sections.

Many of these measures are becoming necessary not just through reductions in company support, but also due to the influence of some of the general trends in leisure. Drink-drive legislation and the trend, particularly in the south-east, for more people to live some distance from their workplace, has exacerbated these trends.

In general, people's tastes are changing – more sophisticated leisure experiences are now in demand, boosted by television advertising and the fashion industry. The commercial leisure industry is growing and filling gaps in the market. Just as many of Britain's manufacturing industries have declined, industrial sports and social clubs in the traditional sense belong to a fast-fading age.

In general terms, many of the more traditional clubs are only used regularly by the older or retired employees for whom the style of facilities remains appropriate and attractive. The younger, more affluent and mobile employees have tended to usurp the sports and social clubs for alternative, more dynamic venues such as the nightclubs, the wine bars, the private health or sports clubs and the restaurants. Clearly, sports and social club committees and their sponsoring companies need to be addressing these trends and defining the future role and nature of recreation facilities for their employees and memberships.

11.7 THE NATIONAL AGENCIES

Central government is not a single entity, but a federation of separate ministries, each with its own policy and ministers. The position with local government is more comprehensive though still fragmented. In providing for recreation, central and local government works with and through a number of quasi-statutory institutions, quangos and agencies. Some have been established by Royal Charter, some by legislation and others by ministerial direction. Central government therefore carries considerable weight and influence on national agencies.

There are a whole range of national, regional and local agencies which assist in providing for public leisure and recreation. They are often hybrids of public authorities and private organizations, and while their primary function is not to provide facilities some of them do, and all of them influence provision through grants, loans, technical advice or support of some kind. The major agencies form a regional network of services.

This section takes a brief look at some of the major national agencies that have an influence on recreation and its management, namely:

1. The Arts Council.
2. Sports Council.
3. Central Council of Physical Recreation.
4. National Playing Fields Association.
5. Countryside Commission.
6. Forestry Commission.
7. National Rivers Authority.
8. National Children's Play and Recreation Unit.

11.7.1 The Arts Council of Great Britain

The Arts Council of Great Britain was established by Royal Charter in 1946. The impetus for its creation was the success of the Council for the Encouragement of Music and Arts which had been established during the Second World War.

The Arts Council's aims are threefold:

1. To develop and improve the knowledge, understanding and practice of the arts.
2. To increase the accessibility of the arts to the public throughout Britain.
3. To cooperate with government departments, local authorities and other bodies to achieve these objects.

The council itself is a body of individuals appointed by the Minister responsible for the Arts after consultation with the Secretaries of State for Scotland and Wales. Scotland and Wales have their own councils.

The *Regional Arts Boards* (previously *Regional Arts Associations*) (established in the 1950s) work closely with the Arts Council but are independent of it, being separate organizations funded from a variety of sources, including the Arts Council, their aim being to promote the development and expansion of the arts in their region.

There are ten boards in England, three in Wales and none in Scotland or Northern Ireland. Different boards place different emphasis on the various art forms and the manner in which they promote them, but the main services they provide are: grant-aiding, the promotion of events, publications and publicity, advice and research, planning and coordination and help for artists.

A working party was set up in 1978 at the request of the Arts Council to examine the council's functions. The report recommended a more efficient and economic organization structure and the majority of its recommendations have by now been carried out with a reduction in the size and number of committees and delegation of more executive powers to the council officers. The recommendations of the more recent Wilding Report [15] aim to shift the emphasis, particularly in terms of funding and organization to the Regional Arts Boards. The changes will dramatically reduce the power of the Arts Council and increase the influence of the regional arts boards.

11.7.2 The Sports Council

The Wolfenden Report of 1960 [16] commissioned by the Central Council for Physical Recreation (CCPR) identified the need for a Sports Development Council. In order to satisfy this need, the Sports Council was eventually established in 1965. Originally it was simply an advisory body, closely linked to the government through the civil service, with a government minister as its chairman. However, in 1972 it was granted independent status by Royal Charter, taking over both the staff and the assets of the CCPR and assuming responsibility for the Technical Unit for Sport (TUS) which prior to this had come under the auspices of the Department of Education and Science.

The implementation of policies and decisions taken by the Sports Council is undertaken by a permanent staff of officers who work for various units which are ultimately presided over by the Director-General. Of particular interest to the Leisure Manager are the Sports Development Unit, the Technical Unit for Sport which provides advice on the design and construction of facilities, the Press and Publicity Unit which produces the Council's bimonthly magazine, and all other Council publications, and the Information Centre which acts as a clearing house for national and international information and holds a collection of material for reference purposes.

The Sports Council has nine regional offices with the responsibility for implementing Sports Council policies with regard to the needs of the particular regions they serve. They provide technical and advisory services to local authorities, voluntary sports bodies and other organizations.

The Sports Council also administers five national residential Sports Centres with the primary objective of meeting the top-level requirements of select sports. The Centres are: Crystal Palace (athletics, swimming and other major sports), Holme Pierrepont (water sports), Lilleshall (soccer, gymnastics, cricket, etc.), Bisham Abbey (tennis, hockey, rugby, etc.) and Plas y Brenin (mountaineering).

The Sports Council provides an important contribution to the field of leisure and recreation management, through its annual recreation management conference and exhibition. The proceedings of the conference are published and provide a valuable source of information on topical subjects related to leisure.

In addition to the Sports Council, there are three national councils. The Scottish Sports Council and the Sports Council for Wales were set up as independent executive organizations by Royal Charter in 1972. They receive annual grant-in-aid direct from central government and perform similar general functions to those of the Sports Council. The Sports Council for Northern Ireland was established by statute in 1974. It advises government on capital expenditure and financially assists voluntary sports organizations in a number of ways. The members of all three councils are appointed by their respective secretaries of state.

In 1976 the Regional Councils for Sport and Recreation, for England, were set up by the Minister of State for Sport and Recreation. These councils supply a forum for consultation among local authorities, local sports councils, various regional bodies of sport and recreation and other interested parties. They are concerned with the planning of facilities and the promotion of opportunities for participation in organized sport and recreation, as well as with informal countryside recreation and the conservation problems inherent in its development. They are independent, autonomous bodies with representatives from organizations which have a major role to play in the development of sport and recreation. Following the DoE Circular 73/77, *Guidelines for Regional Recreational Strategies July 1977* [17]; the regional councils are also responsible for the production of strategy plans for the development of recreation within their regions.

The main aims of the Sports Council are as follows:

1. To promote general understanding of the social importance and value of sport and physical recreation.
2. To increase the provision of new sports facilities and stimulate fuller use of existing facilities.
3. To encourage wider participation in sport and physical recreation as a means of enjoying leisure.
4. To raise the standards of performance.

In 1990 the Sports Council consisted of a chairman, a vice-chairman and members, appointed by the Secretary of State for the Environment. The full Council meets four times per year. It is composed of one Sports Council committee which is advised by a number of consultative groups. The four Sports Councils in the UK, designated 1991 as the National Year of Sport, the aim being to encourage the whole community to become involved in sport at whatever level.

11.7.3 The Central Council of Physical Recreation

The CCPR was formed in 1935 [18]. After the transference of the CCPR's staff and property assets to the Sports Council in 1972, the member bodies of the CCPR voted to retain the CCPR's independence as a forum for the national and governing bodies of sport and recreation. In addition, the Royal Charter setting up the Sports Council specified the need for a 'consultative body' to the council, and the CCPR has been accorded this role.

The CCPR is thus an independent voluntary body with the following objectives:

1. To constitute a standing forum where all national governing and representative bodies of sport and physical recreation may be represented and may collectively or through special groups, where appropriate, formulate and promote measures to improve and develop sport and physical recreation.
2. To support the work of specialist sports bodies and to bring them together with other interested organizations.
3. To act as a consultative body to the Sports Council and other representative or public bodies concerned with sport and physical recreation.

The CCPR also provides a number of services to its member bodies, including a press service, help with sponsorship, legal advice and assistance with fund raising.

During 1989/90, the CCPR's role as an effective pressure group came to the forefront of measures undertaken to alleviate the perceived effects of central government proposals on sporting groups and societies. Its leaflet 'Kick Rates into Touch' outlined an action plan to bear 'pressure and persuasion' on all local authorities, for non-profit-making clubs and associations who are not granted relief from rates under section 47 of the *Local Government Finance Act 1988*.

It is also spearheading a campaign to introduce an internationally accepted code of ethics on standards of sporting behaviour. It is hoped that the 'British Sportsman's Charter', signed by all principal sporting associations, will improve the increasingly degenerate standards of sporting behaviour that are now a regular occurrence in some sports. The charter will outline the codes of behaviour; the form and extent of the penalties but will, however, be at the discretion of the sporting association.

11.7.4 The National Playing Fields Association

Prior to 1925, the supply of public recreational facilities was a local matter with provision being spasmodic and held back by lack of central direction. The National Playing Fields Association, a voluntary body, was founded in 1925 to offer such direction by encouraging the provision of adequate playing fields and recreation facilities throughout the country. The association was incorporated by Royal Charter in 1933; and in 1963 it was registered as a national charity.

Since its inception in 1925, the NPFA has established minimum standards for outdoor playing space. In 1986 the Association reconsidered its own target, set in 1938, for a minimum of six acres per 1000 population of outdoor playing space. This target was reaffirmed for use by local authorities and others, but for the assessing of actual pitch requirements they were referred to Sports Council guidelines.

The main aim of the Association is to stimulate the provision of playing fields, playgrounds and recreation centres by publicity and technical and financial assistance. The work is for the benefit of the whole community, but the major emphasis lies with children, young people and the handicapped.

A small full-time staff implements the policy and decisions of the Association in most counties in England and Wales. There are affiliated Playing Fields Associations and a branch association in Scotland. The Association provides three areas of advisory service, namely technical, grants and loans, and publication and information.

11.7.5 The Countryside Commission

The National Parks and Access to the Countryside Act 1949 created the National Parks Commission and gave it the power to establish national parks. To date, eleven of these parks have been created. Concern soon began to grow, however, about the conflicting claims of conservation and recreation within the national parks and a need was seen to ease the pressure on the parks by developing countryside recreation and conservation in general. To this end, the *Countryside Act 1968* abolished the National Parks Commission and set up the Countryside Commission, with the purpose of keeping under review: 'matters relating to the conservation and enhancement of landscape beauty in England and Wales, and to the provision and improvement of facilities of the countryside for enjoyment, including the need to secure access for open-air recreation'. Independence from the Department of the Environment was granted by the *Wildlife and Countryside Act 1981*, when the Countryside Commission became a grant-in-aid body. Scotland has a separate Countryside Commission, set up under the *Countryside (Scotland) Act 1967*. In 1991, as a result of the Nature Conservency Council being split, responsibility for countryside issues in Wales passed to the Countryside Council for Wales.

The role of the Commission in relation to the countryside is very similar to that of the Sports Council in relation to sport. It does not itself provide facilities, but provides finance and expertise for providing bodies, particularly local authorities. It has the power to aid financially countryside projects, to designate national parks, Areas of Outstanding Natural Beauty and Heritage Coasts, and to advise on countryside planning and management. It undertakes research into all aspects of countryside management and usage and produces educational and informative literature about the countryside in general, and specific areas such as national parks and long-distance footpaths.

11.7.6 The Forestry Commission

The Forestry Commission is the largest landowner in Britain, with 3 million acres. It was constituted in 1919 by an Act of Parliament, being charged with the responsibility for the interests of forestry. Its primary role is that of timber production. In 1935 the Commission recognized the public's need for greater opportunities of access to its forests for recreational purposes and opened the first of its forest parks in Argyll.

In 1970 the Commission set up a conservation and recreation branch at its headquarters and established eleven recreation planning officers in each of its conservancy regions. Recreation plans for each of these regions have been written.

The problems resulting from the primary forest needs, tree planting and felling, and the secondary recreation requirements, need policy sensitivity and diplomatic management. In addition to the user problems, the Commission must make a return on investment. The greater the provision for public recreation, the more difficult it becomes to show the level of profit required.

11.7.7 The Nature Conservancy Council

The Nature Conservancy Council (NCC) was established by *Act of Parliament* in 1973. It has responsibility for 'the conservation of flora, fauna and geological and physiographical features throughout Great Britain'. The Council is an agency, financed by the Department of the Environment, that controls and manages large areas of national nature reserves. In April 1991, the NCC split into three separate bodies, namely the Countryside Council for Wales, English Nature and the Nature Conservancy Council for Scotland, each is responsible for nature conservation in its own area.

11.7.8 The National Rivers Authority

The National Rivers Authority was established by the *Water Act 1989* and became operational the following September. The authority operates through ten regions based upon the ten river catchment areas of England and Wales.

In addition to its responsibilities for environmental protection, pollution control, water resources and flood defence, it is also responsible for the 'promotion of recreational activities such as boating, fishing and walking by rivers'.

11.7.9 National Children's Play and Recreation Unit

Hosted by the Sports Council for a four-year period, the Unit was established in 1989 to 'enhance the range and quality of the childhood experience for all children'. The main objectives of the unit are to:

1. Prepare and carry out a four-year plan of action to place a central service to children's play on a sound basis.
2. Provide a central service to assist existing organizations, both voluntary and statutory, to develop on sound lines the provision of opportunities for children's play and recreation.
3. Consult with and advise government departments, statutory, voluntary and commercial organizations.

Regular mailings from the Unit [19] keep colleagues informed about issues affecting all aspects of children's play and recreation, including legislative issues, demonstration projects, safety, education and training, grants, etc.

Among their initiatives is the 'Accrediting Play Work' project, which aims to give 'credit where credit's due'. The scheme, open to anyone working or intending to work in play, aims to describe and confirm the competence of play workers in England. It is hoped that play workers will then be recognized and rewarded for their work.

In Summary, there are numerous national agencies directly or indirectly involved with the provision of sporting, artistic and recreational opportunity. They are there to fulfil a need, to advise, enable, coordinate, develop, conserve and, in some cases, provide.

This section has outlined very briefly a few of the agencies involved; each source will lead to several more. As a guide to obtaining further information, addresses and contacts are given at the end of the chapter.

11.8 SUMMARY: THE VOLUNTARY SECTOR AND LEISURE

The voluntary sector is extremely large and diversified and is linked with both the public and commercial sectors. It is dominated by clubs, societies and associations. By its sheer volume of organizations and numbers of people, there are more people involved in the 'management' of leisure and recreation in the voluntary sector than in the other sectors. Voluntary organizations give people both the chance to participate and the opportunity to become involved in all levels of organization and management. They also give the opportunity to serve. The range and diversity of voluntary leisure groupings, the motivations of people and the apparent need to belong and to participate with others, are significant factors and as such should be studied by leisure professionals. Clubs offer individuals a group identity. Inter-club competition and rivalries reinforce the identity and sense of belonging. Membership can confer status, offer purposeful activity and a sense of importance.

Voluntary organizations hold one of the keys to personal self-fulfilment; leisure and recreation professionals need to harness their assets and public authorities should enable and encourage their development.

A charitable trust has considerable advantages. It can forge ahead through its own enthusiasm and initiative. It encourages community and commercial support and can save public money. But it needs support from authorities in the way of subsidy, grants, technical advice and help towards capital development costs.

The days of community service having to beg for financial assistance should end and it can do so if local authorities and voluntary organizations collaborate. The trust system can be the bridge between voluntary bodies and statutory authorities; it represents partnership. There is precious little land, money or resources available for organizations and authorities to continue to pay and develop facilities themselves without the widest consultation, cooperation and coordination.

Projects are often well managed where authority lies in a small, strong, high calibre, independent committee, with wide terms of reference and complete control of day-to-day management. This may be easier to achieve in the recreation trust. However, it is important that the committee is independent, has strong powers and is not constantly blown off course by undue political pressure.

Industrial companies provide a large share of the nation's sports facilities. They offer considerable perks to employees and their families and contribute to company cohesion. If these facilities could be more widely available, they would contribute greatly to community recreation. Companies possessing good sports facilities with spare capacity have a ready-made opportunity to demonstrate their goodwill. There are some examples of dual use and extension of club membership to the general community. However, these remain the exceptions.

Although national agencies are not primarily providers of facilities, they have an important role to play in helping to provide resources through financial aid, technical support, research and advice. Some national agencies are not just enablers and semi-government agents, but also employers of leisure and recreation managers. In addition, training for recreation management has been recognized and instigated by agencies such as the Sports Council.

National agencies assist government at all levels and provide help at local level in planning, provision and management. Countryside recreation, for example, is fraught with conflicts of interest between planning, agriculture, forestry, tourism, water resources, sport, recreation and conservation. Leisure management has an important part to play in the network of voluntary bodies and agencies; the Leisure Manager is part of a multi-disciplinary framework for leisure planning and management.

REFERENCES AND NOTES

1. English Tourist Board (1981), *Aspects of Leisure and Holiday Tourism*, ETB, London.
2. Thompson, E. P. (1967), quoted in Tomlinson, A. *Sports Council/Social Science Research Council Review: Leisure and the Role of Clubs and Voluntary Groups*, Sports Council/SSRC, London, 1979.
3. Central Statistical Office (1990), *Social Trends 20*, HMSO, London.
4. English Tourist Board (1981), *Aspects of Leisure and Holiday Tourism*, ETB, London.
5. Tomlinson, A. (1979), *Sports Council/Social Science Research Council Review: Leisure and the Role of Clubs and Voluntary Groups*, Sports Council/SSRC, London.
6. Hutson, S. (n.d.), *Sports Council, Social Science Research Council: A Review of the Role of Clubs and Voluntary Associations based on a Study of Two Areas in Swansea*, Sports Council/SSRC, London.
7. Wolfenden Committee (1978), *The Future of Voluntary Organisations*, Croom Helm, London.
8. Cullen, P. (1966–7), Whither industrial recreation now? *Sport and Recreation*, **7**, 4 October 1966, and **8**, 1 January 1967, Central Council of Physical Recreation, London.
9. Parker, S. (1971), *The Future of Work and Leisure*, MacGibbon and Kee, London.
10. Cullen, P. Industrial Recreation Survey, 1979–80, unpublished data and notes on findings.
11. Ministry of Housing and Local Government Urban Planning Directorate (1967), *Provision of Playing Pitches in New Towns*, MHLG, London.
12. Sillitoe, K. K. (1969), *Government Social Survey. Planning for Leisure*, HMSO, London.
13. Greater London and South East Council for Sport and Recreation (1971), *Industry and Community Recreation: Report on a Working Party*, GLSESR, London.

14. Sports Council Study Group (1968), *The Pilkington Report*, Sports Council, London.
15. Wilding, R. (1989), *Supporting the Arts. A Review of the Structure of Arts Funding, 1989* (Minister for the Arts), HMSO, London.
16. Wolfenden Committee (1969), *Sports and the Community*, Central Council of Physical Recreation, London.
17. Department of the Environment (1977), *Circular 73/77: Guidelines for Regional Recreational Strategies*, DoE, London.
18. E.g. Justin Evans, H. (1974), *Service to Sport – the Story of the CCPR, 1935 to 1972*, Sports Council, London.
19. National Children's Play and Recreation Unit, Information Pack (Summer 1990).

NATIONAL AGENCIES

The Arts Council,
105 Piccadilly,
London W1V OAU

The Arts Council, Scottish,
12 Mannor Place,
Edinburgh EH3 7DD

The Arts Council, Welsh,
Holst House,
Museum Place,
Cardiff CF1 3NX

The Sports Council,
16 Upper Woburn Place,
London WC1H 0QP

Sports Council for Wales,
National Sports Centre For Wales,
Sophia Gardens,
Cardiff CF1 9SW

Scottish Sports Council,
Caledonia House,
South Gyle,
Edinburgh EH12 9DQ

Sports Council for Northern Ireland,
House of Sport,
Upper Malone Road,
Belfast BT9 5LA

Central Council for Physical Recreation,
Francis House,
Francis Street,
London SW1P 1DE

The National Playing Fields Association,
25 Ovington Square,
London SW3 1LQ

The Countryside Commission,
John Dower House,
Crescent Place,
Cheltenham GL50 3RA

The Forestry Commission,
231 Corstorphine Road,
Edinburgh EH12 7AT

The National Rivers Authority,
30–34 Albert Embankment,
London SE1 7TL

National Childrens Play and Recreation Unit,
359–361 Euston Road,
London NW1 3AL

Chapter 12

Leisure provision in the commercial sector

In Chapters 10 and 11 we have focused attention on the public and voluntary providers, and it was shown that there is a level of integration and overlap between them. This chapter is concerned with the commercial sector.

The major difference between the commercial organization and the public or voluntary organization is that the primary objective of the commercial operator is financial profit or an adequate return on investment. The other sectors may make profits but they are established primarily for other reasons.

This chapter, *first*, aims to provide an overview of the commercial leisure sector; and *second*, each of the main constituent elements making up the 'commercial package', relating to the home, social recreation, entertainment, sport, art, tourism, and sponsorship, are covered as distinct units, although their interrelationships cannot be overlooked.

Having read this chapter, readers will learn that while the motive for commercial leisure provision is different from the other sectors, there is still overlap, inter-sectorial involvement and collaboration such that the strict demarcation lines are not indelibly drawn. An appreciation will be gained of the power of the commercial leisure sector to attract mass markets and also the public's attraction to its products.

People's residual income is taken up in large proportion with commercial products and services. Students will learn that commercial operators, while meeting demands and needs by providing what the public wants and is willing to pay for, also create demands, which hitherto people were unaware of wanting. Leisure Managers need to learn some of the skills shown by the commercial sector in developing, marketing and delivering leisure services. Both commercial and non-profit organizations must attract customers – or fail.

12.1 COMMERCIAL PROVIDERS OF LEISURE SERVICES AND FACILITIES

Commercial organizations do not have an intrinsic interest in leisure and recreation, in and of itself, but in leisure as a source of profit. This is not to say that many organizations and managers are not deeply involved in leisure and recreation, nor is it to say that there is no altruism on the part of the providers. Indeed, patronage has long been an element in recreation provision, and commercial support has kept alive many activities which would not otherwise have survived. In addition, the mass media have been responsible for increasing interest and participation in a whole range of leisure pursuits, such as snooker, darts, bowls, golf and even collecting antiques. However, while there is a desire to increase the popularity of a number of leisure pursuits, commercial operations (outside the realm of patronage) will only maintain their interest if there is direct or indirect benefit to the organization.

In terms of numbers, millions of people buy sports equipment and cinema tickets, eat out socially, drink, smoke, gamble, watch television and are entertained in their leisure time through services and products provided commercially. The objective of the commercial provider is to make money by serving the public; the public provider is also concerned with serving the public. Hence the enterprise, whether public or commercial, must attract the public or fail.

However, does the commercial provider provide the products and services that the public actually needs or wants, or is the public persuaded to want them? Is the public obliged to take what is on offer? Product choice is often limited in order to streamline production. For example, a few large breweries control the majority of Britain's public houses. Without voluntary consumer organizations such as CAMRA (Campaign for Real Ale) the specific wishes of people could become secondary to products and distribution efficiency.

The commercial provider is therefore in essence, different from other providers – being, literally, in it for the money. Yet many private businesses are not always 'commercial'; they do not make profits; 40% of American commercial ventures apparently never make a profit, but break even or go under, and 50% of the rest of the companies make only marginal profits. In such a climate, many private/commercial leisure organizations find it hard to stay in business and, compared to public sector business, competition is fierce and many companies and services go under. Changing trends in leisure and leisure spending add to this uncertainty.

In recent years, we have seen a significant increase in the British commercial leisure market and currently this includes sports clubs, squash clubs, indoor tennis, indoor bowls, swimming pools, sports villages and sporting holidays, country clubs, themed restaurants, ten-pin bowling, bingo, etc. Hence the commercial leisure industry is made up of many thousands of businesses, from the neighbourhood sports or hobbies shops to the giant multinationals.

While the industry is widely diversified and contains many retailers with only a few full-time staff and Saturday part-timers, the large companies predominate. The commercial sector is dominant in the provision of hotels, amusement parks, theme parks, holiday camps, cinemas, theatres, bowling alleys, ice skating, horse racing, greyhound and speedway tracks, bingo halls, restaurants, public houses, ballrooms and others. Despite major developments by relatively large companies, however, these providers are dwarfed by the expanding leisure giants – the multinational companies.

The most significant change over the past two decades has been the increase in the size of the multinational companies through mergers, takeovers and diversification of interests. They dominate the commercial leisure industry.

12.2 HOME-BASED LEISURE

Commercial providers have enormous influence in home leisure pursuits. The *General Household Survey* shows the most frequent rates of leisure participation, both passive and active pursuits engaged in at home.

The nature of home-based leisure activities and their enjoyment will be affected by factors such as housing conditions, availability of a garden and standard of living. Leisure-time use will vary according to the home itself, home improvements, family interests and hobbies, and material possessions of the household, which may be leisure 'instruments' in themselves (television, video, radio) or may be time-saving appliances (vacuum cleaners, washing machines) which release members of the household from various tasks, so creating greater leisure time. Another often underrated factor pertaining to leisure at home is the keeping of pets, including many millions of domestic cats and dogs.

Research commissioned by the Sports Council/ESRC [1] into leisure and the home found that four-fifths of all activities and three-quarters of all leisure activities took place there. Activity in the home dominated life in all social groups, especially women, single parents, retirement and pre-retirement age groups, the professional classes and the unemployed. Their research showed little linkage between life-styles, social profiles, housing or household characteristics; However, they concluded:

'Though basic use patterns varied little, different types of homes offered contrasting potential as centres for leisure. People's satisfaction with their homes related to some extent to what they were able to do there and to how well the home accommodated their equipment and activities'.

Three broad areas of home-based leisure have been artificially devised and separated, but only for descriptive purposes in this section. They are (i) the media in the home; (ii) the home as an object of leisure and (iii) the home as an area for recreation and social activity. In reality, the areas overlap or are interwoven. Moreover, elements such as reading newspapers are bound up with going to work, as much as with leisure in the home.

12.2.1 The media in the home

The media have the most influential effect on leisure in terms of what people do with their time. Media in the home revolves around not only television viewing, but also radio, records, tapes, video, hi-fi, newspapers, books and magazines.

The motivations for watching television are likely to include a mixture of needs for entertainment, information, education, social cohesion (e.g. watching television may become a 'family activity') or simply because there is, either through lack of opportunity or apathy, nothing else to do. Furthermore, television is cheap. Viewing appears to be the most frequent among children and the elderly, although overall there has been an increase in the time spent watching television over the past fifteen years.

The commercial sectors' direct involvement with television revolves around the commercial stations which make the programmes and advertise products, and in the manufacture of the television sets themselves. According to the BBC [2], in 1989, the average weekly time spent watching television was 24 hours 44 minutes, a decrease of 1 hour 49 minutes since 1985. With the occurrence of satellite TV, this will undoubtedly rise. The number of cable television franchises for homes in Britain in 1989 is estimated to be 7 million, an increase of 4.7 million on the figure for 1987.

The commercial sector is also involved in a number of other ways with leisure provision via the television. The biggest influence is, of course, that of advertising. A second is the recent expansion of the video recorder market. A third is the use of the television for active participation (i.e. video games). A fourth growth area is the use of the television as an information service, for example, Ceefax, Oracle and TeleText.

Projections for the future use of television indicate that leisure behaviour could be markedly affected by technological advances. Many see mechanisms such as Ceefax as being the forerunners of more sophisticated systems, where not only will information about leisure pursuits such as concerts, sporting events, theater and entertainment, and even clubs and organizations specializing in particular activities or hobbies, be more readily accessible, but it may also be possible to book and pay for tickets, restaurants, etc. via the same system. Only time will show whether such advances will be universally accepted and used. Some have suggested that the growth of home-based leisure could be the embryo of an introverted society. In 1979 a Finnish social psychologist wrote 'The family is alive but not well!' [3].

In relation to listening to the radio, it is interesting to query how much time spent in so doing is purely for leisure, and in fact how much is actually home-based. Often the radio is listened to in conjunction with the pursuit of markedly non-leisure activities, such as doing the housework, cooking and driving to work, and it would be interesting to see whether this accounted for the greater part of radio-listening time. In addition, because of the portable nature of the radio, it is not a solely home-based medium, providing entertainment and information when travelling (either in a car or on foot) and in conjunction with other leisure pursuits such as visiting the beach or sitting in the park.

Listening to records and tapes is another booming home-based leisure pursuit. However, since 1979 the United Kingdom record companies have suffered a slump in business which, in 1983, was only partially offset by the boom in sales of 12-inch singles. 'Singles' carry all the disadvantages of hit or miss and the fees demanded by artists continue to spiral. Some small independent labels in contrast have continued to increase in a modest way. The effects of the video disc and compact disc, in addition, are becoming significant. In 1989 sales of compact disc exceeded sales of long play albums for the first time.

The written word is another source of home recreation although, as with the radio, it is not solely a home-based pursuit. Publication of newspapers, magazines and books is primarily the prerogative of commercial organizations, although private, voluntary and government organizations publish technical and research material that could conceivably be read for pleasure. Direct commercial involvement can also be found with the organization of book clubs, while indirectly leisure behaviour may be influenced by the content of magazines, both in terms of their advertising and the values they promote.

The extent of the popularity of the written word can be found in the National Readership Survey of 1988 [4]. This discovered that 70% of men and 64% of women aged 15 and over read at least one national daily newspaper and 74% of men and 71% of women read at least one Sunday newspaper. On average, 37% of the population (aged 15 or over) read a general weekly magazine in 1988.

12.2.2 The home as an object of leisure

The house and garden can in themselves offer opportunities for leisure activity, depending on whether home improvement and gardening are viewed by the individual as leisure or as an unwelcome commitment. Whatever the motivation, there appears to be an increase in activity in this area. Home improvements together with normal house maintenance entail considerable expenditure on do-it-yourself tools and equipment.

Gardening and the provision of gardening implements is the other area of 'home improvement' in which the commercial sector is involved. The 1986 *General Household Survey* indicated that 43% of the population partake in gardening and the popularity of the garden (either as a place for cultivation or for other leisure activity) is reflected in the recent growth in the number of garden centres, and in the associated increase in the range of products sold.

12.2.3 The home for leisure and social activity

As well as accommodating the various leisure media, the home can be used as a base for recreation and social activity, for the playing of indoor games, for informal gatherings, parties, hobbies and other activities. The commercial sector's involvement here is with the provision of the necessary accountrements and equipment for the pursuit of such activities.

Alcohol is one such provision. The increasing popularity of home drinking is indicated by the increase in off-licence sales, and the rise in the number of off-licences.

The sale of tobacco might also be added to home-based social provision, although as with radios, it is neither an exclusively home-based activity nor a purely leisure one. Its popularity, or rather that of cigarettes, has been waning with a drop in sales over the past decade due largely to greater public awareness of the potential health hazards and the restrictions imposed on advertising. However, there seems to have been a compensatory rise in sales of the 'safer' tobacco products such as cigars and pipe tobacco. While the actual expenditure on tobacco has risen, the percentage of total consumer expenditure has been decreasing steadily since the early 1960s.

Home-based leisure in terms of playing indoor games and playing with toys has been a developing market. The developing 'technology' games, the insatiable demand for more updated board games such as 'Dallas', 'Risk' or 'Trivial Pursuit' and the innovation of world best-sellers like Rubik's Cube stimulate commercial investment and expenditure by the public.

12.3 SOCIAL RECREATION OUTSIDE THE HOME

Moving away from home as an area for and object of leisure activity, provision in terms of social recreation can be divided up in a number of ways – e.g. gambling, eating and drinking out, window shopping and many more.

12.3.1 The sale of alcohol

One institution which seems to perform a unique and distinctive function is the public house. As a focal point for social activity, the selling of alcohol, and often staging live music events, the pub would appear to cater for a variety of needs. The breweries not only cater directly for leisure activity via their own outlets, but also give financial aid to private clubs in the form of grants and loans for the improvement or expansion of premises, usually in return for use of their products. Sales of alcoholic drink associated with eating out are also high.

The alcohol industry is dominated by the few major breweries, although consumer demand, focused through consumer organizations, has led to the growth of some small, independent breweries.

In 1989 the Monopolies Commission released its report into the brewery 'tie'. The report examined a system which permitted six breweries virtually to dictate the habits and tastes of the British pub-going public. The original recommendation stated that breweries should sell all of their pubs over a 2000 limit. After a watering down of the recommendation, it was decided that breweries with over 2000 pubs would be forced to cut the tie with half of their outlets over the limit and be allowed the right to sell 50% of the excess pubs which they cut free from the tie. Undoubtedly, smaller, unprofitable pubs will be sold and the number of pubs will decrease. This could have a dramatic effect on smaller communities.

12.3.2 Gambling

Another favourite area of social recreation is that of gambling. This includes amusement arcades, the football pools, bingo, on- and off-course betting, casinos, lotteries, and even Stock Exchange dealings on the outcome of the World Cup football finals! Gambling turnover – consumer expenditure minus winnings – has increased by approximately 10% over the past few years. It is estimated that over the next few years, with the onset of satellite information service systems, improved facilities including corporate hospitality boxes, restaurants, etc., attendances and spending will continue to rise.

It would appear from all the data available that four out of every five people in Britain gamble in one form or another, despite the drop in the number of betting shops and the drop in spectator attendances. Betting has been encouraged by new government legislation, new technologies and greater commercial marketing. For example, bingo, having been in decline for over a decade, has experienced a formidable turnaround and reaped the benefits of refurbishment, rationalization and the national game link-up. Bingo is even altering its 'older generation' image with a new breed of young players entering the game.

The amount of money gambled in Britain's casinos rose by 9.4% in 1989. The total 'drop' was £1881 million in 119 casinos; this came after two years of falling stakes. The amount staked in the 978 bingo clubs between September 1988 and August 1989 totalled £641.46 million, an increase of 2.4% on the previous year's figures [5]. New government legislation came into force in spring 1986, allowing the sale and consumption of non-alcohol drinks and refreshments in betting shops.

Since the *Lotteries and Amusements Act 1976*, which came into force in May 1977, the Gaming Board of Great Britain is responsible for all local authority and society lottery schemes. Repeated calls have been made on government to introduce a national lottery to help fund health, welfare, sport and the arts.

12.4 ENTERTAINMENT AND THE ARTS

Commercial leisure provision for entertainment and the arts outside the home covers a number of areas, although these can be divided into two basic categories: that which encourages active participation (e.g. ballrooms, discos, dance schools and, perhaps, some other commercially provided education courses such as language learning), and that in which provision is generally geared towards audience and spectators. This section deals primarily with the latter, for active participation can easily fit into other categories of leisure.

Dancing is one of those activities which is difficult to categorize under one heading, probably being as comfortable under social recreation or active indoor physical recreation as it is under entertainment and the arts. Dancing, as revealed by the General Household Survey of 1986, is a most popular entertainment activity, attracting 11% of the population. It is most popular among the 16–19 year age groups.

12.4.1 Audience and spectator activities

Attending the cinema and theatre, going to popular and classical concerts, visiting art galleries or going to shows and cabarets are all part of the audience and spectator activities provided by the commercial sector. Cinema attendances have, however, fallen dramatically from a peak of 1635 million in 1946 to 156.6 million in 1972 and then to an all-time low of 63.1 million in 1983. Yet cinemas, like bingo, are experiencing an upturn in their fortunes. Admissions in 1988 were 78 million, and in 1989, 88 million.

Although there has been a decline in the number of cinema sites, there has been a corresponding increase in the number of screens; this was brought about by the division of many of the existing cinemas into multi-screen units. However, the decline in the number of cinema sites has left many towns without cinemas and commercial organizations now consider 30 000 as the minimum population to support a cinema. This policy can cause problems when new districts are built with a population less than 30 000 but have a high proportion of young people.

The advent of multi-screen complexes with 6, 8, 10 or even 12 screens, many at out-of-town sites, will add further to the accessibility factor and will cater for the mobile populations. The development of multiplex cinemas with well-designed, comfortable surroundings, offering food, car parking, computerized booking and choice has contributed to maintaining and increasing admissions in the United Kingdom.

Going to the theatre is not as popular as going to the cinema. Only a very small percentage of the population attend the theatre, opera or ballet. In 1988 the total number of West End theatre attendances amounted to 10.9 million. Research has shown that the majority of attenders come from the age group 25–34, the fewest being in the age groups 55–64 and 65+ [6].

One-half of the professional theatres in Britain are owned or rented by commercial companies. Of these, nearly one-third are found in London; but West End theatres are finding it difficult to make a profit, owing to competition from subsidized national theatres and now civic suburban theatres, and there is a declining number of commercial theatres in the provinces to accommodate touring plays and musicals.

Visits to museums and art galleries have increased over the past few years. The 1987 *GHS* indicates that 8% of females and 9% of males attended museums and art galleries in the four weeks prior to interview.

There are over 100 commercial art galleries in London, which all tend to be small and specialized, compared with about 10 in the public sector, which tend to be large and comprehensive.

12.5 SPORT AND PHYSICAL RECREATION

All the indications point to the conclusion that sport is an expanding market. More people are playing sport, more sports are being played and consumer spending on goods and services is likely to keep rising during the next five years. Commercial providers are concerned in sport and physical recreation in a number of key areas, for example, active sport participation, spectator sport, facilities, sports sponsorship and leisure and sports goods and equipment.

12.5.1 Active sport

The commercial sector is involved in the provision of facilities for participants in only a limited number of sports. Of the outdoor sports, only golf, tennis and water sports are provided in any great numbers by commercial concerns, and in the case of golf and tennis, these are sometimes provided as part of a leisure complex which also provides squash, table tennis, snooker and other ancillary facilities. The growth and further growth in golf in the United Kingdom, Europe, the Far East and throughout many parts of the world is phenomenal and will be largely commercially led.

Of the indoor sports, snooker, ten-pin bowling, squash, ice skating, indoor tennis and, most recently, leisure swimming pools are being provided by commercial organizations. However, with the onset of Compulsory Competitive Tendering, management will undoubtedly expand to include leisure centres, indoor bowls, swimming pools, etc. currently under the management of the public sector.

Participation in sport and physical recreation, whether in local authority, voluntary or commercial facilities, usually requires an outlay for kit and equipment. The commercial sector is inevitably involved in the provision of such equipment and there appears to be an expanding market for these goods.

12.5.2 Spectator sports

Commercial enterprise tends to deal with only a few sports in terms of spectatorship. Association Football is still the most popular spectator sport (here 'spectator sport' refers to actual attendance, rather than watching via the television set). Soccer spectatorship has declined since the postwar years, when spectators amounted to 41 million attendances in the 1948/49 season dropping to 16.5 million by the end of the 1985/86 season in the English Football League matches. Since 1985/86, there has been a slight increase in attendances to 19.4 million in the 1989/90 season [7].

Spectator sports, apart from some football, rugby and cricket internationals and events such as Wimbledon, are generally less lucrative in terms of receipts from attendance, although many popular indoor spectator sports such as indoor tennis, indoor show-jumping and boxing lend themselves to viewing by comparatively large audiences. There are, however, some indoor sports such as snooker, and more recently darts, which cannot accommodate large audiences on site but which, nevertheless, have become popular spectator sports through the medium of television. Indoor bowls is another sport which has gained popularity through television.

Hence, although there has been a decline in the traditional spectator sports, others have increased in following, many as a direct or indirect result of television coverage and commercial sponsorship. Tennis and golf are examples.

12.5.3 Leisure goods and equipment

A substantial industry to supply leisure goods, clothing and equipment has developed. The manufacture, distribution and retailing of a vast range of goods exists, from yachts, canoes, tents, bicycles and hang-gliders, to tracksuits and special footwear, to rackets, balls, snooker tables, dartboards, trampolines and goal-posts, to hi-fi, records, video, electronic devices and games of every kind, and to gardening implements and do-it-yourself tools.

The Henley Centre for Forecasting states that, in 1991, consumer spending on leisure will reach £81.7 billion. The effects of current high mortgage rates and the Community Charge (or its replacement) will hit leisure spending quite dramatically initially, but forecasts remain optimistic for long-term growth.

12.6 TOURISM AND HOLIDAYS

The commercial sector is closely involved with the tourist industry. This industry might be seen very broadly as providing for three markets in the United Kingdom:

1. Foreign visitors to UK.
2. Britons holidaying (including visiting tourist attractions, day trips, etc.) in UK.
3. Britons holidaying abroad.

Inevitably, the provision for all three markets is interlinked with some facilities and services provided by the commercial sector used by both foreigners and Britons alike, and with British travel agents organizing holidays both at home and abroad. There is also a close interrelationship between the commercial sector and others – private, voluntary, local authorities and government-funded bodies such as the British Tourist Authority (BTA) – who also provide for and influence tourist development.

In 1990 government ministers were quoting a United Kingdom tourist market supporting 1.5 million jobs, with a turnover of over £22 billion. The definition of a tourist according to the English Tourist Board is 'anyone staying away from home for more than 24 hours'. However, within that definition there are various forms, and closely linked to tourism are day visitors or 'day trippers' who return home within 24 hours.

12.6.1 Spending in the United Kingdom

It is estimated that approximately 17.9 million foreign visitors came to the UK during 1990. Spending by these inbound tourists in 1990 amounted to £7.7 billion (excluding visits from Eire). By the mid-1990s, the BTA estimate that over 20 million foreign visitors will come to the UK each year.

In 1990 British residents took approximately 31 million trips abroad. Spending by British residents abroad reached record levels of £9.8 billion.

It is estimated that between 640–920 million day trips are made each year in the United Kingdom [8]. Although there are no accurate estimates, this growth is expected to continue over the next decade as disposable income and the amount of leisure time continue to increase.

12.6.2 Accommodation

Historically, London has been the premier tourist destination within the United Kingdom, attracting consistently high levels of visitors due to its position as the capital city and the seat of government, and the centre for business, culture and entertainment.

The overflow in demand for London bedspace has resulted in a shift to the provinces. This has proved beneficial to traditional tourist centres such as the south coast resorts, Stratford-upon-Avon, York and Edinburgh. The ETB surveys have illustrated that approx. 60% of overseas visitors now travel outside of London during their British visit. However, popular 'attractions' are at saturation and methods of dispersing tourists to other venues is being actively encouraged.

Both foreign and British tourists require accommodation and this could involve any of a number of options, ranging from hotels to camping and caravanning sites and holiday homes. The types of accommodation may be simply a base from which to tour or visit the surrounding area, or it may provide leisure activity in its own right such as holiday camps or hotels that provide sporting and entertainment facilities. At the Aviemore Centre, for example, in the beautiful Spey Valley, leisure facilities include swimming, squash, ice skating and curling. A number of first-class hotels are clustered around the Centre and caravan parks extend the variety of services and self-service accommodation.

Hotel groups such as Forte and Queens Moat Houses are linking leisure facilities to their hotels to increase their attractiveness to visitors. Many prestige hotels, particularly in holiday resorts, have sporting facilities, swimming pools, squash courts and tennis courts within the hotel precinct. A good example is the Gleneagles Hotel at the world famous golf course which has an indoor pool, saunas and spas, tennis and squash courts, in addition to bowls, shooting, equestrian and fishing facilities. Leisure facilities at hotels offer an additional lure to customers, even though only one in ten residents may actually use the facilities. Leisure facilities are, however, becoming particularly important in the short break and business markets.

The proportion of holidays taken in British hotels would appear to have dropped since 1961. A corresponding increase in the use of other forms of holiday accommodation is evenly spread between camping, caravanning, rented accommodation, holiday camps and staying with friends or relatives. Bargain weekend breaks and other marketing initiatives may well have halted this decline.

12.6.3 Holidays

The number of holidays taken by British holidaymakers has increased long term for both holidays in Britain and holidays abroad. Approximately 60% of British residents in the United Kingdom now take a holiday, although the number and length of stay are affected by personal characteristics. Short breaks and particularly activity holidays (ranging from archery to mountain biking and white water canoeing) are becoming very popular as second/seasonal holidays.

12.6.4 Theme Parks

As well as organizing tours, the commercial sector is also involved with the provision and maintenance of tourist attractions such as historical buildings, zoos, wildlife and amusement parks and theme parks.

Over the past several years, there has been considerable growth in the British theme park industry. Theme parks have become very popular since Disneyland resurrected the amusement park industry, in 1955, in the United States. Their philosophy has been one of excellence, cleanliness, courtesy and safety. They create an atmosphere of fantasy, glamour, escapism, prestige and excitement. These parks have been successful in other countries such as Summerland, in Tokyo, and Tivoli, in Copenhagen. Theme parks are privately operated concerns with attractions built around one or more historical or fantasy themes.

Britain's first theme park was Thorpe Water Park at Chertsey, the concept and development of Leisure Sport Ltd, its theme maritime history. The predominant theme is water with activities such as water skiing and tourist attractions such as 'Bluebird' and Viking Longships. Its development encouraged the provision of other 'theme' facilities elsewhere in the United Kingdom. However, many of the theme parks have not been resounding success stories. Britain's only world-rated theme park is Alton Towers, in Staffordshire. It offers a combination of magnificent surroundings, historic heritage and fun and fantasy. Alton

Towers has been transformed from the stately home and gardens into one of the finest leisure parks in the world. Other British examples include American Adventure, Pleasurewood Hills, Camelot, Gulliver's Kingdom, Chessington World of Adventures, Lightwater Valley, etc.

The UK theme market is extremely competitive. Every month several developments are proposed. Britain's history provides numerous ready-made themes, it has a day-trip tradition and it is densely populated; there must, however, be a limit to development. Projection 2000 estimate that admissions could double from approx. 8 million to 16 million between 1990 and the year 2000. Even though all social classes visit theme parks, the C1/2 family is the prime target.

The effects of the Single European Market and the opening of the Channel Tunnel on the theme park industry have yet to be fully determined. However, the construction of 'Euro Disney' – already underway – indicates the level of competition that the market in the United Kingdom is likely to face.

12.6.5 Tourism and transport

This very brief sketch of tourism and the commercial provider's role would be incomplete without some reference to leisure transport. Travel and the mode of transport can be a leisure activity in itself, whether by car, coach, boat, barge, train or plane. The importance of the commercial sector and leisure travel is summed up by Roberts [9]:

'Transport as a leisure activity in itself (pleasure motoring, from home, canal boat tours, sea cruises etc.) as a linkage between home and leisure destinations, or a means of enlarging their destination's attractions (coach tours, car trips, boat trips, fishing excursions etc.), forms a high proportion of leisure expenditure. The commercial sector is directly or indirectly involved in all leisure transport modes in addition to the private car. The sector owns and operates shipping lines, aircraft, coaches, some railways in Continental Europe, taxis, pleasure boats and others. It supplies cars and bicycles for hire; provides catering services; provides the boots for hikers, and the shoes for less ambitious walkers. The supply of equipment generally (for example bicycles) is the prerogative of the commercial sector. Finally, it provides marinas and often owns seaside piers which provide landing stages for shipping'.

The tourism and holiday market is a major commercial leisure industry. It is another expanding area in which the emerging profession of recreation management must consider the management of leisure opportunity for people. Two aspects are worth noting. First, there are a number of personal and social reasons for travel which may be as important as the destination itself. Second, travel is normally expensive and those who can afford it can go further and in greater comfort. Poorer people travel less. Even a journey across a large city with a young family could be formidable. More than most forms of leisure, travel is shaped by cost, both direct and indirect.

12.7 SPONSORSHIP

Sponsorship has been defined as 'the provision of financial or material support for some independent activity which is not intrinsic to the furtherances of commercial aims, but from which the supporting company might reasonably hope to gain financial benefits' [10]. It differs from patronage where the financial, material or professional expertise is given by a commercial company to an activity for philanthropic reasons, without looking for any material reward or benefit.

Sponsorship can benefit the company in a number of ways:

1. By increasing publicity.
2. By helping to reinforce or change its corporate image.
3. By improving public relations, improving trade relations or providing a vehicle for the promotion of company products.
4. By increasing market share.

The scale of sponsorship can vary enormously, from contributions of millions of pounds from a multinational company for national sports to the donation of a cup or prize from a small sports shop to a locally run competition.

12.7.1 Sports and the arts

Sports sponsorship began to develop in the United Kingdom in the early 1960s and dramatically expanded with the ban placed on television cigarette advertising. The cigarette companies had budgeted for television advertising, a large part of which was consequently redirected into sponsorship of sport, since sport had a wide appeal and helped promote a 'healthy image', thus attempting to counteract antismoking propaganda, and probably, most important, lending itself to surrogate advertising through the press and television. However, in 1977 the Minister for Sport placed a ceiling on the amount of sponsorship that cigarette companies could give to sport, and there has been a consequent withdrawal of some companies from this area of sponsorship.

Sponsorship has helped some sports to survive and others to flourish. Snooker and darts are cases in point, but other, once minority, spectator sports are now thriving. For example, basketball has turned from being an insignificant British spectator sport into an expanding one and a deal worth £1.3 million was arranged with Carlsberg, in 1990, and involved amalgamation of the top teams from the two main leagues. Ice hockey and indoor bowls have experienced a similar growth pattern.

The exact amount of sports sponsorship is difficult to ascertain, many companies and governing bodies being reluctant to reveal information. Spending on sports sponsorship events in the United Kingdom is much greater than that for the arts, the latter accounting for approx. 10%. However, there are signs that some sponsors are shifting their ground in favour of the arts. Until recent years, the arts were more the subject of commercial patronage.

Although the majority of sponsorships are a success story, there are some financial disasters; or companies do not achieve expected targets; or the company's name no longer has benefits in one or another direction. The brief history of sponsorship has shown it to be a rapidly changing and fluctuating 'industry'. Among the problems are that the larger the sponsorship investment, the greater the implications on the activity and the greater the harmful effects if sponsorship is withdrawn. With many sport and art events, or leagues or clubs, the need for continuity is essential.

12.7.2 The major companies

It is apparent that although there are many hundreds of commercial companies sponsoring all manner of leisure pursuits and events, national and international sport and art events gain the most from sponsorship. It is also clear that it is the major companies investing heavily in sponsorship that dominate the market financially.

As might be expected, the major sports services and equipment companies have a considerable stake in sports sponsorship. However, in cash terms the major sponsors tend to be the national banks, the oil companies, tobacco manufacturers and brewers. The Whitbread Round the World yacht race and the Virginia Slims Tennis Tournaments are typical.

Why do the 'big four' – banks, oil, tobacco and alcohol – need sponsorship? Although commercially powerful, they are vulnerable to a tarnished public image. Banking and oil are connected with huge profits, drinking is linked with alcoholism and crime, and smoking with lung cancer. Sponsorship helps to buy respectability. Respectability means a good public image. Good images create favourable impressions to buy products and services. The major sponsor's main motive is not to aid sport and the arts, *per se*, but to achieve maximum publicity. Maximum publicity means exposure on television. By far the greatest sponsorship of sport is seen on the two BBC television channels. The BBC's charter, however, explicitly forbids paid advertising. Commercial television cannot sponsor. However, the line between advertising and sponsorship is somewhat tenuous.

There appears to be a qualitative difference between the two. The publication of a company brand name constitutes advertising; the company's name does not. The company nevertheless can get more exposure per hour for its name than would be permissible on the independent television network. During two successive popular weekends taken at random in the summer of 1990, examination of the *Radio Times* revealed that over 30 hours of BBC television (BBC1 and 2) coverage was given to sponsored sporting events during the four days.

Sports and arts sponsorship is big business. Detailed computer compilations costing several hundreds of pounds are available from companies such as Sportscan which give detailed information about who sponsors sport, for how much and why. Since the mid-1980s more and more companies have become involved in the sponsorship of sport and the arts. There has also been a much wider spread of activity across not only events and new events, but in coaching, training, award schemes, youth, women's activities, facilities and equipment, as well as teams and individuals [11]. With the increased popularity of sponsorship, the fourth television channel, breakfast television and satellite television, British sponsorship via the media will increase still further.

From a leisure management viewpoint, whether companies are advertising or sponsoring events and projects, they are all marketing to draw customers to their services and products by creating favourable impressions, so that people will buy what the company has to offer rather than a competitor's product.

12.8 SUMMARY: COMMERCIAL PROVIDERS OF LEISURE

The major difference between the commercial operator and the public or voluntary operator is the *raison d'être* of the business, the primary objective of the commercial operator being that of financial profit or adequate return on investment. Other sectors may make profits but are established and in being for other primary purposes.

Commercial providers of facilities, services and products for leisure consumption have by far the greatest influence on people's use of leisure time. This is seen particularly in leisure in and around the home and in social recreation. The holiday and tourist industry is an expanding commercial market and the continuing rise in active recreation has expanded the leisure and sports goods markets. Sponsorship has made it possible to promote many sports and arts events and has helped to bring major sporting and entertainment attractions of the highest calibre into the homes of millions of people through television.

Despite the overlap between the three main sectors, the commercial sector is different from the others. The commercial provider is in it for the money! In order to reap the best profits and returns on investment, management policies, approaches and techniques are often very different from those employed in the public sector. The Leisure Manager should be aware of the differences and learn which approaches and techniques are best applied to specific situations. Many general management principles will apply to all recreation, whether in the public, private or commercial sectors. However, many specific differences will apply to different management situations. Leisure management is thus both general and specific.

Commercial leisure is a massive industry. It is limited, however, in what is likely to be provided through its market. Capital investment must produce an adequate return on investment and this therefore excludes many costly land-based resources (apart from 'resort' attractions inland and on the coast) and social service elements. The need for coordination between the public, commercial and voluntary sectors is thus of immense importance. Such coordination should fall upon local government in general, and upon leisure professionals in particular.

REFERENCES AND NOTES

1. Glyptis, S., McInnes, H. and Patmore, J. A. (1987), *Leisure and the Home*, Sports Council/ESRC, London.
2. Broadcasters Audience Research Board, BBC Audits of Great Britain, reported in Central Statistical Office, *Social Trends 1991*, HMSO, London.
3. Tolkki-Nikkonen, M. (1979), *Adult Education in Finland*, No. 3.
4. National Readership Survey 1988, reported in Central Statistical Office, *Social Trends 1990*, HMSO, London.
5. Gaming Board Annual Report, 1989–90.
6. City University Research for the Society of West End Theatres, reported in Central Statistical Office, *Social Trends 1991*, HMSO, London.
7. Football Trust (1990), *Digest of Football Statistics 1989*, Football Trust, London.
8. English Tourist Board and Jones Long Wooton (1989), *Retail Leisure and Tourism*, ETB, London.
9. Roberts, J. (TEST) (1979), *Sports Council/Social Science Research Council Review: The Commercial Sector in Leisure*, Sports Council/SSCR, London, p. 12.
10. English Tourist Board (1978), *The Give and Take of Sponsorship*, ETB, London.
11. *Sportscan* (1989), Sports Sponsorship Computer Analysis, July–December, 1984, London.

Chapter 13

Management

The first part of this book has dealt with leisure and the needs of people, and the second part with planning and provision for leisure. This chapter starts the third part, the management of leisure. The assumption has been made that leisure opportunity, services and facilities need management in order to provide for the greater good of the greater number – for effectiveness and for efficiency.

The management of leisure requires the same effectiveness and efficiency which is needed in all good management: the core elements of management will be the core elements of leisure management. Managing leisure will also have its own specialisms. This chapter deals with the general core elements of management, though these are discussed in the context of leisure situations; later chapters deal with the specialisms in greater detail.

First, the fundamental difference between general 'economic' management and service leisure management is introduced. *Second*, the management process is described. *Third*, traditional principles and functions of management are considered. *Fourth*, the job of managing people and the need for appropriate styles of management to meet different situations are taken into account. *Fifth*, two of the primary functions of management – i.e. leadership and decision-making – are studied. *Sixth*, the value of good communication within and between groups is discussed. *Seventh*, the functions of management in the leisure setting are briefly introduced in anticipation of the chapters to follow on the programming, performance and staffing aspects of leisure management.

Having read this chapter, readers will understand that the job of the manager is to ensure the best utilization of resources, including people and money, to achieve short-term objectives and long-term goals of the organization. Policy-makers and managers need to be clear about principles and objectives; know the resources and their value; and understand the performance that is expected.

Readers will learn that three of the crucial tools of management are leadership, decision-making and communication. Leadership provides the direction, the driving motivation and representation. A good leader has to be flexible to meet changing conditions and have concern with both people and results. Decision-making requires adequate analysis, before jumping to conclusions and proposing inappropriate solutions. A high degree of skill in communicating is required because a manager's task is to achieve results through other people.

The quality of management, and hence the quality of the Leisure Manager, is responsible in large measure for the success or failure of the leisure service and organization. But quality does not just happen. It has to be worked for.

13.1 GENERAL MANAGEMENT AND LEISURE MANAGEMENT

Good management of leisure and recreation is concerned with setting goals and meeting objectives and targets, achieving optimal use of resources, achieving financial objectives, meeting priority needs and offering the most attractive services to meet leisure and recreation demands. In order to manage well resources, services and purpose-built facilities, managers need to understand the concept of management and the skills and techniques of management to achieve goals and objectives.

The quality of management determines, to a large extent, the type of use and viability of leisure services and facilities. It is a key component, whether facilities are large or small, whether they are run publicly, commercially or privately or whether they are run by a management committee, board of directors or an owner-manager.

Many leisure facilities in the United Kingdom, which have been poorly designed or have been adapted or converted to recreational use, have nonetheless become hubs of enterprising community programmes. This has been achieved through good management. In contrast, some well-designed facilities have become somewhat lack-lustre community facilities with programme, staffing and viability problems due to poor management.

Management is usually considered in terms of economic efficiency. Drucker [1] claims that it can only justify its existence by the economic results it produces. There may be greater non-economic results, such as the contribution to community welfare, but management has failed, according to Drucker, if it fails to produce economic results. It must supply goods and services which the public wants, at a price the consumer is willing to pay.

This need not be the case, however. 'People service' programmes, including many aspects of leisure management, differ in some fundamental respects from a commercial profit-orientated company. In human service programmes, 'profit' needs to be defined in terms not just of money, but in terms of a whole range of other additional criteria, for example, the physical, social and psychological benefits offered by the programme; the range of users attracted; the meeting of targets for, say, the socially deprived or the handicapped; improving performance; and the numbers attracted from the locality it serves. Here targets are of many kinds, including the level of financial viability aimed for. Extending this idea, some have tried to place an actual financial value on recreation participation.

David Gray is quoted [2] as saying:

'We desperately need a method of planning that permits social cost-benefit analysis. Lacking such a system we are turning control of our social enterprises over to the accounting mind. The accounting mind reaches decisions by a method in which short-range fiscal consequences are the only critierion of value. Recreation and park services will not survive in that kind of environment. Most of the great social problems that disfigure our national life cannot be addressed in a climate dominated by that kind of value system.'

Similarly, Robert Wilder [3] states: 'The modern day name of the game seems to be quantification, justification, competition and cost–benefit analysis.' In search of a management tool by which to measure recreational benefits in terms of 'profit', Wilder presented his 'Economic Equivalency Index' (EEI), which attempts to quantify recreation value in financial terms.

Management therefore can be considered to consist of general, as well as specialist, actions and processes – e.g. being 'profit' orientated. This chapter is concerned with some of these main general aspects of management.

13.2 THE MANAGEMENT PROCESS

Management is both an active human occupation and a process by which people and organizations achieve results.

Management is a distinct type of work. The ability to do a job is not enough. The good physical education teacher, swimming coach, librarian, park ranger or sports or arts administrator does not automatically make the good manager. While technical 'know-how' is important, management is more – it concerns the work of people, effectiveness and accountability for end-results.

What is the distinct type of work which relates to the manager? Management is not a science, with precise laws and predictable behaviour. No foolproof rules exist which can replace the need for judgement, common-sense and related experience. Management is not an art, if by that we imply only intuition and individual judgement, on the thesis that 'managers are born and not made'. Management is not a profession with a code of ethics, standards and ideals (though the British Institute of Management is in the process of establishing a charter of management). Management appears to be a bit of each: 'It is the sum of art and science that makes a manager.'

While management is fundamentally concerned with human behaviour, behaviour is not constant. Management situations vary. Management is concerned with change; it is continually flowing and interacting. Drucker [1] emphasized this aspect of management:

'The job of management is never to be concerned with restoring or maintaining normality because normality is the condition of yesterday.

The major concern of management, if they are to make their business effective, must be in the direction of systematically trying to understand the condition of the future so that they can decide on the changes that can take their business from today into tomorrow'.

Management, therefore, can be perceived as human behaviour and also as a process of handling business; it is both flexible and changeable. It needs a framework, core elements, basic functions and logic to achieve its results, for management is a means to ends.

In order to manage organizations, services and programmes effectively, there must be a clear understanding of the management process and aims by all those within the organization. This is especially relevant in organizations giving services, which call for high levels of motivation, work entailing much of the 'voluntary' spirit and duties often spreading into unsocial hours. Leisure services are a case in point. In addition, understanding something of the essence of the management process renders many of the management concepts and functions less obscure and lifeless. Management is often a matter of adjusting to change and changing conditions, and so gives few opportunities for precise measurement and experiments which provide the basis of scientific evidence. Nevertheless, scientific techniques are now indispensable to many enterprises. Scientific method is objective, it weighs evidence; it tests conclusions.

13.2.1 Management of changing situations

Management has been defined in a whole variety of ways; some explain its purpose at great length, others more directly. Drucker [4], for example, states that management is a 'multi-purpose organ that manages a business *and* manages managers *and* manages workers and work'. If *one* of these is omitted, we would not have management or a business enterprise, according to Drucker. Here management is seen as a structure with functions. Later we will see management described more in terms of a process.

Discussions on management often start with a search for the best definition of the word. A cursory look at dictionary definitions illustrates the problem. The verb 'to manage' can mean 'to direct', 'to handle', 'to influence', 'to exert control', 'to make submissive', 'to contrive', 'to use economically and with forethought' and 'to cope with'. One can 'manage to make a muddle', 'succeed in one's aim', 'make proper use of' and 'manage on one's own'. Managing therefore has diverse meanings and differing interpretations. It also has varied interpreters. Its functions are changing, fluid and subtle.

Management thus depends on a variety of factors, for example, the situation, the information available, the people involved, the organization *and* the people doing the managing; in some significant measure, management depends on the person, or persons, doing the managing. Management relates to people's behaviour. This conditions any definition of management. The qualities found in the good manager are therefore important in any definition of management.

What appears to be abundantly clear is that there is no *one* way, no one 'instant brew' for instant management and no one management principle that is right every time. Management is malleable, amenable to change and flexible in organization. It has many functions. The manager is not just a creator, but he or she is also a planner and forecaster, setting objectives, motivating, leading, deciding, checking and monitoring performance. Management – in the simple idiom of today – is *getting things done with and through people,* and as such management is a social process.

13.3 THE PRINCIPLES OF MANAGEMENT IN HISTORICAL PERSPECTIVE

Contemporary management practices have been influenced by many schools of management thought. Management understanding has progressed from the 'scientific movement' instigated by Frederick Taylor [5] and others at the turn of the century, through the 'human relations movement' influenced by Elton Mayo [6] and the now legendary Hawthorne studies, through the 'classical movement' stressing organization and administration and influenced by Henri Fayol [7] and Max Weber [8] to the behaviourist view of management put forward by Douglas McGregor [9] and Frederick Herzberg [10], who built on the inspiration of Abraham Maslow [11,12].

13.3.1 The 'scientific movement'

Frederick Taylor dominated the beginning of what has come to be known as the 'scientific movement' from the turn of the century until the 1920s. Taylor's ideas are management foundation stones for many organizations and enterprises that sprang up in the first decades of this century. Time study was the basis for Taylor's system and the term 'time and motion study' emanates from his system. His was a system of reward: a fair day's work for a fair day's pay; the higher the productivity, the higher the pay. The belief was born that optimum work environments would enhance productivity. However, one movement in particular – the 'human relations movement' – was to challenge some of the foundations of the scientific movement.

13.3.2 The 'human relations movement'

In the 1920s and early 1930s experiments were conducted at the Western Electric Co. in Hawthorne, Illinois, on the effects of lighting conditions and employee productivity. An experimental group of women worked in one room; and a control group of women worked in another room. Lighting conditions were varied in the experimental group. It was discovered that not only did improved illumination result in improved productivity, but that *all* changes to illumination resulted in improvements, including levels of illumination which were highly unfavourable. In addition, it was discovered that as well as increased production in the experimental group, the same improvements occurred in the control group. Researchers from Harvard led by Elton Mayo were called in to continue the studies [6]. After the illumination experiments, other variables were also manipulated. For example, the experimental group were given scheduled work breaks, a shorter working week and other benefits. Again, productivity increased both in the experimental and the control groups. Mayo's researchers then removed all the benefits from the experimental group. Yet again, production increased in both groups!

What were the reasons for these effects? With the power of the trade unions and the need for fair treatment for all employees, we might not expect to find such results. Why had attitudes to work changed in this situation? Each group was found to be reacting to being an 'object of study' – the consequence of the presence of researchers. Mayo's methodology was to spend considerable time in interviewing both the experimental group and the control group. Employees were made to feel that the company *genuinely cared* for them, cared about their problems and their feelings. Management were seen to be concerned about employees as people. The improved social conditions appeared to be more important than improved physical and environmental conditions. Hence came the dawn of the 'human relations movement' and the discovery that the informal organization and the quality of supervision had a significant effect on morale and productivity. This realization was one of the pivots in the human relations school of management: inter-personal relationships are important, management is a people-orientated business.

The paternalistic concern of management in relation to industrial recreation may well be one of the products of this management movement. Many businesses look to providing a good working environment, offer fringe benefits, social benefits and appear to show genuine concern for workers at work and away from work (Chapter 11). Leisure services, away from the workplace, are people-orientated businesses with considerable face-to-face work and should benefit from such approaches to management.

The human relations movement has, however, had its critics. How widespread were the experiments? Are all satisfied employees the most productive? Mayo's concern for style of supervision, human relationships and employee welfare had challenged the doctrine of the scientific movement; in turn, this people-centred movement was challenged by what has come to be known as the 'classical movement'.

13.3.3 'Classical' management theory

Classical management theory is concerned with the efficient design and structure of organizations – the administration of the business. Building on Taylor's theories, the Frenchman Henri Fayol had an important influence on management thinking. He emphasized five management processes which were applicable to any field of endeavour requiring management: planning, organizing, commanding, coordinating and controlling.

Weber's ideal organization was the bureaucratic administrative structure. As Wren [8] points out: 'Bureaucracy was conceived as a blueprint for efficiency which would emphasise rules rather than men.'

Classical theory is thus concerned with structures and hierarchy. Its fundamental principles have had profound effects on government and industry. Local government, and hence public recreation services, conform to formal structures, organizational charts and hierarchical structures. Considerable support is given to these structures: people know exactly where they stand and what is expected of them; they know their station, their role and their influence; their jobs are defined.

Classical management structuring, however, appears to neglect a people orientation. It is mechanistic, bureaucratic and red-taped! Formal structures tend to put work into tight categories; departments tend to be subdivided into units; labour is divided into specialisms; inflexibility is instilled and top to bottom chains of control – 'chains of command' – become sacrosanct. In public recreation services we find that 'comprehensive departments', so called, may well be a series of tightly closed administrative boxes and specialisms (e.g. administration, finance, programming, catering and maintenance) without lateral linking, or they are divided into parks, baths, youth, aged, disabled – all acting out separate roles in separate units.

13.3.4 The 'behaviourist' view of management

One of the latest management movements is that towards a 'behaviourist' approach which has been in vogue since the early 1950s. It arose, in part, in opposition to the rigid structuring and organizational character of classical methods. It was felt that organization structures should be tempered with flexibility and a greater concern for employee involvement. The inherent possibilities for closed systems and discord needed to be eliminated; harmony would lead to improved work and work relationships. McGregor [9], Herzberg [10], Argyris [13], Likert [14] and others have enlarged management thinking within the behavioural approach, inspired by the work of psychologists such as Erich Fromm and Abraham Maslow and the human relations work of Elton Mayo. Maslow's concern that people should be 'self-actualized' whether at work or play led to the kind of thinking which stressed working patterns that encouraged people to express themselves in work and in leisure.

In an affluent society, most physical and safety needs have been consistently satisfied; consequently, it is the social and ego needs which are dominant. Leisure Managers, like most other people, want to be recognized as individuals, to have some measure of control over the decisions in their working environment and their own jobs, to accomplish something worthwhile – in other words, to see themselves in something that is successful and meaningful. The value system of managers has changed and is changing constantly.

McGregor, in his theory of motivation, added support to the work of Maslow and, influenced by the Hawthorne studies, makes two basic approaches to management based on two main assumptions about human behaviour. The traditional value system of managers he labelled 'Theory X', which he believes is no longer applicable in today's management of people. He proposed his 'Theory Y' as the most appropriate alternative. The Theory Y manager sees work as a natural part of life.

Theory X is the traditional view of direction and control. Most people have to be coerced, controlled, directed and even threatened before effort is made towards the achievement of organizational objectives. The theory also suggests that people prefer to be directed, respond when disciplined, wish to avoid responsibility, have relatively little ambition and want security above all else. In essence, Theory X is the 'stick-and carrot' approach, the carrot being money or reward and the stick being the threat of financial insecurity. McGregor believes that this must be replaced by Theory Y.

Theory Y is the theory of the integration of individual and organizational goals. Effort in work is as natural as play or rest. External controls are not the only means for bringing about effort towards objectives. People can exercise self-direction and self-control when commitment is high. They respond to honest praise and resent punishment. Moreover, people learn, under proper conditions, not only to accept but also to seek responsibility; the capacity to exercise a relatively high degree of imagination, ingenuity and creativity in the solution of organizational problems is widely, not narrowly, distributed in the population, as the old-style management of 'leaders' and 'followers' suggests.

Theory X managers will tend to *push* people to achieve a task. Theory Y managers will tend to *lead* people to achieve a task.

McGregor claimed that those managers operating predominantly towards the principles of Theory Y were generally more successful in the following ways: their departments had higher outputs; staff showed greater motivation; and there were fewer labour problems, lower labour turnovers and less waste and greater profits.

McGregor's work has been enlarged by Likert [14], whose concepts are presented in four management systems: *System 1*, 'exploitative-authoritative'; *System 2*, 'benevolent-authoritative'; *System 3*, 'consultative'; and *System 4*, 'participative'. The nearer the management system is to System 4, the more productive the organization. It produces lower costs, higher earning, better union relations, more positive worker attitudes and higher morale. Conversely, the nearer the management is to System 1, the more it results in lower productivity, higher costs, poorer union relations and resulting lower morale.

The findings of McGregor and Likert confirm that more effective results can be obtained in industry by a people-orientated approach to management. That being the case, then the implications for leisure service management could be considerable. If humanistic approaches to management can prove more effective in product-orientated industries, they should produce more effective results in service-orientated organizations, such as those found in the leisure industry, particularly as people are far more likely to express views and to exhibit wider forms of behaviour patterns.

Herzberg's theory of motivation [10] relates to two main job satisfaction parameters: *hygiene factors* and *motivators*. Hygiene factors are not part of the actual job, but relate to the work environment in its many forms – policies, conditions, relationships, fringe benefits, and so on. These factors may affect job performance but are not part of the job itself. Motivators, on the other hand, are concerned with the job. Is the job challenging? Does it carry responsibility, recognition for achievement, give prestige and esteem? Herzberg is concerned with job enrichment but his theory is limited by being preoccupied with two strands of employment conditions.

Argyris, [13] building on Maslow's self-actualization theme, believes that job enrichment will increase employee initiatives and self-direction. There would appear to be much in common between Maslow's theory, the ideas of Argyris, McGregor's 'Theory Y' and Likert's 'System 4'. They are all concerned with job enlargement, job enrichment and self-fulfilment.

In a leisure context, many writers see Maslow's self-actualization as the goal for the leisure delivery service, particularly for those sections of the community who are not working or working in an environment that provides little opportunity of job satisfaction and self-fulfilment.

But what becomes of these ideals in the practical world of budgets, cut-backs, redundancies, cuts in public expenditure, reductions in manpower and greater costs for less services? In the harsh world of recession the cry from industry is for greater output at less cost. Can the tenets of the 'behaviourist' management school, concerned with life satisfactions, still hold true for leisure services? Perhaps the Leisure Manager could have an even greater role to play in harder times?

13.4 MANAGEMENT FUNCTIONS AND PRACTICES

Most businesses and public leisure services appear to be based on classical management theory. Many writers have revised Fayol's original model but generally the framework and logic have remained intact: *planning* (policies, forecasting, objectives); *execution* (systematic implementation of policies, coordination); and *control* (monitoring performance). More recent writers have added to Fayol's model with additional functions such as motivation, communication, budgeting, creating and staff development.

The functions of management are seen as important because they are the constituents of every management job. The emphasis they receive, however, will vary according to the type of job, the level of the manager, the nature of the environment and many other factors.

It would appear that the classical principles of management theory adapted and modified to meet the needs of different organizations can be used as a basic framework for the management of public leisure services, facilities and programmes, namely:

1. Conceptualizing.
2. Establishing objectives.
3. Carrying out the plan (programme) and obtaining results through people.
4. Seeking improvements and appraising results.
5. Assisting subordinates and inspiring and motivating them.

These processes would seem to have considerable relevance to management in the leisure and recreation field, particularly in local authorities with the current climate of standardization, specification and competitive tendering of services.

There appear to be a core of knowledge and skills that are needed for management at all levels; MacKenzie's classic 3D management process illustrates his 'Ideas–People–Things' model [15]. These core management tasks are basically of three types: conceptual, human and technical.

The *conceptual* skills are developed on an understanding of the overall situations, the nature of the problems and complexities, and the ability to think clearly, analyse problems and plan carefully. These skills in formulating ideas and concepts determine the policies, orientation and objectivity of the organization, enterprise or programme being developed.

The *human* skills are concerned with people. They include the ability to select, develop, motivate, lead, decide, control and monitor performance. Managers must have good judgement and be able to work with and through people to meet objectives.

The *technical* skills are needed to incorporate experience and knowledge of the subject area, a sympathy with and understanding of the management environment and the methods and techniques which are needed to perform the tasks.

In identifying these three areas, Robert Katz confirms that individual management styles vary according to the management position one holds, but as one ascends the management ladder, less emphasis is placed on technical skills and greater importance is given to the conceptual skills. This is illustrated in Fig. 13.1, showing that whatever the management level, all managers need excellent human relations skills.

The Leisure Service Manager

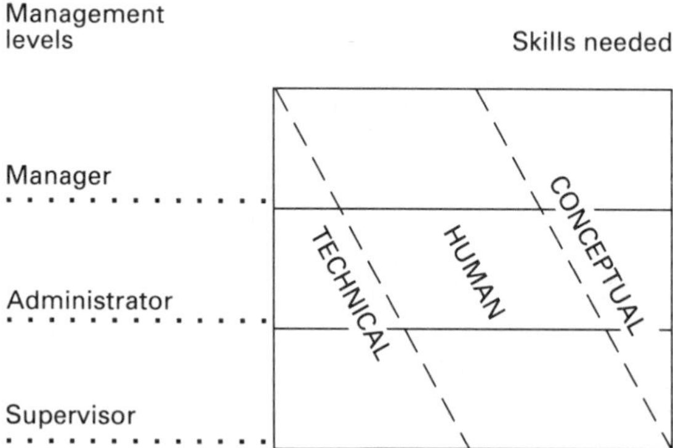

Fig. 13.1 Management skills. Source: adapted from Hershey, P. and Blanchard, K. H., *Management of Organizational Behaviour: Utilizing Human Resources* (2nd edn), p. 9.

However, of critical importance is the appreciation that while management is concerned with planning, execution and control and is concerned also with ideas, people and things, management in and of itself is nothing: it needs a situation, a context. Management therefore is *situational* – i.e. it needs something to manage. In this context, that 'something' is leisure and recreation, which need both general and specialist management.

13.4.1 Management systems

While much management practice appears to be based on the classical movement, many additional management systems and techniques have been added to it or have been introduced in recent years and many have been influenced by the behavioural scientists.

Management by Objectives (*MBO*) has become a popular management system over the past three decades. So well known has the term 'MBO' become that there are now a range of definitions of what it actually is! (Chapter 15). In addition, several systems have been built upon the MBO technique of setting and achieving objectives. Some look to the system being a philosophy of management, others take a more pragmatic view.

George Odiorne [16], thought to be one of the founding fathers of the movement, defined MBO as: 'a process whereby the superior and subordinate managers of an organization jointly identify its common goals, define each individual's major areas of responsibility in terms of the results expected of him, and use these measures as guides for operating the unit and assessing the contribution of each of its members.' Whatever the differences of definition, two main strands of MBO are linked as the cornerstones of the system: the setting of objectives, and the participation by managers from all levels in an organization.

PPBS (*Planning-Programming-Budgeting Systems*) is a specific method of applying systems theory, developed in the early 1960s by the US Department of Defence. Another method, *PERT* (*Programme Evaluation Review Technique*), is a system of planning and control that identifies key activities needed to accomplish a given project successfully. It is frequently used on large projects in the management of resources by identifying when, where and the extent of the resources required. PERT incorporates a system known as *CPM* (*Critical Path Method*), which is a technique based on a network analysis that highlights the activities requiring completion in a particular sequence within a given space of time. A current system in vogue is *TQM* (*Total Quality Management*).

13.4.2 Total Quality Management

Two movements in modern business appear to have gained ground during recent years: the computer–technology revolution worldwide, and the quality–customer care momentum, in which the North Americans have been well in the lead. Markets, including the commercial leisure and tourism markets, have become increasingly competitive. *Pricing*, *quality* and *delivery* have been key determinants in satisfying customers and thereby increasing market share.

Whether managing in the commercial, public or voluntary sectors people have to be attracted to the services and facilities and these should be managed with excellence, that is with quality. But quality does not just happen. It has to be worked for. It has to be managed.

Total Quality Management (*TQM*) is an approach to improving effectiveness and flexibility of business as a whole – i.e. a process from top to bottom, which involves every person in an organization – to ensure customer satisfaction at every stage. TMQ thus focuses on customer needs and builds a logical linkage between these needs and the business objectives.

The British Quality Association provide a definition of TQM:

'Total Quality (TQM) is a corporate business management philosophy which recognises that customer needs and business goals are inseparable. It is applicable within both industry and commerce.

'It ensures maximum effectiveness and efficiency within a business and secures commercial leadership by putting in place processes and systems which will promote excellence, prevent errors and ensure that every aspect of the business is aligned to customer needs and the advancement of business goals without duplication or waste of effort.

'The commitment to TQM originates at the chief executive level in a business and is promoted in all human activities. The accomplishment of quality is thus achieved by personal involvement and accountability, devoted to a continuous improvement process, with measureable levels of performance by all concerned.

'It involves every department, function and process in a business and the active commitment of all employees to meeting customer needs. In this regard the "customers" of each employee are separately and individually identified'.

If quality is synonymous with meeting customer requirements, then this has fundamental implications on leisure. The first item on the agenda will be to find out who are the customers and what are their requirements.

TQM is then a way of organizing and involving the whole business: every department, every activity and every person. It must establish an 'organization for quality'. The principles behind such total quality are identified by Mosscrop and Stores [17]:

1. Excellence as the objective and getting it right first time.
2. Everyone is a customer or a supplier in every transaction – every

transaction in the business, every link in the chain, has a supplier and a customer.
3. Absolute clarity about customers' needs, the perceptions of customers are paramount.
4. Commitment from the top.
5. Measurement of all key outputs: 'We are convinced that control through measurement of key outputs in terms of ratios against past trends, standards and/or targets must become a way of life for all those employed in the leisure sector.'
6. Prevention not blame; sharing responsibility, preventing future occurrences.
7. Training and education from top down.
8. Integration of total quality into the business – a core business activity which permeates every aspect of leisure operations.

In other words, excellence is called for and is worked for by every person in all aspects of the operation. All activity throughout all operations is continuously directed at satisfying customer requirement: 'Total Quality Management in the leisure sector is about securing fundamental changes in attitudes towards colleagues, customers, products, services and quality.'

Oakland (19) believes that Total Quality Management is concerned with moving control from outside the individual to within, the objective being to make everyone accountable for their own performance, and to get each person committed to attaining quality in a highly motivated fashion:

'While an intellectual understanding of quality provides a basis for TQM, it is clearly only the planting of the seed. The understanding must be translated into commitment, policies, plans and actions for TQM to germinate. Making this happen requires not only commitment, but a competence in the mechanics of quality management, and in making changes'.

Clearly, this calls for a strategy and a long-term commitment. According to Oakland, never-ending or continuous improvement is probably the most powerful concept to guide management. The concept requires a systematic approach to quality management, which has the following components:

1. Planning the processes and their inputs.
2. Providing the inputs.
3. Operating the processes.
4. Evaluating the outputs.
5. Examining the performance of the processes.

This system must be firmly tied to a continuous assessment of customer needs. The three basic principles of never-ending improvement are:

1. Focus on the customer.
2. Understanding the process.
3. Involving the people.

Undertaking quality management also calls for the Leisure Manager skilled in leadership, decision-making, communication and the understanding of group and team behaviour. It is to these aspects that we now turn.

13.5 LEADERSHIP

The Chinese philosopher, Lao-Tsu, is reputed to have said: 'To lead the people, walk behind them.' The suggestion here is that not all leadership is waving a flag up at the front. Henry Miller, in *Wisdom of the Heart*, captures the same spirit: 'The real leader has no need to lead – he is content to point the way.'

Good leadership requires an understanding of people – colleagues and customers and their motivations. The handling of people is probably the most important ingredient in the management of leisure. Thus of the three core elements of skill needed by the manager – conceptual, human and technical – this section concentrates on the human factors. The concepts have been debated at length earlier in the book and the technical aspects are to be covered in later chapters.

Leadership cannot be separated from management, though management is not leadership *per se*. Leadership has been described as a mixture of art, craft and humanity. It is an essential part of a manager's job. A good leader is concerned both with people and results.

Good leaders create a vision and define a strategy to get there; they provide:

1. *Direction* – pointing the way, setting objectives and eliminating uncertainty.
2. *Drive* – giving motivation, inspiring confidence and building team cohesion.
3. *Communication* and *representation* – to the outside world and from outside to the team.

Management today is a complex phenomenon as we have seen. Leadership too is multi-faceted. In earlier decades there appeared to be a clear demarcation between 'leaders' and 'followers', based on tradition, class and upbringing, which divided 'boss' and 'workers'. In business management the leader was portrayed as a person, normally male, who was endowed with initiative and the authority to lead men. The Military Academy of Sandhurst joke is of the commanding officer who says of one of his recruits: 'This young officer is not yet a born leader', illustrating a myth that has been perpetuated. Leadership can be a learned skill.

Different styles of leadership will be appropriate to different situations. How can the modern manager be 'democratic' in dealings with subordinates and yet maintain the necessary authority and control in the organization to which he or she is responsible?

Over the past few decades has emerged the concept of *group dynamics*. Social scientists revealed the importance of employee involvement and participation in decision-making. Democratic leadership began to be thought of as solutions coming from the ground floor and autocratic leadership attributed to the boss who makes most decisions himself. Generalizations, lacking research evidence, spoke in simplistic terms of leadership being either 'democratic' or 'autocratic', and even more misleading, these terms became for some synonymous with 'right' and 'wrong' styles of leadership and for others 'strong' leadership and 'permissive' leadership. In this context, a leader should not be confused with the role of the 'head', who is imposed upon a group or organization from above. The person concerned may not have the necessary leadership qualities, yet to be a competent leader these will be essential.

In answer to the question: 'what is leadership?', there appear to be three main schools of thought: first, leaderhip is a matter of *personal traits* (such as initiative, courage and intelligence). These traits must be possessed by individuals and then they are able to lead in most if not all situations. Second, who becomes the leader of a group, and what the leadership characteristics are in the given case, are a function of the specific *situation*; but one person *emerges* as the leader. Third, leadership is a *function*. Any or all of the members of the group may perform, at various times, specific leadership acts or functions which are necessary if the group's objectives are to be obtained. These functions include initiating, regulating, informing, decision-making and maintenance behaviour.

This third view of leadership appears to be currently accepted by most management educators as realistic and appropriate to a successful group in terms of achieving targets. However, all three views are relevant in given situations.

In informal groups, which will apply more in voluntary sector management, the emergence of a leader is needed to satisfy the needs of the group. A leader is needed as a focal point for concerted action as often many groups are pulling in different directions. In these groups, representation, the voice of the organization, is also of importance. In special tasks of leadership, such as in running an event or the maintenance of premises, certain people will emerge as leaders. Different leaders for different situations is a concept worth pursuing in all diverse organizations.

Leadership, one of the core functions of management, is essentially a matter of human behaviour. The modern manager has to ask: 'what is the most appropriate leadership in this situation?' This brings us to leadership behaviour.

13.5.1 A leadership behaviour model

Robert Tannenbaum and Warren H. Schmidt [20] studied the range of behaviour adopted by leaders and presented a continuum or range of possible leadership behaviour available to a manager. In their model (Fig. 13.2) each type of action is related to the degree of authority used by the manager and to the amount of freedom available to the subordinates in reaching decisions. Actions on the extreme left characterize the manager who maintains a high degree of control, while those on the extreme right characterize the manager who releases a high degree of control.

Management

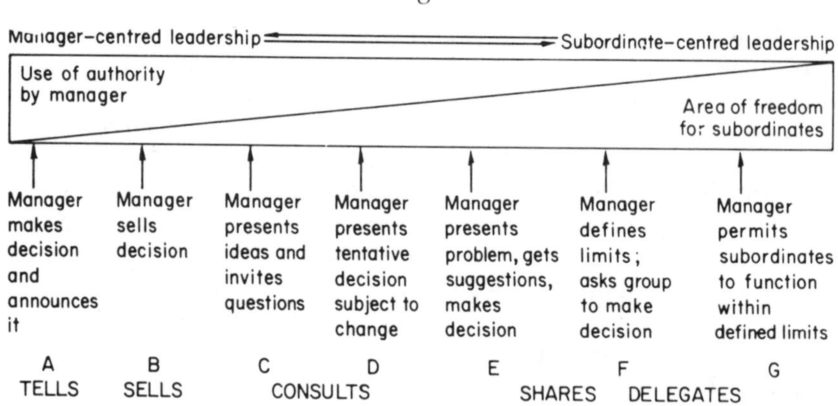

Fig. 13.2 Continuum of leadership behaviour. Note: under F and G, although the manager delegates, he or she must still accept full responsibility. Adapted from Tannenbaum and Schmidt, *How to choose a Leadership Pattern*.

The continuum is important, particularly in three main ways. First, it demonstrates that there are a number of ways in which a manager can relate to the group. In any situation, however, the manager must expect to be held responsible for the quality of the decisions made, even though operationally they may have been made on a group basis. Delegation is not a way of 'passing the buck'.

Second, it is important for the group to recognize what kind of leadership is being adopted. For example, if the manager has already decided what to do and wishes to inform them, it is right that this is done. To adopt a façade of involving the group in the decision-making process would be misleading, and lead to antagonism and frustration.

Third, the democratic manager is not one who gives his or her subordinates the most decisions to make. That may be entirely inappropriate. There may be other more important priorities for them. The quality of involvement and decision-making is important. Involvement only in low levels of decision-making may simply prove to be patronizing to some members of staff.

13.5.2 Deciding how to lead

A leader's style should be flexible enough to change to suit the situation. What factors should a manager consider in deciding how to lead? A false assumption is made in the belief that leaders are born, not made, or that one is either an autocratic, a democratic or 'free-rein' leader. Most leaders tend to use many styles but with a leaning towards one. Much will depend on the circumstances.

In emergencies, authoritative, autocratic leadership is eminently suitable. The authoritarian style can also be very effective when toughness is needed under certain conditions, even at some personal emotional cost to the leader. There is an American saying that 'nice guys don't win ball games' and there is a germ of truth in that, in tough situations. However, in longer-term organizational situations where leadership is an ongoing 'craft', and where the manager is working with and through other staff, then there are four major factors which help to determine the style of leadership which is most appropriate:

1. The personality, make-up and ability of the manager.
2. The characteristics and ability of the subordinates.
3. The characteristics of the organization.
4. The nature of the problem.

(i) The manager

The manager's behaviour occurs as a result of his or her personality, background, knowledge and experience. Among the significant internal forces are the manager's value system and the trust and confidence shown in the subordinates. External forces are also exerted upon the leader, and in order to retain the confidence and alliegance of his or her staff, the person concerned has to conform more to the norms and rules of the 'group' than do its normal members.

(ii) The subordinates

Assistant managers and staff will have expectations of the manager. Each member of staff has his or her own personality and ability factors: the better the manager understands these forces within the group, the better he or she can determine the role to play in achieving the best for subordinates and the organization.

Generally speaking, under the leadership continuum, the manager can permit subordinates greater freedom if the following conditions exist:

1. Assistant staff have high needs for independence.
2. There is a readiness to assume responsibility.
3. They prefer a wide area of freedom rather than simply clear-cut directives.
4. They have considerable interest in the problem and feel it is of importance.
5. They appreciate the goals of the organization.
6. They have sufficient knowledge.
7. They have been 'educated' to expect to share in decision-making; there is a climate of mutual confidence and respect.

(iii) The organization

Management situations vary enormously. Much will depend on the organization itself, its aims and objectives and the efficiency of the group in given situations.

Organizations, such as a local government district council, will have traditional kinds of behaviour which are approved of and other kinds which are not. Its leisure services department may have dispersed sections and sites which preclude effective participatory decision-making. In contrast, a commercial leisure club manager may have to decide prices and controls and meet tight financial targets.

(iv) The nature of the problem

The most important consideration is the problem itself, which will determine the kind of leadership. The problem may need specialist information or be of a complex nature involving many disciplines. The manager will need to be sure all the necessary knowledge is acquired within a given time. The pressure of time is often said to be the biggest headache, even though such pressures are sometimes self-imposed. With 'crisis' decisions, a high degree of authority is likely. When time pressure is less intense, it becomes easier to bring others into a situation where group dynamics – skilfully handled – will become one of the tools to good management.

Day-to-day problems in the leisure field, such as the upkeep and maintenance of the buildings and grounds, the staff systems, the programme, the handling of stock and the accounting for cash, will be more routine and administrative. A leadership pattern has been set and leadership choices are limited; changes are inappropriate.

However, long-term decisions, strategies and solutions to new long-range problems give opportunity to involve others in achieving goals more effectively. For example, a leisure centre's programme and system may have been fixed for the coming 12 months, but a survey has indicated that only 25% utilization is being made by females and that the daytime use by shift workers, the unemployed and the retired is negligible. The manager, anxious to increase the proportions of these customers to meet the aims of the organization, should confer with the assistant managers, initially, and discuss with them the scope of the problem, the constraints to time and money and the need to acquaint the staff and user groups with the problem and the opportunities.

It is in the strategy and the tactics of handling the problem where the manager's leadership skills are put to the test: can he or she raise the level of employee motivation? Can staff and key user groups be persuaded to accept change readily? Can the quality and effectiveness of managerial decisions be improved? Can teamwork and morale be developed? Can the manager both improve individual development and enhance the quality of the organization, and improve the satisfactions of the customers?

13.5.3 Many leisure personnel are leaders

All successful managers must be leaders. Many leaders, however, while doing a managing job are not termed 'managers'. Often they are community leaders, leisure centre supervisors, and the like. In addition to the managers, the supervisors also need leadership training. Indeed, it is they who undertake the majority of the face-to-face work.

The supervisor/leader or community leader is usually employed to get the job accomplished, working through the group of people over whom he or she has control. The leader has three main interrelated areas in which to work:

1. The task to be done.
2. The individuals to work through.
3. The team.

To achieve the task, the leader must be aware that the team needs to work together in harmony and with a sense of team spirit, and that the individual in the team has personal needs which must also be met. He or she must therefore develop the individual and maintain the team. A breakdown in one area will affect the others, it will hamper progress and prevent the effective accomplishment of the task. The overlapping

Fig. 13.3 Effective leadership skills to achieve results.

between the three jobs of work involved in achieving the task effectively is illustrated in Fig. 13.3.

13.5.4 Entrepreneurial leadership

Entrepreneurial leadership is gaining momentum in the public sector as never before, in part due to success experienced in the private sector and the policy requiring local authorities to optimize income and decrease net expenditure. Commercial managers have to be more accountable for financial performance and hence use entrepreneurial skills to increase income. This form of leadership is almost diametrically opposed to the normal manner of operating in government agencies. Public agencies have relied on *the system*, rather than the managers and staff, to provide services. The current climate calls for entrepreneurial, creative managers who are prepared to take chances, be bold and take action and lead, rather than simply react to what happens.

Leisure professionals and managers must be able to teach the skills of leadership to supervisory managers and community leaders. They will need to learn to accept responsibility for leading their teams, have loyalty to the organization and to the team, ensure that each team member knows his or her job, face up to individual and situational problems and 'walk the job' – every day.

In summary, the manager must be a successful leader in order to be effective. The manager must understand himself or herself and the staff and the customers. The manager recognizes that a high degree of subordinate-centred behaviour in helping to run an organization raises employee teamwork and morale. But this does *not* mean that a manager leaves all decisions to the staff. Situations vary and staff vary. Staff readiness and ability are important. The successful leader will behave appropriately in the light of his or her perceptions of the people and the situations, and cannot therefore be categorized as 'strong' or 'permissive'. He or she must have the insight and ability to act appropriately, remaining firm on cardinal principles, yet being flexible to permit degrees of freedom to the greatest advantage. In addition to leading personally, the manager must recognize that many subordinates fill important leadership roles themselves. They too need training in the 'art' of *effective* leadership. Leadership may result in the successful completion of a task, but *effective* leadership occurs when the team of staff not only complete the task, but do so willingly and find its accomplishment rewarding.

13.6 DECISION-MAKING

One of the functions of management is decision-making and a significant proportion of a manager's time is spent in handling problems and making decisions. *How* decisions are made is of importance. Hence the *process* of decision-making, as well as the content of the decision, are important for success. The manager and his or her group, or groups, should have an awareness of alternative decision-making procedures and processes.

Management has moved, and continues to move, from an intuitive 'art' with its 'rule-of-thumb' approach, to decision-making on a more scientific basis. Science, however, is not solely the science of economics, physics or mathematics, but the sciences of people – the psychological processes which affect decision-making.

Traditionally, decision-making has been seen as being undertaken by only those 'at the top'. This has been shown to be wholly undesirable and inadequate. Decisions should be made at all levels of management. Robert Townsend, in *Up the Organization* [21], goes further still: 'All decisions should be made as low as possible in the organization. The Charge of the Light Brigade was ordered by an officer who wasn't there looking at the territory.'

13.6.1 Types of decision

There are three main types of decision identified by Video Arts [22], namely emergency decisions, routine decisions and debatable decisions.

1. *Emergency decisions* are needed under crisis. They require clear, quick and precise decisions, for example, to prevent destruction of the sports hall by a bomb, the possible drowning in the swimming pool, the fight at the discothèque or to make the call for ambulance, fire service or police.
2. The running of an organization and the ticking over of the service revolve around *routine decisions*. Changes to the duty supervisor rota, the change of menu, or giving the blessing for additional staff for the forthcoming major events, are all within an organization's policy framework. Many of these routine decisions simply require a 'yes'/'no' to maintain the status quo.
3. *Debatable decisions* are debatable because they *change* the status quo. They mean changes for people and their work. They are debatable because the chances are that they will be improved through consultations, given effective leadership. They are debatable, too, because there may be a number of different ways of handling the particular situation.

It is these debatable decisions which should occupy a manager's time more than others. It is these decisions which generally lead to harmony or disharmony; and it is these decisions with which this section is concerned.

13.6.2 The decision-making process

Decision-making can be perceived as having five phases:

1. Causes.
2. Possible decisions.
3. Consequences.
4. Evaluation.
5. Choice.

The technique helps managers or groups to highlight the need for information and factual data and the relevance of it to the problem. It helps to analyse logically and so assist in effective decision-making.

Decision-making is therefore a *process* which can be divided into a number of stages. A variety of texts suggest a different number of stages [22,23], though much the same logic is apparent. For the purposes of this chapter, eight simple stages are identified:

1. Defining the problem.
2. Gathering and examining information.
3. Consulting with people and considering their views.
4. Considering choices or alternatives.
5. Making the decision and deciding a course of action.

6. Communicating the decision.
7. Implementing the decision and following up.
8. Evaluation, feedback and modification.

1. *Defining the problem* – the process is dependent on, first, defining the problem; it is so obvious that it is often overlooked! It can be one of the hardest things to do (as many students writing theses will vouch for), but having defined the specific problem, we are a long way forward in finding solutions. We have to be clear: what is *really* the matter and the symptoms must not be confused with the problem itself. What is the decision supposed to achieve?

2. *Gathering and examining information* – what facts and information are needed? When are they needed by? What are the constraints and limiting factors? Are there cash limits, time pressures or staff shortages? Only valid and useful information should be used.

3. *Consulting with people and considering their views* – others may think of ideas which you have not thought of. People need to be identified in the decisions that are reached. The Recreation Manager needs to identify who will be affected by the decision and to discuss with the group the facts and their implications.

4. *Consider choices or alternatives* – consider all possible courses of action. A brainstorming session would help, in this respect, for we often stumble on important ways of achieving results by keeping our minds open to all the possibilities.

5. *Make the decision and decide a course of action.*

6. *Communicate the decision* – in communicating the decision, the manager must be prepared to persuade people of its 'rightness'. This is made all the easier if staff (and customers) have been involved in the decision-making or if the decision has been made by the representative group. Communicating decisions must be undertaken sensitively. For example, receptionists at leisure centres, often working part-time, are rarely part of the central decision-making team (and wrongly so in my opinion); they may learn about forthcoming events from the local newspapers!

Communicating the decision needs care, timing, sensitivity and, above all, the reasons *why* the decision has been made. Some Recreation Managers are careful to inform the staff of the reasons but fail to tell the customers why. How often have we seen 'Sports Shop Closed', 'Keep off', 'No entry' and 'Cafeteria Closed'? People tend to be more understanding and cooperative when they know why, and more so when they have been consulted. In communicating decisions, enthusiasm is important. You only generate enthusiasm in others if you give decisions and reasons with conviction. *How* it is done is important. When briefing the staff team, it is often best to undertake it collectively in order to show an open and frank situation and avoid the grapevine, the contrived gossip and the subsequent miscommunications and misunderstandings.

Recreation Managers often hide behind the memo in communicating decisions. They feel, in this way, that everybody knows, because the written word is clear. However, the written word is sometimes most unclear. It is conceived differently by different people; hidden messages might be imagined; and there may be an air of mistrust. Communication is a two-way process: 'no one can ask questions of the memo'. When preparing the brief – spoken first, then written – the manager needs to envisage how people will *feel* on the receiving end of the decision. Managers have to place themselves in the position of the receiver, into the shoes of the other person.

7. *Implementing and following up the decision* – requires communicating the decision, briefing people together, whenever possible, being ready and willing to sell the decision with enthusiasm and belief and then confirming the decision in writing. Many 'debatable' decisions need a framework on which an evaluation can be made such as timing, targets and implementation. It is important that the manager follows up and monitors progress and sees that areas implementing changes, and which create new problems, are smoothed over, particularly where people's feelings are concerned.

8. *Evaluation, feedback and modification* – most debatable decisions need time to see whether they have been successful or unsuccessful, and to what extent. Even the best preparation may result in the wrong decision being made. Once proof of its 'wrongness' is substantiated, managers need the courage to admit the fact and try again.

13.7 COMMUNICATION

George Eliot once wrote: 'The people of the world are islands shouting at each other across a sea of misunderstanding.'

As we have seen, communicating is far more important than just transmitting a message. The *way* it is done can affect the attitudes and performance of staff. The purpose of communication is to ensure that whoever receives the message understands what is in the mind of the sender. This is not easy; what is obvious to the sender may be obscure to the receiver. One-way communication is fraught with difficulties. A does not know if he is getting through to B.

Many problems of management, in industry and in leisure services, stem from the misunderstanding, misconceptions, mistrust and underlying *feelings* of not being put clearly in the picture, which arise from one-way communications. If the goals of communication are to understand others, to get clear reception or perception, to get understanding, to get acceptance in order to get effective action, then *two-way* communication is essential.

13.7.1 Two-way communications

One-way communication is quick, often satisfying for the sender but often frustrating for the receiver and leads to misunderstanding. While two-way communication takes longer and may be frustrating for the sender, it is essentially more sensitive and more accurate. To communicate, we must understand others. Each one of us is different from everyone else. We are different psychologically and physiologically. We vary in intelligence, education, religious beliefs, social background and experience.

These experiences create different frames of reference with the result that people look at the world around them in a particular and unique way. Our physical and mental make-up and our environment have a direct effect on our perception and judgement. All too often, when interpreting information, we see or hear what we are taught 'ought' to be there and/or what we want to see or hear. Thus there are barriers to communication in ourselves, and these barriers also exist in our subordinates, our peers and our bosses.

The argument for two-way communication is not only a moral one, it is also a practical one because the manager will become more effective by encouraging the group members to make full use of their abilities. Peter Drucker, in a public address, put the argument against the purely persuasive approach to communication in the following way:

'In many cases human relations has been used to manipulate, to adjust people to what the boss thinks is reality; to make them conform to a pattern that seems logical from the top down, to make them accept unquestionably what we tell them. Frankly, sometimes, I think it is better not to tell employees anything rather than to say "We tell them everything, but they must accept it, and it is our job to make them accept it"'.

In this instance, Drucker highlights the problems of forcing one-way communication on to people without their understanding and without understanding them. As Samuel Butler, the 17th-century poet observed: 'He that complies against his will is of his own opinion still.'

One-way communication situations can frequently arise if the sender and receiver are not on the same emotional level. For example, if the sender takes a superior attitude, the receiver will react with some resentment, concentration will decline and the level of interference and distraction is likely to increase.

The advantages of two-way communications are considerable. In small groups, such as those which apply in leisure settings (community arts centres, sports centres, recreation offices or community associations), the advantages can be summarized as follows:

1. Although one-way communication is faster, two-way communication is more accurate, particularly in complex situations.
2. Two-way communication will help both the sender and the listener to measure their standard of achievement, and when they both see that they are making progress, their joint commitment to the task will be greater.
3. The sender may feel under attack as the listener will pick up any mistakes and mention them. This is helpful rather than dangerous because a frank interchange of views will lead to a higher level of understanding and acceptance.

13.7.2 Communication networks

Communication networks have been the subject of much debate in recent years. Kent [24] identified the three most commonly used networks or patterns on which experimental work has been undertaken: the 'Circle', the 'Chain' and the 'Wheel' (Fig. 13.4). (Other variations include the 'Y' and the 'Web'.)

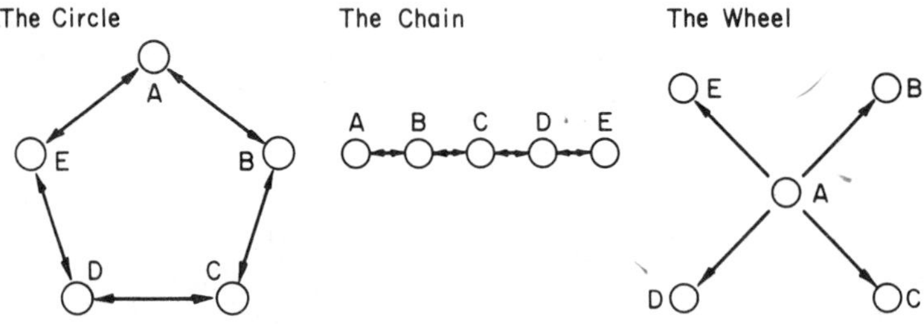

Fig. 13.4 Different communication networks.

Given simple tasks, the *wheel* was a consistently quicker and more accurate means of communication than the other two; the *chain* was the slowest and least effective. However, in terms of job satisfaction, the *circle* was more effective than the other two. The circle was also more adaptable in complicated and ambiguous tasks. The wheel with its central 'gatekeeper' inhibited adaptability to changing situations.

Kent concludes that people never transmit information as well as they believe they do. He outlined commonly identified problems which restrict communication, for example, perceptual bias by the receiver, the distortion of information by the sender, the lack of trust on the part of both sender and receiver, too much information and power used to secrete rather than share information.

The answer is to use more than one communication network. The formal and informal systems of communication Kent groups under four headings: 'hierarchical', 'expert', 'status' and 'friendship'. Further, it is important to encourage the two-way flow of communications and to improve the coordination within organizations: 'A lateral rather than a vertical direction of communications in an organization will avoid the problem of one person becoming the "gatekeeper" of all information, a gatekeeper being a person who can withold or pass on information as he sees fit.'

In both public and commercial leisure management, a substantial level of communication is of the one-way kind. Orders come down from the civic centre, town hall or head office, sometimes by word of mouth through the chain of command and often via the written memo – a system subject to all the misunderstandings and ministerpretations imaginable.

Managers and staff should be trained to handle work through greater levels of two-way communciations for more effective achievement of the task and greater harmony within the team. It should also be stated that written and verbal communication are not the sole methods of communicating and that physical gestures such as facial expressions, through the movement of eyes, or sitting positions, whether made consciously or unconsciously, can convey much to the receiver of the sender's attitude and understanding.

13.8 GROUP BEHAVIOUR IN THE LEISURE MANAGEMENT SETTING

In business, including the management of leisure programmes and services, it is likely that the important decisions are taken in consultation with others. Managers must therefore develop skills in understanding the behaviour processes at work when people are involved in the group decision-making process. It is clear that some behaviour assists in this work, and some behaviour hinders progress.

Two main management parameters are the *task* and the *relationships*. The task is the job that has to be done and the targets that have to be achieved. If these are achieved, as most important ones are, through people, then the relationships, the gel of people working together, becomes very important. The relationship aspects are referred to by some management researchers as 'maintenance'.

What types of behaviour are relevant to the group's fulfilment of its task? What types of behaviour are relevant to the group's cohesion, working together and making the best use of the group's collective resources and strengths? What types of behaviour detract from group cohesion and are self-orientated rather than group/task-orientated [25]?

Our study of management has revealed the importance not only of the manager, but also the importance of the subordinates. Within leisure services the users and clients of all kinds also have considerable inputs into the services and can greatly enhance decision-making, if handled properly. Committees, forums, governing bodies, club officials, sports councils, arts councils, user committees, community groups, and the like, may all be represented in some form within leisure management. Therefore, the understanding not only of managers and their staff, but also the whole gamut of individuals, either singly, in groups or through formal committees, is extremely important.

There are different types of group; two main types can be classified as *primary* and *seconday* groups. Primary groups are made up of a relatively small number of people in a common task. Secondary groups are made up of a larger number and no one member has a clear picture of all the others. These groups can be further classified by their development – i.e. *formal* groups (those deliberately created), and *informal* groups (created by accident). We are concerned here with the primary groups.

13.8.1 Primary groups

Primary groups are made up of a small number of individuals engaged in a common task who have regular face-to-face contact with one another – e.g. the family, the play group, the mother and toddler group, the work group, the club, the church and the youth group. The primary group is an instrument of society through which individuals acquire many of their attitudes, opinions and ideals and one of the sources of control and discipline. The primary group can be one of the main satisfiers of an individual's need for status and emotional security. In the leisure context, the club leader, the society secretary and the sports coach fulfil status and emotional needs.

Primary groups tend to 'appoint' or have a natural leader. Generally speaking, the more harmonious the group becomes, the more efficient will be its performance in most respects. The experience of team spirit, of belonging and sharing defeats and successes, make for extremely strong bonds. Disharmonious groups tend to be less effective. Primary groups appear to exhibit the following behavioural patterns:

1. Initial suspicion towards the newcomer.
2. Set standards of behaviour; non-conformity is often punished by the alienation of the individual; acceptance of standards is rewarded by respect, emotional security and status.
3. Casting members into roles which they are expected to maintain.
4. Indulgence in ceremonies and rituals; these strengthen the group bonding and emphasize the privilege of belonging; for example, there are initiation rites (Masonic, Rotary, Ancient Order of Foresters), intensification rites (annual dinners, stag nights, hen parties, presentations of medals or trophies) and departure rites (parties, gifts and farewell speech-making).
5. Groups, even undirected, set themselves tasks.
6. In group discussions individuals show behavioural patterns which are primarily directed towards the task and/or directed towards improving relations between members of the group.

Leisure Managers dealing with groups need to understand primary group behaviour and respect their standards, ceremonies and collective needs. Harmonious groups working together, helping the newcomer and maintaining good relationships are the groups likely to aid, not inhibit, the fulfilment of managerial goals.

13.8.2 Modes of behaviour within a group

The modes of behaviour within groups have been termed:

1. task-orientated;
2. maintenance-orientated;
3. self-orientated.

Both 'task' and 'maintenance' are important in varying situations, depending on the needs both of management and staff, whereas the behaviour within self-orientated groups hinders or obstructs the achievement of common goals. This behaviour can arise because the individual is faced with certain problems in the group, problems of identity, personal goals and needs vs. the group goals and needs, and so on. These undercurrents cannot be ignored; they should be recognized and attempts made to integrate the individual needs with the group's goals.

The more commitment to a decision which is gained in the group, the higher the likelihood that the group will act in accordance with what has been decided. The process, the procedure and the *way* in which a decision is taken will affect the effectiveness of the decision.

As a guide, Argyris and others [26,27] have put forward ten criteria, based on empirical research that they see as necessary for group competence and effectiveness; they are:

1. Contributions made within the group are additive.
2. The group moves forwards as a unit, is team-spirited and there is high involvement.
3. Decisions are mainly made by consensus.
4. Commitment to a decision is strong.
5. The group continually evaluates itself.
6. The group is clear about goals.
7. It generates alternative ways of thinking about things.
8. It brings conflict into the open and deals with it.
9. It deals openly with feelings.
10. Leadership tends to go (or move) to the person most qualified.

13.8.3 Inter-group behaviour: conflict and cooperation

Individuals, because they have differing goals, needs and ways of looking at the world, often find themselves in conflict with others. If an individual can only gain his or her goals at the expense of others, more conflict is likely.

Conflict, however, is not in itself undersirable; only through expression of differences can good problem-solving take place. For everyone to agree is as unrealistic as expecting that no agreement is possible. But conflict so severe as to disable the participants – prevent the continuation of problem-solving – is undesirable.

Some light may be shed on conflict and cooperation between individuals by looking at the problems of conflict and cooperation between groups [25]. There appear to be strong forces to keep members in the group.

What happens when two (or more) groups are faced with a problem of some kind involving their interest? The problem may be 'solved' by maintaining isolation between the groups, by enforcing unification of the two groups or by allowing one group to destroy the other. By assuming that a real solution is wanted which satisfies both groups, then some kind of joint problem-solving process must take place.

Since group membership is such an important part of our lives, it follows that inter-group conflict is likely to be especially acute. We cannot direct our hostile feelings within our own groups very strongly – to do so would invite rejection. Thus any inter-group problem-solving situation is likely to contain hostility, along with genuine attempts at cooperation. The more the inter-group situation is defined as *win/lose*, the more likely we are to see certain effects leading to confrontation. The more it is defined as *problem-solving*, the less likely the adverse effects. The effects, however, never wholly disappear.

When inter-group exercises have been run in training laboratories, it has been found that *within the group*, the group pulls in close; it sees only the best in itself and the worst in the other groups; it feels that it must guard certain territory; and it demands more conformity from its members.

The interaction *between groups* reveals a tendency for members of one group to become hostile towards the other group; there is a reduction in communication between the groups, and a lack of willingness on behalf of the group to listen to the views of the other; and there is mistrust by one group of the other. On the 'resolution' of the conflict, the *winning group* tends to retain its cohesion or become more cohesive. It becomes complacent ('fat and happy') and there is a release of tension with a reduction in fighting spirit and greater playfulness. There is a high element of cooperation but little work is actually done. On the other hand, the *losing group* splinters, fights, and reorganizes. There is an increase in tension, and the group ('lean and hungry') seeks scapegoats among its leaders and organization. If it sees future 'wins' as impossible, it becomes introspective, self-blaming and depressed. But the group can learn a lot about itself.

Effects like those described above are familiar enough in recreation services, political parties, committees, clubs, departmental sections and are exhibited in inter-departmental problems. The attempted Football League club mergers like Queens Park Rangers and Fulham in England, and Glasgow Celtic and Motherwell in Scotland, vividly illustrate the point.

How can these negative effects be reduced, so that good problem-solving can be maintained at a desirable level of conflict? The answer is to find an *overriding goal* – one which both (or all) groups accept as essential to reach and which *both* can reach – thus '*win/lose*' changes to '*win/win*' and both groups can be satisfied with their achievement.

In recent years, the use of groups – Quality Circles – has become an accepted procedure for problem-solving within an organization. In this way, a group that has a range of abilities and knowledge is more likely to identify all the possible options available, provided that the group environment is receptive to suggestions from all its members and that the size of the group is manageable.

13.9 QUALITY MANAGEMENT CALLS FOR QUALITY MANAGERS

As we have seen, good management is largely the result of good managers, individuals who have the responsibility for providing leadership of the organization and the ability to move it towards its goals.

In a study of successful facility managers in the public and private sectors [28], five essential criteria were found to be almost universal:

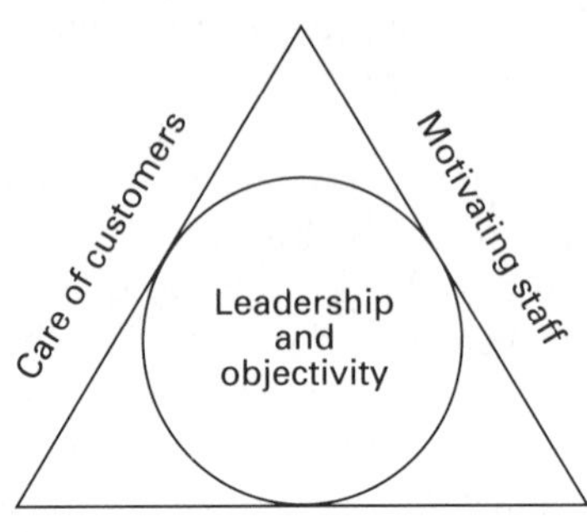

Fig. 13.5 A model for the effective operational management of leisure facilities. Source: based on observation and interviews by Torkildsen, G., reported in *Leisure Management* [28].

sound leadership; objectivity; staff motivation; care of customers; and operational excellence. Fig. 13.5 illustrates the centrality of leadership and objectivity.

In addition to these 'bankers' within the 'effective operational model', management to be effective needs to be flexible to accommodate changing circumstances and to meet the needs of different people. In addition, different managers have different styles of management. The same manager may also have a number of different styles, depending on the different situations. What is becoming clear is that a manager armed with only one style of management may be ill-equipped for the variety of different tasks and people to be handled – just like the golfer with only one club!

The business of leisure, where people choose what to do and where staff have to be flexible and work unsocial hours, calls for styles of management in keeping with providing good customer care and service giving. In these circumstances, the 'democratic' manager with a professional 'executive style' is more likely to succeed. He or she will see the job as effectively maximizing the efforts of others. This manager's commitment to both task and relationships will be evident to all. He or she is not afraid of conflicts and recognizes them as important in understanding the task and the people; such behaviour is seen as normal and sometimes appropriate: these managers often work with a *team*; they are concerned will participation and involvement; ideas can come from any quarter; and the greater number of possibilities explored, the better the understanding of the problem. They still have to lead: they cannot hide behind the team; and they still have to make the ultimate decision but both manager and staff feel involved in the failures and successes. This style of management is an 'objective' art gained with experience and learning, allied to personal flair. Other styles of management will be far easier but it is this quality of management which is essential to the leisure and recreation service.

13.10 MANAGEMENT: SUMMARY

In this chapter we have looked at the management processes, leadership, decision-making, communications and group behaviour and systems such as Total Quality Management. Management must be appropriate to different situations, and the manager must adapt his or her style of management to be appropriate to changing situations.

A manager needs to understand the processes involved in the way people behave within and between groups. It is suggested that the principles of good management apply to any field of collective human endeavour and leisure and recreation is no exception. The management principles and process apply, whether in the public, the private or the commercial sector.

There are many differences between the public, voluntary and commercial sectors but the similarities – in terms of management – are fundamental. Managers in all sectors are managing people and situations in such a way as to provide opportunities for people's leisure. The operation of facilities and the specific technical tasks are secondary to the management of people to achieve results and meet objectives and targets.

The study of management has shown that there are two main management parameters: – the task (the job), and relationships (the people). There needs to be a balance between the two. Other areas of this study deal with aspects of task. This chapter has concentrated on the manager's need to understand people and the relationships between them, whether as individuals or in groups. Without this understanding, and without the ability to communicate, motivate and lead, the manager's chance of successfully and effectively undertaking a task or meeting the needs of his or her customers is considerably reduced. Moreover, management and leadership must be situational and adaptable to change. Wess Roberts (29), in *Leadership Secrets of Attila the Hun*, believes that it is a privilege to direct the actions of others. Leadership flexibility is crucial; no model can anticipate circumstances. Hence quality management requires quality managers and leaders.

REFERENCES AND NOTES

1. Drucker, P. F. (1955), *The Practice of Management*, Pan Books, London, p. 19.

2. Gray, D. E., quoted in R. L. Wilder (1977), EEI: a survival tool. *Parks and Recreation*, August, 23.
3. Wilder, R. L. (1977), EEI: a survival tool. *Parks and Recreation*, August, 23.
4. Drucker, P. F. (1955), *The Practice of Management*, Pan Books, London, p. 30.
5. The work of Taylor is fully considered in Wren, D. (1972), *The Evolution of Management Thought*, Ronald Press, New York, 1972.
6. Mayo, E. (1933), *The Human Problems of an Industrial Civilisation*, Macmillan, New York.
7. Fayol, H. (1930), Administration industrielle et générale (trans. J. A. Coubrough) *Industrial and General Administration*, International Management Institute, Geneva, pp. 40–107.
8. The work of Weber is fully considered in Wren, D. (1972), *The Evolution of Management Thought*, Ronald Press, New York.
9. McGregor, D. (1966), *The Human Side of Enterprise*, McGraw-Hill, New York.
10. Herzberg, F., Mausner, B. and Synderman, B. (1959), *The Motivation to Work*, Wiley, New York.
11. Maslow, A. H. (1954), *Motivation and Personality*, Harper and Row, New York.
12. Maslow, A. H. (1968), *Towards a Psychology of Being*, D. Van Nostrand, New York.
13. Argyris, C. (1957), *Personality and Organization*, Harper and Row, New York.
14. Likert, R. (1967), *The Human Organization: Its Management and Value*, McGraw-Hill, New York.
15. MacKenzie, R. (1969), The management process in 3-D. *Harvard Business Review*, November–December.
16. Odiorne, G. (1965), *Management by Objectives: A System of Managerial Leadership*, Pitman, New York, p. 55.
17. Mosscrop, P. and Stores, A. in association with the Institute of Leisure and Amenity Management (1990), *Total Quality Management in Leisure. A Guide for Directors and Managers*, Collinson Grant Consultants, Manchester.
18. Mosscrop, P. (1990), *Total quality management*, paper presented at Recman '90, Wembley, March.
19. Oakland, J. S. (1989), *Total Quality Management*, Heinemann Professional, Oxford.
20. Tannenbaum, R. and Schmidt, W. H. (1958), How to choose a leadership pattern. *Harvard Business Review*, March–April, 95–101.
21. Townsend, R. (1970), *Up the Organisation*, Coronet Books, London.
22. Video Arts Booklet, *Decisions, Decisions*, to accompany the film, *Decisions, Decisions*.
23. Welsh, A. N. (1980), *The Skills of Management*, Gower, Farnborough.
24. Kent, S. (1981), Good communications. *Parks and Recreation, September*, 27–30.
25. Early ideas were learned from: Sheppard, Moscow Associates (1970), Management Seminars, Eastbourne, January–February, unpublished.
26. Argyris, C. (1976), *Increasing Leadership Effectiveness*, Wiley, New York.

27. Argyris, C. (1966), Interpersonal barriers to decision making. *Harvard Business Review*, **44**, 2, 84–97.
28. Torkildsen, G. (1986), Managers as they see themselves and as we see them. *Leisure Management*, February, **6**(2), 26–31.
29. Roberts, W. (1989), *Leadership Secrets of Attila the Hun*, Bantam Books, London.

RECOMMENDED ADDITIONAL READING

A very useful and comprehensive general management manual is: Elliott G. (ed.) (1990), *The Manager's Guidebook*, Longman, Harlow.

SIMON
6
5

Chapter 14

Programming leisure and recreation services and facilities

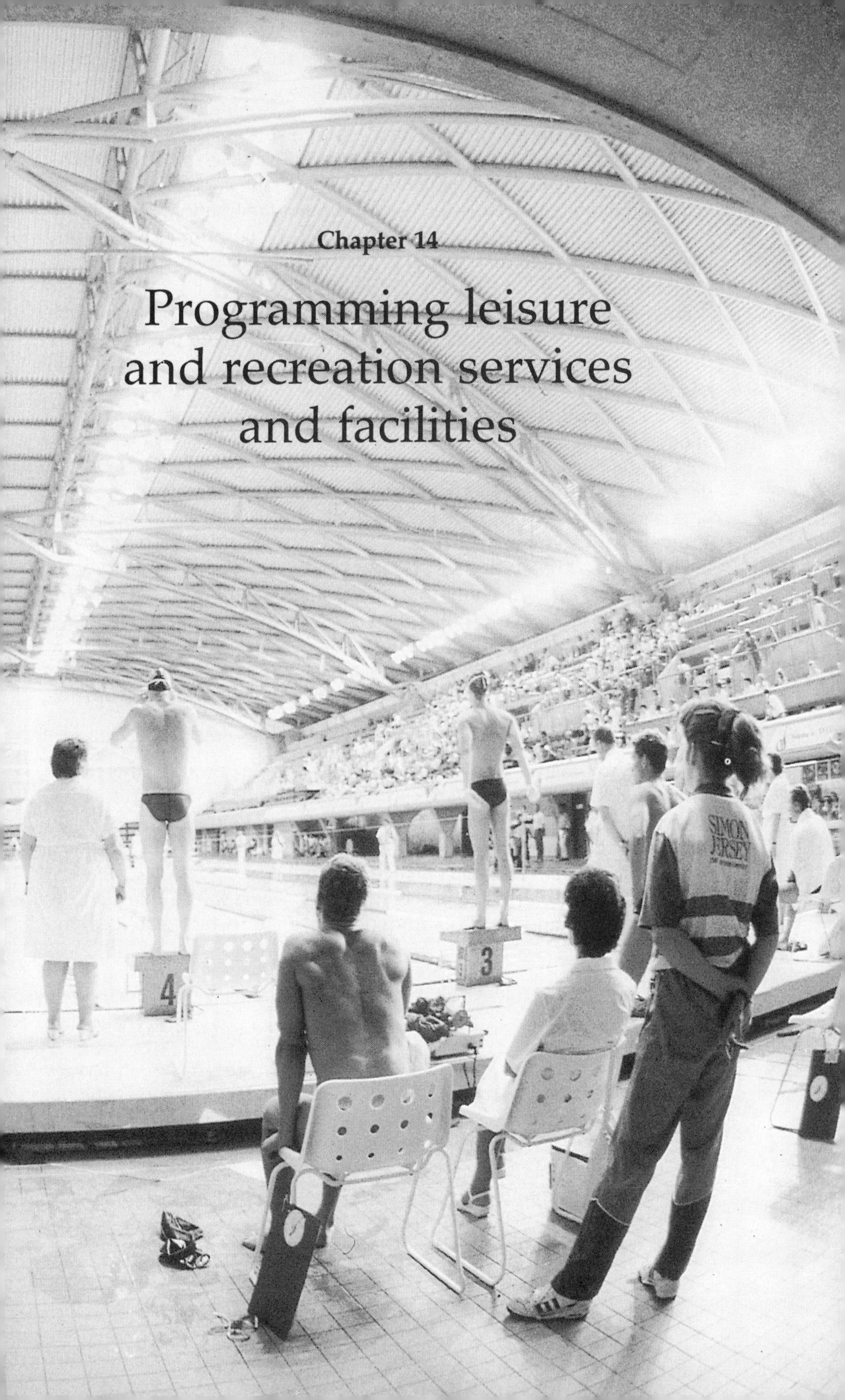

We have seen in preceding chapters that the Leisure Manager, particularly in the public sector, must have sufficient knowledge to assist policy-makers, faced by complex political, economic and social conditions, in establishing guidelines for effective community recreation. The Leisure Manager must also have sufficient knowledge of programming strategies, approaches and methods in order to direct staff in achieving the aims and objectives of the organization.

While social conditions and economic problems must be faced, this chapter concentrates on the programming process and the manager's role in that process. The leisure field is so varied and complex that in giving practical examples to support ideas, there has been a need for selection. Greater emphasis has been given to public recreation services and facility programmes.

First, the question is raised: what is programming? *Second*, two main directional strategies are debated. *Third*, a number of specific programming approaches and methods which fall within the two main strategies are summarized. *Fourth*, the problems and the lessons to be learned from current practices are noted. *Fifth*, the case for greater caring and sensitivity in programming for disadvantaged groups is made. *Sixth*, a leisure facility programme planning process – Programming by Objectives – is proposed.

Having read this chapter, readers will understand something of the complexity of programming and its crucial role in providing leisure and recreation opportunity for more people. It is the means by which objectives are met.

Readers will learn that programming is an ongoing process, that needs a framework and objectivity; it is not a series of activities strung together, but an integrated and planned process. They will learn how to establish aims and objectives, how to set strategies, approaches and methods, how to choose activities and balance a programme and how to measure results. In so doing, recreation activity programmers will be able logically to assign a continuous programming sequence to their services and facilities.

14.1 WHAT IS LEISURE AND RECREATION PROGRAMMING?

Programming is important. It is a highly underrated factor in leisure management. It is a complex process requiring excellent management. Programming must achieve optimal use of existing resources – facilities, manpower and finance – to meet the goals of the organization and the needs of people.

Leisure programming consists of planning, scheduling, timetabling and implementing action which uses resources, facilities and staff to offer a wide range of services and activities – passive, active, routine, guided, graded, varied and special – within the reach of the community to be served.

Programming is a *process* of planning to meet the diverse needs of people. The programme is the essence of recreation services; it is their *raision d'être*. Yet it is important to remember that it is people and their needs which are the reasons for a recreation organization's existence and therefore people's needs must be the focal point of services. Programmes are the tools of the Leisure Manager; they are the vehicles through which leisure opportunity is made available to the community.

The programme is the single most important function of a leisure and recreation organization. Everything that a service or department is concerned with – facilities, supplies, personnel, budgets, marketing, public relations, activities, timetabling and administration – is solely to ensure that opportunities exist for people to enjoy or experience leisure in ways satisfying to them. The opportunity is made available through the programme.

One of the hallmarks of good programming is the extent to which individual satisfaction, individual welfare and the values of the participant are important aspects of the programme. While numbers are important, the individual rather than the aggregate must be the core of the service. Programmes are often judged on how many have attended; qualitative aspects are rarely brought into any evaluation. In order to programme for people, we should bring people into programme planning. It is important not just to dictate, but to work towards participant planning. Within the broad range of leisure programming, a fundamental aspect, for public sector services, is *Community Recreation Programming*.

14.1.1 Which agencies undertake recreation programming?

There are many sponsoring agencies involved in recreation programming; for example, education authorities, local government, commercial organizations, industry, HM Forces, religious organizations and private institutions, associations and clubs.

In terms of community recreation, however, local government should be the *coordinator* of services. Why? Whether by statutory duty or not, it is the only agency with a primary responsibility for provision and promotion of community-wide recreation, using rates and taxes so to do. Therefore, the local government agency needs to plan, prepare, create opportunities and a coordination network to handle community-wide services. It must, first, put its own house in order to ascertain whether it has the resources, knowledge and capability of undertaking this extremely complex task.

Local government has three main functions in the recreation programming process:

1. The provision of resources, facilities and activities.
2. The coordination of resources in the community and assistance to other providers and enablers.
3. Management and leadership.

14.1.2 What constitutes a programme?

What makes a programme? Does it have to be a class, a timetable of bookings, a league or a list of events? Or can it be the planned availability of a playground, a park, a school or venture trail? Or can it exist through the organized distribution of services such as a recreation and leisure information service which collates all that is going on? A programme is all these things and a good deal more. It can take almost any form in the framework of one's definition of what constitutes a recreation experience. However, in terms of practicality, programmes revolve around three basic elements: activities, facilities and services.

1. *Activities* can range from the completely spontaneous variety to the highly structured and all stages in between. Informal activities can be anticipated within a community programme by creating opportunities, encouraging spontaneity, having resources available such as space, time and equipment – e.g. a ball to kick about, a wall to scribble on or deck chairs to sunbathe on. Structured activities, for programming purposes, fall into several major categories such as: arts, crafts, dance, drama, entertainment, games, sport and physical recreation, hobbies, music, nature, social recreation, travel and tourism, and voluntary service to the community.

2. *Facilities* cover all areas, buildings, supplies and equipment within recreation. These can be designed and constructed for special purposes such as public swimming pools; designed for self-directed or spontaneous activity like a park; or simply the natural resources available to the public such as riverside walks, forests and beaches.

3. *Services* cover all methods and means through which people are enabled to enjoy leisure and recreation, for example, lending libraries, transport, community services and information services.

The recreation programme, however, is not a series of individual activities strung together. It is a carefully integrated and planned combination of many activities selected on the basis of individual and group interest, related ideas and themes organized to achieve particular aims. Among these are the realization of personal fulfilment, satisfaction, enjoyment, physical and mental health and the development of positive social relationships. Essentially, programming is the balanced correlation of leadership, required space, facility, equipment and activity, for a customer at an appropriate time and place.

14.2 PROGRAMME CLASSIFICATION

How a programme is classified is not of major importance. However, the *type* of programme needs to be known in order to communicate with the public and avoid preconceived misconceptions. Programmes can be classified in a number of ways, for example, by:

1. function;
2. facilities;
3. people; and
4. outcomes.

By far the most usual classification is functional – i.e. by a listing of the activities offered. Often the functional classification is linked to special groups of people: children, youth, handicapped, aged, beginners, advanced, and so on. Sometimes it may be important to classify the clientele likely to use community recreation programmes.

Sociologists and psychologists tend to group people for classification into life stages. In Chapter 5 changes in the life-cycle and their importance on recreation was discussed. Erikson [1] identified eight stages; six stages up to young adulthood and two stages beyond. Meyer [2] presented four adult stages. Farrell and Lundegren [3] identified a range of activities through eleven life-cycle changes: pre-school, early childhood, late elementary, youth, teenage, young adults, early adulthood, maturity, later middle age, old age and senescence. However, these can be merged for many programmes (e.g. youth, teenager and young adults can be grouped together), or the groups can be further broken down (e.g. pre-school into toddlers, infants and pre-school). Further classification can be made regarding the activities themselves: passive/active, structured/unstructured, planned/self-directed, high risk/low risk, etc.

In summary, the community recreation programme is both the end-product and the means of attaining the aims and objectives of an agency or organization. It has been defined as 'the total experiences of individuals and groups resulting from community action in providing areas, facilities, leadership and funds. These experiences represent a wide range of activities, planned and spontaneous, organized and informal, supervised and undirected' [4]. An essential element that influences the success or failure of the programme to meet its stated objectives is *management*. This is the one ingredient, without which public recreation services lose much impact.

14.3 DIRECTIONAL PLANNING STRATEGIES TO COMMUNITY RECREATION PROGRAMMING

Two major directions for the planning of community recreation programmes, put simplistically, are;

1. Planned programmes directed professionally by officers or authorities.
2. Programmes which emanate from the community itself.

They could be termed 'other directed' and 'community initiated'. Recreation texts describe the directions as *social planning* and *community development* [5].

The social planning approach is the most common. The basic assumption underlying this process is that use of professional expertise and knowledge is the most effective way of meeting needs and solving community problems.

Community development, on the other hand, is a method of organization in which the role of the professional is one of assisting individuals in the programming process, rather than intervening with services to bring about the desired changes. The locus of control is the important factor. Change occurs as a result of community intervention and involvement, not as a result of the diagnosis of a professional or the authority. The process itself and the participation is part of the experiencing; participants assume initiatives for their own development.

The social planning method is *participant dependent* and professional and authority controlled. The community development approach fosters *participant independence*. The distinction of the differing approaches is put cogently by Edginton *et al.* [6]:

'It is important to draw a distinction between the work of a *community developer* and the work of a *social planner*. Perhaps the most important difference concerns the view that each has of the participant. The social planner views the participant as a consumer of his services. The role is to isolate individuals with needs and then intervene directly with services. The community developer, on the other hand, views participants as citizens with whom he or she engages in an interactive process of problem solving. The social planner is primarily involved in fact gathering in an effort to determine the needs of the individuals being served. Once the appropriate information has been gathered, it is used in the decision making process to develop a rational plan for the distribution of available or acquired resources. The community developer, however, maintains a basic strategy of change in which the role is to help individuals identify and bring about change through their collaborative efforts. The community developer works with individuals and small groups, whereas the work of the social planner is primarily carried out in large bureaucratic organisations. The skills needed by the social planner are primarily those of management and administration; the community developer's skills should be particularly strong in the areas of communications and small group behaviour'.

The adoption of a community development approach needs capable, trained men and women 'out in the field'. Community developers have become known by many names: 'encourager', 'enabler', 'catalyst', 'friend', 'adviser', 'activator', etc. The French use the words 'animateur' or 'animateur sociale'. *Animateurs* are well-trained, capable and sensitive people who work towards stimulating individuals to think about their own development and also the development of other people in the community, through community programming. They work to develop the leadership capabilities of others. They assist by supplying information about methods and procedures; they *enable* others to act for themselves.

The relationship between the 'animateur' and the group changes as the group matures. Initially, the 'animateur' fulfils the role of the 'benevolent authoritarian' leader and undertakes the necessary tasks associated with the activities of the group and its maintenance. With continued contact, the role of the animateur changes to that of a democratic leader; and as leaders emerge from the group, his or her role diminishes and the groups largely become autonomous but with support available, should it be necessary. This support is normally required if the natural leaders of the group leave and there are no immediate replacements.

The experience in the United Kingdom has shown that short-term (say, for three years) outreach programmes that undertake a similar function are only successful as long as the support is available. When the programmes cease through lack of funding, the majority of the newly formed groups after a period of time flounder due partly to the lack of physical and/or psychological support.

Traditionally, local authorities have undertaken the social planning approach to programming with much of the work undertaken centrally and away from the facilities. Such an approach has considerable disadvantages:

1. The decision-makers are remote from the potential users of the facilities.
2. There is generally a lack of consultation and sensitivity concerning the needs and demands of the community.
3. The facility staff are not involved in the decision-making process and there is generally a lack of accountability and commitment at

facility level; this manifests itself with poor staff motivation and low job satisfaction.
4. Decision making is slow and programming tends to be repetitive and unimaginative.

In recent years, the tendency has been to decentralize the programming and there has also been a change in emphasis. Initially, the focus was on the facility but this has now moved towards specific activities and groups, while the most enlightened leisure managers have progressed further and are now focusing on the community development approach [7].

With the economic constraints imposed upon local authorities, a new role is emerging for the Leisure Manager. This is as negotiator and coordinator, whereby community access is obtained at commercial and private leisure facilities, such as indoor tennis facilities, at specific times to identified groups.

14.3.1 Twin-directional strategies

Looking across the broad spectrum of recreation programming, it seems clear that to adopt one direction to the exclusion of the other would be inappropriate. Both strategies have merit. A blend of the two is not only possible, but also essential. In addition to the directional mixture, the actual specific approaches and methods can be selected to meet particular sectors of the programme or to suit particular requirements. To achieve a blend and balance of direction and of approach calls for high skills of management and for programme planning objectivity.

14.4 SPECIFIC METHODS AND APPROACHES

Within the broad framework of the two main directional strategies lies a range of specific approaches and methods of programming.

Providing leisure opportunity is so diverse and complex that there is no one approach, system or method which is suitable for all organizations, all situations or all people. The different methods are known by a variety of names; most of them have no agreed formal titles. Most methods appear to evolve as a result of the nature and the aims of the organizations themselves. From nearly 30 approaches which have been identified, including those of Farrell and Lundegren [3], Edginton [8] and Kraus and Curtis [9], this section groups some of these together into eleven broad approaches or methods.

(i) The traditional approach

This has been described as a 'rehash of the same old thing'. The approach, however, suggests that what has gone on in the past and is generally successful is likely to be repeated. It relies on the same format for future programme planning. It is not necessarily based on needs, but on what has worked before. As a *single* approach, it is ineffective. It can be a far more useful approach by learning from the past and making modifications for the future.

(ii) The comparative current trends approach

This approach relies on reacting to recent trends or activities in vogue. This has benefits in meeting some new demands. However, the approach is totally experimental. It is likely to serve only a segment of the market, and what may work in one area may be a total failure in others. Yet fads are important to provide for but must be seen in context.

(iii) The expressed desires approach

By asking people and through questionnaires and surveys it is assumed that desires are ascertained. Therefore, by programming for people's wishes they are given what they apparently want. But will this result in actual participation? And which activities will meet which desires? Such an approach is difficult to administer, but it is a valuable tool for the programme planner; it gives information about people's attitudes and behaviour.

This approach has its limitations, however, as many respondents do not really know what they want and cannot predict with any degree of accuracy what their future leisure behaviour is likely to be. Indeed, prior to the opening of two specific sports centres, the surveys indicated that there was a considerable demand for the use of the sports hall for indoor tennis. Unfortunately, this perceived demand never materialized and the facilities concerned have never been used by the local community for indoor tennis.

(iv) The authoritarian approach

Reliance is placed on the judgement of the controller, head of department or manager. The assumption is that he or she understands what the needs are and what the community wants. This is a quick and tidy approach at its design and planning stage. However, participants are denied any involvement in the programme process. Such an approach makes it difficult to adapt to a more community-orientated strategy.

The 'prescriptive' approach [8], and 'perceived need' approach [9], are very similar to the authoritarian approach. They too require a diagnosis of needs. Programming by perceived needs is a tempting approach to adopt because it *appears* to be based on needs. However, without community involvement, it relies on professional expertise to diagnose other people's needs.

(v) The political/social approach

Edginton *et al.* [8], and Kraus and Curtis [9], both use the term 'socio-political'. In this case, pressure from groups, often linked to social causes, is used as a basis for a community programme. Such causes are invariably grist to the political mill – they carry councillor support. For example, crime, poverty, deprivation, discrimination and social disorder may call for particular kinds of recreation planning and programming. Leisure Managers do not operate in a vacuum, but have to respond to political and social pressure and to changing conditions.

(vi) Action–investigation–creation plan approach

Tillman [10] suggests that a three-phase plan to programming is the most effective. The action plan, in actuality, is reaction to the demands generated by the community. The investigation plan is concerned with fact-finding. The creation plan is the interactive relationship between participants and professionals. The professionals use their own expertise and actively seek the views and involvement of participants. Such a three-phase plan, allied to aims and objectives, could form a logical basis for programming.

(vii) External requirements approach

Here the programme is basically dictated by an authority, an institution or a governing body. It tends to have uniform standards, leadership and resources and there is an external assessment for measuring. A Scout or Girl Guide troop, for example, will satisfy headquarters' requirements. Such organizations normally have vertical management structures, a hierarchical leadership pattern, similar resources, administration and an external reward system. Uniformed groups like British Red Cross, St John Ambulance Brigade and Girls' Brigade and Boys' Brigade, and newer groups like the Majorettes, are clear examples.

(viii) Cafeteria-style approach

James Murphy is reported to have termed this approach the 'cafeteria' style [8]. In this 'smorgasbord' approach, a variety of diverse choices are assembled, giving many opportunities. People can make their own selection. This is a useful approach, in that there is a variety of choice; people may not know what they want and can try things out, 'suck it and see'. Additionally, such an approach is necessary to meet the diverse needs of groups including family groups, which endorses the success of placing leisure facilities in clusters as opposed to stand-alone facilities. It is a safe approach but tends to be expensive. While appearing to be the answer to the manager's dilemma, it is ineffective in the use of resources, in that it can create and provide services which are unused because they have not been chosen. And in addition, it is very difficult to set objectives and measure success – some activities will be winners and others losers, but the reasons may not be known. For example, poor marketing, rather than the activity, may be the cause. Nevertheless, any comprehensive programming will need to indulge in a cafeteria approach for some of its recreation programmes.

(ix) The demand approach: offer what people want

Here programmers rely on consumer input of what *some* people want. This is the most usual form of programming in the public sector. Clubs, associations and interest groups make known their demands. Hence managers are faced with scores of applications requesting specific facilities. However, the most vocal, the most aware and the socially articulate will make their demands known most readily. The approach is not concerned with equitable distribution and may result in narrow segmental programming. Many people and groups will not be aware of the recreation options and benefits. Most comprehensive programmes, however, will and should include this approach within the overall plan.

(x) The community orientation approach

This is a process based on using people's talents and capabilities. Here individuals are involved in the planning process. The approach is only possible by using professionals or capable amateurs to meet people on their own patch, for example, through outreach programmes, associations and community counsellors.

The *discovery approach* is an extension and continuation of community orientation. It assumes that people can work together, there being no superior or subordinate relationships. One's knowledge, skills, abilities and interests are used to meet another's needs without necessarily imposing value systems or external expectations. The approach is a people-to-people approach of interactive discovery requiring community face-to-face leadership.

(xi) Community leadership approach

Here consumer input is made possible through advisory boards, user committees, tenants' groups and other action groups. They represent concerns of the community. This approach assumes that individual interests are represented by their group. This, of course, is not wholly possible, but it does indicate community interaction and a level of democracy. As Edginton *et al.* emphasize, it opens channels of communication between providers and consumers [8]. It is a valuable tool for the recreation programmer.

In summary, this section has described some specific approaches to community recreation programming albeit briefly. Which approach or method is the most appropriate? Which direction should Leisure Managers take? The review has brought to light several important factors to be borne in mind when programming; it has unveiled many problems and it offers some solutions. The next section considers the problems, the lessons to be learned and suggests a solution to some of the problem areas – a logical approach to community recreation programming.

14.5 THE NEED FOR A COMPREHENSIVE, COORDINATED, OBJECTIVE APPROACH

Leisure and recreation organizations are faced with the twin dilemma: which strategic programming direction should be taken? Which methods should be adopted to meet objectives?

The manager is the key person in finding solutions. This is were the manager should come into his or her own. He or she will be trained and experienced to 'read' the situation. One of the guiding principles will be that programming must be situationally and culturally specific. There are different communities, different problems, different aims and therefore different objectives. The good manager must be a realist and use whatever approaches and options are open to meet needs and demands effectively and to be efficient in planning and operating the programme.

Needs assessment is complex. Part of the solution is gradually to make it possible for people to interpret their own needs and plan their own programmes. Managers must therefore learn how to involve people in programme planning. The Leisure Manager must:

1. Understand the lessons to be learned from the various strategies and approaches.
2. Understand the problems within current community recreation programming.
3. Devise a logical and objective approach to his or her own situation, bearing in mind the resources available and the constraints to programming.

14.5.1 The lessons to be learned

Many programmes have become excellent with improved management performance. Important lessons have been learned about programming from observation of over 100 recreation centre programmes [11], as follows.

1. There are serious problems within recreation programming and many ineffective programmes. The accent has been on efficiency and tradition, not on effectiveness and community need.

2. There appear to be two major strategic directions in which programme planning can be undertaken. One relies on using programmers to 'dictate' what the programme shall be (this is the most usual). The other starts with communities – the role of the professional being one of enabling and assisting. A combination of the two is necessary.
3. The strategy balance and the specific approaches employed depend on the organization, department capability, the aims, the community to be served, other providers, staff skills, money, facilities and a whole variety of other factors. Programmers are thus often caught in the system of 'having' to proceed along certain lines.
4. Most programmers do not use a single approach. Most use a number of approaches, but they are often an untidy mix, a 'hotchpotch', overlapping and uncoordinated.
5. Programmes are often the result of educated guesswork and are built up on hunches. This results in a hit or miss approach and lack of predictability; it is certainly not built on people's needs, but rather on managers' ideas.
6. Programming is a continuous and changing process requiring constant monitoring and thorough evaluation. This assumption leads logically towards a programming approach which is geared to systems which are tailor-made to particular settings and situations.
7. Due to the complexity of the programming process the task of programming should be undertaken by a senior member of staff.

Integral to the lessons to be learned and the problems encountered in recreation programming, is the fact that many managers in community recreation have little knowledge, limited experience and poor training in the context of recreation programming.

14.5.2 Specific problems within recreation programmes

In order to get the objectives right, Leisure Managers should consider the problems of many of the programmes currently practised. Working from operational experience, a wide range of problems occur constantly within recreation facility programmes:

1. Demands are not assessed.
2. Objectives are rarely measurable.
3. Programmes tend to be too traditional, static and much 'the same old thing' – the same activities, same methods and same people.
4. Programmes lack variety and novelty.
5. Often a 'take it or leave it' approach is adopted, regardless of whether the programme is appropriate to the target groups in the community.

6. The advantages and disadvantages of membership systems are not evaluated fully.
7. The need to balance casual use with club use and events is not based on policy, but expediency.
8. The need to analyse the benefits and problems of different activities is rarely considered.
9. User life-flow patterns such as regular, habit-forming activities are broken into by insensitive programming.
10. Programme patterns, such as seasonality, are not given due consideration.
11. Incompatible activities are sometimes programmed together.
12. Insufficient programme flexibility and the need to adapting to given situations which require sensitive management.
13. Ways of expanding an already busy programme are insufficiently explored.
14. Programmes must be more socially acceptable.
15. Programme organization and administration require greater efficiency.
16. Many programmes which are claimed to be comprehensive contain imbalance: clubs, leagues and classes abound in recreation centres, table tennis and discos in youth centres and there are generally few community-orientated programmes in community facilities. This is a myopic view of a programme.
17. Programme worth is increasingly judged on numbers allied to financial viability. Qualitative programming gives way under such strain.
18. Risk avoidance leads to a lack-lustre approach, having a lack of creativity, stifled programmes, lack of adventure and non-appeal for young people.
19. Some facilities are used for single purposes which occupy only a proportion of time and attract a narrow market segment.
20. Many resources – e.g. schools, church buildings, factory canteens and industrial recreation facilities – remain underused.
21. Programme monitoring and evaluation are rarely carried out to change and improve programme content.

14.6 COMMUNITY RECREATION MANAGEMENT AND DISADVANTAGED GROUPS

It has been shown unequivocally, that the public sector leisure facilities are used disproportionately by those who are more affluent and mobile than those who have social, economic and other hardships. Such social hardships, in relation to leisure participation, have been highlighted from a number of sources, including, Griffiths's survey in Greenwich [12], Torkildsen's survey of lone parents in Harlow and use of public leisure facilities [13] and in the work of a number of leisure researchers. Haywood and Henry's 'Policy developments in community leisure and recreation – implications for management' [7] offers insights into non-traditional ways of developing services for communities and targeting disadvantaged groups.

Effective community recreation management can be measured in part by the degree to which a reasonable balance of the various population market segments within a community have been attracted across the range of services. Torkildsen's study found that those least likely to use leisure facilities are characterized by having low incomes, poor mobility and dependent young children. The problems are exacerbated if children are being cared for by a lone parent. Recreation and leisure do not appear to be of much relevance to the lot of disadvantaged people due to a combination of factors, including constant responsibility for children, lack of money, no use of a car, loss of confidence and lack of a partner.

It is the continuing theme of this book that leisure participation can lead to building up of self-image and self-confidence. Management flexibility, to cope with the different needs of different customers, deserves far greater attention. Clearly, Leisure Managers need to make contact, to articulate with disadvantaged groups.

14.6.1 How can providers and managers help?

Providers can assist greatly by lightening the heavy burdens that some members of their community face. This will also help managers to give a better service. Authorities need to provide, and make known, concessions and opportunities on a far wider front. They need to support voluntary groups. They need to assist in a variety of ways – a helping hand, even in *small* ways, may be the catalyst that many people may need. Others will need more substantial help, as one professional worker put it: 'the disadvantaged need to be met more than half-way.'

Concessions and benefits to disadvantaged people will enable them to exercise greater choice and enjoy the relative freedoms which are open to people enjoying greater advantages [13]. For lone parents, for example, these could include financial and programme benefits, outreach initiatives and marketing strategies:

Financial

- Cost subsidies
- Reduced/free memberships
- 'Passports', 'Leisure Cards' or free passes (*not* just for children)
- Avoidance of lump-sum payments
- Bus passes

Outreach

- Assistance to self-help groups
- Crèches at minimal cost
- Transport, e.g. mini-bus shuttle
- Baby-sitting services
- Neighbourhood contacts
- Neighbourhood facilities
- Mobile facilities

Programmes

- Play schemes and family holiday programmes
- Specific target groups including Women's programmes
- Leisure skill learning – arts, crafts, sports
- Taster courses
- Family events
- Open days and days out
- Social and community programmes

Marketing

- Leisure counselling
- Advertising benefits
- Help-line services
- Leisure information service
- Links with other communtiy services and voluntary groups

The single most limiting factor for many disadvantaged groups, such as lone parents, is said to be the *cost* of taking part. Yet, even by providing facilities free of charge, *still* the manager will need sensitively to market and provide support and backup services such as more crèche facilities, taster sessions and mother and child activities, and far more sessions and attractions for women generally, and women with children in particular.

The style of management, and the in-house operational services also, are important. Customers lacking in confidence are the most vulnerable to 'take-it-or-leave-it' services and will be easily put off. First impressions count. The approach of leisure centre staff to some users was described as 'intimidating', particularly at receptions [13]. Procedures, regulations, membership cards and having to *ask* for information about concessions, for example, are daunting for some potential customers. An abrupt voice at reception can ruin a person's leisure experience. Disadvantaged people, who outwardly look perfectly capable, may need welcoming and encouraging. The need for sensitivity is paramount. Managers and staff must be both sensitive and reactive to the needs. People market leisure. Therefore, training in customer service is of vital importance.

14.7 PROGRAMMING BY OBJECTIVES AND LEISURE FACILITY PROGRAMMES

The basic assumption was made at the start of this chapter that programming is a process. It is logical therefore to use a programming system which is a systematic process, a system which takes a wide and open view of the variety of possibilities. First, the approach must be capable of incorporating both major strategies: social planning and community development. Second, the approach must be capable of handling any of the options, from the wholly authoritarian-directed service at one extreme to the participant-controlled programme at the other.

Different approaches will suit different situations at different times. The *Programming by Objectives* method, outlined below, builds on the principles of Management by Objectives. It is a planning approach to achieve measurable targets, which lead to ultimate aims. It coordinates the network of several specific approaches; it sets targets, plans, implements, controls and monitors. It is a practical, objective approach which gets things done. Of all the approaches, it embraces several styles, yet avoids needless duplication because there is a coordinated network plan. It is businesslike; it is a professional approach.

Building on the lessons learned from the directional strategies and the specific programming approaches, this section is concerned with reaching a sequence of interrelated actions which go to making up a community recreation programme. A logical progression is needed:

1. Interpret policy and establish aims.
2. Assess demand and resources.
3. Set objectives and targets.
4. Plan the programme.
5. Implement the programme.
6. Evaluate and monitor progress.

(i) Interpret policy and establish aims

A programme needs to be based on a sound philosophy. It needs principles on which to guide its course, and policies on which to plan and establish effective procedures. The *philosophy* can be regarded as the broad conceptual framework of the organization and its purposes and principles. It gives the organization a *rationale* – a justification for its existence. The *purpose* is synonymous with the rationale, the basic reason for an organization, department or programme existing.

The *principles* are the fundamental beliefs arising from within the philosophy and purposes of an organization. The principles lead to major *policy* guidelines. These guidelines give direction and, for local authority services, can be summarized into statements which are the consensus of the community. These statements become the *aims* of the organization, the department, the service or the programme. Many local authorities have no stated aims and, in such circumstances, the council policy has to be interpreted from previous action and aims set and subsequently approved.

The aims of a community recreation service (which will need to be converted into measurable objectives and targets) could include, for example:

1. To serve and give substantial leisure opportunity to all people in the community regardless of race, colour, creed, age, sex, ability or disability.
2. To meet significant social needs.
3. To involve people in the community in recreation programming.
4. To provide the most appropriate service to serve the greatest number of people in the community and also serve those in greatest need, recognizing the need for balance between majority and minority interests.
5. To market community recreation effectively to discover need, to supply appropriate services and to attract participants.
6. To give range, diversity and balance to programmes.
7. To provide programmes which are flexible enough to cope with changing demands.
8. To make the fullest use and most imaginative use of all resources.
9. To give a large measure of choice through which variety, novelty and depth of programming is possible.
10. To stimulate community initiatives and spontaneous activity.
11. To manage services and facilities with capable and suitably qualified and trained personnel.
12. To evaluate progress regularly and systematically.

(ii) Assess demand and resources

The Leisure Manager collates all the marketing information and discovers as much as possible about the community and the range of interests. This will include determining the user profile for the community and identify gaps in the range of opportunities currently on offer. Next the manager evaluates what resources are available – the areas, facilities, organizations, agencies, personnel and finance.

In programming at a recreation facility, such as a sports centre, the manager will need to establish who are the potential customers, together with the non-participants. This is more specific than a community demand assessment. It arises out of the assessment and helps with the setting of objectives.

To what extent will the facilities and activities attract individuals, casual users, recreational groups, clubs, leagues, classes, courses and events? Will schools, industries and other institutions be hiring for their own communities? From the experience at other centres, the manager will know that different people have different needs. By recognizing this, managers are able to add another important factor to programme balance.

(iii) Set objectives and targets

Objectives are different from aims. Aims are long-term, ultimate goals, which reflect the purposes of an organization. Objectives are short-range, attainable ends, leading towards fulfilling the aims. They must be measurable. Objectives should be written as statements that are quantifiable with some dimension of time. Objectives answer questions such as: what? how? when by? how measured? Objectives describe the way in which action is to be carried out and how results are to be measured. Objectives can also be broken down into several shorter-term *targets*.

In addition to objectives which are measured quantitatively, some objectives are needed which can be measured by more qualitative criteria. Objectives such as 'to maximize use', 'to serve as many people as possible' or 'to provide activities for the whole community' are meaningless unless they have some yardstick with which to evaluate the results. In short, they must be measurable. For example, take a hypothetical case of an indoor recreation centre where the programming aim is: to provide a balanced and broad-based programme of opportunities that meets the leisure and sporting needs and demands of the different sections of the community.

The community consists of players of high and low standards of ability, young and old, male and female, able and disabled, sports persons and non-sports persons, highly competitive players and socially orientated players, etc., and the programme has to cater to some extent for their diverse requirements. Consequently, objectives can be set in respect of:

1. the range of opportunities (sporting and non-sporting activities) to be offered;
2. the range of leagues, competitions, ladders, etc., to be provided in specific sports;
3. the range of courses to be offered in specific sports for adults and juniors at different levels of ability;
4. the specific opportunities to be provided to identified market targets such as:
   - disabled
   - mothers with young children
   - the 50+
   - the unemployed;
5. the range and type of non-sporting events to be staged;
6. the balance of the programme with specific elements being restricted in terms of time and space, e.g. clubs not to exceed 30% of the week-day evening programme.

Additionally, where objectives are likely to be in conflict, there is a need to establish priorities, particularly with regard to the programming of, say, a leisure centre's main hall, where at peak times the demand is likely to exceed the supply.

(iv) Plan the programme

The programme offered represents the practical application of the purpose of the facility or service and the fulfilment of the set objectives.

To ensure that the proposed programme is well balanced, there is a need to analyse the activities offered, the space allocated and the anticipated profile of different users.

It is also necessary to ensure that no sections are ignored and that the incompatibility of activities and users is avoided. To some extent, the breadth of the programme will be affected by the resources available (e.g. facilities, personnel and finance) and the activities offered will, of necessity, have to be provided within the allocated budget.

(v) Implement the programme

To ensure that the potential participants are aware of the opportunities offered, it will be necessary to promote both the centre and what it offers. Programmed time within a facility is a most perishable product, hence the general and specific awareness of a facility is of the utmost importance.

In order to be able to manage the programme efficiently, a range of systems needs to be developed that deal with specific aspects associated with programming. These include the booking system, the administrative system relating to internal leagues and competitions, the payment of coaches and tutors, the collection of entry fees, issue of invoices, etc.

In order that the programme runs smoothly, it is advisable to anticipate any problems that might arise. By so doing, an alternative strategy can be planned and introduced, should the need arise. In this way, crisis management and panic reaction can be avoided.

(vi) Evaluate and monitor progress

In the United States considerable work has been undertaken on recreation programme evaluation [14]. In the United Kingdom comparatively little has been achieved in this area, particularly in terms of community recreation. It is crucially important to evaluate the programme. How else can a manager know whether the objectives have been met, the goals reached? Evaluation is often thought of only in terms of the end-result of a programme – the 'bums on seats' approach. However, this is merely part of the evaluation picture. Evaluation is methodically appraising a programme's worth, taking into consideration:

1. The input – how much has gone into the programme, planning and organization.
2. The process – what has actually occurred during the programme.
3. The outcomes – what were the end results and how did these compare with the target objectives and performance objectives.

The *input* is the planning stage. What were the total costs of the exercise? How many resources were used? How many staff and how much time and effort were put into the operation? What promotion was undertaken? In other words, what was involved in putting the programme together?

The *process* is concerned with the running of the operation. What actually went on? This gives clues as to why a programme was successful or unsuccessful. It refreshes one's memory. It lets others know about the running of the programme and what methods were employed, what management style was predominant, what leadership techniques were successful.

The *outcome* involves comparing programme objectives with actual performance. Why have objectives if you do not gauge them with what has been achieved? Outcomes are often too heavily weighted on financial performance. While this is paramount in the commercial setting, in community recreation programmes financial yardsticks are but one measure. The question is: *did the programme fulfil its purpose?*

When, how and who should evaluate are further questions to be considered by the Leisure Manager. Both *inside* and *outside* evaluation makes good sense as the evaluation can be both situational and objective. Feedback from as many as possible – policy-makers, officers, staff and customers – makes for greater understanding, validity and improvement to the existing programme.

We have seen how employee motivation improves performance when they are involved in the decision-making process. Staff and leaders are closest to people; they and the participants are first-hand observers. Therefore managers should endeavour to collect information from everyone. What was good? What went wrong? Why? How can the programme be improved? This style of evaluation needs skilful and sensitive handling.

14.8 PROGRAMMING: SUMMARY

Community recreation programming is a process. The recreation programme is the means to achieve the aims and objectives of the recreation organization. There are many agencies, authorities and organizations whose function it is to provide recreation. The local authority, however, has a special enabling and coordinating function in addition to supplying its own services and facilities.

Programming hinges around five main factors: the policies; the people; the activities; the facilities; and the management. There are many ways in which programmes can be classified, including by function, by areas and facilities, by people and social interaction and by the expected outcomes of the recreation programme. The classification into functional activities is the most common.

There are different approaches to programming. Two major directions can be loosely termed 'social planning', where the locus of control is with the authority and professionals, and 'community development', which is a more people-orientated direction. There are a great variety of specific methods of approach. In practice, a mix of approaches is tried but without a sound coordinating network.

'Programming by Objectives' is an approach which overcomes many of the inherent problems in other more subjective methods. In this approach, the Leisure Manager undertakes several actions, including working with policy-makers to establish aims, setting objectives, choosing activities, and promoting and presenting the programme. This will include sectors of the programme where community initiatives are given full rein, enabled by organization resources. It will also include several approaches: meeting demands, giving choice and trying experiments. The programme will be constantly monitored: it is important to keep in touch with the programme and the people. Finally, the programme is evaluated; the evaluation is concerned with the input (what has gone into the planning), the process (what has occurred) and the actual outcome. Programming is perceived as an ongoing continuous process, and while there are steps in the procedure, different sections will be at different stages – the whole programme will be changing and evolving. This is why high-quality management is needed to coordinate and control the entire operation. Recreation programming needs quality managers. As way of a summary, and a checklist, a 'seven step' guideline to successful community leisure and recreation programming is outlined below.

PLANNING BY OBJECTIVES – SEVEN STEPS PLANNING GUIDE (See Fig. 14.1)

1 INTERPRET POLICY, ESTABLISH AIMS AND OBJECTIVES
Understand the purpose of your organization, its philosophy and its fundamental beliefs.

1.1 Produce a 'Mission Statement' – i.e. the aims and goals of the organization.

1.2 Produce policy guidelines and directional strategies.

1.3 Where no written philosophy/policy exists, top managers should interpret the organization's purpose and adopt a written policy statement. Obtain committee endorsement and communicate for all to know what you are in business for.

2 ASSESS RESOURCES AND CURRENT AND POTENTIAL DEMAND
Produce a profile of the current and prospective consumers and the type of services and activities to meet their needs and demands.

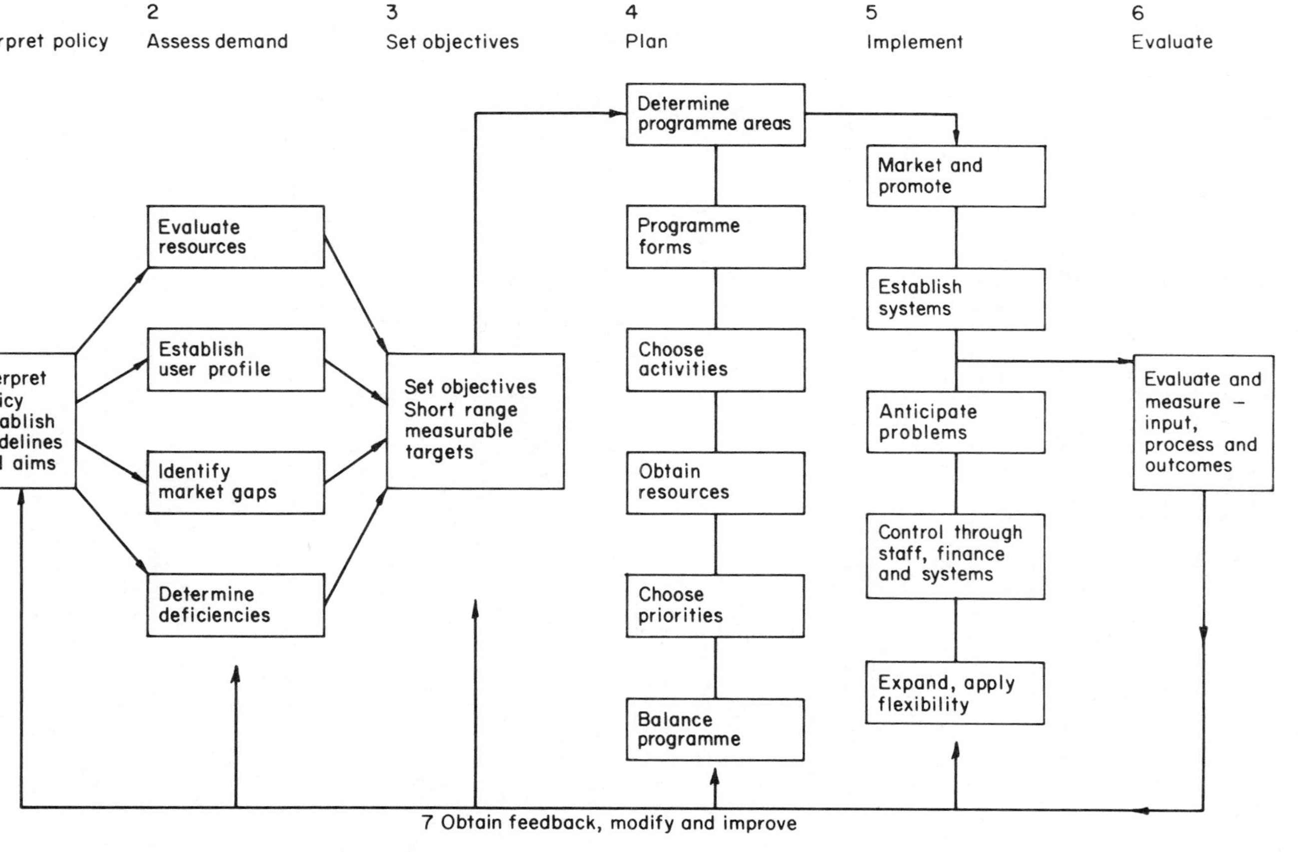

1
Interpret policy
2
Assess demand
3
Set objectives
4
Plan
5
Implement
6
Evaluate
Interpret policy Establish guidelines and aims
Evaluate resources
Establish user profile
Identify market gaps
Determine deficiencies
Set objectives Short range measurable targets
Determine programme areas
Programme forms
Choose activities
Obtain resources
Choose priorities
Balance programme
Market and promote
Establish systems
Anticipate problems
Control through staff, finance and systems
Expand, apply flexibility
Evaluate and measure – input, process and outcomes
7 Obtain feedback, modify and improve

Fig. 14.1 Seven stage community recreation programme planner.

2.1 Evaluate current resources, facilities, organizations, services, programmes and opportunities.
2.2 Assess forthcoming year's new resources – e.g. historic celebrations, sponsorship and campaigns.
2.3 Evaluate the contribution made by other agencies – e.g. voluntary sector, commercial enterprise, education and industrial clubs.
2.4 Evaluate the current performance of facilities and services; determine the level of spare capacity, etc.
2.5 Collate all marketing information. Use surveys, suggestions, community councils and recreation organizations.
2.6 Establish a community profile – i.e. the community to be served.
2.7 Establish a profile of potential users – i.e. the individuals and groups likely to participate.
2.8 Identify market gaps and determine areas of deficiency in terms of services and programmes.

3 SET OBJECTIVES
Translate policies and market demands into action, first by setting objectives. Involve policy-makers, staff and community in the setting of objectives.
3.1 Set short-range targets in each area within a precise time period: weeks (e.g. holiday programmes); months (e.g. leisure courses); and years (e.g. financial targets, social objectives, etc.).
3.2 Make each objective measurable and within a time span.
3.3 Set an appropriate balance between community-orientated and professionally-directed approaches.
3.4 Set balances between passive and active leisure, between sport, recreation, art, social, entertainment, etc. to meet the aims.
3.5 Agree financial income/expenditure ratios, subsidies and targets.
3.6 Establish priorities with regard to objectives: (a) because there will be conflicting objectives, and (b) no programme can meet all demand.

4 PLAN THE PROGRAMME
Adopt the programmer's motto: 'Proper Prior Planning Prevents Poor Performance.'
4.1 Time is the basis on which the programme operates. Establish hourly, daily, weekly and seasonal patterns of use. Consider both fixed and flexible timetables.
4.2 Determine programme areas (arts, sports, social, etc.).
4.3 Determine programme forms (clubs, courses, events, etc.).
4.4 Recognize the different needs of different people: recreational, competitive, beginners, high standard, older, younger, etc.
4.5 Because of conflicting claims, it is necessary to establish priorities.

Balance the programme providing width and depth – balance implies diversity.

4.6 Choose activities and methods which collectively are most likely to meet objectives.

4.7 Analyse the activities in order to provide the appropriate conditions.

4.8 Avoid totally exclusive use, it narrows the field.

4.9 Avoid totally casual use, it also narrows the field.

4.10 Build flexibility into the programme. It will lead to variety, wider use and greater balance.

4.11 Consider how the programme fits into the marketing strategy – e.g. corporate approach to marketing, specific promotions?

4.12 Consider the staffing implications and management style, division of labour, responsibilities, etc.

4.13 Train staff to undertake responsibility and gain success. Train staff for a customer-orientated approach.

4.14 Avoid administration problems by establishing easily handled and easily understood systems and methods – i.e. easy for the user and easy for the organization.

4.15 Establish a wide network of communications through community development strategies.

5 IMPLEMENT THE PROGRAMME

Construct, promote and implement the programme with vitality, enthusiasm and charisma.

5.1 Implement the agreed marketing strategy, using the most appropriate promotional methods. Spend time on promotion.

5.2 The flexible approach needs skilful management to enable individuals to participate in the way *they* want to. Flexibility is needed to meet changing situations.

5.3 Give sensitive care to staffing aspects, especially with regard to community development. Staff/helpers are needed to support newly formed groups until they become self-supporting. Consider some outreach approach.

5.4 Try new technologies to programming – e.g. video, computers, giant screen for information, visuals to show court availability, self-service, do-it-yourself bookings, etc.

5.5 Control the programme through staff span, financial and systems control.

5.6 Develop monitoring systems to provide management with information relating to current level of usage, profile of users, changing trends.

5.7 Anticipate the likely problems; be ready with alternatives.

5.8 Avoid incompatible activities in terms of health and safety, noise, age, level of play, etc.

5.9 Expand the programme with new activities, new methods and new people.
5.10 Sell 'packages', not just single items.
5.11 Try some experiments; try out regional and national activity trends, yet always enhance *local* success.
5.12 Extend product life-cycles through changes, variety and new ways of selling.
5.13 Use pricing flexibility as a marketing tool; consider the benefits of differential pricing.
5.14 Keep all informed of what is going on. Use a variety of communication systems.

6 EVALUATE
Evaluate – or how else will you know whether you are doing a good job?
6.1 To what extent has the programme been successful or unsuccessful? Measure its effectiveness – i.e. to what extent have objectives been met?
6.2 Measure the efficiency of the operation: how well has the job been carried out?
6.3 Evaluate the process and the outcome – i.e. the operation from beginning to end.
6.4 Use several criteria, not just financial, to measure 'profits', both quantitive and qualitive; throughput; social mix; use by less-advantaged; age mix; income generation; subsidy per user; levels of sponsorship achieved; etc. Measure cost-effectiveness.
6.5 Determine any changes in user profiles, catchment areas.
6.6 How effective have the marketing methods been?
6.7 How adaptable has the organization been to the changes in the programme?
6.8 How adequate has the staffing been; how well have staff performed?

7 OBTAIN FEEDBACK AND MODIFY PROGRAMME
Think of programming as an ongoing process. Therefore, every cycle should see some change or modification.
7.1 Ask how can the programme be improved? Modify the objectives and targets accordingly.
7.2 Obtain feedback through the community network and community leader resources.
7.3 If the programme or elements of it have been unsuccessful
– first, determine the causes for failure to meet targets;
– second, consider staff training or retraining;
– third, consider changes in staff areas of responsibility;
– fourth, consider the effectiveness of the management style.

REFERENCES AND NOTES

1. Erikson, E. (1963), *Eight Ages of Man in Childhood and Society* (2nd edn), Norton, New York.
2. Meyer, H. D. (1957), The adult cycle. *Annals of the American Academy of Political Science and Society*, **33**, 58–67.
3. Farrell, P. and Lundegren, H. M. (1978), *The Process of Recreation Programming*, Wiley, New York.
4. Butler, G. D. (1976), *Introduction to Community Recreation*, McGraw-Hill, New York, p. 231.
5. Edginton, C. R., Crompton, D. M. and Hanson, C. J. (1980), *Recreation and Leisure Programming: A Guide for the Professional*, Saunders College, Philadelphia, Pa, pp. 28–43.
6. *Ibid.*, p. 38.
7. Haywood, L. and Henry, I. (1986), 'Policy developments in community leisure and recreation, part one'. *Leisure Management*, July, **6**(7), 25–9.
8. Edington *et al.*, *ibid.*, chapter 2.
9. Kraus, R. G. and Curtis, J. E. (1977), *Creative Administration in Recreation and Parks*, C. V. Mosby, Saint Louis, Mis.
10. Tillman, A. (1974), *The Program Book for Recreation Professionals*, National Press Books, Palo Alto, Calif., pp. 57–8.
11. Author's observation from: The Sports Council Sports Centre Management Award; Polytechnic of North London DMS (Rec.) Centre Visits and author's surveys of managers and centres, 1973–87.
12. Griffiths, G. (1981), Recreation Provision for Whom?, unpublished dissertation, Cranfield Institute of Technology.
13. Torkildsen, G. (1987), Recreation Management: A Framework for the Effective Management of Community Recreation Facilities, unpublished PhD dissertation, Polytechnic of Central London.
14. Theobald, W. F. (1979), *Evaluation of Recreation and Park Programs*, Wiley, New York.

Chapter 15

Performance appraisal based on management by objectives

In Chapters 13 and 14 it has been shown that all organizations, public and private, need to set objectives and evaluate the results. This chapter concentrates upon the performance appraisal of leisure services and facilities in the public sector.

The introduction of the Community Charge (poll tax) and the Compulsory Competitive Tendering legislation has forced many local authorities to concentrate on improving the managerial efficiency of their leisure facilities. As part of the tendering procedure, a detailed service specification has to be produced which stipulates the nature of the service to be provided, together with the minimum managerial performance required. This latter factor should cover not only the net revenue cost, but also the efficient and effective requirements for the facility.

In order to produce the service specification, there is a need, first to undertake a performance appraisal of the facility or centre concerned. To do this, it is necessary to identify suitable performance indicators that can give an appraisal of the overall performance of the facilities and services. Second, one has to develop a system that incorporates the specification as performance objectives and targets.

This chapter is written in the following sequence. *First*, the range of 'Performance Indicators' are described and include: input, output, efficiency, effectiveness and programme indicators. *Second*, management information systems are noted. *Third*, the implementation of a performance appraisal, allied to the system called Management by Objectives (MBO) is proposed and the requirements for a successful MBO are discussed. *Fourth*, examples of a Performance Appraisal/MBO undertaking are given.

Having read this chapter, the reader should be able to identify a range of performance indicators and apply these to determine the overall performance of a facility or a service. By using an applied version of the Management by Objectives system and incorporating many of the performance indicators as objectives or associated targets, a performance appraisal system can be established that is comparatively easy to implement and operate.

15.1 MANAGEMENT BY OBJECTIVES – WHAT IS IT?

The key to ensuring that the performance appraisal is undertaken in a meaningful way is to ensure that the management system used is tested and found to be operative and that the performance indicators are appropriate. The recommended management system to be used in such circumstances is an applied version of Management by Objectives, normally known as MBO; this is not a new concept and can be defined as a management approach that incorporates a systematic management process that can monitor the organization's progress and links the pursuit of the organization's aims with the needs of the individual manager. It differs from the establishment of a set of rules, a series of procedures or a set method of managing. It is a particular way of thinking about management, in fact a management philosphy that determines the direction that management should follow.

Contrary to many misconceived beliefs, MBO is not the panacea to resolve all management problems. The success of an oganization to manage its problems is not only dependent upon its management approaches and systems, but more important, its success largely depends on the quality and ability of its individual managers and staff.

Generally an organization that has no quantifiable objectives is unable to evaluate how well it is performing. It is not possible to assess an organization's performance without some prior expectations against which this can be measured. A manager is unable to perform with maximum effectiveness if he or she is unaware of the organization's goals and objectives or how well he or she is doing in relation to these goals or objectives. Without objectives, it is not possible even to determine whether an organization is going in the right direction or not. Within this context, the performance indicators will be used as quantifiable objectives or targets.

15.2 PERFORMANCE INDICATORS

It is perhaps surprising that until recently few leisure facilities undertook any form of performance appraisal apart from comparing the actual net operating costs with the set budget for the year. At a time of economic constraint, this non–action can be wasteful and is tantamount to neglect of duty. Even at facilities where no aims, objectives or targets are set, an assessment can be made of its efficiency, (and whether it is operating at an optimum level of usage), and if the service is being effective and fulfilling its expected role – (i.e. in attracting the customers it is intended to serve).

Some local authorities' sole measure of performance is based on how much it costs to operate a centre. In such cases, a facility that manages to operate within the stated budget is perceived as performing well, although it may be underused, with high staffing levels (and hence high subsidy levels per attendance) and attracting the more affluent members of the community who could well pay an economic participative fee. Hence such an approach that uses a single performance indicator is inadequate, particularly as in this example it relates to an input indicator.

Performance indicators represent a direct or indirect method of measuring whether the centre is achieving a good level of performance, and will include both quality and quantity indicators. In many respects, these indicators will provide the management with the necessary information to determine whether the centre is being managed efficiently and effectively.

Performance indicators fall into the following categories:

1. input indicators;
2. output indicators;
3. efficiency indicators;
4. effectiveness indicators;
5. programme indicators.

15.2.1 Input indicators

Traditionally, local government has measured inputs rather than outputs and other forms of indicators, hence they have not been concerned with meeting the needs and demands of the community. The input indicators, in this context, are the resources placed at the disposal of the management of the facility or service, namely the finance available, the facilities provided and the staff employed. The number of staff (including management) employed will depend on the nature and range of facilities provided and the stated philosophy of use, while the finance provided relates to the net operating cost (although in most local authorities the accounting systems used tend to regard the operation costs (gross expenditure) and the income generated (gross income) as separate elements). Hence the level of the operating costs and the amount of staff costs are input indicators in relation to the range of facilities provided.

An indication of the level of performance can be obtained by making a comparison with similar facilities and in the case of sports/leisure centres a comparison can be made with national norms. It should, however, be said that a comparison with other facilities has its limitations as no two facilities are identical. They differ in the range of facilities on offer, their philosophy of use, their location and accessibility and the environment in which they are located. None the less, a good indication of the level of performance can be obtained by using a range of performance indicators. Also a comparison of a facility's performance with those in preceeding years can also give an indication of whether the facility's performance is improving or deteriorating.

Hence Input Performance Indicators can be regarded as:

(i) *Finance*
- Gross expenditure costs
- Net expenditure costs (operating costs)
- Variable operating costs
- Staff costs
- Energy costs

- Other variables/costs (supplies, maintenance, equipment)
- Fixed Costs.

(ii) *Facilities*, e.g.
- Swimming pool
- Sports hall
- Gymnasium
- Squash courts
- Training room 1
- Training room 2
- Sauna suite
- Bar and catering area.

(iii) *Staff*
- Number of staff employed
- Qualifications
- Training.

15.2.2 Output indicators

Those local authorities that use output indicators have tended to rely on total attendances as the indication of the level of output of a service. This quantitative measure, however, as a sole indicator, has its limitations and should not be confused with the number of users. For example, if a leisure centre has 300 000 admissions per year and if on average every user visits the centre 50 times a year, then the number of users (i.e. separate individuals) is 6000 which will probably represent around 5% or less of the catchment population. Therefore, to obtain an accurate picture of a centre's performance it is necessary to obtain a greater range of indicators.

A further output indicator is the level of utilization. That is the amount of space and time sold, which is generally represented as a percentage of the capacity of the facility. This method of assessing a centre's performance is suitable as one of the performance indicators for assessing 'dry' facilities such as sports halls, squash courts, etc. (It should be stressed that the sale of such facilities is very much a perishable commodity and cannot be resold the following day.) With regard to facilities such as swimming pools, sauna suites and conditioning rooms, the total admissions based on weekly, monthly, quarterly and annual attendance levels is a more meaningful indicator.

Although we have previously stated that the net operating cost is an input indicator (i.e. gross expenditure less gross income), the income generated is in itself an important output indicator. It would therefore appear that the output performance indicators are:

(i) *Income generated*
- total income
- break-down of income by types of user, facilities, service, activities

- membership
- hire of equipment
- sale of goods
- rents
- hire of charges
- course fees
- special events
- bar and catering
- sponsorship
- grants

(ii) *Admissions*
- total
- facilities used
- activities participated
- nature of participation – casual, club, course, etc.
- user category – junior, adult, OAP, etc.

(iii) *User numbers*
- total individual users

(iv) *Level of usage*
- level of utilization as % of total capacity of facilities such as sports hall, squash courts.
- total users of specific facilities such as swimming pools, weight training, solarium.

15.2.3 Efficiency indicators

At a time of economic constraint, and with the advent of CCT, it is more important than ever that the service is managed as efficiently as possible. Efficiency, in this context, is defined as the optimum use of resources; that is, the facilities are utilized to (or approaching) their optimum, the staff are used to generate the highest level of productivity, while the financial resources are used to generate the maximum 'output' returns. Efficiency can therefore be measured by means of ratios between inputs and outputs, as illustrated in Table 15.1. For example, the Al ratio – Total Income: Operational Costs – is an important ratio and is commonly known as the 'Recovery Rate'.

Other possible ratios include:

1. Total Income: Staff Costs.
2. Staff Costs: Operating Costs (gross expenditure) (less loan charges and central establishment charges)
3. $\dfrac{\text{Net Operational Costs}}{\text{Total Attendances}} = \text{Subsidy per Attendance}$
4. Total Income: Staff numbers (FTE).
5. $\dfrac{\text{Gross Profit of Bar/Catering} \times 100}{\text{Cost of Sales}}$

6. Variable Costs: Operating Costs (gross expenditure) (less loan charges and central establishment charges).

For many of these ratios, there are national norms which can be calculated from CIPFA publications [1] and these can provide valuable guidelines to the level of performance of a centre. The Sports Council [2] have issued recovery targets together with targets for the subsidy levels per attendance. Although the subsidy targets were made in 1981, these can be updated through the use of the retail price index.

Other ratios may form only part of a total input or output indicator. However, it must be stated that it will not be necessary to utilize all the efficiency indicators illustrated in Table 15.1 to make a performance appraisal, even if all the necessary data is readily available.

A further valuable efficiency indicator that does not appear in Table 15.1 is 'The Spend per Head', especially when applied to the centre's Bar and Catering Service.

In order to make a comparison of ratios more meaningful, it is advisable to reduce the number of variables as much as possible. Hence it is recommended that the loan charges and the *central establishment charges* (i.e. the indirect costs levied by most local authorities to cover the cost of the support services such as legal services, personnel) be omitted from the gross expenditure or operating costs and that only the net (or loss) trading surpluses – e.g. bar and catering service – be taken into consideration.

15.2.4 Effectiveness indicators

Although effectiveness is usually defined in management terms as the degree to which an organization fulfils its objectives, it is also associated in a leisure management environment with providing the right service at the right place, and at the right time – in other words, a *service that meets the needs of the different sections of the community*. Ideally, in such circumstances, the user profile of the centre should match that of the neighbourhood surrounding the centre. It is therefore desirable that a record of the different types of users be maintained. Much of this can be obtained if a centre is using a computerized entry system that registers different categories of users – e.g. adult, junior, gender, OAP and unemployed. This should, however, be supplemented by undertaking a user survey at least bi-annually. The size of the sample should be related to the total number of users (and not attendances), and even in the larger facilities, a sample of 350 to 450 respondents should be ample. Apart from obtaining the user profile, the survey could also be used to determine information relating to catchment area of the facility, frequency of visits, activity participated, etc., together with more in-

Table 15.1 Efficiency indicators

Input	*A* *Operational costs ex loan*	*B* *Variable costs*	*C* *Staff costs*	*D* *Staff nos (FTE)*	*E* *Net expenditure*	*F* *Facilities cost centres*	*G* *Input/output mix – progress–activities/nature*
Output							
1 Total income – income centres	A1	B1	C1	D1	E1	F1	G1
2 Attendances	A2	B2	C2	D2	E2	F2	G2
3 Users	A3	B3	C3	D3	E3	F3	G3
4 Level of utilization	A4	B4	C4	D4	E4	F4	G4

tangible indicators such as satisfaction and level of attraction. From the responses in the survey, it would be possible to determine the actual number of users and the level of penetration from within the facility's catchment area.

The Effective Indicators can include the following:

1. Agreed aims, objectives and targets.
2. User profile:
   - age
   - gender
   - occupation
   - resident
   - use by target groups, e.g. disabled/disadvantaged.
3. Frequency of visit (indication of attraction).
4. Catchment area.
5. Level of penetration within catchment area.

15.2.5 Programme indicators

An important aspect of the service specification is that which relates to the programme content. Although it is neither an input nor output, it does involve *effort*, and because it is one of the main managerial functions, it merits a category of its own. Indeed, the programme should be the practical application of the facility's philosophy for use.

The programme indicators could include:

1. Range of activities offered.
2. Availability of casual opportunities.
3. Courses – range of activities;
– level of ability.
4. Centre clubs.
5. Activities specifically for target groups.
6. New initiatives.

15.2.6 The appraisal process

Performance appraisal is an essential part of any leisure service as it is only in this way that the management can determine whether they are doing a good job or not. By using the above indicators, it is possible to determine the level of performance of a leisure facility and identify areas where improvement is necessary. With facilities that are performing well, the findings of the appraisal process can be used to justify the existence of the facility, its programme and the level of subsidy provided.

15.3 MANAGEMENT INFORMATION SYSTEM

To be able to undertake a performance appraisal quickly and efficiently, a good *Management Information System* is required, so that the vital information is provided in a programmed way to ensure that the facility is on course to achieve its targets, etc. With the aid of a microcomputer, the following management information data could be provided.

1. *Booking Systems*

   (a) Individual services (e.g. lessons, courses, squash, badminton, tennis, etc.)
   (b) Special events
   (c) Group and club (e.g. leagues, pitches, main hall, block bookings, etc.)
   (d) Individual and group registration/membership

2. *Income*

   (a) Income per facility – *cost centre* approach
   (b) Income per activity (badminton, five-a-side, etc.)
   (c) Income per user (adult, junior, unemployed, etc.)
   (d) Income by time (morning, afternoon, lunchtime, etc.)
   (e) Income from sales of goods/products (bar/catering, vending, etc.)
   (f) Income from hire of equipment (rackets, etc.)
   (g) Income from use of equipment (lockers, hairdryers)
   (h) Income from special events
   (i) Income from membership
   (j) Income from entry fees

3. *Expenditure*

   (a) Expenditure into different categories (staff costs, controllable costs, etc.)
   (b) Expenditure per facility – cost centre approach
   (c) Expenditure per components listed in (2) – contra items

4. *Levels of Utilization*

   (a) Number of attendances – total throughput, including participants and spectators
   – facility
   – activity
   – type of user
   – time (morning, afternoon, etc.)

(b) Occupancy (%)	– per facility – per activity (badminton) – per time
5. *Efficiency indicators*	– subsidy per attendance – spend per head – spend per head bar/catering – gross profit on bar/catering sales
6. *Financial Ratios*	– income: staff costs – income: operating costs – staff costs: operating costs

15.4 PERFORMANCE APPRAISAL – ITS IMPLEMENTATION

In order that the performance appraisal has the biggest impact and is taken seriously by management and staff alike, it is necessary for the appraisal process to be incorporated into a management system that is universally accepted as being a proven approach. From practical experience it would appear that a modified version of a Management by Objectives management system could be adapted to meet the specific requirements of each leisure facility.

15.4.1 Benefits of introducing an MBO/management system

By setting objectives associated with performance indicators that collectively are realistic and quantifiable and which have to be achieved within a predetermined time span, an organization can evaluate its own level of performance. Other benefits which an organization can incur are:

1. By establishing common organizational objectives, and by identifying individual contributions and targets within the organization, the MBO system enhances the opportunities for developing a coordinated team effort without eliminating individual initiative. Managers learn to concentrate on the *end-results* rather than on the means to an end.
2. Managers know what is expected of them, what constitutes a good performance and what constitutes an unsatisfactory performance. Both managers and staff can measure performance in a realistic way, which is a logical basis for identifying managers for promotion and for ensuring the effective use of resources.
3. Not only are tangible results such as lower operating costs, increased revenue and greater level of utilization easily recognizable

under an MBO management system, but the organization also benefits along its *intangible* plane through the reduction of inhibiting factors within a bureaucracy such as the quality of the service, staff morale, communications, role conflict, role ambiguity, etc. Managers and staff feel identified and very much an integral part of the organization.
4. The organization learns to focus on the areas within the service, where it is vital to be effective and prioritize tasks to be undertaken. This can avoid taking on time-consuming, non-essential tasks. It also provides managers with the necessary guidelines to make the right decisions.
5. The system provides the manager with a warning of any deviations from target in sufficient time to take remedial action.
6. MBO highlights the training needs of both the organization and the individual managers and staff. The skills and knowledge required to fulfil each objective should be determined and compared to those of the staff concerned.

Such benefits far outweigh the limitations associated with an MBO system. These limitations usually relate to those few objectives that are not quantifiable and where a performance appraisal can only be undertaken subjectively. Additionally, some managers claim that MBO, at the more efficient centres, has only a minimal effect, particularly where continued improvement in performance becomes most difficult or nigh-impossible to achieve. Although to achieve such a level of performance the organization probably used an objective-based system, even if it is not formalized.

15.4.2 Situation required for a successful MBO/management system

In order to reap the best rewards from the introduction of an MBO management system, it is necessary to create the most conducive environment. It is apparent from research undertaken that MBO produces the best results where the following situation exists:

1. An MBO management system must run in conjunction with the organization's budgeting programme. This is necessary as many of the objectives and targets are financially based. In the public sector the fiscal year commences annually on the 1 April, and hence each MBO cycle should run in parallel and be completed on 31 March annually.
2. MBO demands that the organization concerned, must determine its current and future role. It must state what it wants to achieve, state its current position and determine how it can close the gap.

3. Research indicates that the success of MBO depends largely on the objectives being *specific*. Poor objective writing is one of the most common errors made when introducing an MBO management system. Vague statements about what should be achieved are not objectives and as such are practically useless.
4. The set objectives and their associated targets must be *realistic*. Staff given impossible targets will get discouraged, lose motivation and will not try very hard, while easily achieved targets will not stretch the staff and the organization will suffer as a consequence. Hence the set objectives and targets should contain a challenging element. This would be of benefit to both the staff and the organization.
5. The *commitment* of all levels of management and staff is essential for the success of MBO. Consequently, it is important that individual managers and staff be consulted as part of the process that establishes the objectives and targets. If staff are involved in the planning process that impinges on their work, they are more likely to consider the system as being fair. They will also tend to react positively if they are given an opportunity to contribute in the setting of targets. These often become commitments and staff generally will try harder to meet them.
6. The commitment of senior managers to establish and maintain *accountability* for achieving objectives and targets is essential. There is a need to recognize good and bad performances by managers. Failure to react to sub-optimum performances and, when appropriate, be critical of subordinates undermines the effectiveness of MBO.
7. All managers must be able to identify the *key areas* of their individual jobs in order to recognize the essential tasks that have to be completed in pursuit of the organization's goals.
8. In order to be able to achieve the set objectives and targets, managers must be provided with regular and accurate *feedback* information. Without such feedback data, managers will not necessarily make the right decisions as they will be forced to use, to some degree, elements of judgement or chance.

15.4.3 A suggested MBO approach

The manner of the practical application of MBO theory is largely dependent upon the nature of the business involved and the structure of the organization. Experience suggests a *modified* approach is best suited to the management of sports/leisure centres and swimming pools. This approach is illustrated in Fig. 15.1.

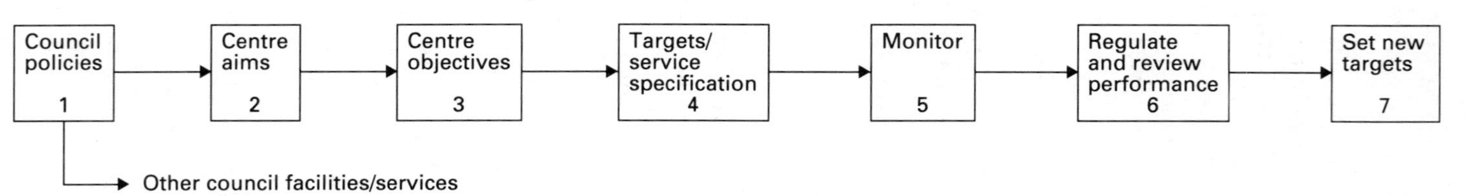

Fig. 15.1 A suggested MBO approach.

The suggested approach has seven distinct phases, as follows.

1. *Council policies*
How the council perceives the benefits that can be obtained by individuals and the community from leisure participation can influence the nature of the services provided. Such policies are also the starting point for the development of an MBO system at the council's other leisure facilities and services and collectively form a hierarchical structure.

2. *Centre aims*
Likewise, the centre's aims should also reflect the council's policy. These aims or goals are what the organization strives to achieve (although in reality this is hardly ever accomplished). In written form, these are expressed as general statements of purpose and could cover such areas as efficiency, programming, staffing, marketing, public relations, effectiveness, etc.

3. *Centre objectives*
These objectives will include performance indicators, which are themselves quantifiable or have measurable targets associated with them. Other objectives relating to the key areas of responsibility within the centre will also be set in an attempt to meet the centre's aims. Wherever possible, these should relate to the centre as a whole and to individual cost centres within it.

4. *Targets*
Along with the establishment of objectives, the setting of realistic targets is of the utmost importance, as it is against these targets that the performance of the centre is measured. The targets can include input indicators (e.g. net expenditure level), output indicators (e.g. total attendances) and targets that represent efficiency indicators. Additionally, targets can also be set to cover the more intangible aspects such as the quality of service and motivation of staff.

5. *Monitor*
The monitoring of the usage of the centre, the income generated and the usage by different target groups, etc., is essential not only to enable the management to make a performance appraisal, but also to improve the centre's programming.

6. *Regulate and review performance*
This phase of the process should not be restricted to a period at the end of the cycle for a performance appraisal, but should be a *continuing* process. This would enable the management to identify areas that are

under-performing or areas that are problematic, so that remedial action can be taken, and the training requirements of both the organization and the individual can be recognized. At this phase also it may be necessary to reassess the level at which targets have been set.

7. *Set new targets*
For the forthcoming fiscal year, new or repeated targets have to be set. These will largely be based on the previous year's experience and taking into consideration such factors as the appointment of new staff, changes in leisure trends and the local environment.

15.4.4 Implications on staff

By giving staff adequate feedback about their work performance, this should assist in improving the quality of their work and increasing their level of productivity. This is achieved through improved levels of motivation and increased efficiency. It is not only the organization that benefits from the introduction of a performance appraisal/MBO approach, but the staff also benefit. One of the basic human needs is that of the need for recognition, and by fulfilling the set objectives and targets, the staff concerned are recognized and appreciated. In this way, job satisfaction is enhanced and the staff motivation maintained.

New members of staff will also benefit from this approach, particularly if an operating handbook is produced for each facility or service. The staff will know exactly what is expected of them in terms of tasks and performance and how these relate to the expected overall performance of the facility or service. They will also be able to assess their own performance and, to some degree, plan their career advancement through the knowledge of their own strengths and weaknesses.

15.5 APPLICATION OF THE MBO/ PERFORMANCE APPRAISAL MANAGEMENT SYSTEM

Figure 15.2 and Table 15.2 illustrate how the MBO/Performance Appraisal Management system can be applied to a leisure centre. The council policy for the centre is stated as being 'the provision of an efficient and effective service, from the available resources, that provides a range of sporting and leisure opportunities that meets the needs and demands of all sections of the community', and arising from this six general aims have been set covering the centre's main areas of responsibility:

1. efficiency;
2. programming;
3. staffing;

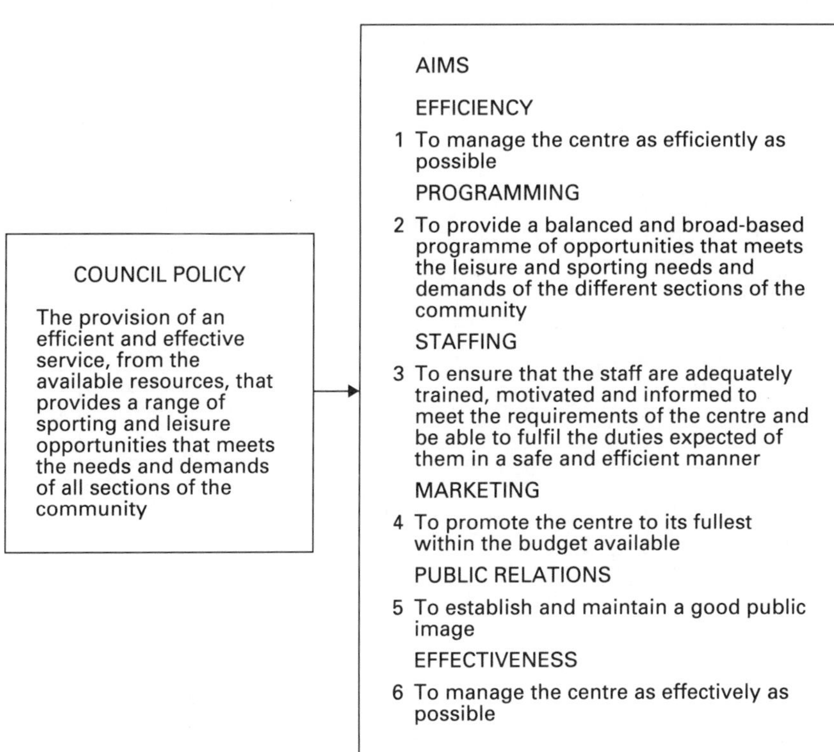

COUNCIL POLICY
The provision of an efficient and effective service, from the available resources, that provides a range of sporting and leisure opportunities that meets the needs and demands of all sections of the community
AIMS
EFFICIENCY
1 To manage the centre as efficiently as possible
PROGRAMMING
2 To provide a balanced and broad-based programme of opportunities that meets the leisure and sporting needs and demands of the different sections of the community
STAFFING
3 To ensure that the staff are adequately trained, motivated and informed to meet the requirements of the centre and be able to fulfil the duties expected of them in a safe and efficient manner
MARKETING
4 To promote the centre to its fullest within the budget available
PUBLIC RELATIONS
5 To establish and maintain a good public image
EFFECTIVENESS
6 To manage the centre as effectively as possible

Fig. 15.2 An example of aims of a leisure centre arising from the council policy.

4. marketing;
5. public relations;
6. effectiveness.

Linked to each of these aims are a number of objectives with associated targets, and Table 15.2 gives an example of the kind of objectives that can be set in order to achieve the efficiency aim. It should be stressed that this approach can be adapted to meet a range of different aims, in addition to those listed above (Table 15.2).

15.6 CONCLUSION

The MBO/Performance Appraisal Management approach is a method that enables the management to control the organization by making sure that the various functions and tasks are undertaken and on time and that the overall performance of the facility matches its stated expectations. The approach enables sub-optimal performance of both

Table 15.2 Example of an aim, objectives and targets

Aim	*Objectives*	*Suggested targets*	*1990/91*	*1991/92*
To manage the centre as efficiently as possible	1 To attract an increasing *number* of attendances	Total attendances	630 000	700 000
		Swimming pool	304 056	335 000
		Junior swimmers	108 704	130 000
		Sauna/solarium	6 539	16 000
		Conditioning gym	27 227	40 000
		Crèche	4 000	4 500
	2 To attract an increasing *level* of usage	Peak – squash)	52%	75%
		Off-peak – squash)		45%
		Sports hall	73%	78%
		Gym	75%	80%
	3 To generate an increasing level of *income*	Total income (exclusive of VAT)	£546 000	£580 000
		Financial ratio – income: operating costs*	0.57	0.67
	4 To obtain an increasing level of *productivity* from management and staff	Financial ratio – income: staff costs	1.20	1.31
	5 To *reduce the subsidy* level per attendance		£0.65	£0.39
	6 To ensure that the centre is managed within the set *expenditure limits*	Operating costs (gross expenditure) (less loan charges)	£956 000	£857 000
		Staff costs	£453 000	£440 000

* Less loan charges and central establishment charges.

the organization and individual key staff to be identified and remedial action taken. In this way, the facility's performance can continually improve with the staff also benefiting from increased job satisfaction. The customers will also benefit from an improved customer-orientated service that is reflected in a reduction in waiting time and the elimination of errors.

15.7 ASSIGNMENTS

This assignment is to test your knowledge on appraisal based management.

Waterville Leisure Centre – Efficiency Objectives and Targets
Set economic objectives and targets for the Centre for the forthcoming year. The set economic aim is 'to manage the Centre as efficiently as possible'.

The Centre's actual income and expenditure data and other information for the previous 12 months operation are given below.

15.7.1 Assignment

Waterville Leisure Centre Actual Last Year

	Expenditure	*£'000*
(i)	*Employees*	
	Wages	110
	Salaries	120
	Bar/Catering staff	60
	Central Establishment Charges	60
(ii)	*Premises*	
	Repair & Maintenance of Building/Plant	65
	Maintenance of Grounds	3
	Fuel	58
	Rates	62
(iii)	*Supplies/services*	
	Bar/Catering (cost of sales)	70
	Equipment & Tools	1
	Clothing & Uniforms	2
	Laundry	1
	Refuse Collection	1
(iv)	*Transport*	1
(v)	*Estalishment expenses*	
	Printing stationery, etc.	10

	Advertising	10
	Telephones	2
	Insurance	5
	Miscellaneous	5
(vi)	*Loan charges*	70
	Total gross expenditure	716

Income	*£'000*
Fees and charges	290
Courses	21
Lockers/Machines	8
Special Events	5
Bar/catering (including Vending Service)	101
Miscellaneous	5
Total income	430
Net expenditure	286

Attendances	
Adults	245 000
Children	65 000
	310 000

REFERENCES AND NOTES

1. Chartered Institute of Public Finance and Accountancy (1989), *Leisure and Recreation Statistics 1989–90 Estimates*, CIPFA Statistical Information Service.
2. Sports Council (1981), *Making Better Use of Resources: Regional Recreation Strategy Subject Report*, Greater London and South East Council for Sport and Recreation, London.

RECOMMENDED ADDITIONAL READING

Audit Inspectorate (1983), *Development and Operation of Leisure Centres (Selected Case Studies)*, HMSO, London.

Sports Council (1988), *Measuring Performance, Management Papers*, Occasional Papers in Recreation Management Issue No. 1 Sports Council, Greater London and South East Regions, London.

Theobald, W. F. (1979), *Evaluation of Recreation and Parks Programms*, Wiley, New York.

Chapter 16

Marketing of leisure and recreation

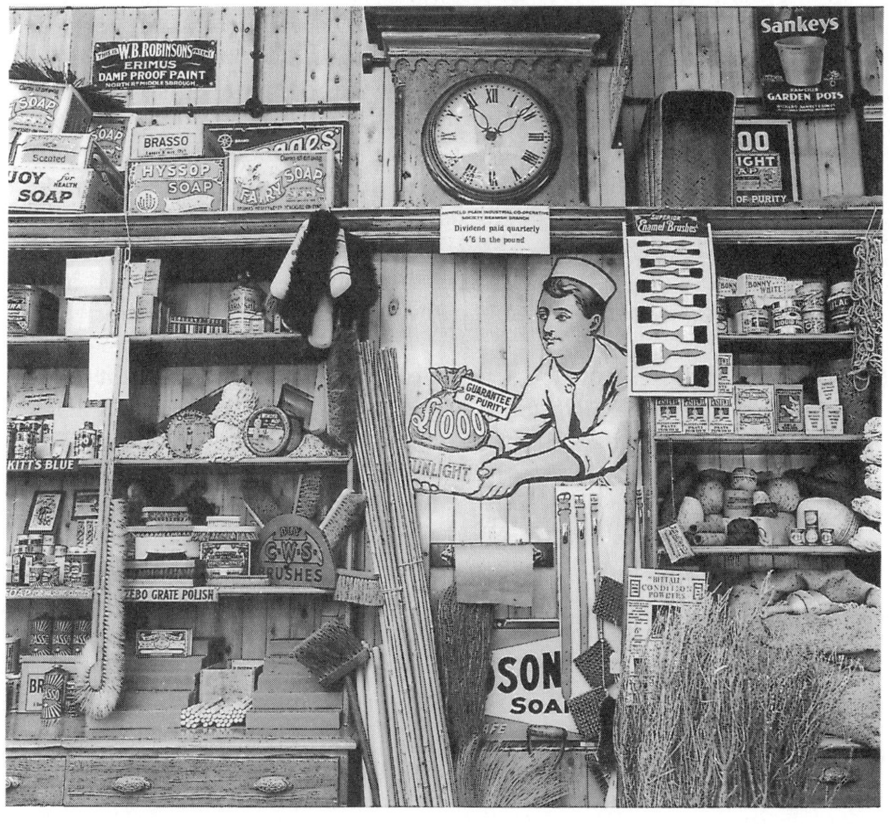

Marketing was developed for selling products profitably. The marketing of leisure, particularly public service leisure, is relatively new. However, marketing (of some kind) is undertaken by all those involved in providing services, resources and goods for recreation and leisure, whether in the public, private or commercial sectors. Public knowledge, or lack of knowledge, about services and facilities and the image they portray are essential components of marketing. It could be argued therefore that every organization in the leisure business is already 'marketing'. The question is whether they are marketing well or badly.

Marketing, promotion and customer care have received a good deal of attention of late in training courses and literature within the field of leisure management. This chapter deals with the concept, moving flexibly between theory and practice, with examples and anecdotes from working experience; it provides approaches, messages and clues to providing attractive public leisure services to customers at a social 'profit'.

This chapter is structured around four main themes. *First*, the concepts of commercial marketing, social marketing and public service marketing are described and distinguished one from another. *Second*, as the *raison d'être* of marketing is selling to customers, the motivations to buy and the demotivators are described. *Third*, the constituents of the 'marketing mix' – i.e. product, price, place and promotion – are considered in a leisure context. *Fourth*, approaches towards achieving a marketing plan are proposed.

Having read this chapter, readers will be made aware of the substantial influence of marketing on the buying habits of the public and what motivates and demotivates customers. They will also be aware that marketing starts with customers and their needs, not with products and organizations.

Students will learn what comprises the 'marketing mix' and that commercial marketing will need to be adapted to suit the social, political and institutional structure within the local government setting. They will learn about market segmentation and positioning.

Leisure Managers will be reminded of the need for customer care training for all levels of staff and that the face-to-face employees need particular motivation. They will learn how to set up a marketing strategy and the process to be followed, to set objectives and to achieve them.

16.1 INTRODUCTION

Modern marketing came about as an answer to increasing difficulties and competition in selling products in capitalist economies. In part, the growth in marketing is a response to the ever-increasing consumer choice and proliferation of industrial and commercial goods and services.

We are all influenced by marketing. In Western civilization marketing is part of the fabric by which we go about our daily business. 'It is part of the modern survival kit – because we depend on it' [1]. Marketing is simple. There is no mystique about it. Some treat it with reverence, as a formal, academic subject. Others take a more liberal and relaxed view. Robert Townsend [2], in *Up the Organisation*, captures the latter spirit: 'If you can't do it excellently, don't do it at all. Because if it's not excellent it won't be profitable or fun and if you're not in business for fun or profit, what the hell are you doing here.'

16.2 MARKETING: WHAT IS IT AND WHO DOES IT?

In the commercial world marketing has proved to be an effective means of staying in business and making greater profits. For leisure services in the public and voluntary sectors, it can also bring greater success.

The purpose of maketing is to earn profit by 'adding maximum value at minimum cost' [1]. Put simply, marketing is concerned with satisfying customers – profitably. However, 'profit' should be measured not just in terms of money, but also by satisfactions, the quality of the services, the turnover, the range of people, the choice and scope of the programme, the improvements made and other relevant criteria.

Marketing is a process and coordination network that analyses, creates, develops products and services, packages, prices, promotes, distributes and sells. It is a beginning-to-end process. This process is usually aimed at a segment of the public or a target market.

The marketing process is coordinating the activities of the business in the pursuit of adding maximum value at minimum cost. It is a linkage function for saleable goods or services. Its point of origin is consumer demand.

One feature of the concept of marketing is that of *voluntary exchange*: 'It calls for offering something of value to someone in exchange for something else of value' [3]. For example, public recreation is provided for the community in exchange for people's money, time and level of community charge.

Commercial 'product' marketing and public 'service' marketing have some aspects in common but there are conceptual differences. In the commercial field the product is subordinate to the fundamental aim – achievement of sales targets and the making of financial profits. In the services field the quality of the service is paramount.

Many people treat marketing with suspicion:

'It's an unfortunate fact that marketing – the profession, trade, way of life or what you will – is held in pretty low esteem by the public at large. It's probable, of course, that the public at large doesn't actually understand what marketing's about, but for many, the term has too close an association with the street trader, who would sell his sister if the price were right.

'The whole panoply of consumer persuasion, from advertising and PR, through sales promotion, packaging, point-of-sale display and salesmanship itself, is bundled together in many minds as prima facie proof that marketing is immoral, in practice if not in theory' (*Marketing*, April, 1984).

16.2.1 The marketing approach

Marketing is not a single function in a business or service organization. It is a business philosophy, a business way of life. It starts in the market place with customers. It is about selling satisfactions.

Traditionally, many companies are process-led and product orientated; they have a predetermined product or service. They find customers and convince them they want the product. The approach is, 'This is what *we've* got – now sell it'. Local government services often work in this way. For example, facilities are built, equipment is installed, markings are put on to the floors, programmes are devised, times are decided, charges are determined, systems are established, and the council will proudly announce that the facility is open. Many councillors will then say of the facility, 'It is there for them to use; if they don't use it that is their lookout. We provide plenty of opportunity in our town.' This approach is concerned with providing facilities.

The marketing way reverses the process and starts with the customer. It is market-led. It says, 'This is what the customer wants – now make it'. It then designs, produces and delivers the satisfactions for the customer, at a profit. Using the findings of a market research programme – i.e. information received – management organizes its business to ensure that the product is *tailor-made* for the market. By knowing who your customers are and about their wishes and wants, it is possible to produce appropriate products. When wants have been ascertained, sales resistance is apt to evaporate. The Japanese perfection in mass production, efficiency and knowledge of what the public wants in design, looks, performance and price has reaped a harvest in the motor cycle, motor car, home-based leisure and other industries. And indeed, the leisure manager's greatest competitor is leisure in and around the home. The question for Leisure Managers is: what does the public want from leisure services? Ted Blake [4] says: 'Sports centres, pools, theatres, art galleries, libraries, museums, gymnasia, are merely warehouses holding tangible and intangible products that have no value except that brought to them by customers.'

Potential customers need to know therefore about the 'products' and be attracted to them. Local authorities have to compete for a share of the market. The financial profit motive, however, is not normally an issue, although greater stress on viability and commercial approaches are being employed. Viable services are important but service to the public at large is pre-eminent. Marketing could be used to enhance social and community programmes. However, local government constraints in the United Kingdom could make for difficulties in this direction.

An emerging marketing myth is that local authorities can market public recreation in exactly the same way as one can market breakfast cereals, cameras or holidays. While local authorities have elements within their services which could be commercially orientated, and while marketing techniques can be used to promote recreation programmes, the overall purpose of the authority is not to make financial profit, but to meet need and demand. Moreover, the recreation product is extremely difficult to define and quantify, and quality of the service is difficult to measure. The aims and objectives, too, are decidedly different from many commercial undertakings: financial yardsticks are only one measurement and should normally be quite secondary to other criteria. Local councils have political, governmental, traditional and institutional constraints, in addition to social and moral obligations. Marketing is needed but the *way* in which it is processed should also be different because the commercial product and the local authority service 'product' are not identical. Public sector marketing is a hybrid of approaches which have evolved historically and are now caught up with commercial approaches, primarily to limit subsidy or to help make the facilities pay for themselves. With the advent of Compulsory Competitive Tendering in respect of public services (including leisure and recreation services), leisure managers are under far greater pressure to 'perform'.

16.2.2 The concept of social marketing

Marketing is typically defined in business terms as the planning, pricing, promoting, distribution and servicing of goods and products. It has been concerned with economic exchange of goods. As such it has been associated with business objectives to sell products and to learn about the kinds of product that the public would like to purchase.

The concept of marketing, however, can be interpreted as much broader than just economic exchange and could also 'logically encompass exchanges dealing with social issues and ideas' [5]. Most people are familiar with recent attempts to project politicians and political platforms through marketing: 'For example, an individual participating in an election exchanges his vote for the promise of the enactment of a particular political platform if his candidate is elected. Thus, this situation involves exchange' [5]. Marketing, it is argued, includes the facilitating of social exchanges as well as goods and services.

Kotler and Zaltman [6] define social marketing as 'The design, implementation and control of programmes calculated to influence the acceptability of social ideas and involving consideration of product planning, pricing, communication, distribution and market research'. Marketing, then, can encompass political campaigns, community programmes and social causes, such as environmental 'green' issues, pollution control, family planning, health, stop smoking campaigns, equal opportunities, anti-apartheid and peace campaigns. (The success of 'Live Aid' and Mandela concerts, 'Sport Aid', BBC's *Children in Need* and ITV's *Telethon* are testimony of the power of marketing social causes in recent years.)

Any new trend is likely to have both positive and negative effects. Marketing can improve the chances of useful social and community programmes coming to fruition. However, marketing can also be seen as having potential ethical problems. Those who are economically powerful could use marketing techniques to enhance ideas which may promote causes that are *not* socially beneficial.

Social marketing can be utilized in the leisure field for causes and community projects and to assist in recreation planning. A whole range of causes could be brought to public attention, for example, retention of open space, recreation for the disabled, health and fitness, 'Sport for All', 'Art for All' and Music for All' campaigns. However, its sensitive application is enormously important to avoid the criticism of indoctrination, for social marketing could be a powerful instrument which can affect the way people think, speak and act. This, of course, is the purpose of some marketing and this is why the causes and issues must be debated and adjudged by society to be beneficial. How important it is to put philosophy and principles *first*.

16.2.3. Marketing of public authority leisure and recreation services and facilities

Local authorities provide a number of services such as housing, refuse collection, social services, and so on, and citizens have little choice in the matter. But they *can* choose whether or not to use local authorities' leisure facilities and services. The facilities are said to cater for the whole community. Clearly, they do not. Some are not aware of their existence; others are aware but are not motivated to use the facilities –

they are not prepared or able to exchange what they have for what is on offer. Indeed, the facilities are disproportionally used by those who are more able, more mobile and more socially and financially advantaged.

The broad conclusion of studies by Cowell [7], in the late 1970s, was that there was 'no major evidence of marketing being applied to local authority recreation and sports centre planning and provision. However, the question now raised is whether it is reasonable to expect that marketing could and should be applied to this area.' There were exceptions to the general finding and since then marketing has received greater attention. Even so, the overall picture is one of limited evidence of marketing application. Demand assessments are rarely undertaken; the 'product' appears to be 'a portfolio of activities, events or facilities'; and there are few price experiments or use of prices as promotional devises and promotional budgets are small and inadequate.

Cowell states that the absence of substantial marketing should not necessarily be seen as criticism. Should marketing be practised? Three main possible explanations were put forward for the relative lack of marketing: *general constraints, institutional constraints* and *service constraints*. Marketing has been developed in economic contexts. Is marketing relevant in times of scarcity and restriction? Marketing has only recently been concerned with social and service issues. These general constraints have made it difficult for local authorities to adapt to a marketing approach:

'Providing for everybody's needs may make good political sense; it is unlikely to make sound marketing sense where segmentation is in vogue. Organisational structures too are often extended and are rarely designed for speedy response to the market place; political interests cloud issues; the committee system can delay decision making; local authorities interpret their sport, leisure and recreation responsibilities differently' [7].

Many authorities see recreation as a social service. The nature of what is being 'sold', however, is only partially understood. What is actually being marketed? In the commercial sector financial profits are used as measuring criteria. In local authorities, financial pressures lead to ambivalence. Panic measures may demand that income be maximized and expenditure minimized. This may mean that expenditure in one vital area is reduced, which could then work against achieving the objectives – a treatment least likely to effect a cure.

It is clear that, while marketing may have considerable benefits in local authority provision and management of recreation, the use of marketing approaches must be adapted to suit the social, political, economic and institutional structure within the local government setting.

16.3 CUSTOMERS AND THE INFLUENCES UPON THEM

A caption in *Advertising Age* exemplified the susceptibility and vulnerability of potential customers to persuasive promotion: 'In very few instances do people really know what they want, even when they say they do.'

Customers have many similar needs. But their demands may vary as do their levels of disposable income. In addition, in times of economic recession, the disposable income of many people diminishes, while the costs of goods and services increase. Not only do customers vary one from another, but the same customers may vary from one situation to another, from one mood to another and from one inclination to another. Therefore in leisure we must market for both the *similarities* and *differences* of customers.

Many factors affect demand, as we have seen in Chapter 6: social class, age, family, education, looks, personal aspirations, income, government restrictions, hire purchase, fashion, social attitudes, choices, motivations and many more. Customers are under constant pressure, whether as individuals or companies. In the past there were small, concentrated and highly profitable markets. Now there are widespread mass markets with affluence. There is far greater choice.

Customers are not static, unquestioning beings, but dynamic and often highly irrational people. They do not remain the same. Situations can change people. Therefore there is a need for flexibility in management style. Managers must vary their responses so that they continue to be appropriate to changing situations. In leisure services we cannot satisfy all of the people all the time, but we can go a long way towards satisfying most people. As Ted Blake [8] believes, it is by treating them with *importance, attention* and *understanding*. This underlines the importance of staff training in customer care.

In leisure services there is often the tendency to treat managers, processes, systems and organizational structures as important. Such services are not customer orientated, and may not meet customer expectations. Even in times of financial pressure, organizations should not be greedy and kill the golden goose. How many authorities are saying 'Put up the price of aerobics and fitness; there is demand; they'll pay'. This will work when demand outstrips supply; but when supply outstrips demand; then one is into a highly competitive market. In addition, the amount of one's disposable income influences decisions. But how much will *they* pay? How many of the young or less well-off will continue to pay? Are there alternatives or substitute activities for them? There are many 'thems'. At leisure centres, for example, the customers are a variety of people. They include the individuals, their friends, their families, the organizations (who buy for others), the supporters, spectators, schools, parents and visitors. Each link in the chain is a customer. The network is wider than we at first imagine, the chain is longer.

In order to market leisure successfully, we must sell benefits to customers. These benefits go to make up the picture of success. Local authorities have special benefits to give, particularly to those who are least able to fend for themselves; special groups include the old, the young, the handicapped, the unemployed and especially the jobless school-leaver. Here the problem is compounded, in that they have *more* free time, *less* disposable income and *poor* mobility. Young people, for example, need a favourable image of themselves; they need to realize some of their dreams. The marketing of leisure can assist in this image seeking. Yet the young are susceptible to marketing; commercial enterprise has been quick to seize the opportunity to provide what they are looking for. Pop culture, fashion, music and drink take a massive share of leisure spending. The pub is the leisure centre for many young people.

Suffice it to say that, in terms of marketing, the customer is the key – is the King! In leisure management we must therefore be customer orientated.

However, potential customers can be influenced in a variety of ways, some of which are beneficial but others harmful both to individuals and communities. It is worth considering therefore some of the motivating factors.

16.3.1 Motivation and the depth approach to marketing

All of us can be influenced and manipulated, far more than we realize, through marketing. Efforts are constantly being made to channel our *unthinking* habits, our buying decisions and our thought processes through the use of sciences such as psychiatry. 'Typically these efforts take place beneath our levels of awareness, so that appeals which move us are often, in a sense, hidden' [9]. Some 'manipulating' has been amusing, and some disquieting. The 'depth' approach, as Vance Packard calls it, is being used in a variety of fields and on a variety of unsuspecting people. 'The use of mass psychoanalysis to guide campaigns of persuasion has become the basis of a multi-million dollar industry. Professional persuaders have seized upon it in their groping for more effective ways to sell us their wares – whether products, ideas, attitudes, candidates, goals or states of mind' [9].

The 'persuaders' are looking for the whys of our behaviour; for example why wives are drawn into illogical purchases or fill shopping baskets in a supermarket as though under hypnosis, or why men buy certain drinks or cars. Packard believes that the 'persuaders' see us typically as 'bundles of day-dreams, misty hidden yearnings, guilt complexes, irrational emotion blockages. We are image lovers given to impulse and compulsive acts' [10]. It seems that our subconscious can be 'pretty wild and unruly'. The persuaders stop at nothing. Nothing is immune or sacred. Agencies seek to discover the psychological effects of the female menstrual cycle on the purchasing of certain food products; psychiatric probing techniques have been used on impressionable young people anxious to be attractive; and public relations experts are advising church ministers on improving communications to their congregations. Cheskin [11] adds support to Packard:

'Motivation research is the type of research that seeks to learn what motivates people in making choices. It employs techniques designed to reach the unconscious or subconscious mind because preferences generally are determined by factors of which the individual is not conscious ... Actually in the buying situation the consumer generally acts emotionally and compulsively, unconsciously reacting to the images and decisions which in the subconscious are associated with the product'.

Marketing is, then, potentially powerful and equally potentially dangerous. What people tell interviewers at a surface, conscious level could have little bearing on how they will actually behave in a buying situation. The manipulators are working *beneath* the surface of conscious life. Most leisure research concerned with public sector provision has been based on surface-level surveys and questionnaires and on quantitative analysis. Research which is more qualitative and looks beneath the surface is required to help to understand people's motivation in making recreation choices.

16.3.2 What motivates people to 'buy' leisure and recreation?

What motivates people in making choices? The realization that there are 'hidden persuaders' makes us aware that there are factors of which the individual is unconscious and that people do different things from what they say they will. For example, *impressions* could decide the customer's response. First impressions count. Leisure facilities must therefore create the *right* impression. Marketing slogans preach: 'it is not the product but the *promise*'. There is a need in leisure to be selling both the product and the promise.

The selling of 'pop music' singles is often marketed on what are sometimes termed 'hookers' – i.e. those lines, rhythms or jingles which you catch on to and cannot get out of your head, however hard you try. Puccini's 'Nessun Dorna' sung by Pavarotti was BBC TV's introduction to the 1990 World Cup in Italy. The single and LP were massive 'hits' both for the records and for 'selling' the BBC and the World Cup. A Eurovision Song Contest No. 1 is another example. One of the best-selling Top Twenty hits of 1973, 'Tie a Yellow Ribbon', was revived in 1981 to welcome home to the United States the Iranian hostages, and again in 1985 for the hostages from Beirut. The jingle had not been forgotten, the *message* had not been forgotten. The ribbon symbolism was used years later as a mark of peace on the fortieth anniversary of the dropping of the first atomic bomb on Hiroshima and again after the Gulf War in 1991.

Some marketing slogans can become part of the product itself and hence a great deal of marketing can be undertaken at very little cost. Leisure equipment, clothing and fashion can carry slogans, messages and communications which become embedded in the minds of consumers. To return from shopping in London's West End carrying a Harrod's carrier bag confers a kind of status on the carrier. The trefoil or the laurel wreath seen on a sports shirt carries the name and markets the goods: 'carrying an Adidas sports bag and wearing an Adidas sports shirt confer status beyond what might be expected from association with the names of professional sportsmen' [12].

Cooperative marketing spreads the burden of promotional expenditure. Kelloggs, for example, support promotions of toys, video recorders, sports bags, tennis rackets and bathroom scales. The television and radio media are flooded with advertising jingles. The jingles may remain in the head and promote products for an appreciable length of time. Wilson and West [12] recall that, in 1971, Coca-Cola commissioned a jingle for a new advertising campaign. This was heard repeatedly on television and in cinemas throughout the world. The copyright was assigned to a musical company and a new lyric was written. The former commercial jingle entered the singles record charts as 'I'd like to Teach the World to Sing'. But the pop song never lost its association with the Coca-Cola advertisement: 'So the company not only recovered much (if not all) of the original investment; it also continued to enjoy a promotional benefit.'

16.3.3 The leisure demotivators

Bad news travels fast. It is passed on more readily than good news. Marketers (i.e. Leisure Managers) must therefore not only have concern with what motivates people to recreation, but also with what demotivates. Nothing demotivates more than poor handling of customers: rudeness, a 'take it or leave it' attitude, ruined expectations, dissatisfactions and broken promises. The package holiday scandals of holidaymakers being sent to the wrong place, or double-bookings, demotivate for example.

Leisure and recreation, as we have seen, is marketed largely through people. Managers and staff have important roles to play. Since the reorganization of local government there has been a very considerable increase in the number of personnel, services and facilities. Much attention has been given to the emerging 'profession' of leisure management. Time and effort have been expended on gaining 'professional status', on guarding professional jealousies, on the rights of staff, pay scales and conditions and on manoeuvring into positions of importance. Managers' over-concern with their own positions, and preoccupations with administrative technicalities and systems, can take the time, the capacity and the heart out of marketing for people and militate against customer orientation. If managers become greedy, judging success by their personal goals, then an unwelcome aura can be engendered, demotivating both colleagues and customers.

Leisure service is primarily concerned with customers; it is about *their* needs. Townsend [2] believes that good service is given and things get done because of men and women with conviction. In current leisure management, the 'light of conviction' is often seen in the eyes of junior staff, who may not have the necessary experience but can, with enthusiasm, 'reach the parts others cannot reach'! They should be encouraged, for leisure can be best marketed by people who are involved, committed and who undertake their work with conviction and enthusiasm.

Satisfying customers brings benefits. Success in selling leisure and recreation lies not in leisure departments, centre management, committees or even in the facilities themselves, but out in the market, in the minds and pockets of the customers.

16.3.4 Training for customer caring

Who should do the selling to customers? The British Productivity Council estimate that in 95% of cases there must be *face-to-face* selling. Commercial organizations spend considerable effort in training and briefing staff, teaching staff how to talk with, meet with and communicate with customers.

Training of staff in public facilities is poor by comparison. Many who are in the greatest need of training are those who manage facilities and are not released by their authorities for training or those who work at a face-to-face level with customers. It is these staff at the 'sharp end' – i.e. the receptionists, the caretakers, groundsmen, park keepers and supervisors of all kinds – who have the job of meeting and motivating the public. With some notable exceptions (such as many reception staff), face-to-face employees are so often the least capable of communicating with and handling customers. They have not been trained, encouraged, motivated, made to feel important or supported. Yet it is they who are called upon to undertake the most important job, namely that of communicating with people. People market leisure and recreation – customers and staff. Staff need help in carrying out this important function; they need training. Regrettably many leisure services, far from motivating people, sometimes serve to demotivate them, achieving the complete opposite of that which was intended.

Customer care and quality of service in the leisure service is probably more important than in any other service because the leisure 'product' we are dealing with is satisfying experiences for customers. As we have seen, a visit to a leisure event which is badly managed and results in bad experiences, is unlikely to be bought again. Now, if people are seeking pleasure experiences, they can find these in all kinds of leisure activities, not just those that your organization is promoting.

At leisure facilities and events, customers need to enjoy their experience or to have found it worthwhile. If they do, they will probably come again and they will let others know about it. Customer caring therefore involves the whole team of management and staff at a facility.

16.4 THE MARKETING MIX

Marketing is concerned with providing the right products and services and then forging the best relationships between customers and products and services.

The *'Marketing Mix'* is the means by which that relationship is expressed. It has a number of ingredients, the most important being:

1. product (including service);
2. pricing;
3. place;
4. promotion (pre-purchase);
5. performance (post-purchase).

There are a number of factors which need emphasis in deciding how the ingredients are going to be mixed in order to be appropriate to the market. Sandy Craig [13] points to some:

'Firstly, the nature of the product or service influences the balance of the ingredients. Products with a high fashion content, e.g. designer sportswear, emphasise the product itself through product development and design and promote heavily. Price and availability are not so important. By contrast, staple foods such as canteen food emphasise price and ready availability with promotion and product playing less important roles. (If the 'canteen'/cafe in your facility provides fast food the availability becomes more important, product development (including packaging) becomes more important and price less important. If it provides health food (or healthy food) then product development (including packaging and presentation) becomes even more important, and price less important).'

The emphasis between leisure products in the commercial sector and products in community recreation services will be decidedly different. The sections which follow deal with the main ingredients in the 'marketing mix' and, first, the product.

16.5 THE LEISURE PRODUCT

The *product* (including the service) is the basis of all marketing. It is the unit of exchange with the customer. If it offers the customer satisfactions, he or she may continue to buy it.

Products exhibit life-cycles. With most commercial products that life-cycle revolves around a product start, growth, development and decline and the replacement by better products. In leisure services many products have been with us for decades, but even well-established activities like squash may currently be on the decline and have to be packaged differently to redress the present trend. What is needed is product development to provide a continuous stream of new or changing products.

The leisure product we are talking about is described in Chapter 7. In essence, it is the satisfying or worthwhile experience derived from participation in or involvement with an activity in a person's time for leisure. Therefore the product is not goods, but the experiencing of satisfactions. Let us use the analogy of tennis. As Jon Johnson reminds us [14] you can buy a tennis racket, feel and handle it, pay for it and keep it. It is tangible. But leisure is intangible, until you experience it.

The tennis racket not sold today can be sold tomorrow. The tennis court space or theatre seat not sold today is lost for ever. Its 'sell-by' date is in advance of the activity! Leisure, in this sense, cannot be stored.The product is perishable.If you are rich you might own a tennis court, but most of us simply rent it for an hour and we have a choice of waiting our turn at the park courts, booking in advance at the sports centre or taking part at a tennis club.

As well as being perishable, the product is fragile and unpredictable. It is easily damaged. John McEnroe can smash his racket on the ground and may still be able to play with it. But a customer treated rudely at reception, double-booked on the court or unable to get a drink can take her or his custom elsewhere. Leisure behaviour is less predictable than work behaviour. In leisure customers have choice and are fickle.

The leisure 'product' therefore is somewhat of an enigma – diverse, changing, intangible, perishable, fragile and fleeting – and, in many instances, dependent on the person giving the service, namely the coach, tour guide or performer [14]. Leisure products and services are provided by the public, voluntary and commercial sectors. Commercial leisure normally has a finite answer and a measurable target. For example, at squash club the object could be to enrol 1000 squash members at £200 per head and sell 70% of court space during the 80 hours of opening at £4 an hour. But even in this simple objective of selling memberships and utilizing space, there are many service elements – efficiency, attractive facilities, ambience and après-squash – all of which go to make up the product and bring satisfaction to the user.

The leisure product in local authority services is rarely spelled out. The selling of spaces, times and activities is understood. What is not understood is the creating of an environment in which people can experience recreation through an activity of their choice. Demand for a product may arise out of choice, out of opportunity, from the facilities themselves or from the policies of management. On the other hand, demand for a product can be stifled by restrictive policies, limited opportunities, highly exclusive clubs, lack of choice, vested interests and other demotivators. For example, a sports facility requiring a playing-in standard, or an enrolling fee, or a proposer and seconder on an application form, may attract better players, more affluent people and those who can handle the whole 'joining' process; others may find the joining process itself intimidating and a major stumbling block to participation. The objectives determine the leisure products and their promotion.

Facilities, opportunities and 'welcome' can stimulate demand and dramatically expand a leisure market. For example, the *opportunity* to play squash provided by those from *outside* squash circles (public and commercial providers) made it into a boom sport. Sponsorship and exposure has done the same for other sports such as snooker, darts and indoor bowls.

Most recreation programmes, even those designed with major speciality areas, such as drama or cycling, tend to market more than one product. How many products are to be marketed? In the public sector, it has been shown in recent years, not only that a combination of facilities attracts greater use and is more economical, but also that the spin-off to other activities expands the market [15].

Markets rarely remain static. Managers should therefore avoid putting all their eggs in one basket. In addition, if the aim of a council is to give the public a level of freedom of choice, then it is important to give that choice and variety within the overall service.

Some products will cease to contribute to 'profits' or 'benefits'. New products may be the life-blood of some static leisure services. The answer may be to introduce *new looking* products to create new images: 'New looking products carry advantages to stress new customer benefits' [8]. What do potential customers think the product is? *Their* notion of what it is and what the benefits are is what matters.

Products may decline, but demand for the type of product may still be rising. Skateboarding's rapid growth and decline hides the creation of new looking activities on wheels such as roller skating, roller surfing, roller disco and roller hockey.

Product development and improvement are therefore of importance. Packaging different products can generate customer benefits at all levels of participation – e.g. a daytime leisure centre package might include: sports activity, dietary clinic, sauna and a crèche for the children.

16.6 PRICING THE PRODUCTS

The pricing policy is an important factor in financial planning and in the overall strategy. It is a vital part of marketing. Should we price high and then reduce; price low for a quick penetration of the market; price at one rate for all the customers; or offer special rates, discounts and packages? Commercial marketing is profit orientated; therefore, it is price sensitive. Products must be gauged at the right price to attract customers to buy. Discussion is often centred on keeping prices low, but in many exclusive establishments pricing high can achieve the type of response aimed to meet objectives.

Local authority pricing is largely based on tradition, and what is an 'acceptable' level compared with other authorities. There is great similarity between authorities in terms of pricing levels, although there may be a range of charges levied for different activities or services. These can be expressed in theory along a charging continuum, which extends from a social service approach, where no charges are imposed, to a commercial approach at the other end of the continuum. Table 16.1 illustrates this charging continuum within the public sector, together with its user implications.

Where the social service type of approach exists, the basis of such a policy is based upon the belief that the intrinsic value of leisure and recreation is beneficial both to the participants and the community and that the opportunities should be equally available to all members of the community. Consequently, no charge for using the facilities and services is made. The facilities that fall within this category are the parks, the libraries and the community centres.

The economic approach is based upon the belief that the benefits

Table 16.1 The charging policy continuum in the public sector

		Break-even	
Charging continuum	←- - - - - - *Subsidy*	| *Profit* - - - - - - →	
Type of charge	*No charge*	*Economic charge*	*Commercial charge*
Basis of policy	Social service – all residents have a recreational need – facilities available to all	Participants are main benefactors, hence have to pay full costs	Benefits participants exclusively. Charges include Full Costs + Profit Charges based on what market can bear. Profit used to subsidize other facilities
Type of facilities	Parks Libraries Community Centres	Entertainments Golf courses	Indoor tennis Squash Sauna Sun beds
Profile of Users	Representative of neighbourhood	Middle-income groups Youths/young adults	Middle to high-income groups

Note: Within the continuum, facilities such as swimming pools, sports halls and sports grounds will fall between the 'no charge' and 'economic charge' bands; fitness activities could fall between economic and commercial bands.

obtained are largely confined to the participants themselves, and hence the charges levied include all costs in an effort to break-even. Generally this approach is becoming more popular within the public sector and with many local authorities charging an economic rent for entertainment and facilities such as golf courses.

The commercial approach is based upon the belief that the benefits obtained are exclusively restricted to the participants, hence the charges levied not only cover all costs, but also a profit that can be used to subsidize other activities. Thus at this end of the continuum, the charges made are what the market can withstand. Examples of activities that frequently fall within this category include squash and the use of sun-beds.

In recent years, the high running costs of leisure services and centres has called for a more objective financial appraisal. Authorities are asking themselves: is it possible to cover running costs? Should subsidy be given in greater measure to certain sectors of the community?

There is fierce competition in the commercial world. Competitive pricing and good margins are valuable weapons for salesmen. There are special bonuses for stockists; discounts apply. Attractions in the form of stamps, wrappers, competitions, free glasses at petrol stations, incentive schemes, holidays for two and a host of other methods are tried. The promotional inventiveness is endless. Commercial marketing is not just concerned with the product (it is quite secondary to other factors), but with the benefits to the customers, if they *buy* the product and to the salespeople, if they *sell* it.

Local authorities are not under such fierce competition. Authorities have far greater scope to use resources to enlarge opportunities and help to meet people's needs. But local authorities must, first, discover needs and wants and then attract people to the services offered. Leisure products could be offered at no charge at all and still people will spend their time and their money on other apparently less worthy products! But well-managed and promoted Passport to Leisure schemes have clearly shown that even the price of swimming can be a deterrent to some sections of the community.

Price therefore may not be as important after all. Cheapness is one criterion, especially for the financially disadvantaged, but not necessarily the only criterion. Rambling, camping, tennis, museums, theatres and athletics, for example, are relatively cheap activities, yet they attract only certain small segments of the population. Marketers (i.e. managers) have the task of changing images in order to draw people to the leisure product. The level at which prices are set can also be used to control the demand for a particular activity (e.g. golf courses), while at others it may be used to extend the capacity of a facility (e.g. indoor tennis courts).

Pricing has always been a vitally important element in commercial business. It is now to be more important for local authorities through *Compulsory Competitive Tendering*, *Local Management of Schools* and the financial constraints imposed on local government. Local authorities will need to examine their marketing strategies in terms of subdividing their products by price and quality and consider the advantages and disadvantages of pricing high, medium or low and the implications of these policies on the service. Maintaining a principle of accessibility for all will be sorely tested. One of the keys may be in price flexibility, allowing managers to gauge the sensitivities of the market.

16.7 PLACE

The *distribution policy* should be based on the market research about customers, the products and the prices: how important it is for services and facilities to be placed in locations which customers can get to easily. (This aspect has been covered in some detail in other parts of the book, particularly in Chapter 6 on factors which influence participation.) In addition to the distribution of resources, a distribution policy needs to be formulated relating to location of key elements within facilities – e.g. access to créche, cafeteria and to all the programme allocations of time and space, opening hours and a balance between activities. (These aspects are taken up in Chapter 14 on programming). In addition, the level and quality of service at the right place and time are important.

Many leisure facilities will be inaccessible to segments of the population. In these cases, needs can be met by managing mobile services – e.g. library, toy library, play bus, travelling theatre and by appointing artists in residence, sports motivators, animateurs, etc.

Services may well be available, accessible and at the right price but customers may still not take advantage of the opportunity. This is where promotion and communications come into play.

16.8 PROMOTION

So far we have looked briefly at the customer, the products, pricing, buying, motivating and selling. Another ingredient of the 'marketing mix' is promotion. It is a process of familiarizing, reminding and creating favourable attitudes and a willingness to buy. The process is one of pulling customers to the product using words, music, pictures and symbols to present an image of the product that is attractive, if not compelling.

Promotional activity has been defined as

'an exercise in communications. Its role is to facilitate exchanges with potential client groups by communicating the benefits offered by a programme or service. It seeks to inform, persuade or remind' [16].

The promotion consists of four major components:

1. *Personal contact* – this involves a verbal presentation to one or more potential customers with the objective of selling a service or a product.
2. *Advertising* – this represents a paid form of non-personal presentation about the organization and/or the programme of opportunities offered.
3. *Incentives* – these represent a financial offer that is made to potential customers with the objective to encourage them to purchase a particular service or product.
4. *Publicity* – this represents a favourable form of communication in the media (e.g. print or broadcast) at no direct cost to the organization concerned.

16.8.1 Personal selling

This is probably the most common form of promotion within the leisure industry. Leisure industry personnel generally have an outgoing personality which enables them to interact well with their customers. To be effective in personal selling, it is necessary that the person concerned does it with enthusiasm, that he or she is perceived as being credible and has similar attitudes and norms to the potential customer. Selling to community leaders and 'Queen Bees', with an extended social network of receivers, can do much to spread the 'word'.

The function of personal selling involves a two-way communication process and can provide valuable feedback information about existing and potential recreation programmes.

16.8.2 Advertising

Advertising encompasses many forms of communication and includes:

1. Posters.
2. Brochures and leaflets that describe the facilities, services and programmes on offer.
3. Advertisements placed in the local media – i.e. newspapers and radio.
4. Newsletters and fully paid supplements in the local newspapers.
5. Direct mailing enclosing new information, e.g. changes in programmes offered to members

In comparison to publicity, advertising does not provide immediate feedback and can be an expensive form of promotion.

Televison advertisements are extremely expensive, as are paid advertisements in the press. In contrast, the local cinema can be a relatively cheap form of advertising. As cinema-going audiences are largely young people, then products, activities and services that appeal to young people could be effectively advertised in local cinemas. Local radio advertising can vary in cost but in getting across to young people local radio could pay dividends. Poster advertising can be very indifferent compared with face-to-face communication (i.e. human communication), which makes a greater impact. The message to Leisure Managers appears to be to look at the whole variety of ways of communicating, to try out various forms and 'shop around' and then act positively, measure results and make appropriate adjustments.

Promotions, then, will include all the methods designed and packaged to sell the benefits of the services and products on sale. They include the marketing research information, advertising, packaging, sales promotions, public relations and in the leisure facility environment membership schemes, 'passport' schemes, discounted prices, price packaging and a host of others.

In order to ensure that the communication messages are effective, there are general guidelines that can be helpful in attracting the attention of potential customers:

1. Colour attracts the attention of the reader far more than black and white material.
2. Unusual or novel design catches the eye of the reader.
3. Taller shaped material appears to be more effective than wide-shaped material.
4. Large materials tend to attract more attention than small exhibits.
5. Communications that involve more than one sensor (e.g. sight and sound) appear to have the greatest impact.

Further, in any written form the importance of the headline cannot be overemphasized. The headline must be catchy to stimulate the reader to read the full message. Often this takes the form of a question with the answer or solution appearing in the text below. Current questions that touch on aspects of health, fitness and beauty tend to arouse adequate interest for potential customers of sports centres to read further. Also the text should be persuasive and demand action from the reader such as 'telephone *now*' or 'complete the attached form *now*'.

A self-testing criterion for an advertising communication is that it should produce positive answers to the following questions:

1. Is it eye-catching?
2. Is the layout attractive?

3. Does the headline stimulate the reader to proceed further?
4. Does it provide adequate information?
5. But at the same time, is the message clear and simple?
6. Is the text persuasive and creditable?
7. Does the advertisement create a favourable public image of the organization?

16.8.3 Incentives

In contrast to the other forms of promotional activity, incentives should not be used on a regular basis and when offered should be restricted to a limited period of time. The main objective of using incentives is to stimulate participation from identified market targets. The incentives can take the form of an introductory offer – e.g. centre tee-shirts, discounts (e.g. two tickets for the price of one), awards and badges.

The offer of discounts such as reduced off-peak pricing without adequate advertisements and publicity is unlikely to have a great impact on generating increased levels of utilization. Permanent discounts appear to have a minimum impact and can lead to questions being raised on whether the pricing levels are good value for money.

16.8.4 Publicity

Since most local authority leisure services departments have a minimal promotional budget, this has resulted in many concentrating more on publicity. This normally takes the form of press releases, feature articles and in some instances, a leisure centre may write its own weekly column in the local newspaper. It is a useful method of conveying information to customers, and potential customers, about changes in a programme and informing the community of the results of fixtures in the local leagues and competitions. To keep a facility continually in the public's mind, it is necessary periodically to have general interest stories relating to the facility in the local newspaper since not all readers read the arts and sports pages.

Although publicity does not directly involve financial expenditure, the true cost of preparing the publicity material may be considerable, particularly if many senior personnel are involved. Also the editorial staff may reject the 'press release' or leisure centre prepared copy on the grounds that it is not adequately newsworthy.

Coverage of a leisure programme or event or issue can fix an image in the mind of the public. Such an image is difficult to eradicate, particularly if the image is a poor one. The press can give a negative image in minutes; and the press is often seen as challenging, questioning and embarrassing to the local authority. Therefore, the only effective approach is to influence the control of the image-making and take a hand in managing the coverage. This can be achieved by informing and involving them and keeping them up to date with news. Good press coverage will help the public to say that their money on a leisure facility is well spent.

16.9 TOWARDS A MARKETING PLAN – MISSION, POSITION AND SEGMENTATION

Managers have leisure services and products to sell, and markets to sell them to. There are basically four courses of action:

1. Selling existing services and products to existing markets – i.e. market penetration (which includes extending product life-cycle and increased level of consumption).
2. Selling the existing services and products to new markets – i.e. market development.
3. Selling new or re-modelled services to existing customers – i.e. product-service development.
4. Selling the new services to new markets – i.e. market diversification.

The ethos of an organization can be encapsulated in what is now being termed a *mission statement*. It exists to promote the organization within and without, stating why the organization exists and what it hopes to achieve, what it believes in, how it should behave, what its strategies are and what image it wants to promote. As Ted Blake puts it in his succinct manner [17]:

'Everybody is looking for meaning in their lives. The *right* kind of mission gives this meaning. Meaning, in addition to fair pay and good working conditions, inspires greater trust, cooperation, commitment and loyalty through better job clarification and satisfaction; better decision-making; clearer communication; and greater ease of delegation with less need for supervision and inspection. Recruitment becomes less subjective and the mission makes it easier to define, recruit, promote and develop the "right kind of people"'.

Another term in vogue is market *positioning* and, like many marketing innovations, emanates from the USA with its highly competitive selling of products. Products and services have long-term 'personalities', just like people. For example, the Bank of England – safe and dependable; Wimbledon – the pinnacle, traditional values, class; or Richard Branson's Virgin products – innovative, creative, daring, adventurous. Kelloggs, Heinz, Harrods, Ascot and hundreds of other 'institutions' have a position in our minds and in the market place, as has DisneyWorld and even local government 'baths' services! But market positioning can be re-positioned. Lucozade used to be sold in chemist's shops for people who were ill. The Daley Thompson promotions repositioned Lucozade as a refreshing energy drink for athletes – from the sick to the fit!

Ted Blake [17] paints the picture vividly:

'Coca-Cola is teenaged, ubiquitous and very American. Hofmeister is a smart "with it", street-wise lager. Bisto is simple, tasty and dependable like Mother. Guinness is friendly, classless with comforting strength, warmth with a touch of humour.

'Jerry Hall helped Bovril re-position itself as a *must* nutrition for the ultra-figure conscious'.

Positions, however, take time to establish. 'Positions are the users' perception of facts that have been simplified and organized for easy retention and recall. Feelings are facts that linger in the public mind ... that can be evoked, dramatised, and rendered more important and urgent by advertising and other promotion options.' Leisure facilities, particularly those in the public sector, do not at present engender such perceptions; and consequently, they are frequently not utilized to the optimum level.

16.9.1 Market segmentation

It has often been claimed that the problem with municipally managed leisure facilities is that they try to cater for all the community rather than concentrate and penetrate a segment of the total market.

A painter or a potter creating a work of art for a special gift provides an exclusive service. Teaching the piano or tennis through private one-to-one tuition also provides an exclusive product designed for the individual. With mass markets, however, it is impossible to provide exclusive products for each individual, but it is possible to tailor-make products for segments of a market. Low-income earners do not buy Rolls-Royce cars, nor join the most expensive golf clubs, nor book seats at Covent Garden Opera House (Sir Thomas Beecham is reported to have said: 'God has yet to invent a faster way of spending money than putting on an opera'). However, there are many dissimilar individuals who can still be segmented because of their similar characteristics – e.g. the same age, the same sex, the same fashions, similar interests, and so on.

Targeting to like-minded segments, with appropriate products, is much more likely to achieve success than a hit or miss strategy. Local authorities tend to avoid market segmentation because they believe they should be providing for all their customers. The problem with this view is that the service given may not be wholly appropriate to any group, in particular: trying to suit everybody, may suit very few.

A market segment, then, is any homogenous subdivision of a market that is likely to be attracted to particular products or services. A local authority or a company can choose different kinds of segmentation to attract people to their products and services:

1. *Differentiated markets* separate products and services for each segment (e.g. Junior Sports and Senior Citizens Old Time Music Hall).
2. *Undifferentiated markets* sell one product to all buyers within a catchment area (e.g. Town Festival which caters for all segments).
3. *Concentrated markets* focus on one or just a few lucrative or popular 'brands' (e.g. five-a-side football and badminton in a sports centre or country club golf and tennis).

The process of segmentation needs good market research, understanding of groups and people's life-cycle needs. It requires strategies and selection of segments which match particular products within the overall service.

16.10 CONSTRUCTING A MARKETING PLAN

In order to market successfully, there needs to be a marketing plan based on the aims and objectives of the organization. This involves seeking answers to fundamental questions: what business are we in? What are our services and products? What is the market structure? Who are the competitors? Who are the customers? What are the products? Such an initial approach provides information, but it is only information. It will not make decisions; it represents a reconnaissance of the market. It needs to be turned into a plan of action.

Having undertaken the reconnaissance and arrived at a profile of the community or market sector or target group, the manager must then construct a *marketing plan*. An example of how a marketing plan for a new swimming pool can be developed is illustrated in Fig. 16.1 and consists of nine distinct stages.

MARKETING PLAN: A NINE-STAGE PLAN FOR MARKETING A NEW SWIMMING POOL

Stage 1: council policy

- Determine council policy.
- In the absence of aims and objectives, establish purpose of facility.
- Have any policy issues been determined?

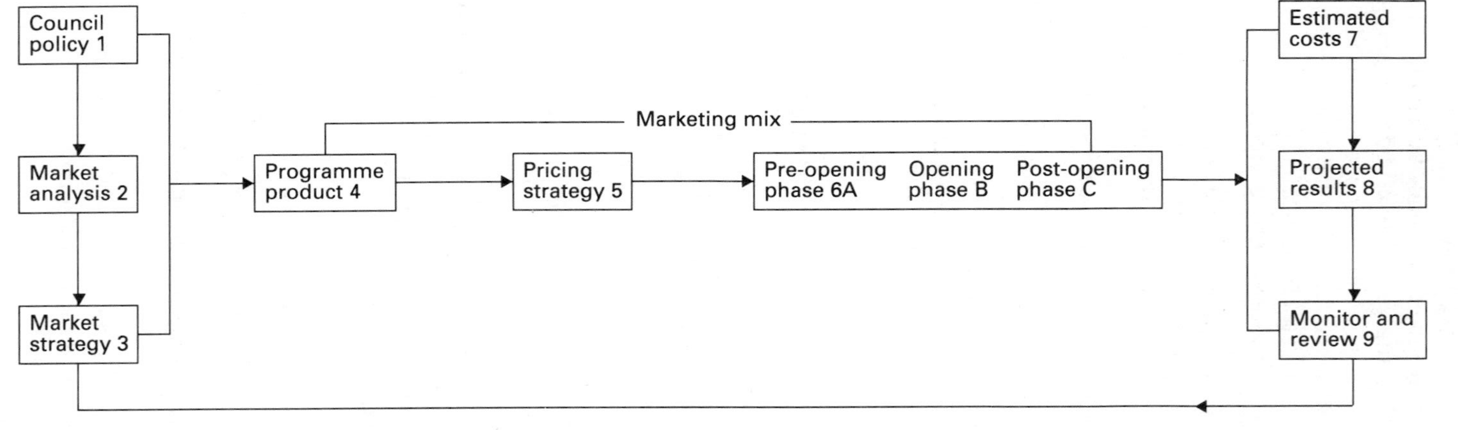

Fig. 16.1 A marketing plan for a new swimming pool.

Stage 2: market analysis

- Determine potential of facility.
- Undertake population analysis of perceived catchment area (having taken location and accessibility into consideration).
- Undertake survey of programme requirements of local clubs, schools and organizations.
- Examine competition in the area.
- Determine potential demand in the area.
- Examine competence of staff to undertake promotional tasks.

Stage 3: market strategy

- Provide centre with identifiable logo (local competition).
- Establish programme guidelines to cover:
  - casual use by public;
  - education;
  - range of activities to be offered;
  - club usage;
  - courses.
- Establish target groups:
  - women;
  - 50+;
  - unemployed;
  - disabled;
  - under 5s.
- Determine potential of total attendances.
- Propose areas to secure sponsorship (to supplement promotional budget).
- Establish objectives.

Stage 4: programme (product)

- Produce practical suggestions for programming – i.e. to meet council policy:
  - range of activities;
  - range and ability level of courses to be offered;
  - proposed competitions;
  - proposals for establishment of facility-based clubs;
  - specific programme for different target groups;
  - suggest role in borough/district sports development plan.

Stage 5: pricing strategy

- Suggestions to ensure:
  - value for money image;

  - maximum penetration in local catchment area;
  - maximum impact on target groups.
- Consideration to be given to:
  - discounts for target groups;
  - cost per participant for courses.
- Suggested prices for peak or off-peak:
  - club use;
  - hire for galas.
- Suggestions for gross profit levels on trading activities.

Stage 6: promotions

(a) Pre-opening phase

- Identify methods to create high levels of awareness among potential users.
- Maintain high level of press coverage throughout the development phase.
- Communicate with clubs and organizations and representatives of education service.
- Introduce newspaper pull-out supplement to enhance public image of facility (and obtain sponsorship and sale of advertising space).
- Produce brochures providing information relating to:
  - scale of facilities;
  - activities to be offered/opening hours;
  - availability of courses;
  - prices to be charged;
  - programme for target groups;
  - booking procedures.
- Distribute brochures at locations accessible to public.
- Produce 'give-aways' – e.g. stickers, badges and balloons.
- Suggest design/layouts for posters and advertisements.

(b) Opening phase

- Suggest programme for official opening – e.g. displays, competition.
- Obtain star/personality to undertake official opening.
- Draw up list of official guests and VIPs.
- Suggest buffet for guests and VIPs.
- Draw up invitation list of local clubs and organizations.
- Place advertisements in local media.
- Organize house-to-house invitation drop.

(c) Post-opening phase

- Consolidate early successes.
- Identify programme areas that are under performing and reassess.

- Organize and promote special events on regular basis.
- Review programme on regular basis and modify if necessary.

Stage 7: estimated costs

- Estimate gross cost of:
  - printing brochures, posters, etc.;
  - advertising in local media;
  - star/personality fee;
  - cost of artwork;
  - cost of promotional 'give aways'.
- Estimate income from sponsorship.

Stage 8: project results

- Project:
  - level of utilization;
  - total attendances;
  - total users (e.g. adults, juniors, club usage);
  - attendance on courses;
  - total income;
  - user profile.

Stage 9: monitor and review

- Assess effectiveness of promotional strategy.
- Compare facility performance with set objectives and targets.
- Amend programme if necessary.

16.11 MARKETING CONCLUSIONS

Marketing approaches to leisure products and services, using a marketing plan, will increase the probability of success in both public and private sectors. The marketing approach ensures that when a product or service is made available to the consumer, it has been planned, designed, packaged, promoted and delivered in such a manner that the customer is not only persuaded to buy, but also to repeat the experience as often as possible. While impulse buying, like attending an event or 'having a go' are important, repeat visits and repeat buying of the leisure experience are even more important. People get 'hooked' on products. Once caught with the bug of pottery, painting, jazz, playing golf, squash, snooker, sauna bathing or yoga, we are anxious to participate even more. Impulse buying may attract people but this needs to be capitalized on, for new-found satisfying experiences want to be bought again and again. They become habit-forming.

Marketing needs a budget. The crumbs that local authorities spend, usually under the heading 'Advertising' are minimal. Many seaside resorts, theatres and festivals are well publicized and some are marketed well; however, the general picture is poor. For example, many authorities have a revenue expenditure at leisure centres in the region of £1 million and more yet spend less than 0.5% on marketing and promotion.

The marketing process will need to be adjusted to meet the conceptual differences to be found in local authority services. Local authorities have great opportunities to market their services to meet their aims and objectives. Their services on the whole fail to attract the majority of the underprivileged and lower socio-economic groups. Indeed, one might argue that the higher up the social scale you go, the more of your entertainment, such as opera, ballet and music, is paid out of public money. Great opportunities exist to meet community needs and demands but sensitive, humane handling of the marketing process must be achieved.

At the start of this chapter, it was stated that marketing is concerned with voluntary exchange and that community leisure services are provided in exchange for people's money, time and rates and taxes. If the public does not want what is provided and is not prepared to pay the costs and give up the time, then local authority support could well be reduced. Therefore, leisure managers must be concerned with the questions: are the customers satisfied with the leisure products; are they experiencing satisfactions? It is not just how many participated, but whether the market target groups were reached with satisfying results and whether objectives were met. Community leisure and recreation marketing is concerned with identifying and responding to what the community needs and wants and is prepared to support.

In summary, marketing needs objectives, a plan, action and measurement. Marketing need not be a highly sophisticated and learned process. A marketing plan is a statement about what actions are to be undertaken to meet objectives. Marketing affects people's attitudes. It affects the way they speak, look, think and behave. Managers of leisure should encourage people to look more favourably towards themselves and towards the products and services being offered by their organizations. What is of greater importance is that managers should ascertain first what is likely to be most satisfying to customers and try to provide what is needed. This can be undertaken more successfully through marketing approaches adapted to meet the demands of the situation.

REFERENCES AND NOTES

1. McIver, C. (1968), *Marketing* (3rd edn) (revised and edited, G. C. Wilson), Business Publications, London.
2. Townsend, R. (1970), *Up the Organisation*, Coronet Books, London, p. 96.
3. Kotler, P. (1975), *Marketing for Non-Profit Organisations*, Prentice-Hall Englewood Cliffs, NJ, p. 5.
4. Blake, T. (1985), Image, *Leisure Management*, November, **5** (11), 14–15.
5. Laczniak, G. R. *et al.* (1979), Social marketing, its ethical dimension, *Journal of Marketing*, Spring, **43**, 29–36.
6. Kotler, P. and Zaltman, G. (1971), Social marketing: an approach to planned social change, *Journal of Marketing*, July, **35**, 3–12. Fox, K. and Kotler, P., The marketing of social courses: the first 10 years, *Journal of Marketing*, **44**(4), 24–33.
7. Cowell, D. (1978), Marketing's Application to Public Authority Sport, Recreation and Leisure Centres. Paper presented at Marketing Education Group (MEG) Conference, Hull College of Higher Education.
8. Quoted by Ted Blake in several presentations on Marketing Sport and Recreation.
9. Packard, V. (1965), *The Hidden Persuaders*, Penguin, Harmondsworth, p. 11.
10. *Ibid.*, p. 14.
11. Cheskin, L., quoted in *ibid.*, pp. 14–15.
12. Wilson, A. and West, C. (1982), Effective marketing at minimum cost. *Management Today*, January, 72–8.
13. Craig, S. (1989), *Marketing Leisure Services*, Leisure Futures, London.
14. Read a series of articles by Jim Johnson (1987), in *Leisure Manager*.
15. This is the general finding coming out of a number of surveys undertaken by the Sports Council, Built Environment Research Group of the Polytechnic of Central London and others.
16. Howard, D. R. and Crompton, J. L. (1989), *Financing, Managing and Marketing Recreation and Park Resources*, W. C. Brown, Dubuque, Iowa.
17. Read a series of articles by Ted Blake (1990), in *Baths Service and Recreation Management*.

Further information:

A Scottish Sports Council project has demonstrated the impact on the performance of local authority sports centres achieved by the use of professional agencies to implement a strategic approach to marketing. The Council and Northern Enterprise Management produced a video presentation describing the project.

Several series of articles on marketing have appeared in leisure management literature and journals during the late 1980s; for example:

Blake, T. in Leisure Management series, 1985–6.
Blake, T. in Baths Service and Recreation series, 1989–90.
Johnson, J. in Leisure Manager series, 1986–7.

Drinkwater, R. and Davies, I. in Leisure Management series, 1987.

Cowell, D. (1979), *Marketing in Local Authority Sport, Leisure and Recreation Centres*, Local Government Studies, July–August, 31–41.

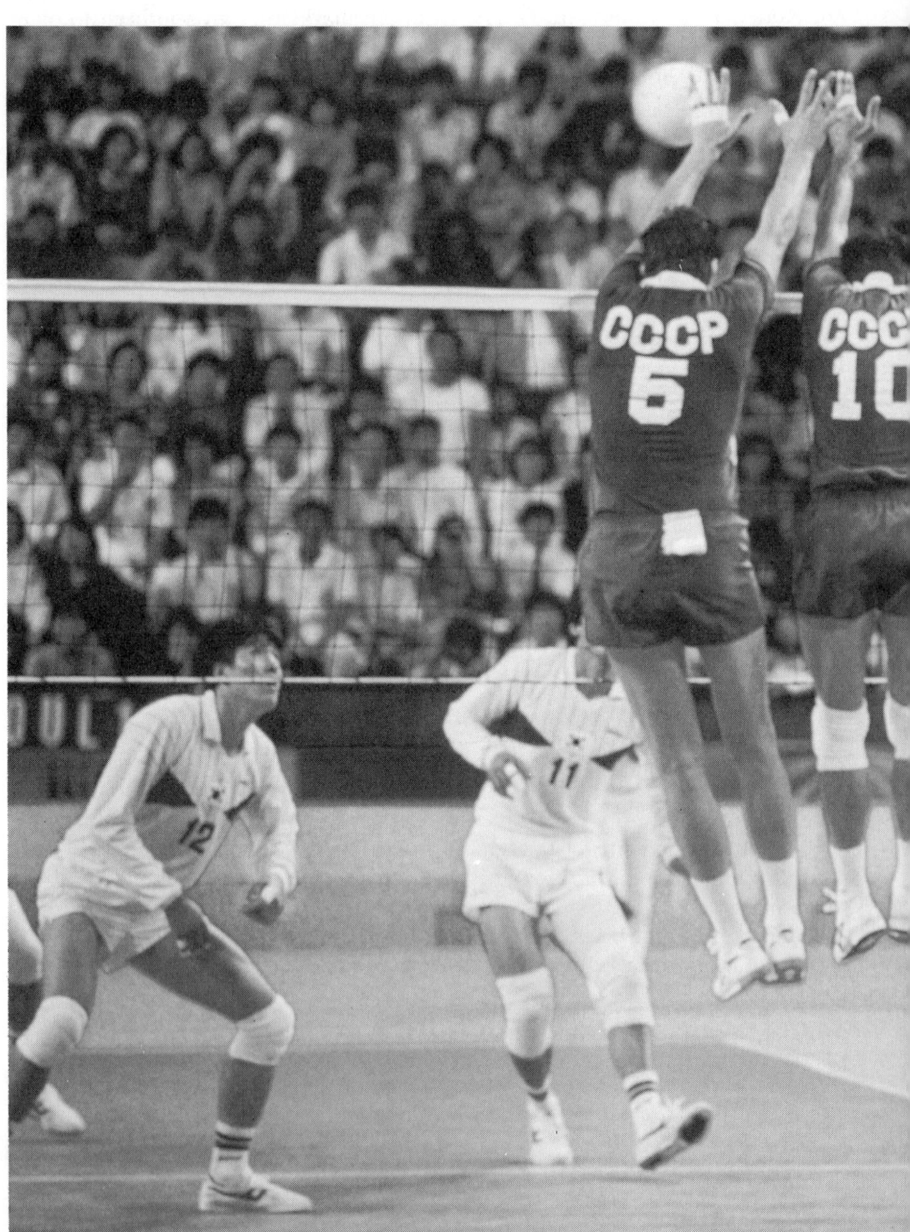

Chapter 17

Organization of major events

Events are an important part of any comprehensive leisure and recreation programme. They have appeal; they capture the imagination. Events can involve the community, increase awareness and help put an organization or an activity on the map. Events can attract top-class performers, entertainment, novelty, adventure and fun and bring glamour to a programme.

Well-organized events can therefore be a boon to any organization; badly organized, they can detract. The public has become more sophisticated in its taste when it comes to the organization of events. Leisure Managers must be capable of leading or controlling the planning of major events.

This chapter is intended, primarily, for the Leisure Manager who is responsible for special events which are scheduled in addition to his or her overall leisure and recreation programme. It is written in the following sequence. *First*, the question is raised: what is a major event and what makes it special? *Second*, the formulation of policies and event organization strategies are considered. *Third*, organization structures are discussed. *Fourth*, budgets are shown to be integral to all major events. *Fifth*, the special staffing requirements are considered. *Sixth*, the need for detailed and meticulous planning is shown. *Seventh*, all events are subject to problems – and learning from these is an important clue to better future events. *Eighth*, as part of the chapter summary, an event planning guideline, an event checklist and an event planning process model are put forward as an approach.

Having read this chapter, event organizers will be in no doubt as to the importance of events within a comprehensive leisure service and that they should be embarked upon with clear vision and concise objectivity. Organizers will understand that events need military precision not just in their presentation, but in their preparation; the free-rein or flexible style of management will not be appropriate. Unlike the ongoing programme, events have precise starts and finishes and are encapsulated into absolute parameters of time and space. The clearest lesson to be learned is that an event needs one coordinator, around whom the event organization is controlled. Events lend themselves to clear objectives, tight administration and budgets, preparation deadlines, entrepreneurial flair, excellent preparation and honest evaluation.

17.1 MAJOR EVENTS IN COMMUNITY LEISURE

The management of major events is beginning to receive far greater attention in the United Kingdom as people are increasingly being exposed to professionally produced events, and as the British arena event industry develops. Currently there is limited experience of the management of indoor arenas. Although there are many large conference and exhibition halls, only Wembley Arena, the National Exhibition Centre, Birmingham, the London Arena, Sheffield Arena and Birmingham National Indoor Arena can be classified as comprehensive event arenas and even these do not cater for the range of community events held in the majority of British leisure centres.

The emerging arena industry is highly competitive with most of the arenas appealing to many of the same markets. Excellent promotional and operational efficiency is called for. The management of event arenas is considered at length in the publication *Arenas* [1], so arena events as such are not covered in this chapter. Suffice to say, however, that all events need good planning and organization. While most top-level major events are organized by promoters or by governing bodies and associations outside the control of leisure facility managers, the community-related events, joint promotions and 'own promotions' call for considerable expertise on the part of leisure managers.

This chapter is written for Leisure Managers who have to present major events throughout the course of the year as part of the total leisure and recreation programme. The principles and many of the methods will apply to all event organizers, but it is recognized from the outset that some organizations are set up as specialized event producers. In local authorities, too, there are specialized event departments and committees to stage the county show, or annual festival. In national sports administration committees and staff exist to administer international events. While all event organizers can learn something from this brief chapter, it is the Leisure Manager, whose special events are *superimposed* on all his or her other tasks, that this is primarily intended to serve.

17.2 SPECIAL CHARACTERISTICS AND FUNCTIONS OF MAJOR EVENTS

What is a major event? It can be a special event, 'happening', project or attraction of any kind that is outside the 'run of the mill' of attractions. It usually has some significance. It usually attracts a crowd or draws the attention of the media. An event can be international, national, regional or local. It can include sport, art, music, drama, festival or tournament. It can be competitive, fund-raising, social or just 'plain good fun'. It can be the town annual show or the village fête, the athletics championships or the Boy Scouts' sports. It can be an exhibition, a meeting, a rally or a talk. The scope of major events is as wide as the scope of the leisure and recreation spectrum.

Major events carry a number of features which distinguish them from other elements within a leisure and recreation programme, including the four outlined below:

1. *Events have distinctive characteristics* – all major events are perceived as being something special. All events have a starting and finishing point. They are tightly bound in time and space. They have fixed deadlines. For the general manager, these are usually superimposed on other work.

2. *Events carry advantages to improve programming and management* – events can capture the imagination of 'sellers' and 'buyers'. They can be a means of promoting the organization and creating favourable images. Their organization crosses administrative and departmental boundaries; hence they can unify the organization. They call upon all the resources of an organization and test them, revealing strengths and weaknesses. They may break new ground and could present the organization as a pioneer.

3. *Events pose many problems to all organizers* – most problems can be anticipated but many will be unforeseen. The event unlike the normal ongoing programme is speeded up and delivered within a short space of time; this concentrates all the advanced planning and actions into specific hours and moments. Problems can thus be dramatic and could prove devastating. One problem is that managers and event organizers cannot depend on established routines. Another is that there are dangers in dates slipping by in preparation, targets not being met and budgets being overspent. In addition, there are dangers in lack of coordination, bringing inadequate linkages, miscommunications, omissions, duplications, wasted effort and inadequate controls.

4. *Events lend themselves to certain management styles and methods* – first, events need a coordinator; his or her role is paramount. Second, they need precision, deadlines and fast decisions and this differs from most normal programming issues. Third, tight administration, using flowchart organization and checklists can help to meet deadlines and objectives. Fourth, entrepreneurial skills, allied to good administration, can be put to best effect. Fifth, because events are task orientated, a more authoritarian style of leadership or 'benevolent dictatorship' may be required, particularly in the late stages of detailed preparation and on the day itself.

Events therefore are a special and specialized aspect of leisure and recreation management.

17.3 EVENT PLANNING STAGES AND ORGANIZATION

All events need good planning and organization. Regrettably, all events are not well planned and organized, even many of some significance, particularly in the voluntary and public sectors. Leisure Managers must guide and support event organizers in the basic principles of planning and organization.

The management approach to an event will depend on the particular circumstances, but it is worth recognizing ten interrelated planning stages in the life-cycle of a major event:

1. Policy formulation.
2. Feasibility and decision-making.
3. Appointment of organizing committee and coordination.
4. Objective setting.
5. Budgeting.
6. Organization structure.
7. Staffing and personnel.
8. Detailed planning.
9. Event presentation, including preparation, closure and clearing.
10. Evaluation, feedback and modification for future events.

17.3.1 Policy formulation to objective setting

First, formulate the idea. Debate, reason out and answer fundamental questions: *Why* is the event proposed? *What* is it for? *How* will the event be run? *Where* will it be held? Who will be responsible for its planning and operation? *When* will it be held? If the idea is a good one, planners can take the idea to the next stage of considering its feasibility.

Second, in considering the feasibility of an event it is important to explore in greater depth the questions already raised. What are the benefits? What are the costs not just in terms of money, but in terms of manpower, time and effort? Will the effort result in meeting the aims of the event? Can the problems be overcome?

If the event is not feasible, planners should have the courage to say 'no'. Regrettably, many events have taken place without considering their feasibility and they should never have been held. If the event is feasible, and there is positive commitment to the project, then it is important to make a firm decision, allowing ample time for forward planning and detailed planning. Coinciding with the decision to go ahead, certain crucial tasks should be undertaken, namely:

1. Announce the decision to hold the event.
2. State clearly the nature of the event and the aims of the event; commit these to paper.
3. Appoint an events main committee – a *working* committee.
4. Appoint the key figure in the planning and control of the event – *the coordinator*.
5. Set objectives.

In setting objectives, be clear and unequivocal in stating them as measurable targets. Make them unambiguous. Include all main areas and units of the programme. In particular, be precise about the financial estimates and budgeting. In formulating the objectives, the coordinator should consult with the policy-makers and the key personnel involved in it, whether as representatives of organizations or as unit or team leaders. Set the dates, times, specific deadlines and critical dates in the planning stages.

17.3.2 Budgets

All major events need a *budget*. The extent to which they do, depends on the nature of the event and on the objectives. Is the event designed to give a free service to the public: an open day in the park, free band concerts, children's festival or a sports centre open day? Is the event designed as a crowd puller on a break-even financial exercise: an entertainment talent contest or a sports tournament? Is the event a sponsored event to draw in the crowds and capture the eye of the media: a national basketball tournament or a one-day county cricket match? Is the event totally sponsored such as a firm's exhibition or a television *Super Stars* or *It's a Knockout* programmes? Is the event primarily designed to raise funds for the organization or another charitable cause?

Most local authority sponsored events are heavily subsidized – i.e. by the rates. Town shows, orchestral concerts, free pop festivals in the park, old-time music halls, painting competitions, exhibitions and many thousands of events are run because they enhance the quality of life of citizens and are part of our heritage and traditions. Two key aspects concern:

1. Evaluating true costs.
2. Setting budget targets.

17.3.3 Evaluating costs

As far as the Leisure Manager is concerned, all events, even those totally subsidized, in reality, cost a great deal of money. They must all have budgets and must all achieve the income/expenditure balance or ratio set in the objectives. Even more important is that the event be run with excellence. The principle for the Leisure Manager to work to is that of being *professional*. Regardless of whether the event is free, the facilities are free or the staff are already paid for, the manager should always evaluate the *true costs*.

It will normally cost money to use, hire or acquire facilities and make them functional and attractive for the event. There will be costs for electricity, water and technical and maintenance aspects. There will be costs of transport. Equipment may need to be hired, purchased, borrowed and transported. Additional staffing, stewards, voluntary helpers and personnel connected with the event will be required. Administration costs will include not only the promotion, printing, tickets, posters, financial costing and preparations, but also the whole office backup and administrative services, such as telephone, stationery and man-hours. There will normally be costs for mounting the event itself, the programme costs, the cost of artists, hospitality, the additional insurances and legal costs. The hidden costs of most events are enormous. The good manager should know what they are. They may not be of great importance to one event, but they could be to the next.

Most events will accrue some income. Even events which are 'free' to the consumer may be raising income from some sources such as grant aid from the local authority. Income can be derived from direct methods and indirect methods. The direct methods include gate receipts, programmes, bar and catering, car parking, cloakrooms and costs of other services. The indirect methods include advertising, donations, sponsorships, sales, raffles and fund-raising of a variety of sorts. Sometimes the amount of effort put into running the annual dinner raffle is more than that put into the whole event itself!

17.3.4 Budget targets

Events, then, need a budget and all events need expenditure limits. A large proportion of events also need income targets. If budget targets are known to all from the outset and are included in the objectives of the event, then everyone is working to the agreed targets for the event. Many events lend themselves to a break-even figure, for example, an entertainment festival may cost in cash terms £2000 and is to run for one week; the objective could then be to attract a minimum of say, 4000 customers at an average spend of 50p; or 2000 customers at an average spend of £1. Numbers over this become a bonus, but normally not a profit. Extra income that might accrue will normally help to meet hidden costs or help the organization or boost the funds for the charity.

The risk element with most events is very high, particularly when they are at the mercy of the weather, or the call of the television on Cup Final Day, or when new ideas are being tried or when dealing with an unknown quantity. There are risks enough without taking even greater financial ones such as overspending budgets or minimizing income. Events therefore need not only the budget but also a coordinator to ensure that financial targets are worked to.

17.4 EVENT ORGANIZATION STRUCTURES

Organization is concerned with planning, establishing an organization structure and developing working relationships and methods to achieve objectives. Organizational structures cover the chains of command, the spans of control and the discrete units, teams or working parties dealing with the various areas of work. The structure must cover the broad spectrum of the event. An event such as a leisure festival involving community groups might have several units, for example:

1. *Programme and content* – activities, organizations, etc.
2. *Budget* – accounting, income and expenditure in all areas.
3. *Promotion* – awareness, publicity, media, etc.
4. *Personnel and staffing* – contracts, duties, etc.
5. *Administration* – programmes, printing, box office, legal, etc.
6. *Technical* – resources, equipment, preparation, etc.
7. *Services* – parking, cloaks, information, first aid, etc.
8. *Catering and social* – routine, special entertaining, etc.

There should be a working group for each area and a section leader who accepts the responsibility and links with the main coordinator. It is important to agree: the precise roles and responsibilities of each group and each leader; and the organization, tasks, target deadlines and dates.

17.4.1 Roles and responsibilities

Everyone involved in an event should know to whom they are responsible, who is responsible to them, who they are working with and what exactly their function is in the organization. Areas of responsibility and tasks to be done should be handled in discrete units, linked together through a coordinated network.

Key factors in the make-up of the organization are:

1. The people carrying out the planning.
2. The task units.
3. The heads of the units.
4. Their span of control.

There must be sufficient keen and knowledgeable people prepared to give time and effort to the tasks. But there must also be an efficient organization to make the best use of such people.

People need an optimum amount of responsibility. In Chapter 18 on staffing we learn that a person's span of control depends on many factors, and that there are dangers in either too wide or too narrow a span. We also learn that although formal structures are important, the informal structures are also critical to the harmony and efficiency of an organization. Unfortunately, with many event organizations, the structures are poor and without coordination. The result is that informal dealings flourish without coordination; misunderstandings and miscommunications abound, leaving many parts of the planning to fall between two stools. 'It will be all right on the night' [2] is a totally inadequate substitution for good organization. On the day, organizers have found that there is no staging, no public address or it does not work, lights will not come on, the changing rooms are in the nearest school a mile away, the VIPs are standing in the rain trying to convince the doorman that they have been invited, the performers cannot get into the ground because the entrance is blocked and the grand piano has been delivered to another venue. At one national leisure event, catering for the conference banquet had not been arranged! The lack of coordination and delegated task responsibilities are evident in such situations.

17.4.2 Organization, tasks and dates

Once principles have been agreed and objectives set, then the structure for organizing the event can be put together. The use of an organization chart is helpful. It helps to clarify any ambiguities and provides an overall picture indicating the various responsibility areas. Its main disadvantage is that it shows only the formal relationships. However, this is not too limiting for events. Events are finite, fixed occasions, requiring task operations that need to be controlled and, particularly in the later stages, handled autocratically to meet deadlines. For major international events such as an international tournament, an organization handbook will be necessary in addition to an organization chart [3].

In addition to the structure, a work flow-chart indicating critical paths will be valuable for programming and timetabling the work of committees, task units and sections. It should indicate the flow pattern, the critical dates, the deadlines, the merging of two sections at appropriate times and the interrelationships between sections.

17.5 STAFF AND PERSONNEL

All events need personnel. The number and type will depend on the nature of the event. However, all events need:

1. A coordinator.
2. Support staff.

17.5.1 The coordinator

The coordinator does not organize directly. He or she is the leader, the link person, the informer, *the* one person who knows what is going on in each unit, section or team. The coordinator does not have to know every detail, but needs to know who has the knowledge and whose responsibility it is. The coordinator must control and monitor progress using the most efficient methods – i.e. meetings, sectional heads reporting, work flow-charts. He or she needs to be an encourager, yet firm in handling situations. Towards the later stages of the planning, in particular, the coordinator will have to exert pressure and make authoritative decisions in order to meet the deadlines. He or she is the key figure in any event organization and the leader, the link and the controller.

17.5.2 Support staff

For large events, the coordinator will normally work with a team of sectional heads. Each team head, and each discrete unit, will have its clear responsibilities, duties, times, deadlines and calendars, but all within the overall organizational design. Without linkages, it is possible for one unit to function independently, making its own contribution unilaterally, and sometimes competitively, without thought to the overall success of the project.

Events are run with many different types of staff and helpers. Large-scale events will have full-time staff, part-time paid staff, paid casual staff and volunteers and will also delegate certain functions to organizations or concession others. Information to all concerned throughout the planning is essential to keep people motivated, involved and committed, in addition to keeping abreast of information. So often, those in the firing line are ill-informed.

Paid staff will need to know well in advance their pay, the times and the conditions; trade unions may well be involved; and there will be irregular hours, different rates of pay and insurance aspects. Volunteers will also need to know exactly where they stand, what their responsibilities are and how far these extend. Legal problems are always to be borne in mind with special events; contractual problems, insurance details and promotional aspects will call for professional legal advice.

Staff and helpers need to know what their job is, what is expected of them, who they are responsible to, who is responsible to them and what they have to do to be successful. They must be highly committed and involved. This is the job of the coordinator and the team heads. The answer is never to be complacent, nor to take people for granted.

Motivation, acknowledgement, praise and thanks are important. People want to see something of themselves in a successful venture.

17.6 DETAILED PLANNING OF THE EVENT AND THE EVALUATION

The event itself should be preceded by detailed planning and rehearsals. It should be excellently presented, with a memorable start and finish. A careful evaluation and follow-up should also be part of the whole process.

The detailed planning can be assisted by the use of work flow-charts, critical paths, checklists, targets and dates. Five steps must be taken in the final stages for many major events:

1. The detailed final plan must be produced.
2. Checklists must be carefully followed.
3. Contingency plans must be formulated.
4. The event should be practised or components rehearsed, including staff duties.
5. All possible elements should be double checked.

The event itself, having been thoroughly planned, should normally go well. However, there will invariably be problems. The coordinator of a large event must be totally free to make objective decisions, should these be required. Section leaders also need to be relatively free to control their own sections.

The ending and closure is an important component of the whole event. Closing ceremonies, hospitality, the thanks to all, cashing up, stock checking, clearing up and motivating workers to carry things through to the end, all make for ultimate success. After the event, the accounting, reports, lessons to be learned, making good damage and writing of 'thank yous' must be undertaken. A social event to thank the workers should be considered, in addition to thanking them on the day itself.

In the cold light of day, a full evaluation is needed which assesses the preparation, the organization structure, the event, the results, the feedback from spectators, participants and staff and the lessons for future events. A report should be prepared both for record purposes (sometimes queries continue for several years!) and to assist in the future planning of events.

Having considered the theoretical base from which to stage events, it is salutary to consider the range of problems that can occur leading up to events and at the events themselves. Some of these problems are raised before summarizing conclusions.

17.7 MAIN PROBLEM AREAS IN STAGING MAJOR EVENTS

In order to run efficient, memorable events, it is wise to consider the problems of previous events. Some main, and some minor, faults are listed below. Eight areas have been identified. The first mentioned is possibly the most critical, yet the most frequently violated.

1. *Insufficient consideration of the aims and objectives and organization structure at the outset* – this invariably leads to poor communication and duplication of effort, but even more serious, lack of direction, authority and controls.

2. *No appointment of a coordinator* – this is the key figure. There are usually a chairman and heads of committees but often no coordinator with the authority and responsibility for operational control.

3. *Failure to maintain accurate written records of all that transpires during the planning stages* – if good records are kept, they act as reminders and checks for work to be carried out. Rarely are there flow-charts with deadlines plotted. Much is kept in one's head. This leads to misunderstandings and recriminations on the day.

4. *Organizations give themselves insufficient planning time* – even when they do have sufficient time, so much effort is put in at the last moment. This can lead to overloading and frustration through poor planning.

5. *Committee and unit structures are, in many cases, either too narrow or too unwieldy* – many are far too large; others leave matters to just one person. These individuals invariably take on far too much. They see the event rather as their own. They may be so keen to do the job that they will not share responsibility or delegate duties. Some very busy people take on events as social obligations and over-commit themselves. These problems are typical of an amateur approach but must not be part of the professional Leisure Manager's repertoire.

6. *There are often problems with 'governing' bodies* – this usually stems from lack of agreement on principles and organization in the first place. There are problems with looking after guests. Relationships with staff (who have heavy additional duties in addition to their normal work) are often strained.

7. *Unusual technical problems are encountered* – the technical problems are considerable, for example, noise from other parts of a building, keeping the audience informed, the import of a whole range of additional

equipment, the extra floor markings or take-up of markings, the additional stage lighting, décor, the need for additional seating and many others.

8. *Some problems should not be tolerated* – no matter what the organization, certain problems must be ironed out for the next event. They include lack of clear objectives, weak coordinator and sectional heads, faulty public address, keen but ineffective announcers, insufficient staff, insufficient food and drink, failure to inform the police, no first aid, no plans for inclement weather, no press coverage, no litter containers, embarrassing pauses between activities, programmes overrunning, no hospitality for visitors, untidy and careless presentations, no colour, no glamour, no heightened emotion – no umph!

Some problems can be put right immediately for the next event, others need time and consideration and planning. This is the role of the Leisure Manager.

17.8 EVENT MANAGEMENT: SUMMARY

Experience of running events shows that although all events differ one from another, in terms of management approaches, the similarities are greater than the differences. While policies, programme and content will differ considerably, a planning sequence similar to the one proposed in this chapter serves the requirements for many events. See Fig. 17.1 for a seven stage event planner.

No one method of organizing a major event is best and all others second best. The method will depend on the event and the circumstances surrounding it. However, some ways are more effective than others; they are more objective, they are better planned, costed and controlled.

What experience has shown is that there has very often been insufficient thought given to the planning and organization of the event *before* committees are set, jobs allocated and decisions made to go ahead. Forward planning, organization structure, objective setting and communications are integral main issues to successful event management.

Events are important strings of the Leisure Manager's bow. Their organization is important to his or her repertoire of skills. Events lend themselves to certain styles of management such as Management by Objectives. They need a sound, logical framework, with a starting and finishing point. Events need thorough planning, imaginative marketing and excellent presentation.

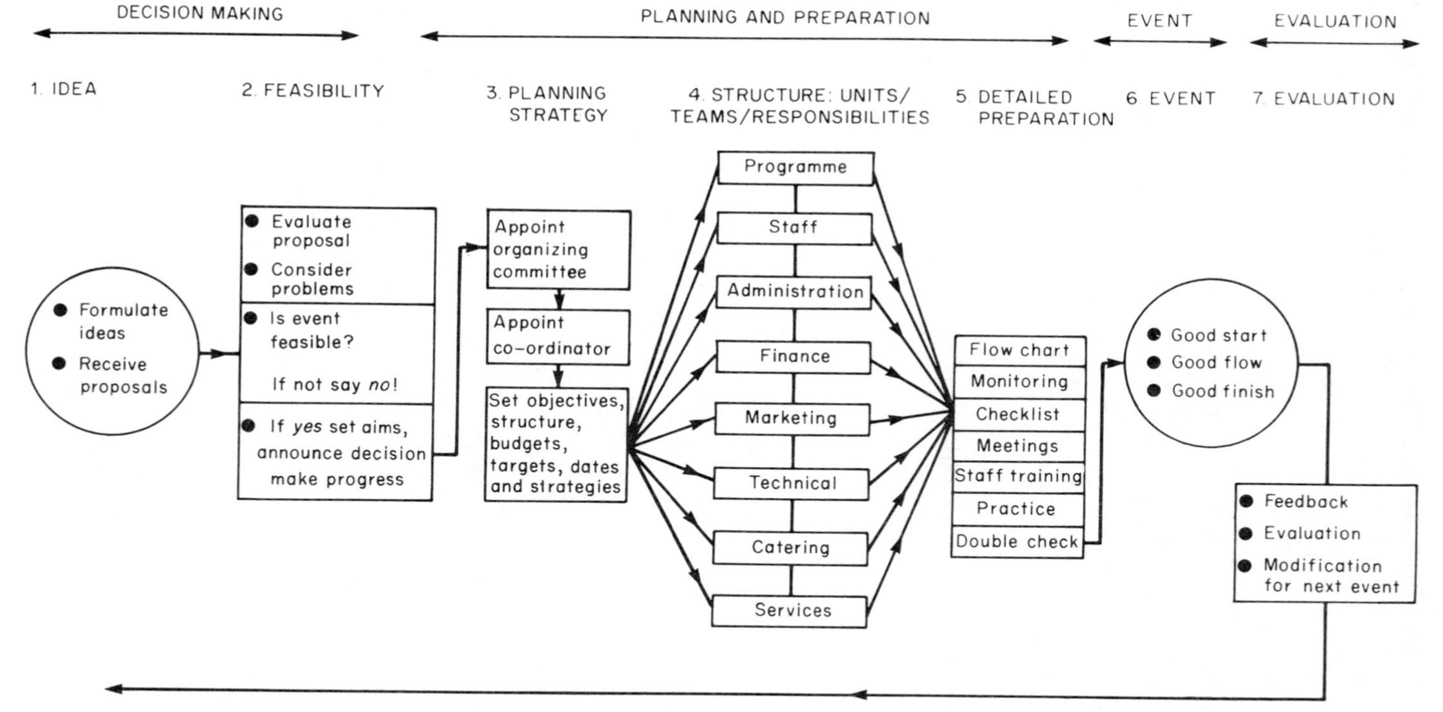

Fig. 17.1 Seven stage event planner.

Well-run events will have the following features:

1. Clear and agreed objectives to which all are committed.
2. Discrete units to undertake specific tasks yet work as a whole.
3. A coordinator of calibre and authority.
4. Unity of effort.
5. Efficient lines of communication.
6. No duplication of effort or waste of time.
7. 'Professional' presentation with some glamour, novelty, surprise, tension or heightened awareness or emotion – an *experience* people will want to buy again.

REFERENCES AND NOTES

1. Shields, A. and Wright, M. (eds) (1989), *Arenas: A planning, design and management guide*, Sports Council, London.
2. Read: *What Every Exhibitor Ought to Know* (1975), the companion booklet to the films *It'll be OK On the Day* and *How Not to Exhibit Yourself*, Video Arts Ltd.
3. The Scottish Sports Council (1980), *Major Events: An organisation manual*, SSC, Edinburgh.

RECOMMENDED ADDITIONAL READING

Event organization information can be obtained from the Sports Councils, Arts Councils, governing bodies of sport and many other agencies, such as The National Outdoor Events Association.

Read: *Community Arts Festival Handbook*, Greater London Arts Association.
Planning Your Course or Conference, Municipal Entertainment supplement.
Spencer, P. J. (1982), *OK On The Day*, National Association of Youth Clubs, Leicester.
Organising a Swimming Competition, Amateur Swimming Association, Dec. 1989.

Chapter 18

Staffing and staff structures in leisure services

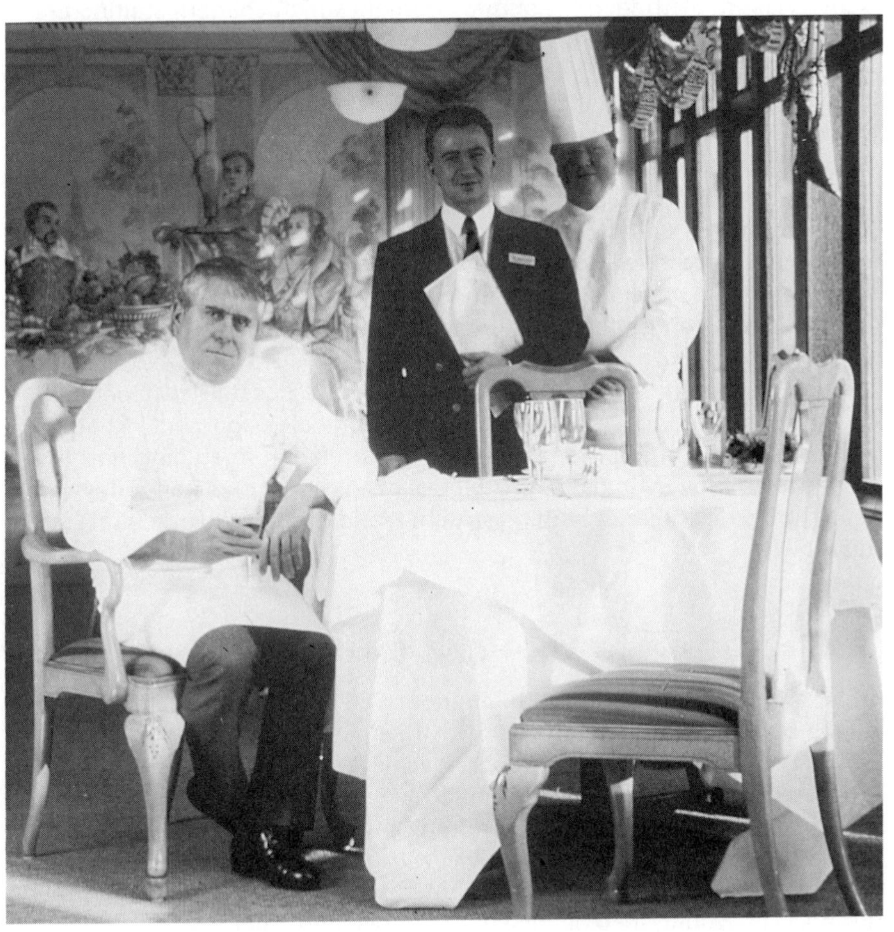

Excellent staff are as important as excellent facilities. Therefore, senior professionals and managers in leisure services must have knowledge, experience and understanding of staff matters: selection, staff relations, staff motivation, organizational structures and something of the law as it relates to employment.

In Chapter 13 we have dealt with many of the general management aspects: principles of management, leadership, motivation and decision-making. This chapter deals with some aspects of staffing, mainly within leisure services departments. *First*, the problems associated with staff and staffing structures within leisure service organizations are examined and emphasis is placed on the need for more effective organization of staff. *Second*, the principles of management which concern staffing are considered. *Third*, the formulation of organization and staffing structures are critically examined. *Fourth*, some legislation relating to staff employment is summarized. *Fifth*, a brief analysis is made of the recruitment and selection of staff; and *sixth*, the production and use of a staff handbook is advocated.

Having read this chapter, readers will be in no doubt that the effective handling of staff and the way the staff are organized and employed are essential for effective and efficient management. Good handling of staff is important, but needs to be structured fairly and professionally for greater effectiveness and efficiency and also for legal, economic and social reasons.

Students, in particular, will learn of basic principles of staff management: 'chains of command', 'span of control' and 'logical assignment'. Readers will be introduced to a number of the laws relating to staffing and the duties of employers and responsibilities of employer and staff. They will learn how to formulate a staffing structure and produce an essential staff handbook.

18.1 THE CHANGING LABOURFORCE

Most employers in the United Kingdom will find the labour market is changing as a result of many factors, principally changes in population. This was the warning of the report *Young People and the Labour Market*, produced in 1988 by the National Economic Development Office (NEDO) and the government Training Agency and was followed in 1990 in the report, *Defusing the Demographic Time Bomb*. The need was shown for a better-educated and trained workforce at a time when the number of young people leaving schools and colleges was falling sharply.

The leisure industry, a major employer in the United Kingdom and abroad, has become used to employing young people (and part-time female employees) often because they represent cheaper labour or availability in holiday periods and at weekends, and also because they are flexible in hours and duties and provide the energy and adaptability required in the leisure industry.

Yet the changes taking place in the labourforce are about much more. Employers have to consider their future skill needs in the wider context of changes in technology and quality and competition from abroad and the development of the Single European Market. There needs to be a more stable, committed and highly motivated workforce, with more flexibility to respond to the challenges of the 1990s.

18.2 STAFF AND STAFFING STRUCTURE IN LEISURE ORGANIZATIONS

Staff are the most important resource in any organization and its cost should be regarded as an investment rather than an expensive item of expenditure.

One of the key areas in the management of leisure and recreation services departments and facilities is the staffing and staffing structure. The way in which staff are organized is a crucial factor in the performance and level of success of management. The structure represents the way in which the work is organized and shared out and the manner in which an organization is managed.

Every leisure and recreation service from the smallest to the largest has an organization and staffing structure of some kind. Used effectively the structure provides the framework through which the work operations proceed in an orderly manner towards achieving organizational objectives. The staffing struture has an effect on the programme just as the facilities themselves affect the programme. That is not to imply that the more staff one has, the better or more varied the programme. Rather the *way* staff are organized, deployed and motivated will have decided effects on the results.

18.2.1 Staff and structures vary

Staffing structures, the types of staff and the levels of staffing in leisure services vary considerably from authority to authority, organization to organization and from centre to centre, even where facilities are comparable and where policies appear to run parallel.

In public recreation, financed in large measure by rates and taxes and subject to bureaucratic administrative systems and standardized procedures, one might expect to find a considerable level of uniformity. However, in the United Kingdom there are almost as many different structures as there are authorities and it is difficult to find two precisely the same. While different localities have different facilities and different circumstances, it is understandable that variations exist. However, the variations in structure, methods, approaches and personnel are so wide – from a small subsection to a comprehensive department, in towns of the same size and with similar ranges of services – that comparative studies are needed to highlight the benefits and limitations of different systems. By way of illustration, at some similar, large leisure complexes in the United Kingdom, staff numbers can vary from 50 to 100.

Not only are structures different, but also the types of staff vary. In addition, staff vary within the same organization from full-time to part-time, temporary, casual and voluntary. There are recreation executives, senior, middle and line managers, recreation officers, wardens, park-keepers, coaches, teachers, community workers, youth workers, play leaders, artists, caterers, technicians, supervisors, administrators and the whole range of technical, clerical and maintenance staff. They have variations in Contracts of Employment, job descriptions, training and benefits. They work different hours and different shifts and many work long, unsocial hours. With most comprehensive leisure facilities, opening hours are lengthy, as much as 100 hours a week. In these circumstances, even the most dedicated manager is in essence a part-timer!

The allocation of revenue expenditure towards staffing, particularly in public recreation facilities, takes the largest share of operating costs. For example, salaries and wages account generally for 55%–60% of the operating expenditure, plus the statutory and other 'on costs'. In times of economic stringency, and with the introduction of compulsory competitive tendering (CCT) in Britain, reduction in staff is one method of reducing deficits. How important it is therefore to demonstrate clearly the appropriate levels and duties of staff as a means towards achieving objectives.

18.2.2 Inadequate staff structures

In many public leisure and recreation organizations the staffing structure is inappropriate to the needs. The structure of, say, an arts centre may be unhappily embedded within a local authority departmental structure with a hierarchy, levels and status positions which have little relationship to programming needs, the needs of staff and, possibly least of all, the needs of users. Fitting new types of facility and services into outmoded structures highlights the problem even more clearly.

Many new leisure centres require managers with considerable decision-making powers and senior staff to take full responsibility in unsocial hours (usually peak hours, in terms of attendances, events and programme variety). They need structures which are flexible enough to respond to changes, in order to meet less predictable community demand.

Despite local government reorganization, the upsurge in facilities and the emergence of an embryo profession of leisure and recreation management, staff in some cases are having to fit into structures and systems designed in times past to suit the Victorian 'parks–pitches–pools' era. In one London borough, pre-CCT, a vast community sports and recreation centre had its director replaced by an administrator, so that the centre's organization structure could fit into the borough's departmental structure! The bureaucracy could not handle flexibility, not even at one centre, which had demonstrated itself to be unique, something outside the normal run of the mill.

18.2.3 Staffing flexibility

Many leisure facilities, particularly in the voluntary sector, are managed by a leader and many volunteers. They take responsibility for facilities, plant, programme and personnel. Even in public leisure and recreation centres the level of part-time staff can be high. It is not unusual to find a leisure centre at 10.00 p.m. manned by a supervisor or receptionist and a few part-timers, managers and senior staff having long since gone. Nor is it unusual to find a part-time receptionist carrying out the programming.

Different forms of management may be needed to optimize, promote and encourage leisure and recreation. Part-time paid staff, coaches, helpers, community workers and volunteers may be needed to help to meet the needs, particularly of those who find it difficult to make use of public recreation facilities.

It is apparent that leisure and recreation services call for special, sensitive handling of staff. Staff have a variety of duties and the facilities are open for long hours. The nature of the job – that of creating satisfaction for people in their leisure time – requires that good staff have personal commitment and an understanding of customer requirements: *if staff flexibility is required, then organization and employer flexibility are also required.*

18.3 STAFFING AND PRINCIPLES OF MANAGEMENT

Some top-level managers and senior personnel are concerned with the formulation of policies and organizational structures. Most managers, however, are appointed to positions in existing organizations, to which they have to adapt. It is important that managers at all levels understand the organization structure, the principles on which it is based and the components which go to make it up.

According to the International City Management Association [1], three basic principles of management must be considered in establishing an organizational structure, namely:

1. Unity of command.
2. Logical assignment.
3. Span of control.

18.3.1 Unity of command

The principle of *unity of command* states that each individual in an organization should be responsible to *only one* superior. Adherence to this principle establishes a precise *chain of command* within the organization.

Situations exist in recreation organizations which do not follow such a principle. For example, at one recreation centre the head groundsman is answerable to both a centre manager and an assistant technical officer at the town hall. At another, a Recreation Manager is responsible to both a centre director and a borough recreation officer. At another establishment, while the principle of unity of command exists (in that the centre manager is responsible to only one person), he is answerable not to the borough director of recreation, but to the chief executive!

18.3.2 Logical assignment

The principle of 'logical assignment' states that staff doing the same work should be grouped together and that work is planned and scheduled in a logical order.

Situations exist in leisure management where structures and departmentalism are put first, and the job in hand second. Without logical assignment, there will be duplication, overlap, confusion, resentment, power struggles, drawing in of responsibilities to heighten status, keeping things close to the chest, and not sharing, which all lead to poor performance. Here again, personalities are blamed but the greater responsibility rests with those responsible for the structure and its implementation.

18.3.3 Span of control

The principle of *span of control* is something of a misnomer. The principle states that there are limiting factors which must be considered in deciding the number of subordinates a member of staff can effectively handle. Span of control may be more accurately defined as *span of management* because the limiting factors are many. They include the number of *people* that can be supervised, depending on the quality of staff and level of delegation, the *distance* over which control can be exercised, the amount of *time* in which to exercise control, and the number of *activities* that a manager can effectively manage. The span of management is, then, a statement of those *limitations*.

It is not possible to state the exact number of people a manager should 'control'. Much depends on the competence of subordinates and the manager's own knowledge, ability, time, energy, personality, leadership style and the environment and situation in which work must be undertaken. The type of work, in addition to the capacities of the manager, must also be considered. Too few staff under one's control can lead to under-utilization of a manager's talents; efficiency and effectiveness will be limited by too many staff.

In local government recreation services many managers have responsibility for a large geographical area. Members of staff directed by a specific manager should not be situated too closely if this results in over-supervision. However, they should not be located too far away as this can lead to under-supervision.

Time is a very limiting factor. Every manager has to allocate time to:

1. Routine work which is usually delegated but must be supervised.
2. Regular work a manager must do himself or herself.
3. Special work and assignments.
4. Creative work.

Executives and senior managers often give very little time to the routine supervisory work, the kind of face-to-face work with the work-force. Many pool supervisors, green-keepers, community art workers and play leaders would not be able to recognize the director of leisure services or head of department if he or she walked into their work situation!

It is clear that a manager's ability to manage staff is limited. A narrow span of 'control' makes it possible to supervise work tightly but it does not give assistant staff the opportunity to make decisions or feel a sense of commitment and achievement. Leisure Management needs highly motivated staff. It also needs many specialists such as coaches, community leaders, music teachers, community artists, park wardens and outdoor activity specialists, who need guidelines and support, but also a level of autonomy rather than overt control and supervision.

It seems logical therefore to have as broad a span as possible [6] because of the following:

1. There are fewer levels in the structure. This reduces the remoteness of managers from staff.
2. The lines of communication are shortened. This reduces paperwork and increases information flow.
3. Broad spans tend to stretch and develop future managers.
4. Less tiers of structure should save money and time, in addition to improving communication.

Additionally, staff develop skills and special expertise peculiar to the job. This technical know-how can be harnessed to improve job satisfaction and involvement in decision-making processes, which impinge on their area of work.

18.4 ORGANIZATION AND STAFFING STRUCTURES

It is important for managers in leisure services to have knowledge, experience and understanding of staff, staff relations and organizational structures. Managers will have to work within structures, often not of their choosing; they will have to be negotiators, decision-makers, communicators and understanders of a wide variety of professional and lay staff. Effective structures and good handling of staff are essential for effective management.

A good organization and staff structure will assist greatly in the achievement of the goals of any organization. However, it is not a panacea or alternative to good management. Rather, *it is a means to an end*. A 'good' structure as such does not exist in isolation; it is only good if it is good for the organization it serves. Furthermore, organization structures provide only a framework for management and staff to work within. To get the best from a department, the manager will need to use the organization to achieve its objectives, through staff motivation and commitment.

Structures will depend on several important factors:

1. The nature of the controlling body (local authority, commercial entrepreneur, private club).
2. Aims and objectives of the organization (profit making, service orientation).
3. The environment.
4. Distribution of facilities.
5. Financial targets.
6. Scale and nature of the facilities and resources.
7. Layout and design of facilities.
8. Nature of the service to be provided.
9. Levels of performance (top level, casual, formal, informal, beginners or a comprehensive range).

10. Quality of management and staff and the level of delegation.
11. The hours of operation.

18.4.1 Formulating a staff structure

In some situations staff structures have been charted even *before* an organization has outlined its policies, objectives and target programmes. In such cases, assumptions have been made that it is possible to strike the right balance on paper, bearing in mind the levels of staffing in other authorities or organizations, the hierarchical system within the overall authority and the funds which are likely to be available for staffing. Such mismanagement is born out of the belief that it is the way in which squares and rectangles fit neatly into a comprehensive family tree and which lends support to the status quo that will find favour. But the first step should not be the discussion of a structure, rather an analysis of the organization and its policies which the structure is *to serve*.

Many leisure centres in the United Kingdom have tried to copy or to emulate a structure which has been developed elsewhere. Some standardization is useful and makes for efficiency. However, different areas have different priorities; each has its own identity; each has its own budget targets; and each has its own style. Structures must be developed which meet the needs of the situation.

Organization and staff structure should not be *static*, determined and fixed forever. Structures must be changed to meet changing situations. For example, a manager usually comes into a structure previously determined, and finds ways of improving performance or ways in which the staff will respond to his or her ideas. Programmes will change; staff will develop and some will move on; and financial forecasts will alter. Therefore, appraisals, say, after one or two years should be undertaken and changes implemented to meet the new situation. It is said that we can be certain of only one thing – change. Changes in structure, changes in style and changes in objectives are always necessary but seldom implemented in public recreation services. Commercial organizations must of necessity change the way the structure works to be effective and financially sound.

18.4.2 Departmental structures

To be effective, managers must divide the workload into manageable parts. The main purpose of dividing the work is to establish methods of determining individual groups, and section responsibilities, the distribution of authority to individuals and the processes of delegation.

The most used method of dividing work is departmentalization, that is dividing the workforce into units and departments.

According to Grossman [2], there are four avenues managers can follow in creating departments:

1. *Function* – these are departments in which staff are grouped according to function, for example, sports coaching, arts and crafts and maintenance.
2. *Clientele* – these departments are grouped according to the clientele they are to serve, for example, junior, youth and senior citizens.
3. *Geographic* – staff are grouped according to the area in which they work, for example, a large borough could have Area or District departments.
4. *Process* – these are usually service-giving departments and grouped according to the process used in providing the particular services, for example, an information service or counselling.

Most managers use a combination of these strategies or adjust elements of specific strategies to create the appropriate departmental structure. However, the structure often evolves haphazardly and lacks planning and coordination. What is important is that the manager knows the possibilities and the alternatives and logically thinks through them, broadening his or her horizons to accommodate the variety of methods and approaches to develop the most appropriate departmental structure.

18.4.3 Formal and informal structures

Once the work is departmentalized, managers must make decisions relating to levels of authority. It is these decisions which establish chains of command within an organization. Authority levels establish the organization's power structure. Staff appointed to high authority levels normally have more power. They have a greater say in group management decisions.

Inflexible, bureaucratic adherence to chains of command, however, are inappropriate for much of the 'gelling' of an organization. The structure is there as a framework. Within and around the formal structure there is very soon built up an *informal* structure: 'It is the informal structure which provides for cross-communication rather than going through the channels' [3]. Much of the important 'human' work which makes an organization 'tick' is undertaken through cross-communication. A recreation department and youth department, for example, often work out joint problems without going through their department channels.

An example of good cross-communication is shown at a leisure centre in Essex. Daytime integrated sports coaching classes are run for adults and college pupils – i.e. within the same space/time allocation, utilizing coaches from either organization. The possibility of these classes being held would have been remote if procedures and communications had been conducted through the formal structures of the county council and the technical college. The informal structure and communications network enabled those with first-hand knowledge to make decisions relating to work, which they are the best to advise upon. This informal process cuts across organizational boundaries, budgets, space and time allocations, staff and administrative red tape. One of the skills of the good manager is to permit, within certain limits, a level of face-to-face work which in essence *bypasses the chain of command*.

Nancy Foy [4] believes that it is time we 'humanized' our systems. We need not scrap them, as long as they remain human in scale. While organizations and the people in them need rituals and regular checkpoints, they also need information about their own work groups, their own outputs, and so on: 'A lot of information that can't be transmitted can normally flow informally, with complete credibility and confidentiality, once people believe they are hearing the truth and able to tell it as well.'

18.4.4 Line and line and staff organizations

Organizational charts normally depict either 'line' or 'line and staff' organizations. In *line* organizations authority is passed on from the highest to the lowest levels via a *chain of command*. In *line and staff* organizations staff personnel are incorporated, in addition to 'line' staff. 'Staff' personnel are frequently specialists who service 'line' personnel, for example, financial, programming and personnel specialists. In many recreation organizations 'staff' sections have line staff under the direction of a sectional head. A director of coaching, for example, may be responsible for individual coaches who may work with specialist duty supervisors. The principle of 'logical assignment', however, needs sensitive manipulation. The Financial and Technical officers at one leisure centre carry out their 'staff' functions in office hours, and their 'line' functions as duty managers in the evenings and at weekends.

'Line and staff' organizations are more flexible than 'line' organizations. They permit 'line' personnel to carry out the regular work – the use of the resources and the facilities by the public – leaving certain specialist functions to 'staff' personnel. The International City Management Association [5] differentiates the functions of line and staff as follows:

Line functions:	*Staff functions*:
Line directs or orders	Staff advise
Line has responsibility to carry out activities from beginning to end	Staff studies, reports and recommends, but does not carry out
Line follows chain of command	Staff assists line but is not part of chain
Line decides when and how to use staff for line use	Staff always available
Line is the doing part of the organization	Staff is the assisting part of the organization

Separate staff function advantages include reduction in costs (one finance officer for several sections), an arm's-length objectivity, longer-term stability and specialist inputs into the organization. This provides service, advisory and planning information for managers and the organization [6]. A potential disadvantage is that staff departments tend to grow at a faster rate than other departments, leading to greater overheads, administration and 'tail-wagging-the-dog' inclinations.

18.4.5 The organization chart

The organization chart is the most common approach to portraying the organization's structure. It illustrates the hierarchy, functions and chain of command. Strict adherence at all costs to charts and family trees is not advocated, but as a general framework it helps staff within an organization to visualize and understand, to see clear lines for efficient accomplishment of its objectives. Where a recreation service is geographically spread, or where there is difficulty in perceiving the roles of particular departments, the organization chart has considerable advantage. The organization chart, however, must not be given permanent status, as though it was indestructible. It portrays the organization, acts as a framework for sharing the work and indicates levels of responsibility. It should be used to further the work of the organization.

The structure is not infallible; it has limitations. First, it is skeletal, in static form. It is representative only as long as the status quo remains. Second, it has little flesh about the skeleton; it is not precise about amounts of authority and responsibility. Third, and most important, it does not portray the essential informal structure and relationships. Some managers become over-concerned with preserving and enhancing the organization structure itself, rather than with helping to meet the organization's aims and objectives. However, the organizational structure, used wisely, is one of the tools to promote successful management performance.

18.4.6 Designing a structure

The various organization structures used in the delivery of leisure services fall along a continuum between a *mechanistic model* (which is rigidly structured) at one extreme to an *organic model* (which is flexibly structured) at the other (Fig. 18.1).

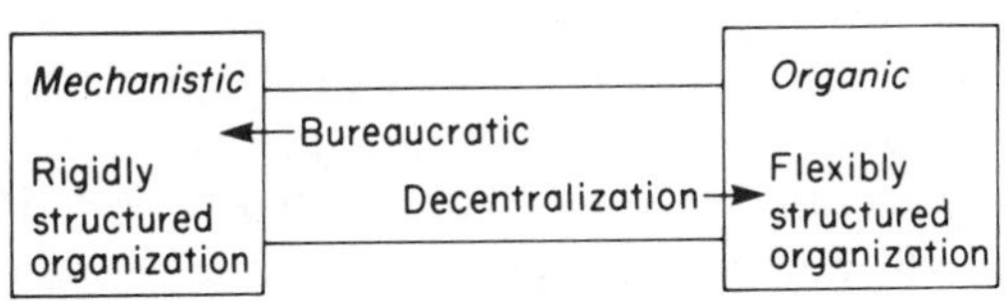

Fig. 18.1 Organizational models.

The characteristics of the two different models are outlined below, together with the characteristics displayed of being either more 'vertical' or more 'horizontal', and more or less 'bureaucratic':

1. *Mechanistic organization*
   - Operates more effectively when the environment is stable.
   - Control, authority and communication usually follow hierarchical patterns.
   - The work is broken down into differentiated tasks with precise instructions that become highly standardized.
   - Interaction tends to follow hierarchical lines between superior and subordinate.
   - There is a general assumption that those higher up the hierarchy are better equipped to make the more important decisions.
   - Operational actions tend to be governed by instructions issued by superiors.
2. *Organic organization*
   - Better suited to operate in an environment where change is a factor – it is adaptable to changing conditions.
   - One's special knowledge and experience are looked at in terms of what they can contribute to the overall task.
   - Problems are not pushed upward, downward or sideways – i.e. 'buck-passing' is discouraged.
   - Control, authority and communications move through a wide network rather than a single hierarchical structure.

– Communication tends to be more lateral than vertical and content consists of information and advice rather than instructions and decisions.

3. *Vertical and horizontal structures and decentralization*
Vertical organizations tend to be highly structured and the role expectations of staff strictly controlled, leaving little room for individual discretion and initiative. In contrast, horizontal organizations tend to be more loosely structured, with fewer constraints, leaving staff with considerable discretion to define their own roles in achieving the overall objectives. The right balance for maximum effectiveness must be achieved.
Peter Drucker [7] has often spoken of the need to de-centralize structures: 'Performance will be improved by de-centralization. It will make it possible for good men, hitherto stifled, to do a job effectively. It will make better performers out of mediocre men by raising their sights and the demands on them. It will identify the poor performers and make it possible for their replacement.'
Decentralization can lead to decisions being made more quickly and nearer to the point of action. It reduces lines of communication, reduces status problems and provides greater job satisfaction [6]. However, decentralization is not appropriate to all situations.

4. *Bureaucracy*
The bureaucratic model is the most widely implemented form of organization. It is a vertical structure. Authority is located at the top of the hierarchy and flows downwards through the organization. The division of labour emphasizes the hierarchial structure and establishes a superior/subordinate relationship. This allows the various activities to be subdivided into a specific set of tasks with the roles of individuals clearly defined.

18.5 STAFFING AND LEGISLATION

The employment of staff and staff relations are governed, to a considerable extent, by government legislation. In recent years, there have been fundamental changes in the law in the United Kingdom, which have far-reaching consequences for employers and employees. Recent legislation has set new standards in personnel policies and in employer–employee relationships and has provided statutory bodies to enforce the new standards.

There are well over thirty salient Acts of Parliament which have a bearing on staff relations and employment, 50% of which have been introduced or have been changed in the past two decades. Most legislation has put obligations and constraints on employers and extensive rights have been given to unions and to the employees. An exception was the *Industrial Relations Act 1971*, which while imposing restrictions on management, had far more effect on unions; this Act, however, was repealed in 1974.

The new Acts have undoubtedly improved the working conditions and job security of employees in general (outside times of recession!). The effects of the new legislation have been most dramatic on industry. They have been less dramatic in the public sector where many of the new obligations were already being practised, for example, equal pay. For all employers and employees, the position is now much clearer than in times past. Employees now have a much clearer idea of their position within their authority or place of employment; employers have a detailed procedural guide to employment matters. *In theory*, if the procedures are carefully and sensitively followed, there should be less conflict. However, despite legislation, tribunals and procedural guidelines, problems of employment and staff relations exist. They are primary factors in poor public relations, poor communications, mismanagement and low morale, all leading to less successful business enterprises, whether in the private, commercial or public sectors and whether in the context of factory, school, swimming pool or opera house.

Problems still arise and statutory bodies have been appointed to ensure that the law is adhered to. For example, Industrial Tribunals were established by the *Industrial Training Act 1964* as a type of court which is suitable for hearing matters of industrial relations legislation. The tribunals cover not only matters arising from that Act, but also the *Equal Pay Act 1970*, the *Sex Discrimination Act 1975*, the *Employment Protection Act 1989* and the *Race Relations Act 1976* and several others. Appeals go before the Employment Appeals Tribunal.

Much of the work carried out in the field of recreation and leisure is subject to these Acts. For example, much of the work is undertaken in unsocial hours when there are pressures of urgency relating to, say, mounting a major sporting spectacular, a town festival, a major concert or television programme. Unsocial hours, special duties and overtime hours of full-time staff have to be handled along with part-time staff, volunteers and temporary staff. The kinds of work and the complex nature of recreation programmes often produce the pressures which cause tensions and can lead to disputes. Managers should be aware of the laws which regulate staff relations. A thumbnail sketch of some of the relevant Acts of Parliament follows.

18.5.1 Sex discrimination

The *Sex Discrimination Act 1975* makes it unlawful to discriminate in employment, education and training in Britain on grounds of sex, or marriage. The Equal Opportunities Commission was established to enforce the legislation and individuals have the right to complain to courts and industrial tribunals. The law covers recruitment and existing employees in matters like promotion. The employment provisions were amended by the *Sex Discrimination Act 1986* to bring legislation in line with the European Community directives on equality and restrictions on the maximum hours of women employed in industrial undertakings were repealed.

The *Employment Act 1989* amends the *Sex Discrimination Act 1975*, in pursuance of the directive of the Council of the European Communities, on the implementation of the principle of the equal treatment for men and women as regards access to employment, vocational training and promotion and on working conditions.

18.5.2 Race relations

The *Race Relations Act 1976* makes it unlawful to discriminate on grounds of colour, race, nationality or ethnic origin. Individuals have access to civil courts and industrial tribunals. The Commission for Racial Equality was established to enforce the legislation.

18.5.3 Health and safety

The *Health and Safety at Work Act 1974* has the purpose of 'securing the health, safety and welfare of people at work and to provide for the protection of the public whose health and safety might be affected by work activities'. The 1974 Act is superimposed on previous acts of legislation, some of which still apply. Previous legislation, however, only covered two-thirds of the labourforce; now everyone, except domestic staff, are covered. The general principle underlying the Act is that employers, in consultation with their employees, will draw up health and safety arrangements, within the broad obligations of the law to suit their own work areas.

The 1974 Act established the Health and Safety Commission, responsible for developing policies, including guidance, codes of practice and proposals for regulations. The Act also set up the Health and Safety Executive, which includes a government inspectorate covering a number of work activities.

Regulations introduced in 1988 to control exposure to nearly all substances hazardous to health in all places of work represent the most significant health and safety legislation since the 1974 Act.

18.5.4 Equal payment

The *Equal Pay Act 1970*, amended in 1984 by the *Equal Pay (Amendment) Regulations*, requires men and women to be paid the same rates of pay for doing the same or broadly similar work, or work of equal value. The purpose of the Act is to eliminate discrimination in pay and other employment matters: holidays, sickness benefit, bonus, overtime, etc.

18.5.5 Employment protection

The *Employment Protection Act 1975* and the *Employment Protection Consolidation Act 1978* (as amended by the *Employment Act 1982*) provide the machinery for promoting good industrial relations and give employees certain rights, including: guaranteed payment after four weeks, if the employer is unable to provide work; maternity rights; rights for time off work either paid or unpaid for certain reasons, written statements of main terms and conditions of employment, an itemized pay statement for employees and unfair dismissal. The 1975 Act also set up ACAS, the Advisory, Conciliation and Arbitration Service.

18.5.6 Employment of children

The employment of young people and children in certain occupations is governed by the *Young Persons Employment Act 1938* and the *Employment of Children Act 1973*. These Acts make provision for the employment of young people under the age of 18. These are divided into two groups: young people over school-leaving age but under 18, and children below school-leaving age. Section 10 of the *Employment Act 1989* makes amendments relating to the employment of young persons.

18.5.7 Employment liability

Two Acts were passed in 1969, the *Employers Liability (Compulsory Insurance) Act*, which stated that all employees must be insured, by the employers, against industrial injury or disease; the certificate must be placed where all can see it. The *Employers Liability (Defective Equipment)* Act stated that any injury suffered by an employee, through defective equipment was deemed to be the employers's fault. The employer can counter-claim against the supplier or employee for negligence.

18.5.8 Trade union and labour relations

The *Trade Union Act 1984* repealed the *Industrial Relations Act* 1971 but re-enacted its unfair dismissal provision, restored status of unions and employers' organization and repealed workers' right not to belong to a union, leading to closed shops.

Major changes to trade union legislation have been introduced by the government through four Acts: the *Employment Act 1989*, the *Employment Act 1982*, the *Trade Union Act 1984* and the *Employment Act*

1988. During much of the 20th century, trade unions and their officials and members have enjoyed immunity from legal action when organizing certain industrial activities. The *Trade Union Act 1984* removed legal immunity from trade unions which call a strike without first holding a properly conducted secret ballot of members concerned and securing a majority vote for this action.

The *Employment Act 1988* provided for the removal of the remaining statutory support for the closed shop. The Act made it unlawful to organize or threaten industrial action to establish or maintain any sort of closed shop practice. The *Employment Act 1989* removed civil law immunity from those organizing certain forms of secondary action and limited lawful picketing to peaceful picketing at the pickets' own workplace.

18.5.9 Contracts of employment

The 1972 Act requires all employees to be given a contract. Minimum periods of notice must be given. Contracts must give details of dates, rates of pay, hours, holidays, sick leave, pension rights and discipline and grievance procedures. The Act establishes the right of employers and employees to a minimum period of notice.

18.5.10 Redundancy payments

This Act, passed in 1965, was a major step forward in job security. It requires an employer to make a lump-sum compensation to an employee who is made redundant after at least two years or more of service since the age of 18, unless the employer can prove to a tribunal that the employee was fairly dismissed and not made redundant. The amount of compensation is regulated by the *Employment Protection (Variation of Limits) Order*.

18.5.11 Employment

The *Employment Act 1980* made alterations to closed shop agreements. Alterations to unfair dismissal shifted the onus of proof from employer to employee. This Act reduces the former rights of individual employees and their trade unions. The 1980 Act was amended by the *Employment Act 1982*, which further strengthened the position of employers in cases of industrial disputes and provides for the payment by the state of compensation to former workers dismissed for non-membership of a trade union.

In summary, these Acts of Parliament and other legislation illustrate the legal and contractual implications of employer and employee and these laws affect leisure organizations. What follows – the recruitment of staff and production of a staff handbook – are thus of relevance.

18.6 STAFF RECRUITMENT AND SELECTION

Staff selection is one of the most important functions of employers and managers. Successful management is dependent on good staff. Good staff assist in leading an organization towards its goals. They work together to achieve objectives; they overcome difficulties, they solve problems. They are flexible in both spirit and deed.

Poor staff are a millstone. They make for ineffective organizations and lack flexibility and create blockages in the system; they become a noose around the neck of the organization, resulting in redundancies, at best, and to ineffective organizations at worst; and they expend considerable funds of energy of the organization, which could otherwise have been effectively applied to meeting objectives. How important it is therefore to select staff wisely.

18.6.1 Methods of selection

Selecting the right people for the right jobs is of crucial importance to an organization's prosperity. Selecting staff is basically about judging other people and their abilities and their appropriateness for the job.

In addition to the standard letters, curricula vitae and application forms, there are many methods or combinations of methods to shortlist or select staff:

1. Promotion internally.
2. On recommendation.
3. 'Head hunted'.
4. Written presentations.
5. Verbal presentations.
6. Discussion groups.
7. Personality testing.
8. Agency shortlisting or recruitment.
9. Consultancy advice.
10. Interview.

Personnel selection has become a major sphere of management and has been subject to considerable 'scientific' investigation. Measuring the qualities of leadership potential, emotional stability, and the like, have been part and parcel of civil service selection boards, for example, throughout this century. However, in spite of the research and development of psychological tests of intelligence and personality, the job of selection remains inexact and subjective.

The interview, in spite of its critics, remains the primary method of assessing and selecting staff. The standard local government format with leisure and recreation posts is that of:

1. Application form.
2. Shortlist.
3. References.
4. Half-hour interview by a panel.

18.6.2 The right man or woman for the right job

Who will make the judgement? People's innate skills at judging and selecting staff varies and some, given the responsibility, are wholly inadequate. Finding the right person for the job is a time-consuming and expensive business. It becomes even more expensive when tackled badly because the wrong person may be selected.

Two of the main problems employers bring on to themselves is either choosing a poor candidate or finding a good candidate, but one who does not fit the post. This may mean changing the job to meet the qualities of the candidate or living with a mismatch.

In leisure, wages, salaries and associated costs form a significant proportion of operational costs. The efficient recruitment and utilization of manpower is an important management responsibility and can offer scope for both improved performance and cost savings.

18.6.3 Job descriptions, conditions and person profiles

The job 'description', 'condition' and the 'specification' of the qualities needed to fit the job are quite distinct. The job *description* describes the job, its functions, responsibilities and what the employers' expectations are in terms of carrying out the job. Its major concerns are with the nature of the work itself and the achievements necessary to meet the goals of the organization.

Job descriptions for senior posts should never be fixed and strictly demarcated, or they will become a straitjacket, limiting the development of the job and the person. They should serve as parameters and guidelines encouraging initiative, growth and job enrichment. Staff should have titles and job descriptions which give them a broad scope of duties and which do not limit their function.

The *person specification* sets out the ideal credentials required from candidates, to fit the job. The specification is not a detailed description of the job. The job *conditions* set out what the employer has to offer in terms of conditions of service, pay, benefits and prospects. The person 'specification' and the 'job description' are often combined in one document, but selection panels ought to match personal credentials to the requirements of the job.

18.6.4 Learning from professional selectors

The leisure industry has much to learn from professional selectors of people. Leisure employers, by the nature of their function, usually lack the continuous interviewing experience and the knowledge needed to probe the job market effectively. Too often local government interview panelists, for example, pride themselves on their ability to make instant decisions about people. They work on feelings and hunches. With good judges of people's character and ability that may be fine, but with biased or poor judges the results can be disastrous both for the organization and the new employee.

Interviewing and selecting staff are difficult and inexact exercises, but guidelines or 'outside' or 'informed' help can reduce uncertainties and chance. For example, a *good* agency or consultancy service will have a selection procedure which has been rigorously tested through practical experience and good results.

18.6.5 A simplified selection process

Selecting the right person is made more effective if a logical sequence is followed, which is based on proven successful methods. Video Arts films [8] illustrate selection techniques and the need for a methodical process.

In simple terms, there are five key steps:

1. *Describe and define the job.* Should you fill the old one? Should you create a new one? Can you re-allocate the workload? It is wise to avoid seeking a replica of the previous job holder as no two people are alike and the job will have changed. Instead use the vacancy to bring about necessary change and improvement. The job description defines the job.
2. *Specify or 'profile' the person whose qualities are likely to meet the requirements of the job.* Detail the expertise, experience, skills and qualifications that are likely to fit the job. Describe the personal qualities being sought, the demands of the job and the people already working in the team.
3. *Set out the conditions of the job* – i.e. pay, benefits and prospects.
4. *Choose methods of communicating and publicizing the job vacancy, seeking to match the person to the job.* This may require a range of internal communications, outside advertising and professional advice from specialist recruitment sources.
5. *Select sensitively, carefully and methodically.* Haphazard selection can be ineffective and unfair. Probe, search and enable candidates to express their capabilities, enthusiasm, weaknesses and strengths. Selection is choosing the right and best person who fulfils the needs

of the job, the tasks and the relationships with others and who is well satisfied with the conditions for employment.

Selectors need to satisfy themselves on main points:

1. Is the candidate capable of doing the job?
2. Does he or she have the qualities and real credibility in the field?
3. Will the candidate fit well into the organization and get on well with people?
4. Is he or she the best of the capable candidates?
5. Is it the right person for the right job?
6. Does he or she have the courage to do the right things, not just the ability to do things right and so assist the organization towards its goals successfully?
7. Is the candidate happy with the terms and conditions?

Investment in people pays off. Staff employed will require a high level of dedication if the full potential of leisure service and facilities are to be realized.

18.7 STAFF HANDBOOK

The right staff need to be employed, trained, nurtured and enabled to perform well for the organization and themselves. A staff handbook is a useful communications document but only if it is read, understood, accepted and used, and as long as it is sufficiently flexible to meet changing circumstances. Working by the rule-book, can be like 'working to rule' – the kiss of death to an organization, if ever there was one! Peter Drucker has said: 'Many companies have magnificent personnel policies on paper – that is all they are' [7].

The information-giving handbook can provide a valuable source of reference for managers and staff. It should back up and support the face-to-face, two-way communications and staff training. It should welcome, introduce, inform, explain and give new and existing staff a picture of a businesslike, friendly organization that cares about its customers, its staff, its products and services.

The handbook's production should be clear, unambiguous and authoritative. It should be attractive and well produced, but not an expensive, impracticable, glossy. It needs to be indexed for easy reference, personal and friendly in its style and suited to its readers, yet factual and concise.

The handbook is basically an exercise in communication. It is essential therefore that management and staff are consulted fully as to its contents and style and its distribution, in order to achieve cooperation and acceptance. An *aide-mémoire* in producing a comprehensive handbook [9] is set out below.

PRODUCING A HANDBOOK FOR STAFF: A GUIDELINE OF 20 KEY SECTIONS

1. *Introduction and welcome*
   - Personal message of welcome from Chairman or Chief Executive.
   - General aims of organization, its background and history, the current position and priorities.
   - The products and services and their value to the customers.
   - The organization structure and committee, departmental and staffing structure.
   - An employment and personnel policy statement.
   - A policy statement on excellence in relationship with the public and customer care.
2. *Recruitment and selection*
   - Documentation required – references, medical certificate, etc.
   - Personnel records and notification of changes.
   - Probationary or trial periods.
3. *Contract of employment*
   Inform new employees they will receive a written statement within the legally permitted time and what that statement will cover. Inform staff of their legal rights in these matters.
4. *Induction, training and assessment*
   The sooner a new employee can be used effectively, the greater the organization's effectiveness. The job and the environment are inextricably linked:
   - Induction and familiarization systems.
   - Essential training provided and additional training opportunities.
   - Methods of appraisal and assessment.
   - Job evaluation and review.
   - Opportunities for promotion.
   - Career development.
5. *Salaries and wages*
   The lawyer in the employer is matched by the lawyer in the employee! The handbook must be unambiguous:
   - Statement on payment system.
   - Precise methods of payment.
   - Deductions – e.g. income tax (PAYE), national insurance contributions and any others.

- Additional payments – e.g. special, overtime, bonus.
- Allowances for particular duties or circumstances of unsocial hours.
- Expenses – e.g. travel, car, refreshment.
- Procedures relating to pay reviews, alterations to pay, etc.
- Incentive pay or bonuses.

6. *Hours of work*

- Normal working hours.
- Flexitime.
- Timekeeping, starting and finishing times.
- Evening, weekend, overtime and other special hours.
- Meal and rest entitlements.
- Variation of hours.
- Time off in lieu.

7. *Time off and absence*

- Procedures for notification of absence.
- Time off and under what terms for public duties – e.g. political, magistrates, jury service.
- Maternity rights.
- Sick pay scheme and Statutory Sick Pay (SSP) entitlements.
- Medical certificates.
- Unauthorized absence.
- Requests for special unpaid leave.
- Hospital, dental and other personal appointments.

8. *Holidays*

- Annual holiday entitlements.
- Holiday increases for long service.
- Public holidays and 'in lieu' entitlements.
- Holiday pay and special pay on termination of employment.

9. *Fringe benefits*
Fringe benefits are part of the total job environment. The handbook should set out in general terms the opportunities and benefits open to the staff as a whole:

- Housing scheme.
- Insurances.
- Medical scheme.
- Car purchase.
- Educational and training opportunities.
- Social, leisure and recreation opportunities.
- Incentive schemes and other benefits.

10. *Amenities and facilities*
Leisure organizations will have services and amenities to offer employees. These benefits make up the job environment and can help maintain harmony and goodwill. They can also be a source of discontent if handled unfairly or perceived to be unfair! The handbook should set out:

- Use of the telephone – a statement to say in what circumstance.
- Use of 'company' facilities and products.
- Personnel, welfare, medical and information services.
- Staff meals and refreshments.
- Free memberships or use of leisure facilities.
- Discounted services and facilities.
- 'Company' clubs and societies.
- Social amenities.
- Use of amenities by family members and friends.

11. *Trade unions*

- The right to join a trade union.
- The unions and their position within the organization.
- Trade union representatives.

12. *Health and safety*
Responsibility, legally, falls on both employer and employee. Set out those responsibilities.

- Policy statement, including safety officer role.
- General procedures and sources of information.
- Safety regulations.
- Fire precautions and drills.
- Hospital, doctor, first-aid procedure.
- Emergency procedures.

13. *Property*

- Security of the business plant, supplies, equipment, money and property within and outside the premises.
- Security of personal belongings.
- The right of search.
- Lost property procedures for public and staff.

14. *Disciplinary rules and procedures*
Rules are needed for safety, fairness and efficiency. However, careful and sensitive wording is needed to convey collective responsibility and good individual conduct, rather than penalites for misconduct.

15. *Grievances*
    The law sets out procedures to enable staff to seek redress of any grievance. The handbook should set out the legal procedures and the three grievance stages that must be followed.
16. *Staff counselling and personal problems*
    Problems may stem from inside or outside the job.
    In the work situation counselling is needed before rules and procedures come into play.
    Home circumstances or personal and domestic problems can lead to low morale and poor efficiency.
    Good listeners are essential. Counselling, far from offering advice, is most often non-directive – i.e. a manager helps a colleague to come to terms with the situation and find the solution himself or herself.
    The handbook should inform staff where to go for help and what to do.
17. *Staff involvement*
    It is good practice to involve staff in the decision-making process. Marketing a successful organization with a good public image makes for a high staff morale and *esprit de corps*. The handbook should explain the ways in which staff can take a 'share' in shaping and keeping a successful organization:

    - 'Shares' in the success of the organization.
    - Joint consultative committees.
    - Staff representation.
    - Meetings.
    - Suggestion schemes.
    - Notices.
    - 'In house' magazine.
    - 'Company' events – for itself, staff families, charity, etc.
18. *Retirement and pensions*
    Organizations should prepare staff for retirement:

    - Retirement policy and entitlement.
    - Voluntary early retirement and benefits.
    - Pensions.
    - Retirement courses and planning.
19. *Termination of employment*

    - Notice entitlements.
    - Redundancy.
    - Discharge.
20. *New clauses and changes*

18.8 LEISURE SERVICE AND FACILITY GUIDELINES

Outlined below are 15 suggestions for improving leisure service staffing.

GUIDELINES FOR FACILITY STAFFING AND STAFF STRUCTURES

1. *Select staff wisely and logically*
   Match the qualities of the candidate to the job – the right person for the right job.
2. *Train and deploy*
   The way staff are trained and deployed affects results.
3. *Study legislation* Legislation affects both employer and employee.
4. *Understand management principles*
   Recognize the limitations of span of control and use of 'unity of command' and 'logical assignment'.
5. *Create formal structures*
   Provide for clear lines of authority.
6. *Permit informal structures*
   Recognize the importance of cross-communications.
7. *Present sound structure proposals*
   Essential levels of staffing, responsibilities and roles are needed to gain the support of authorities.
8. *Create team management*
   Recognize the value of team management to coordinate long hours and a varied programme.
9. *Use 'line and staff'*
   Avoid rigid 'line' structures. Consider appropriate hybrids to meet particular situations.
10. *Make conditions flexible*
    The complexity, hours and patterns of use of leisure facilities call for flexible organization staff attitudes which do not limit their function.
11. *Construct departments and decentralize*
    Divide the work into units and identify functions. Identify tasks and responsibilities attached to each position. Encourage decentralization.
12. *Produce staff handbook*
13. *Start with essential staff*
    When opening new facilities, start with essential staff only and then build up as needs dictate. The full-time staff positions should be limited to immediate recognizable functions. To cope with initial, additional demands, use part-time staff.

14. *Consider alternative structures*
    Appraise the relative value of additional, different forms of community recreation management – train and support voluntary assistants, outreach service workers, animateurs, etc., consider job sharing. Consult with trade unions.
15. *Use structures as means, not ends*
    A structure chart is a management tool. It must be used. It must be changed to meet changing situations. Do not be preoccupied with structures and family trees. Structures are means towards ends, not ends in themselves.

18.9 STAFFING: SUMMARY

This chapter has been concerned with staff and staffing structures within leisure and recreation organizations. It is clear that Leisure Managers should understand the way in which staff are employed, trained and deployed in order to maximize efficiency, bring out the best in staff and lead the organization towards its goals.

The manager should understand relevant employment legislation and the principles of management as they relate to staffing, the formulation of organization structures and the specialist responsibilities of selection and staffing functions within leisure and recreation services and facility management. However, managers should not be preoccupied with organizational charts and family trees. The organization chart must not be given permanent status, as though it were indestructible. Jobs need to change because situations change. Structures therefore must also change.

REFERENCES AND NOTES

1. International City Management Association (1965), *Basic Concepts of Organization. Bulletin 3, Effective Supervisory Practices*. ICMA, Washington, DC.
2. Grossman, A. H. (1980), *Personnel Management in Recreation and Leisure Services*, Groupwork Today, South Plainfield, NJ, p. 64.
3. *Ibid.*, p. 65.
4. Foy, N. (1981), The human side of information. *Management Review and Digest*, October.
5. International City Management Association (1965), *Basic Concepts of Organization. Bulletin 3, Effective Supervisory Practices*, ICMA, Washington, DC, p. 5.
6. E.g. Elliott, G. (ed.) (1989), *The Manager's Guidebook*, Longman, Harlow, Section 4.6 (Instalment 5); for other personnel aspects, see Section 9.
7. E.g. Drucker, P. F. (1955), *The Practice of Management*, Pan Books, London.

8. See Video Arts films, and read Briefcase booklets, *When Can You Start?*, *How Am I Doing?*, *The Reed Executive Guide to the Selection Interview* and *Can You Spare A Moment*, Video Arts, London.
9. Specific practical evidence was gained from the General Manager and staff at Harlow Sportcentre.

Chapter 19

Leisure and recreation management education and training

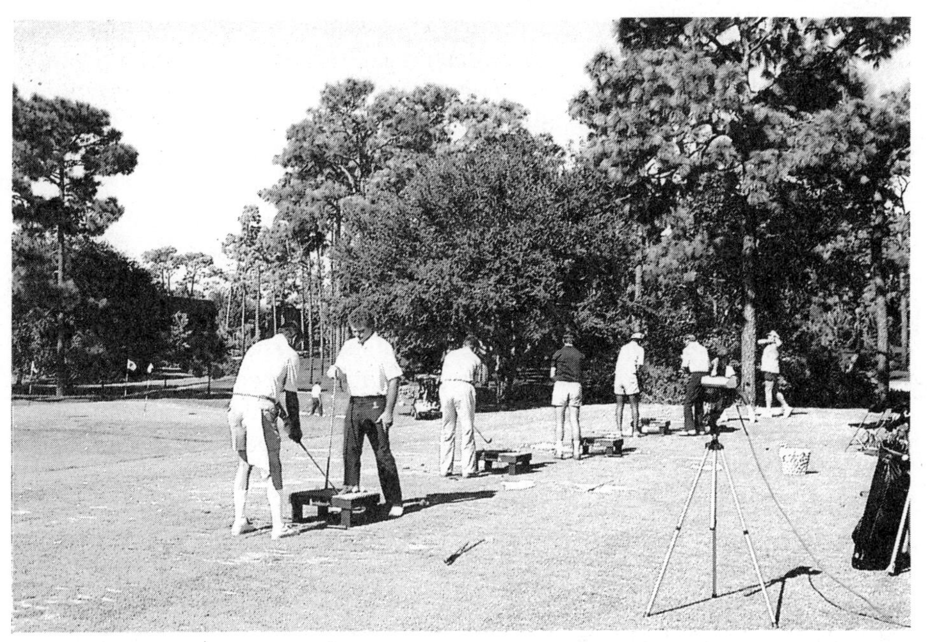

Leisure is a growth industry of national significance both in social and economic terms. Jobs in tourism and leisure amount to approximately 2.5 million, 6% of the workforce in the United Kingdom. Employment on this scale raises substantial questions about training and career development in the emerging profession of leisure and recreation management. In a time of change, growth and complexity, there need to be sound principles, objectivity and excellent leadership. In a relatively new industry, without adequate professional foundation stones, these factors are of significance in establishing a professional ethos.

Education and training therefore are of vital importance at all levels of leisure and recreation management. Without men and women of vision and standing at top management level, and without qualified and trained staff at all levels, no leisure service can hope to be efficient, let alone effective in meeting the needs and aspirations of its customers.

This brief chapter is written in the following sequence. *First*, the problems with training in the United Kingdom are highlighted. *Second*, the difference between education, training and development is described and the word 'training' is used to encapsulate the various aspects; a process to identify and meet training requirements is developed. *Third*, the potential market for training and the types of training are identified also. *Fourth*, in discussing the content of courses, the question is raised: is leisure management a discipline in its own right or is it composed of separate elements – i.e. leisure and management, or an area of knowledge with specialisms, or several subdivisions? *Fifth*, current thoughts on training requirements are debated and current courses are shown to be loosely grouped into further education, higher education and continuing education, including government initiatives and professional agencies. *Sixth*, the question of whether leisure management is an expanding profession is discussed.

Having read this chapter, readers will appreciate the need for training in order to provide the most effective and efficient management. They will understand that a need exists for education, training and career development and that it is only through a systematic process that the needs of staff and the organizations can be met effectively. The structure and the learning process must revolve around the needs of the people and organization to be served. Training must be of value to meet management goals.

Course organizers will be able to consider the implications of a wide variety of approaches and methods and areas to be covered in the content of courses. They will be made aware of the shortcomings of a number of current courses in the United Kingdom and also the dangers in 'turning out' standardized, technically orientated Leisure Managers.

19.1 LEISURE AND RECREATION MANAGEMENT TRAINING – PROBLEMS ADN COMPLEXITY

The concept of leisure and recreation management, as we know it today in the United Kingdom, has only emerged since the mid-1960s as a direct result of the development of indoor sport and recreation centres. Prior to that time, various 'professional' bodies had been running training courses and awarding institution qualifications for many years, with some institutions going back to the 1920s. However, these qualifications were of a technical nature and did not cover the broad spectrum of leisure and recreation management.

Despite the expansion of courses in recent years, particularly those at the lower ranges of operation and management, with the introduction of City and Guilds, and the Business and Technician Education Council (BTEC) courses, considerable criticism is still levied at the range, quality, relevance and accessibility of training opportunities available.

A frequently stated criticism is the lack of adequate resources, with only a limited range of books and journals being available in the library and a general lack of simulated practical material such as case studies and management games that are used on the courses. The lack of relevance of many of the courses relates to the limited knowledge and experience of many tutors and the general lack of leisure management content within the syllabuses. All too often, commercial financial management techniques are taught on courses targeted to public sector employees, while other courses convey false levels of expectations to potential students about the quality of the course and the type of post they might expect upon successful completion of the course. Finally, the distribution of courses is not made on any strategic basis and hence access to certain categories of courses in different areas of the country might not be possible. Additionally, the concentration of full-time courses in middle and top management restricts courses for many potential students.

19.1.1 Education, training or development?

In the various reports, and in college courses themselves, there exists some confusion and conflict over the use of the three terms 'management training', 'development' and 'education'. At times these terms appear to be interchangeable, and sometimes one term may be all-embracing, encompassing three meanings in one.

Management *education* may be seen as a process of active learning and enquiry (including learning from one's peers), with learner input a necessary part of this process. Management *training* may be seen as an input process from teacher to learner, whereby the learner is equipped with the specific job-related knowledge and skills needed to carry out his or her job successfully. Management *development* may be seen as encompassing both management education and training, increasing the manager's adaptability and flexibility, maximizing his or her strengths and overcoming weaknesses.

Although all three terms are identified here, for the sake of simplicity when discussing the issues the term 'training' will be used to embrace all three, although it is recognized that it is a far from satisfactory description.

19.2 THE NEED FOR TRAINING

The need for professional management of sports centres prompted the Sports Council to set up a working party which reported its findings, *Professional Training for Recreation Management*, in 1969 [1], which led to the first postgraduate/post-experience courses and qualifications.

The reorganization of local government in 1974 brought about new comprehensive leisure departments and a greater awareness was created as to the benefits of improved management of recreation in the public sector. There was also the growing realization that recreation management should be applied to a much broader field than was once appreciated. This growth led to the instigation of a government working party.

The Recreation Management Training Committee (the Yates Committee) was appointed in 1977 by the Secretaries of State for Education and Science and for the Environment to 'review and make recommendations on the training of staff in the management of resources and facilities for sport and for all forms of outdoor recreation' [2]. The report called for a coordinated, strategic approach to the planning of recreation management training. It took several years to produce the final report and its actual publication [3] was further delayed until 1984, which reduced the expected impact of the report upon the industry and, to some extent, its credibility also suffered.

The Yates Committee recommendations were never implemented. One of its cornerstones – the enhancement of Regional Management Centres (RMCs) – was thwarted, with the demise of many of the RMCs. Further, another of the recommendations in the report, of creating a single professional institute, had been overtaken with the formation of the Institute of Leisure and Amenity Management (ILAM), although the industry is still some way from establishing a single, all-embracing institute for leisure management. In addition, a number of training initiatives have emerged since publication such as the development of the ILAM Certificate and Diploma and the growth of BTEC leisure courses. However, the rapid pace of change in local government leisure services, as a consequence of the demands of compulsory competitive tendering (CCT), meant that there was a need for an up-to-date analysis of training needs in local government. Several surveys were undertaken [4] and the Sports Council published the CELTS Report, *Recreation Management Training Needs,* in 1990 [5].

The need for training is generally described as the need for employees to learn new areas of knowledge and skills, so that they undertake the tasks associated with their post more effectively. In this way, the needs of both the individual and the organization are fulfilled.

Not only is it necessary to provide training for staff to acquire new skills to meet the requirements of new technology such as computerized booking systems, but there is also a need for the key personnel to acquire the necessary knowledge (e.g. the product, factors that influence or inhibit participation, etc.) to ensure that the service provided is effective. There is also a responsibility (although not a legal responsibility) for the organization to develop its staff (in respect of their abilities and skills) and motivate them through more challenging areas of responsibility and experience. This will give employees the opportunity to achieve a greater self-worth in the job, while the organization will benefit through having a more productive and flexible workforce.

The staff further benefit if the courses they successfully complete are recognized by the leisure industry (such as the Institute of Leisure and Amenity Management, Institute of Baths and Recreation Management and Government Training Board courses) as they form an integral part of the person's career structure.

Although the knowledge, skills and techniques required by personnel in the public sector of the leisure industry have been identified by the Yates Committee and more recently by CELTS, it does not necessarily follow that these requirements equally apply to the same staffing and management levels throughout the country. It should also be stressed that no two leisure organizations are identical; they differ in their structure, the basis for their divisions of responsibility (e.g. functional or geographical), their philosophies, the range and distribution of facilities and services, etc. Hence there is a need to identify the training requirements at local level. This should be interpreted as the gap that exists between what an organization or individual staff member actually does, as opposed to what they *should* be doing.

This task is rarely (if ever) undertaken; and even when it is undertaken, it is normally completed by a local authority centrally located training unit that tends to be unaware of the specific requirements of a customer-orientated service. The process required to identify and meet the training requirements of leisure organizations are given in Fig. 19.1.

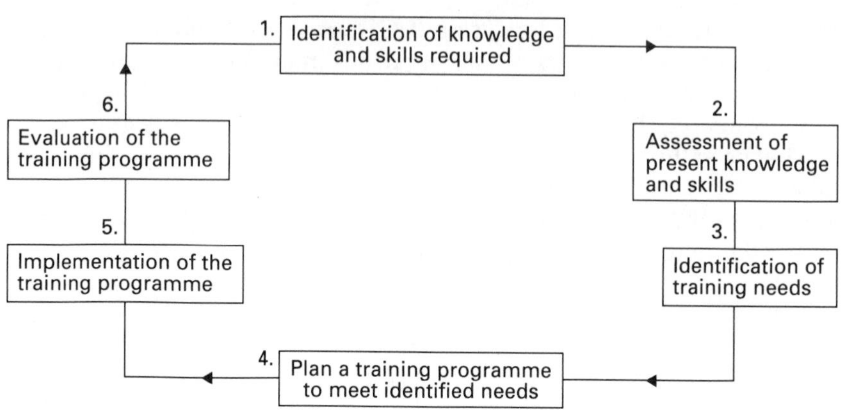

Fig. 19.1 Process of developing a local training programme.

An important and generally forgotten stage of this process is the *evaluation*. Evaluation is an integral part of any training programme. Not only is it concerned with determining whether the objectives of the programme have been fulfilled and what improvements are required to make it more cost-effective, but more important, improvements or changes should be measureable in the following elements:

1. *Learning* – there must be evidence that new knowledge and skills have been acquired.
2. *Change in behaviour* – not only should there be evidence of improved competence in undertaking the set tasks, but one would expect an overall improvement in the person's attitude to work with a more flexible approach, a greater understanding of the requirements of the service and a greater level of job satisfaction.
3. *Greater contribution towards the organization's goals* – this could be measured in terms of improved input, such as greater productivity, improved quality of service and improved staff morale.

It is only in this systematic way that the training needs of the staff and the organization can be effective.

Although we have only discussed in general terms the need for training within the public sector, there is also a considerable requirement within both the voluntary and commercial sectors for the training of their respective staff. The voluntary sector, in particular, is a neglected area and apart from the courses organized by, for example, Arts Councils and the Central Council for Physical Recreation, there are few other courses available for voluntary arts and sports clubs' officials.

19.3 POTENTIAL TRAINING MARKET

Any coherent system of training must be structured around the needs of the people it is intended to serve. If training is to be effective we need to ask, 'who is it for?', before we can ask, 'what should it be?'.

The leisure industry is a vast one; and the number of people employed both as managers and subordinates has increased substantially over the past twenty years. Although it is difficult to determine the precise number of people employed in the leisure industry, in 1988 it was estimated that this was in the region of 1.6 million (excluding the voluntary sector), of which approx. 1 million were in what one may loosely term 'tourism' [6]. The approximate breakdown of the employees is shown below, based on numbers emanating from the Office of Population Censuses and Surveys and the Conservation Association Central Office during the early 1980s:

Hotels and guesthouses	254 000
Pubs, bars	243 900
Restaurants, cafés, snackbars	190 000
Clubs	149 700
Contract catering	117 800
Other tourist accommodation	51 900
Tourism and other services	39 300
Libraries, museums, art galleries	63 500
Sport and other recreation	263 900
	1 374 800

Since that time, the leisure industry has expanded but the general picture appears to be similar. In 1990 [6], it was estimated that there were over 750 000 leisure 'managers' in the voluntary sector, nearly all of whom are unpaid and occupy official posts such as secretaries, treasurers, bar chairmen, etc.

Hence the potential training market is exceptionally large, and this can be subdivided into three main categories:

1. Personnel employed within the leisure industry; this includes personnel involved in the public, voluntary and commercial sectors, covering arts, sports, play, entertainment, etc; and it also includes a range of posts in junior, middle and top management, supervisory level staff, technical/manual staff (incorporating pool, bar, catering staff, etc.) and administrative/reception staff.
2. Personnel in other industries that have connections with or require leisure management knowledge and skills; this category includes managers and staff employed in dual use centres, industrial sports clubs, outdoor pursuit centres, activity youth clubs, etc.

3. Individuals seeking employment within the leisure industry. Within this category are school-leavers, college students who already possess a qualification and those wishing to change career.

This illustrates something of the range of courses required to meet the training needs of the above personnel.

19.4 TYPES OF TRAINING

The choice of a course that an employee, or potential employee, follows may not be simply related to the needs of the individual concerned or the present or future needs of the organization or the cost-effectiveness of the course, but based solely on the course's accessibility.

19.4.1 Full-time

Undoubtedly, full-time courses that are relevant, accessible and appropriate to the ability and skill level of the person concerned are normally the most effective method of acquiring new knowledge and skill. On such courses, the students are able to concentrate fully on their course work and their attention is not diverted to problems associated with their work.

With the current emphasis of central government on producing an 'economic service' and reducing operational costs in real terms, it is unlikely that many staff in the public sector will be given secondment to attend such courses. Likewise, full-time management courses for middle and top managers are normally of a postgraduate level, and as such local education authority students' grants fall into the category of a discretionary award; and in the present economic climate, such a grant is unlikely to be forthcoming. Consequently, students able to undertake full-time courses are school-leavers who are eligible for mandatory grants.

19.4.2 Part-time

Part-time or day release courses that lead to nationally recognized qualifications or to membership of professional institutions have certain advantages. Students can benefit from mixing with students from other organizations which can broaden their perspective. However, off-the-job training can be difficult in transferring skills and knowledge learnt in the classroom, unless the examples given and the problems set are provided in a simulated working environment.

Other forms of 'off-the-job training' can be seminars and conferences organized by professional institutions (such as ILAM and IBRM) and national agencies (such as the Sports Council, Arts Council and Tourist Boards). However, in some circumstances, these may be expensive, and because such training tends to lack reinforcement and evaluation, it is unlikely that direct learning from the lecturers and talks is cost-effective.

19.4.3 Distance learning

The potential of distance learning material has never been exploited sufficiently by the leisure industry. Indeed, in recent years, in terms of physical recreation, this method of learning has largely been restricted to the package offered by the IBRM. The advantages of this method are that it can make courses accessible in areas that do not offer such courses and gives the individual the freedom to choose the time he or she wishes to study. The disadvantages associated with this method are that it can be costly to produce and will require amendments and updating from time to time, although the biggest disadvantage is probably the absence of the discipline associated with a formally structured course with its programme of learning and assignments.

19.4.4 In-house

'On-the-job training' is preferred by commercial leisure organizations, particularly among its manual and low-level staff where skills are learnt by doing. The public sector is beginning to follow suite and many local authorities have recently organized 'in-service' training in such areas as customer care, marketing, first-aid, and so on, but unlike the commercial sector, these are often haphazard and lack continuity, reinforcement and monitoring of results.

19.5 CONTENT OF TRAINING COURSES

The basis of most arguments on what to train, essentially revolves around how specialist or how general such training should be, with the arguments tending to fall into one of three categories:

1. That leisure management is composed of two *separate* elements – recreation and management – and that the management element is applicable to any management situation. This seems to be the present basis of most academic college courses.
2. That leisure management is an area of knowledge within its own right, with a set of *specialist* skills that are applicable across the recreation sphere.
3. That leisure management is composed of specialist management

subdivisions (e.g. baths management, countryside management, arts management), with particular skills unique to that subdivision.

These three viewpoints are discussed below.

19.5.1 Leisure Management is composed of two separate elements

The arguments in favour of this concept tend to perceive the leisure element as comprising an essentially technical body of knowledge, and that the management element will be applicable in varying degrees to all management situations. Drucker [8] states that 'Businesses are different, but business is much the same regardless of size and structure of products, technology and markets, of culture and management competence. There is a common business reality.'

This approach was supported by the findings of the recreation centres survey [9], conducted on behalf of the Yates Committee and by the education institutions that offered the earlier postgraduate leisure management courses. On many of these courses the management and leisure elements were treated independently, taught by separate staff from separate departments with little effort made to integrate the two. Many of the management elements were taught in a way that had no relevance to public sector leisure services, with commercial financial management techniques, production line problems and product sales being integral parts of the course. Indeed, at some polytechnics, some post graduate leisure management courses are no different to other management courses, apart from an optional extra which, in some cases, represents little more than a dissertation on an area of leisure management (Fig. 19.2).

19.5.2 Leisure management is an area of knowledge in its own right

This viewpoint holds that management skills are not necessarily applicable to any situation, but are specific to the context in which they are being used, depending on whether recreation management is viewed as a general or a specific situation. Rosemary Stewart [10] states that:

'the job of the manager is varied; the differences may be as much, if not more than, the similarities. These lists of management functions ignore the diversity of management; the job of the top manager bears little resemblance to that of the junior manager, or that of being a coke manager in a steel mill is hardly comparable with being an advertising manager to a popular shoe manufacturer. These jobs differ because they have different functions, but even more because the situation of the firm is so dissimilar'.

facility orientated. Such an approach may fail to ask the fundamental question of whether the facility is needed and what its function is. Without considering the purpose of the service and the needs and demands of its potential client the facility may become more important than the people it is intended to serve.

19.6 THOUGHTS ON TRAINING REQUIREMENTS

The CELTS study [5] collected information on the nature and relative importance of skills and knowledge required for jobs related to sport and recreation, the in-service training needs and the education and training needs for the next five years from 1990. It concluded that job-related skills and training requirements are best regarded as a continuum, rather than a series of distinct grade-related breaks.

The high priority given to the basic management skills indicates the widespread lack of formal management training among leisure service personnel. Given the presumed radical changes associated with compulsory competitive tendering (CCT) (contractor–client relationships; performance monitoring and evaluation; increased consumer orientation; and stricter financial management), the need for these skills will become more urgent.

The study found that local authorities appeared to regard training as a *cost*, while commercial organizations regarded training as an *investment*. However, it was suggested that because of CCT, local government leisure services were shifting from a vague philosophy of public service to a more precise statement of aims, objectives and values:

'The bureaucratic and fragmented approaches of local government needed to be replaced by a more coherent, integrative organisational culture – one based on approaches and values described variously as "consumer orientation", "entrepreneurialism", "enterprise" or "commercial attitudes"'.

Clearly, competition in the industry is increasing. In local government there are pressures on managers to become more entrepreneurial and to compete with commercial companies for the right to manage efficiently. These developments have implications on the current and future roles of leisure managers.

In view of the findings of the CELTS Study and the criticism levied at the present courses, a more appropriate approach may be that which is illustrated in Fig. 19.3. The technical aspects are learnt prior to embarking on a management course, while management theory and concepts remain the foundation of the course, but with the emphasis being placed on the applied and operational aspects in a leisure environment. Likewise, the managerial, administrative, communication, etc. skills should be taught in a simulated leisure situation. This would ensure

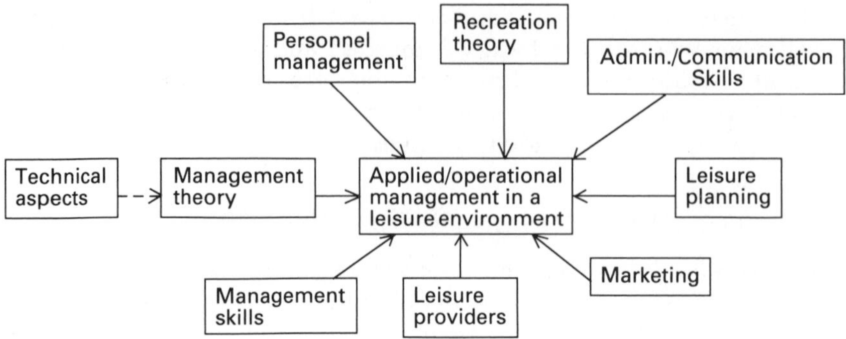

Fig. 19.3 Illustration of the basis of a proposed approach to leisure management training.

that the course content is relevant and that the learning can easily be transferred to the workplace.

A report of a survey that was undertaken on the training needs in recreation centres in Kent [4] states that:

'Training requirements in the recreation/leisure industry have historically tended to receive less attention than other service sectors, and there is clearly an urgent requirement for systematic identification of both existing and future training needs, and for the development of appropriate training provision to meet these needs'.

The Kent survey demonstrates that there exists a high level of demand for training but that there is a poor level of provision of suitable training packages for meeting the variety of training needs. However, with most colleges and polytechnics currently experiencing a reduction in the level of resources available, there is a possibility that the quality of the courses may deteriorate further!

19.7 CURRENT TRAINING COURSES

Over the past twenty years in the United Kingdom, there has been something of a confusing plethora of courses in recreation management. This complex picture has been streamlined of late with the standardization of some of the qualifications. However, the courses tend to be taken up more by the public sector and many commercial leisure companies run their own courses.

Courses provided in the institutional sector can be loosely grouped under 'further education', 'higher education' or 'continuing education':

1. *Further education* includes courses at a basic level of entry, run by colleges of further education or technical colleges; further education courses include BTEC First and National, as well as City and Guilds courses and SCOTVEC National Certificate modules.

2. *Higher education* includes courses entered at post A-level (or Scottish Higher) standard, run by polytechnics, colleges of higher education and universities. Higher Education courses include Higher National courses, degrees, higher degrees and postgraduate diplomas.
3. *Continuing education* includes courses entered by mature students who have some management experience and wish to study on a part-time basis. The BTEC Continuing Education Certificate (Leisure Management) courses are run by a range of educational institutions. There is a significant move towards competence-based qualifications, following the establishment of the National Council for Vocational Qualifications, and the implications for leisure awards and courses are considerable.

The following covers the main kinds of courses, grouped according to level of entry, certificate courses are part-time, Diplomas are longer full-time courses:

Entry point	*Type of course*
School-leavers of 16+ with qualifications	City & Guilds 481 Recreation & Leisure (Studies) BTEC First Courses in Leisure Studies SCOTVEC National Certificate Modulus
School-leavers with qualifications	BTEC National Diplomas and National Certificates in Leisure Studies SCOTVEC National Certificate Modulus
School-leavers with 1 A-level or more	BTEC Higher National Certificates/Diplomas in Leisure Studies SCOTVEC National Certificate modules and Higher National Diploma courses
School-leavers with 2 A-levels or more	CNAA and university degrees in various relevant disciplines
Graduates	Various CNAA and university diplomas and masters degrees
In-service courses for junior leisure staff	City & Guilds 481 (Recreation and Leisure Studies) IBRM Technical training schemes NEBSM Certificate courses with Leisure specialism BTEC First Courses in Leisure Studies

	BTEC National Certificates in Leisure Studies
	SCOTVEC National Certificate Modulus
In-service part-time courses Leisure Managers	BTEC Continuing Education Certificate in Leisure Management
	BTEC Higher National Diploma in Leisure Studies
	CNAA and university post-graduate diplomas and masters degrees
	SCOTVEC Higher National Certificates in Leisure Management (Scotland)
	Note: Institute and Leisure and Amenity Management Certificates and Diplomas are accessed via BTEC Continuing Education Certificates and Diplomas in Management Studies (DMS), respectively.

19.8 GOVERNMENT INITIATIVE ON TRAINING

A programme has been initiated, under the auspices of the Department of Employment Training Agency, designed to provide a trained and qualified workforce to meet the demands of a changing society. The programme applies to all sectors of industry, including the leisure industry. Each section of industry has an Industry Lead Body (ILB). There are approx. 150 ILBs, 4% of which have a direct involvement in leisure: Amenity horticulture, Arts and Performing Arts, Hotel and Catering, Museums and Art Galleries, Retail Travel, Tourism and Leisure and Sport and Recreation.

The programme is designed to improve work performance through a system of vocational qualifications and training. National Vocational Qualifications (NVQs, or SVQs in Scotland) are being developed, based on 'standards of competence agreed and accepted by both employers and employees from the industry'. These vocational qualifications are being designed to demonstrate what an individual can do at work and how well he or she can do it.

The NVQs are approved by the National Council for Vocational Qualifications (NCVQ), and SVQs are approved in Scotland by SCOTVEC. They reflect the standards of work performance set by each industry; NVQs are grouped into a framework which identifies the level of work for which a person is qualified – i.e. from basic tasks to supervisory and management skills. Armed with an NVQ as an acknowledgement of a person's skills, it will be easier for employees to progress within an industry and help employers to select the right people with the right skills for the right job [13].

The 'Competence Standards' are the tasks an employee undertakes at work and the skills and knowledge the employee requires to fulfil these tasks. The Industry Lead Bodies believe that setting standards will benefit employee, employer and customer:

1. For the employee, there will be –
   - Qualifications and training geared to the needs of the industry.
   - Better employment prospects.
   - Clear career progression.
   - Recognition of experience and ability.
2. For the employer, there will be –
   - A properly trained workforce.
   - Qualifications relating to the industry.
   - A consistent national standards framework.
   - The right people applying for the right jobs.
3. For the customer, there will be –
   - A better trained and qualified workforce which will mean an improved quality service.

However, the leisure industry is, as we have pointed out, vast, volatile and managed by so many different sectors that uniformity and standardization may be inappropriate in many respects, primarily because leisure behaviour is different from work behaviour which is far more predictable and far less discretionary.

The NVQ also presupposes that all tasks can be predetermined and hence will not take into consideration the unusual situation where a degree of flexibility is required. Also the system does not adequately reward the individual who uses his or her initiative. Indeed, it tends to reinforce the bureaucratic type of organization, with emphasis on job demarcation, the means to undertake a task as opposed to the end-result and upon efficiency rather than effectiveness. This situation could have a detrimental effect upon staff initiative, morale and motivation which, in turn, can influence the quality of the service offered and the level of productivity of the staff.

19.9 THE 'PROFESSIONAL' BODIES REPRESENTING LEISURE MANAGERS

Leisure and recreation attract large numbers of representative bodies, including associations and institutes with many overlapping interests. The *professional* bodies in the United Kingdom, include:

- Institute of Leisure and Amenity Management (1983) (an amalgamation of Association of Recreation Managers, Institute of Leisure Management, Institute of Park and Recreation Administration and Institute of Municipal Entertainment).
- Institute of Baths and Recreation Management (1921).
- Chief Leisure Officers' Association (1976).
- Tourism Society (1977).
- Library Association (1877).
- Museums Association (1889).
- Leisure Studies Association (1975).
- Institute of Entertainments and Arts Management (1982).
- The Physical Education Association (1899).
- Recreation Managers' Association (1956) (formerly Industrial Sports Clubs).
- Association of Playing Fields Officers (1958).

Many of the above, including ILAM and IBRM, have their own training programme and career structure and make a valuable contribution to the training of their members.

19.10 RECREATION MANAGEMENT: AN EMERGING PROFESSION IN THE UNITED KINGDOM?

Whether the managers in the leisure industry consider themselves to be professionals is dependent upon their perception of the nature of their work and its value to society, and their capability and standing within the community.

Not surprisingly, managers within the industry perceive themselves as professionals. It is, however, questionable whether the rest of society view Leisure Managers in the same light as the high-status professions or occupations. Although there is no generally accepted definition of the word 'profession', there appears to be an acceptable criterion for evaluating whether an occupation is of professional standing.

Sessoms [14], writing about the evolution of recreation professionalism in the United States, has described a profession as implying 'a defined and distinctive body of knowledge attained through a disciplined, formal education process prior to sanction for practice. It bridges technique and immediate application with theory, sets standards and serves social needs.' Murphy [15], in 1980, claimed that while accepting the concept that recreation management encompasses a relevant body of knowledge, it is not adequately defined and lacks 'a formal education process for entry into the occupation'.

Although both 'recreation' and 'management' can only be regarded as secondary disciplines, they do however draw on primary disciplines such as sociology and psychology. Entrance to some of the main leisure and recreation management institutes is by means of a formal examination, and in the case of ILAM proof of practical competence is also required. It would thus appear that the leisure and recreation management occupation has significantly advanced towards or along the professionalization continuum. However, it has a long way to go and it could be argued that recreation is becoming more occupational rather than professional.

The church, law and medicine are often considered as the original 'professions'. Other professions like education and accountancy are placed somewhere on a continuum between these originals and those which are classed as 'occupations', like advertising and coaching. Leisure and recreation management, as an emerging profession, albeit with a growing body of knowledge, does not yet fit into the main strands of the professional continuum. The service areas and job tasks have been identified, public recognition is very slowly coming about and formalizing structures and training is beginning through the government's Training Agency initiative. However, there is a wide gap between public and commercial leisure training and the adoption and enforcement of ethical codes, found in the original professions, is a long way away. Indeed, the wide interpretation of what is, and what is not, acceptable leisure, make the enforcement of ethical codes difficult.

With the widening of knowledge and the dawn of the technological and computer age, many emerging professions have been slowed down in their professional recognitions. The profession of physical education, for example, is increasingly being challenged by the advance of professional coaches, sports psychologists, fitness experts and aerobics teachers. Similarly, in the arts and music professional artists have an important role to play in teaching. The self-governance of schools, the involvement of parents and the heightened use of volunteers can fill gaps, normally the province of the 'professionals'.

In this book we have shown that provision for and management of leisure and recreation is made by major sectors: public, institutional, voluntary and commercial. The Leisure Managers represented by the institutions and associations discussed in this chapter and the managers that emerge from the courses and training schemes represent only a small part of the world of leisure and recreation and its management, primarily those areas in the hands of public or semi-public bodies. The range and scope of leisure and recreation requiring management, however, is very wide. The non-public sector, made up of thousands of voluntary organizations and commercial bodies, is barely touched by current levels of leisure management training. Even in the public sector many areas of leisure and recreation are not encompassed, for example, in the education-related leisure field.

Whether working in the public or non-public sector, Leisure Managers are concerned with creating opportunities for people to have satisfying leisure experiences. They must attract the public or fail. Leisure and recreation is a 'people orientated' business. Training therefore must see itself primarily as a people-oriented service. Training is a means of acquiring new skills and new knowledge because things are always changing. Managers and organizations must evolve as demands change, rather than simply becoming more efficient, consolidating the status quo and thus becoming less effective. Yet no amount of training and management education will guarantee making a successful manager, but with education and training, leisure personnel are more likely to become good managers.

REFERENCES AND NOTES

1. Sports Council (1969), *Professional Training for Recreation Management: Report of a Working Party* (Chairman, D. D. Molyneux), Sports Council, London.
2. Department of the Environment (1978), *Recreation Management Training Committee: Interim Report* (A Discussion Paper) (Chairman, Anne Yates), HMSO, London.
3. Department of the Environment (1984), *Recreation Management Training Committee: Final Report*, HMSO, London.
4. E.g. MSC/Mid-Kent College Local Collaborative Project (*c*. 1989), *Training Needs and Training Provision Requirements in Sports/Recreation Centres in Kent*, Mid-Kent College of Higher and Further Education.
5. CELTS (Centre for Leisure and Tourism Studies) (1990), *Recreation Management Training Needs*, London, Sports Council.
6. Central Statistical Office, *Annual Abstract of Statistics* (1990 edn), HMSO, London.
7. Dartington Amenity Research Trust (DART) (1980), Discussion Document: Links between the Public and Non-Public Sectors (Recreation Training Committee), unpublished.
8. Drucker, P. F. (1969), *Managing For Results*, Pan Books, London.
9. Torkildsen, G. (1978), Report to the London Regional Management Centre for the Recreation Management Training Committee (Yates Committee) on Sport and Recreation Centre Management Staff, in collaboration with N. Stang and the Polytechnic of North London, unpublished.
10. Stewart, R. (1970), *Managers and their Jobs*, Pan Books, London.
11. Pick, J. (1978), Training: the future. *Municipal Entertainment*, **5**, No. 10, June, 11.
12. Kahn, D. and Katz, R. L. (1966), *The Social Psychology of Organisations*, Wiley, New York.
13. National Council for Voluntary Qualifications (NCVQ), publicity literature.
14. Sessoms, H. D. (1975), Our body of knowledge: myth or reality? *Parks and Recreation* (USA), November, 30.
15. Murphy, W. (1980), Professionalism and Recreation Management, Occasional Paper, unpublished.

Chapter 20

Towards effective leisure and recreation management: some conclusions

This book has set out to further an understanding of leisure and recreation and the improving of its management. We have also sought to revise, update and improve upon the original book, which carried the same title.

The book has been written in three main parts. In the first part we were concerned with leisure and the needs of people, spanning Chapters 2–7. In the second part we were concerned with planning and provision, covered in Chapters 8–12, and in the third part with management in both general and specific terms, in Chapters 13–19, culminating here in our conclusions, which point in the direction of more effective mangement of community leisure and recreation.

Three pivotal chapters which link the whole study together are: Chapter 7 (the leisure product), Chapter 8 (the planning process) and Chapter 13 (management). They provide the linkage between leisure philosophy and the needs of people, leisure planning and resources and the management process, which will enable a new approach to a model framework for the effective management of leisure services and facilities to be considered.

This chapter undertakes three functions. *First*, a broad overview and summary of findings is given of the three main parts of the book. *Second*, a new approach to leisure management in the form of an approach to a theoretical framework is described. *Third*, a discussion of some of the ideas, and more personal conclusions and philosophy, is set out.

20.1 INTRODUCTION

Effectiveness is concerned with meeting the goals of an organization. An effective leisure and recreation service for the greater good of the greater number of people needs to be based upon four pillars or planes:

1. Leisure opportunity, to achieve the potential of leisure.
2. Meeting the needs of different people.
3. Management excellence, including planning and provision.
4. Sound organizational policies, aims and objectives.

20.2 LEISURE OPPORTUNITY TO MEET LEISURE POTENTIAL

Potentially, leisure can provide experiences and satisfactions which enhance the quality of people's lives. We have described leisure in Chapter 2, and refined upon this in Chapter 7. Leisure, for individual people, was perceived as experiencing activities, chosen in relative freedom, that are personally satisfying and innately worthwhile and that can lead to self-actualization and, ultimately, to a self-fulfilling life.

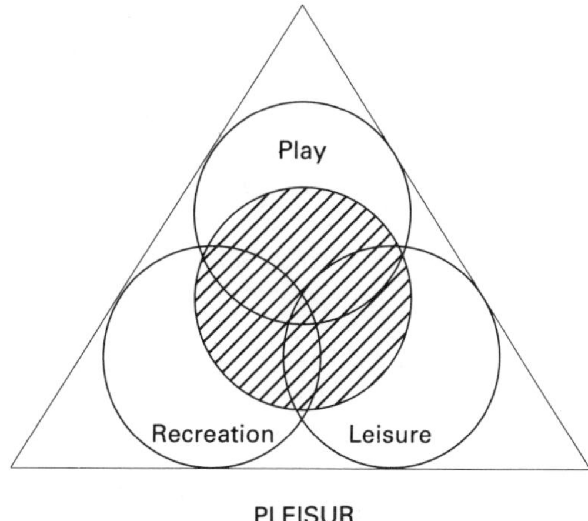

Fig. 20.1 'Pleisur' at the heart of play, recreation and leisure.

By 'self-actualization', I mean realizing fully our potential, to be or become what we are capable of becoming. Leisure then, ideally, can be an integral part of our way of living.

Alas, most of us do not live in an ideal world and many of us choose not to accept the gift of leisure, nor to sacrifice what we already have for something which, potentially, could be far better. This may be because we have not had the opportunity, nor seen the potential of leisure: this is where the leisure professional comes in.

In terms of planning for and managing leisure services and facilities, Leisure Managers can perceive leisure as a framework of opportunity for people to be attracted, to choose and to experience satisfactions, which lead to interests and life-enhancing pursuits.

Leisure's potential includes the possibility of achieving innate experiences through chosen activities, very similar in quality and feelings that can be found in the experiences of play and 're-creation'. In Chapter 7, I called this wordless experience, 'pleisur', a derivative and acronym of the words *play, recreation* and *leisure* (Fig. 20.1).

If, as leisure professionals, we want to provide a choice of activities and opportunity for people to experience and develop leisure potential, then such experiences are more likely to occur for individual people if the setting and circumstances are favourable; there need to be:

1. The right conditions with levels of freedom, choice, absence of necessity, self-initiating, and spontaneity.
2. Satisfactions in the doing with levels of self-expression, challenge, novelty, stimulation, playfulness, quality experiences including peak experiences and re-creative moments.

3. Positive outcomes, such as physical, emotional, social and psychological wellbeing, levels of achievement and heightened self-esteem.

These innate, worthwhile experiences give satisfactions. Satisfactions lead to consuming interests. Individuals are therefore more likely to realize their potential and this can lead towards achieving personal self-worth and self-actualization – goals of leisure. It has become clear that, whether a way of living or not, leisure is linked inextricably to other elements in life and specifically to the needs of people.

20.3 MEETING THE NEEDS OF PEOPLE

The needs of people were considered in Chapter 5 and further refined in Chapter 6, which was concerned with the influences brought to bear on people in their time for leisure; in Chapter 7 in relation to play, recreation and leisure; while in Chapter 8 our concern was with a people-orientated approach to leisure planning.

PEOPLE'S NEEDS

People have diverse needs, and different people have different needs, which change according to their circumstances and stage in life. Leisure needs, as such may not exist, but some of the needs of people can be met through involvement in leisure pursuits.

People have a whole range of needs, some of which are basic to survival, some essential to coping with living in an uncertain social world and others at the apex of a complex human network which seeks to find balance, harmony and self-worth. People want to be 'somebody'; it is therefore in this latter category where leisure opportunity can help people to meet some of their needs, to find themselves and have a favourable personal identity.

Hence other aspects of life cannot be separated from leisure. Emotional stress, financial and family worries, work obligations and crisis points in life may dominate to the extent that leisure becomes peripheral. For example, leisure for many disadvantaged people is likely to remain low, while major life constraints persist such as lack of income, poor housing, poor mobility and unrelieved pressures of parenting.

All these life factors support my contention that leisure cannot be divorced from other elements of life. Therefore, effective public leisure services require local authorities to play attracting, enabling and supporting roles, examples of which we have given in Chapter 8.

20.4 PLANNING, PROVIDING AND MANAGING LEISURE

The potential of leisure offers opportunities not only for individuals, but for groups and for society as a whole to blossom. In the community context, leisure and recreation services have to fit into our culture, institutions and systems. In Chapter 8, on planning, we have proposed a greater interrelationship between planners, leisure professionals and the community. 'Putting people into plans' was the developing theme.

Chapters 10–12 respectively dealt with the major providers of leisure services and facilities – public, voluntary and commercial. Choice is essential, but planners, providers and managers need to be aware of the implications of making certain choices. Powerful commercial attractions have a magnetic draw and products may also have significant value for jobs and the economy; yet there is a need for people to learn to choose not only activities which are superficially pleasurable alone, but also activities which are intrinsically worthwhile. Leisure advocates must not lose sight of or inadvertently destroy the leisure 'gift' which is there for the taking.

Each of the providers has valuable contributions to make. The commercial sector can provide pleasurable social, physical and entertaining activities. The public sector, despite changes in its role and the constraints upon it, still has many roles to play, namely that of planner, provider, enabler and manager. The voluntary sector, in particular, provides great opportunity for many millions of people to develop consuming interests and to express themselves in company with like-minded people and to achieve together the goals of their organizations.

If leisure is a freedom to choose, *personal* management is of far greater importance than management by someone else, particularly the faceless 'someone'. However, in our culture effective 'professional' management is needed to open up opportunity for more people.

20.4.1 The management process

In Chapter 13 we have dealt with the management process and in Chapters 14–18 with leisure programming, performance objectives, marketing, event management and staffing, all essential within the process of management.

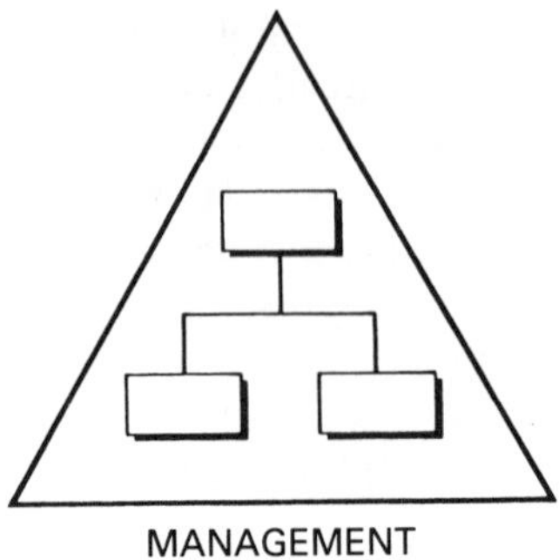

The job of the Leisure Manager is to manage effectively and in doing so meet the goals of the organization and the needs of people. Effectiveness is measured by the degree to which an organization achieves its goals and objectives. This applies to all organizations, whether in commerce or leisure. In public leisure services effective community leisure management can be measured, in part, by the degree to which a reasonable balance of market segments has been attracted. For example, if a leisure centre purports to be a centre for the community, it follows that it too should attract a cross-section of the local community.

Two key elements are (a) the interaction between the organization and those who use the services – i.e. it is as a people-orientated business, and (b) managers are involved in the achievement of goals. Implicit within these elements – within community leisure and recreation – is the desire to meet the needs of people through leisure opportunity.

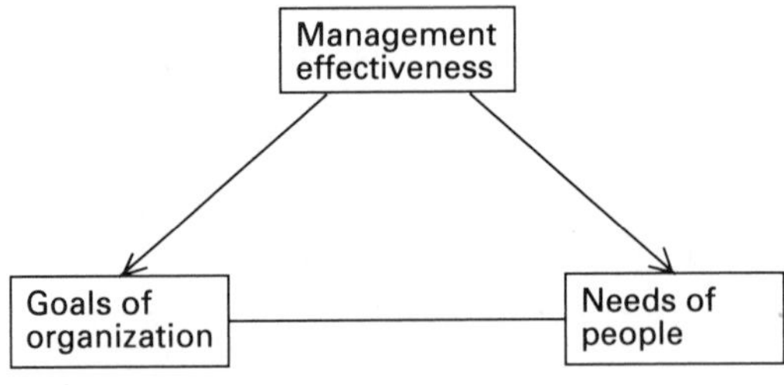

20.4.2 Leisure Management

A leisure and recreation organization is a business whose functions include the creation and distribution of services, programmes and activities that are used by individuals and groups during their time for

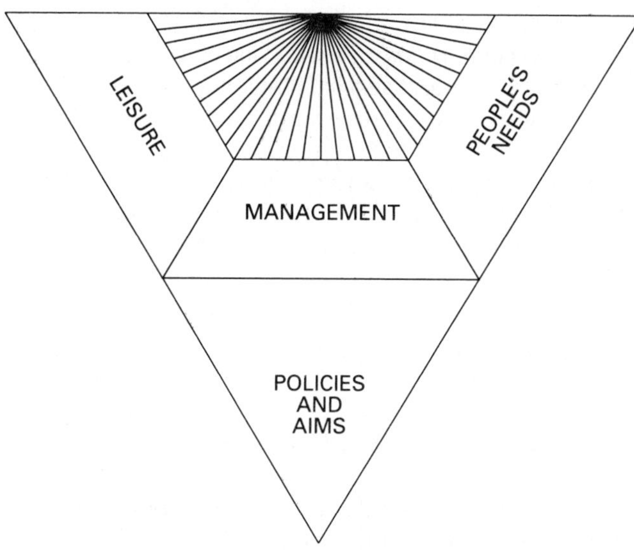

goals of the organization, the situation and the current emphasis. Therefore, for efficiency and measurability each of the three planes will need to contain levels of performance to meet objectives and targets. For simplicity and illustration only, this is represented in the 'model' as three levels: the lower tier or basic level, the middle tier or secondary level and the upper tier or primary level.

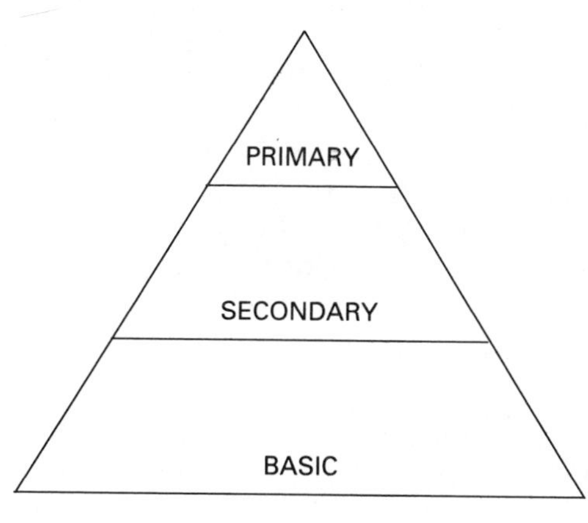

LEVELS OF EFFECTIVENESS

Basic

At the lower, basic, level managers would seek to achieve a wide range of choice of activities, general service efficiency, high levels of throughput and income and a broad programme of casual, club and special events. The basic level therefore represents the numbers game – i.e. a head-counting and money-counting exercise. Many authorities and organizations measure success only at this point – i.e. an organization survival level! They stop at this point!

Secondary

At the next, secondary, level we could expect to see, in public services, a user profile reflecting broadly the catchment population and the target markets which the organization is aiming to attract. At this level, managers would seek to have a balanced programme to meet some of the needs of the different people and groups in the area. Greater emphasis will be given to customer service, the encouragement of community initiative and meeting the standards and quality of service expected by the manager, organization and community.

Primary

At the top, primary, level the manager will be concerned with individual customer and group needs, sensitive handling of customers, the needs of the disadvantaged, the quality of experience of the individual and the encouragement of long-lasting activities that are perceived by the individuals to be personally worthwhile and of importance.

The apex of the pyramid serves to illustrate the goal of leisure management – i.e. personal self-actualization or self-fulfilment of individual people through leisure opportunity. It thus represents the highest quality of leisure experiences that people will want to 'buy' again and again, the satisfactions that can lead to an enhancing of the quality of life. It is to this goal of quality leisure and recreation that a manager must strive in order to give a service that can truly be called 'excellent leisure management'.

20.5.2 Value of the 'model'

This broad, simplistic conceptual 'model' serves as an illustration only of the components which go to make up effective leisure management of public leisure facilities. Although only skeletal in form, it endeavours to capture the essential ingredients. It is also illustrative of the theory that an individual is like all people having the same basic needs (the basic level of the pyramid), like some other like-minded people sharing the same interests (the secondary level) and like no

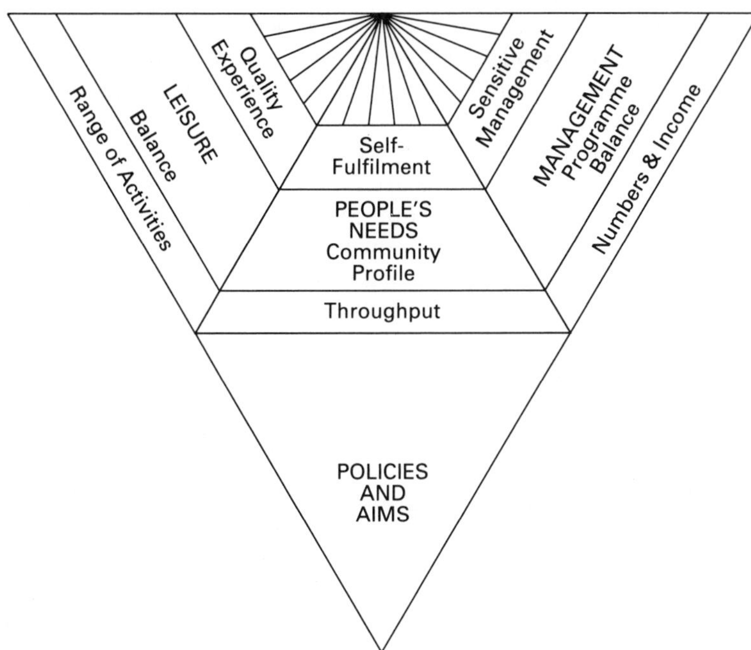

other person – a unique individual at the apex of the pyramid. At the top point of the pyramid there is no room for more than one.

The value of a theory is the degree to which it explains and predicts and is of practical use. To make operational sense of the various elements within the framework, the ideas and themes can be incorporated by Leisure Managers into a process for effective and efficient management from various starting points, for example, in terms of operational management and performance objectives, as outlined in Chapter 15, or in programming by objectives as set out in Chapter 14 or as part of a marketing plan as described in Chapter 16.

From whatever direction, there will be a sequential and continuing process of providing a balanced service to meet both the goals of the organization and the needs of the people to be served. The framework also allows for maximum flexibility, so that Leisure Managers can vary their responses to be appropriate to given situations. Good management needs to be flexible management, but the greater the flexibility, the greater the need for management excellence.

In summary, the first tenet of management is to know what we are in business for – i.e. what it is we are supposed to be managing. Leisure Managers are not only managing parks, pitches, pools, theatres and sports centres, but creating opportunities for people to experience leisure in ways satisfying to them.

To provide real leisure opportunity for people, there must be effective management – i.e. management concerned with what is below the surface as much as what is above it. Measures of effectiveness must therefore include not only throughput, income and expenditure, but the range of people, the scope of the activites and the quality of the experience. Managers must ask themselves: 'to what extent have we met the needs of the people we are here to serve?.'

To provide more effective community leisure management, a theoretical framework has been built upon the three interlocking aspects of *people, leisure* and *management,* visualized as the three planes of a triangular pyramid, with the base of the pyramid as a representation of the purposes of the organization. Hence a new approach to community leisure and recreation management has been fashioned which calls for a re-orientation towards a better people and process management approach.

One of the purposes of this book has been to examine the linkages between leisure philosophy, resources and management and to forge bridges between them in an attempt at improving the management of community leisure services and facilities. At the outset, three propositions were put forward, as follows:

The first was that providers and managers should be concerned with the *quality of experience* for the individual and not just with the quantity of facilities and numbers attending.

The second was that *leisure opportunity* can lead to satisfying leisure and recreation experiences which, in turn, have positive effects on the quality of life of individual people.

The third was that *management* policy and performance can be powerful influences on both people's participation and non-participation.

The study undertaken in writing this book confirms these three propositions. The theoretical framework illustrates, in conceptual form, the components which make for effective community leisure management. *There is nothing more practical than a good theory – if you put it into practice!*

20.6 DISCUSSION

Leisure has emerged over the past three decades as an important sphere of life. It now has less to do with former definitions of time and specified activities and more to do with satisfying experiences. As a choice of life-style and a form of personal expression, it should now become less a reflection of demographic and socio-economic status and more a reflection of who we are and what leisure means to us.

Leisure consumption is one of the few growth areas in the current economic climate in the United Kingdom. Well into the foreseeable future there will be an increasing demand for centres of interest to satisfy the rising expectations of people in all walks of life and all sections of the community. Well-researched patterns of social change show that the trend will continue well into the 21st century. Therefore, new facilities specially selected for their leisure and social value should be developed. In addition, existing services, facilities and operations should be improved to take full advantage of a positive leisure climate.

The benefits of providing for these trends will include, it is hoped, a healthier and more relaxed population, more effective use of leisure time and, above all, greater personal fulfilment. The case for leisure and recreation investment and support is well made. I believe, and evidence exists in this book to show, that leisure opportunity can be the vehicle through which people can play and find recreation and in so doing meet some of their human needs.

The correlation between leisure and recreation participation and variables, such as social class, education and income, is high. The extent to which participation is influenced or conditioned by such factors is not clear and the question is raised whether leisure and recreation policies and management can overcome many of the apparent constraints to wider participation. I believe that good management *can* remove many of the artificial barriers and that planning, location, perception, accessibility, choice, social acceptance, the attitude of managers and the quality of management have very important effects. In a social and community context, leisure can help to give people self-worth and confidence. Resourceful people are those who can overcome obstacles and find preoccupying activities and interests. All people appear to have a quest for personal identity; leisure and recreation management has much to offer in the way of enabling people to develop skills, to discover themselves and reach beyond their immediate grasp.

Leisure Managers must, above all else, be good *managers*. They need an understanding of general management principles, processes, practices and the ability to handle people. They must have skills of leadership, decision-making, communications and administration. They have to choose, train and deploy staff wisely. They need objectivity, financial acumen and marketing ability. Management must be appropriate to different situations, and the manager must adapt his or her style of management to be appropriate to changing situations.

In essence, Leisure Managers are no different from other managers. Whether they operate in the public, voluntary or commercial sector, a part of their job is to provide people with opportunities to experience satisfactions through leisure activities. Managers must understand the nature of the leisure experience and what motivates people to leisure and recreation. They must create environments in which leisure can flourish. Then they can define managerial objectives, develop skills for the job and utilize the resources at their disposal. Managers need multi-skill qualities for *both* general and specialist management. All providers and managers must attract people or fail. Leisure and recreation is thus a people-orientated business.

As we have pointed out in Chapter 1, a Leisure Manager is not someone who comes out of college with a certificate. Nor is he or she someone who, through experience, can operate a facility but fails to appreciate what it means to achieve an effective service. A grasp of theory accelerates the learning through job experience. However, the opposite is not necessarily true. Job experience may, or may not, accelerate a grasp of theory. In this book, a theory – practice orientation – is advocated to produce the most effective Leisure Managers. Yet no amount of training will guarantee to make the manager: he or she is someone with a mixture of objectivity, craft and humanity.

There is much to be said for practical, simple, commonsense approaches to management. We have somehow managed to make management something academic and difficult, particularly in the public sector, with many levels of bureaucracy and training only at senior levels. Mechanistic and institutionalized systems are prevalent. Some institutional managers get stuck in a rut; then they do not respond positively to change and management practices; and far from enhancing leisure, they may well militate against effective management! While knowledge, logic and technical ability are important, there is also an important place for enthusiasm and empathy, even charisma. There is room for belief and conviction. Managers should have the ability to recognize need and plan to meet it with objectivity and sensitivity.

Leisure opportunity is a tangible means of improving the lot of individuals in society. The message to policy-makers is clear: make savings on capital if you must, but never on good management. A great deal can be done without major capital expenditure. There exists a gulf between well-meaning public providers and the actual public themselves. There is inarticulation and miscommunication at the interface between people and providers. Leisure Managers can help to mesh together the resources that already exist, help to make the connections and the linkages. Enabling, encouraging and supporting can be achieved in a thousand and one small ways. 'Small things make a big difference', particularly when it is personal satisfactions with which leisure management is ultimately concerned.

Leisure professionals must develop a 'helicopter' view of their leisure services: the higher they go, the greater the vision. They need to view, not just the array of facilities, but the interconnections, the junctions of the various pathways, the fuels that make the processes effective, and the blockages that cause the hold-ups.

Leisure Managers should develop more people-serving concepts, with an emphasis on concern for the customer. Policy-makers, planners and managers should challenge the assumptions of traditional leisure services by re-examining the justification for provision and services. They must continually question the assumptions on which we plan and manage. Policy-makers and managers must focus their leisure orientation within the context of the total human experience. Such a perspective broadens the basis of leisure expression.

Here, then, is the conflict, the dilemma: leisure and recreation is concerned with human experience. It defies management. But management is the instrument by which environments can be shaped, opportunities can be given and people can be taught to cope. The challenge therefore is not just in facilities, programmes, costs, income or even in numbers, but whether leisure services can provide opportunities for leisure and re-creation to occur for people, and where individuals can choose, learn, find pleasurable and satisfying experiences and control the content of their leisure behaviour.

In this book, emphasis has been placed on effectiveness. It has been shown that effective management cannot be measured solely in terms of numbers and income. We desperately need a method of evaluation that permits a social cost-benefit analysis. We do not want to promote the slogan 'Leisure for all who can afford it'! Allowing the accounting mind to dictate social policy will be a tragedy for people, for art, for sport and for the nation.

'Leisure for all', should be concerned with individual people achieving a personal harmony through satisfaction in participating in art, music, sport and recreation. Those who can experience the joy of participation and exhilaration of movement, and who can reach beyond the ordinary, have greater opportunity to find a better and more satisfying life.

In these days of standardization, bureaucratic institutions, financial accountability and competitive tendering, our attention is being drawn towards mathematical results and quantitative performance ratios. Facilities are being planned for entertainment, eating and drinking and all the fun of the fair because these attractions achieve volume traffic and greater spends per head – the right mix for profitability. But other provision (often unprofitable) is also needed to help to meet the goal of leisure. Furthermore, too much time and energy is being spent on *who* is going to do the managing – public departments or private companies. But it should not matter who is managing, but rather what is being managed and how, and what are the benefits. Disney has taught us that treating customers with attention, understanding, consideration and courtesy – 'quality services' – brings quality results. Let us focus on the results for people.

The major resource that this world has is people, at the community level. Many of our social systems – including leisure – make people dependent on directed programmes and services, without the inputs from community groups. Building on the theme of Dr Nellie Arnold (from her pre-Commonwealth Games address in Brisbane) our untapped resources are in the community sector:

1. We need to create an *enabling environment*, returning much leadership to the community – play, leisure and recreation are born at the grass-root level.
2. A *supporting environment*, providing a resource, an economic and administrative base, aided by local authorities and agencies.
3. A *connecting environment*, linking people to agencies, clubs and voluntary bodies: our role as advocates is crucial.

Leisure and recreation management is concerned with policies, politics, planning, provision, programmes and people. But at its core it is concerned with individual and collective behaviour. While numbers are important, the individual rather than the aggregate must be the core of the service.

Leisure is not new. 'With what activity should we occupy our leisure?', asked Aristotle. 'Let each become all he or she is capable of being' could have been his modern-day slogan. Jacob Bronowski believed that leisure activity has potential for a deep sense of appreciation which can lift us to a higher plane, where we discover peace, beauty and joy in this world. This can carry over to an increased appreciation of life itself. Julian Huxley, in the *Bulletin of Atomic Scientists* states: 'The leisure problem is fundamental. Having to decide what we shall do with our leisure is inevitably forcing us to re-examine the purpose of human existence, and to ask what human fulfilment really means.' I believe that leisure management should be concerned with such fulfilment, with a love of life, for people and for the human expression that leisure opportunity affords. At the end of the day, it is about one person and his or her experience.

The House of Lords Report captured the belief and the spirit in which this book is written:

'Many people suffer from a lingering feeling that leisure is something of a luxury. As an escape from the commendable pursuits of earning a living and making a contribution to the national economy, leisure seems tainted. When carried to excess it is called idleness. But the Committee believe that it is time for the puritan view of leisure to be jettisoned. Leisure is as much a part of life as work and it plays an equally important part in man's development and the quality of his life . . . In its own way it is almost as important to the well-being of the community as good housing, hospitals and schools'.

The world may change, but some things are changeless; we have been given creative, changeless gifts. It is through play, recreation and leisure that our talents for discovery, invention, music, art and sport are realized. My hope for leisure providers and managers is that they will not just concentrate on efficiency, finding more administration to satisfy less activity, but to aim for effectiveness and put their talents into ideas and activities for more people to find self-fulfilment. The spirit of the world cannot be changed through money, facilities or bureaucracy, nor by government, but by imagination and ideas. Those ideas need the backing of our enthusiasm, confidence and vision.

The leisure experience which I have described in this book stems from *intrinsic,* rather than extrinsic rewards: it is person-centred. Each society should respect the individuality of each of its people. The community, encouraged by its local authority, should endeavour to provide the opportunity for each person to engage in leisure of his or her choosing. Society, in turn, will benefit, for people who function at their optimal potential can help society to reach a far better level of *collective* well-being. As the Select Committee of the House of Lords put it: 'When life becomes meaningful for the individual then the whole community is also enriched.'

Answer guidelines

ASSIGNMENTS 8.7 (p. 165)

Blackroad Sports Centre – additional squash courts

Assessment of demand

1. *Standards approach*
   Squash Rackets Association recommends one court per 6000 population,

   $$\therefore \text{ recommended provision } = \frac{16\,400}{6000} = 2.73 \text{ courts, say, 3 courts.}$$

   Current provision = 2 courts,

   ∴ deficiency = 3 − 2 = 1 court.

2. *National participation rates – General Household Survey*
   Assumption (i) that population under 16 years represents 23% and (ii) that occupancy of squash courts in the region is 65%.

   Number of potential players = 16 400 × 77% × 2.4%

   Participation rate = 303 players.

   $$\text{Number of games per week} = \frac{303 \text{ players} \times 1 \text{ frequency of play}}{2 \text{ players per game}}$$

   = 151 games per week.

   Weekly capacity per court = 14 h/day × 7 days/week × 1.5 games/h × 65% occupancy
   = 95 games per week.

   $$\therefore \text{ Number of courts required} = \frac{151}{95} = 1.58 \text{ courts, say, 2 courts,}$$

   deficiency = 2 − 2 = 0.

3. *Expressed demand*

   Level of utilization

   Income from 2 squash courts = £14 600,

cost of participation = £2.80 including VAT for 40 min
= £4.20 including VAT per h
= £3.58 excluding VAT
say, £3.60 excluding VAT.

Financial potential of existing courts = 2 courts × 98 h/week × 51 week × £3.60 = £35 985 pa.

$$\text{Current level of utilization} = \frac{14\,600}{35\,985} \times 100\%$$
$$= 40.57\%$$
$$= 39.75 \text{ h/week,}$$

but peak times occupies 60% of utilization;

peak hours	– 46 h/week	– utilization =	23.85 h/week
off peak hours	– 52 h/week	– utilization =	15.90 h/week
		Total utilization	39.75 h/week.

Hence, there is considerable spare capacity available with only some 50% occupancy at peak hours.

Capital cost – £40 000 × 2 courts = £80 000, assume borrowing at 15% interest over 40 years.

Operating costs – first year of operation		
loan charges	– capital repayment	£2000
	interest	£12 000
	total loan charges	£14 000
other costs	– fuel, cleaning, etc. say,	£ 1000
	Total operating costs	£15 000

Although the provision of additional courts will undoubtedly generate additional usage and hence income, at peak periods when it is assumed that currently there is a degree of total occupancy, it is unlikely that this will generate much usage that cannot be accommodated in the existing provision.

Additional income not able to be accommodated in existing provision, say,

= 2 h/day × 2 courts × £3.60 × 7 days × 51 weeks
= £5140 pa.

Therefore, from a purely financial point of view, there is no justification for the provision of a further two squash courts.

However, with a further two courts, the management has greater programme flexibility (e.g. organizing courses) and the provision of four courts would make the venue more attractive for club fixtures.

(ii) Soccer Pitch Provision – general notes

Assumptions

(a) That the number of players required to sustain a soccer team and provide the necessary cover for sickness, injury, holidays, etc. is 16;
(b) that a team plays home once in two weeks – but almost all the matches are played within the Borough;
(c) that the pitches are used once on Saturdays and once on Sundays. (Although it is acknowledged that the quality of the drainage of the pitches, the changing accommodation and the flexible attitude of the teams and the leagues can influence the playing capacity of pitches.)

Therefore, the weekly player capacity of each pitch is

= 16 players × 2 teams × 2 games/week = 64 players

Hence, the number of pitches required

$$= \frac{200\,000 \text{ population} \times 2.7\% \text{ participation rate}}{64 \text{ players}} \times 1.25 \text{ freq/week}$$

= 105 pitches

ASSIGNMENT 15.7 (p. 337)

Waterville Leisure Centre

To be able to set targets, it is necessary to undertake a performance appraisal.

Financial ratios

(a) *Analysis of data*

Operating costs (gross expenditure) including net bar/catering service and excluding loan charges and Central Establishment charges

			£'000
			= 716
Less loan charges		70	
Central administration charges		60	
Bar/catering staff	60		
" cost of sales	70	130	260
			456

Income	*£'000*
Gross income	430
Less bar/catering	101
	329

Staff costs excluding bar/catering service	
Wages	110
Salaries	120
	230

Bar/catering service	
Sales	101
Cost of sales	70
	31
Staff costs	60
Net loss	29

Net Expenditure (including net trading on bar and catering service, but excluding loan charges and Central Establishment charges)

	£'000
Gross expenditure	456
Gross income	329
Net expenditure	127

(b) *Financial ratios*

Income: staff costs = 329 : 230 = 1.43
Income: gross expenditure = 329 : 456 = 0.72
(operating costs)
Staff costs: gross expenditure = 230 : 456 = 0.50
(operating costs)

$$\text{Subsidy per attendance} = \frac{127\,000}{310\,000} = 0.409.$$

To make these ratios more meaningful, they can be compared with the Centre's previous year's performance, other local centres and national norms.

(c) *Bar and catering service*

(i) The net financial situation regarding the bar and catering service was a loss of £29 000.

(ii) Gross profit on turnover

	£'000
Sales	101
Cost of sales	70
Gross profit	31

$$\text{Gross profit on turnover} = \frac{31}{101} \times 100\% = 30.69\%.$$

This is disappointing and below the norm for such a service.

(iii) Spend per head on bar and catering service.

$$= \frac{\text{sales}}{\text{total attendances}} = \frac{£101\,000}{310\,000} = £0.325.$$

To set targets, one should make an allowance for the rate of inflation and for any improvements required in the performance of the centre.

Index